Bearing Witness

Bearing Witness

Intersectional Approaches to
Trauma Theology

Edited by
Karen O'Donnell
and
Katie Cross

scm press

Published in 2022 by SCM Press
Editorial office
3rd Floor, Invicta House,
108–114 Golden Lane,
London EC1Y 0TG, UK

www.scmpress.co.uk

SCM Press is an imprint of Hymns Ancient & Modern Ltd
(a registered charity)

Hymns Ancient & Modern® is a registered trademark of
Hymns Ancient & Modern Ltd
13A Hellesdon Park Road, Norwich,
Norfolk NR6 5DR, UK

British Library Cataloguing in Publication data
A catalogue record for this book is available
from the British Library

ISBN: 978-0-334-06117-5

Typeset by Regent Typesetting
Printed and bound by
CPI Group (UK) Ltd

This book is dedicated to all those whose lives and trauma are complicated.
Your stories, in all their complexity, matter.

Contents

Section Three: Trauma Theology and the Whole Body

Section Four: Poverty and Privilege in Conversation with Trauma Theology

Acknowledgements

When we first invited contributors to this volume, we had no idea we would be asking them to write chapters on trauma theology at the same time as dealing with the Covid-19 pandemic. We want, therefore, to begin by acknowledging and thanking our phenomenal contributors for producing these outstanding essays during some very difficult times. We are very grateful to you for your willingness to continue working on these themes. You have been a pleasure to work with! We would also like to thank David Tombs for his generous reading of this volume and the writing of a Foreword that helps to put this work into context. Thank you also to our wonderful colleagues at SCM Press who worked so hard to make *Feminist Trauma Theologies* such a success and have been so open and enthusiastic about this subsequent volume.

I, Karen, would like to thank my brilliant co-editor Katie Cross. Katie, you are such a pleasure to work with and it's an absolute joy to produce this kind of work with such a good friend. Thank you for all your work and your encouragement of both me and the contributors. I am also grateful to my students, one of whom is included in this volume, for their hard work and inspiration that never fails to excite me and get my theological brain working. My thanks also go to my lovely colleagues at Sarum College who are so patient with me and so encouraging. Finally, my thanks go to my wonderful family, and especially to James, who is still waiting for a cheerful book.

I, Katie, would like to thank Karen O'Donnell, who, over the course of two volumes, has become both a theological co-conspirator and a dear friend. Thank you, Karen; your work and your passion for witnessing to trauma is changing lives. I am so glad to know you. Thanks, too, to my students and colleagues at the University of Aberdeen, who inspire and encourage me in this work. I am especially grateful to my friends, family and chosen family for their love, guidance, support and humour; in particular, my parents, Nicos and Christine, and my brothers, Andrew and Peter Scholarios. Lastly, I could not do this work without Peter Cross and our wee dog Merlin, who brew me strong cups of coffee and take me for regular walks (respectively). Thank you for loving me so well.

List of Contributors

Tyler Brinkman is an independent scholar and theologian with a Masters of Divinity from Anabaptist Mennonite Biblical Seminary. His research interests include theological anthropology, trinitarian theology, trauma studies, intersexuality, embodiment theology, pneumatology, social ethics – especially from a Wesleyan perspective. He lives with his wife and son in Elkhart, Indiana.

Cláudio Carvalhaes, from Brazil, is an ecologist, theologian, liturgist and artist. He is the Associate Professor of Worship at Union Theological Seminary, New York City and author of *Ritual at World's End: Essays on Eco-Liturgical Liberation Theology* (Barber's Son Press, 2021).

Alex Clare-Young is a transmasculine non-binary person, currently completing doctoral research into trans theology, ministering in Cambridge city centre, and speaking, writing and consulting on diversity. Alex's book *Transgender. Christian. Human* was published in 2019. In 2021, their article about trauma experienced in identity-related ecclesial conversations was published in *Theology and Sexuality*.

Susannah Cornwall is Professor of Constructive Theologies at the University of Exeter. She is the author of various books and articles on Christian theology, sex, gender and sexuality. She was a member of the Theology working party for the Church of England's Living in Love and Faith project.

Micah Cronin is a PhD student at the University of Bern. His research interests include queer negativity, constructive and systematic theologies, and trans masculinities. Micah holds an MDiv from Princeton Theological Seminary and is a candidate for Holy Orders in the Episcopal Church.

Katie Cross is Christ's College Lecturer in Practical Theology at the University of Aberdeen. Her research and teaching focuses on theologies of trauma, disaster and church practice. She is the author of *The Sunday Assembly and Theologies of Suffering* (Routledge, 2020).

Brandy Daniels is Assistant Professor of Theology and Gender, Women's, and Sexuality Studies at the University of Portland. Her research explores the place of difference within communal identity in Christian thought and practice. Brandy co-chairs the Queer Studies in Religion unit of the American Academy of Religion and the LGBTQIA+ working group of the Society of Christian Ethics, and is an ordained Disciples of Christ minister.

Sara Gillingham was born with intersex traits and underwent surgeries in childhood. On learning the truth in adulthood, she shared her story to combat secrecy and stigma. She participated in the Church of England's Living in Love and Faith project, before leaving for the United Reformed Church. She has commented in national media on intersex, religion, and NHS clinical guidelines.

Nuam Hatzaw is a PhD candidate at the University of Edinburgh. Her research critically examines theologies of hybridity and identity from the perspective of migrant Zomi women from Myanmar. Nuam's wider research interests include World Christianity, postcolonialism and anthropology. She is also co-host of the Voices of World Christianity podcast.

Margaret Kamitsuka is the Francis W. and Lydia L. Davis Professor Emeritus of Religion at Oberlin College, Ohio. Her most recent book is *Abortion and the Christian Tradition: A Pro-choice Theological Ethic* (2019). Margaret serves as the book editor for the American Academy of Religion's Academy Series for new dissertations.

Adriaan van Klinken is Professor of Religion and African Studies at the University of Leeds, and Extraordinary Professor in the Desmond Tutu Centre for Religion and Social Justice, University of the Western Cape, South Africa. His research focuses on religion, gender and sexuality in contemporary Africa.

M. Cooper Minister is Associate Professor of Religion and Affiliated Professor of Gender and Women's Studies at Shenandoah University. They are the author of two monographs and the co-editor of three volumes. Their most recent work is on transmuting illness, time and death on the dancefloor.

Karen O'Donnell is Director of Studies at Westcott House, Cambridge. She is a feminist, constructive theologian with particular interests in trauma and bodies. Karen's most recent book is *The Dark Womb: Re-Conceiving Theology through Reproductive Loss* (SCM Press, 2022).

CL Wren Radford is a postdoctoral research associate at the Lincoln Theological Institute, University of Manchester. Passionate about developing collaborative research with marginalized communities, their work focuses on how lived experiences are engaged as a basis for theological reflection, drawing on liberative theologies alongside qualitative and creative methods. They are the author of *Lived Experiences and Social Transformations* (Brill, 2022), and they publish and teach on areas around practical theology, research methods, and literature and theology.

Anupama Ranawana is a theologian and political economist with research and teaching interests in religious thought, feminist theology, liberation theology and international development. She is a Research Specialist with Christian Aid and is also writing a monograph on the relationship between Asian feminist theology and literature at the University of St Andrews.

Anthony G. Reddie is the Director of the Oxford Centre for Religion and Culture in Regent's Park College, in the University of Oxford. He is also an Extraordinary Professor of Theological Ethics and a Research Fellow with the University of South Africa.

J. A. Robinson-Brown is Assistant Curate at St Botolph-without-Aldgate in the City of London and Visiting Scholar at Sarum College, Salisbury. His research interests are in patristics, early Christianity and bodies, gender, sexuality and ethnicity in late antiquity. His most recent publication is *Black, Gay, British, Christian Queer: The Church and Famine of Grace* (SCM Press, 2021).

Chris Shannahan is an Associate Professor in Political Theology at the Centre for Trust, Peace and Social Relations at Coventry University. His research, which is informed by many years as an inner-city church minister and community organizer, focuses on the intersection between poverty, inequality and Christian social action, as seen in his recent 'Life on the Breadline: Christianity, Poverty and Politics in the 21st century' project.

Selina Stone is Tutor and Lecturer in Theology at St Mellitus College in London. Her research and teaching focuses on the themes of power, justice and ethics. Dr Stone's PhD thesis 'Holy Spirit, Holy Bodies? Pentecostalism, Pneumatology and the Politics of Embodiment' offers a womanist analysis of Pentecostalism.

Catherine Williams is an Anglican priest, spiritual director and writer. Catherine regularly contributes to a variety of spirituality resources, including *Daily Prayer* and *Daily Reflections* (Church House Publishing), *Pray-As-You-Go* (Jesuit Media Initiatives) and *Fresh from the Word* (International Bible Reading Association). She is also the current editor of *The Canterbury Preacher's Companion* (Canterbury Press).

Claire Williams is an associate lecturer at Regents Theological College, Malvern. She is working towards her PhD studying the faith lives of women in Newfrontiers churches and is currently writing a liberation theology for neurodivergence for SCM Press. Claire was diagnosed with autism as an adult.

Foreword

DAVID TOMBS

Anyone who is interested in the brokenness of the world and how theology might address this brokenness with faith, compassion, healing and hope, should be grateful to the contributors and the editors for what follows in these pages. This book is a demonstration of the creativity which comes from wrestling with difficult questions. It is not an easy or comfortable read, but it offers scholarly and pastoral insights from a wide range of experiences. As the editors explain in their Introduction, in some ways it is an extension of their first collection, *Feminist Trauma Theologies*.[1] However, this second collection is shaped by a more intentional concern for intersectionality. It covers a wider range of subjects across race and ethnicity, gender and sexuality, economics and poverty, and health and well-being. As such, the work gives attention to areas that have received insufficient attention in the past and opens up significant new directions for further work.

My own entry point into theology and trauma was my research in the 1990s on the sexual violence that accompanied state terror practices in Latin America. My initial interest had been understanding the development of Latin American liberation theologies and how these had emerged as a voice of justice within the Church in the 1970s and 1980s. However, the more I read about the context in which these theologies developed, the more I noticed a disturbing silence. Sexual violence had been a common instrument of political repression in Latin America, and was widely documented in the Latin American torture practices of the 1970s and 1980s. Yet despite the trauma of sexual violence being well known in some ways, significant attention to sexual violence was unusual in scholarly literature, and almost completely missing from theological discussion. It was not that acts of sexual violence within the wider violence were unknown. On the contrary, some of the most egregious cases had received worldwide media attention and prompted a global outcry. Yet at the same time, these traumatic experiences were also cloaked in silence. Almost nothing was said about them beyond the bare facts that they happened. To speak of these experiences was to enter into a realm that trauma scholar Judith Herman appropriately describes as the 'unspeakable'.[2]

My understanding of the silences and denials that so often accompanied traumatic experiences developed through a sequence of conversations with Flora Keshgegian in the early 2000s. We met regularly at the Annual Meeting of the American Academy of Religions. Keshgegian's presentations addressed many core issues central to trauma theology. Her book *Redeeming Memories: A Theology of Healing and Transformation* (2000) is one of the pioneering works in the emerging field of trauma theology.[3] As a first-generation Armenian American family who had survived the Armenian genocide, Keshgegian writes of the hold that the traumatic past had on her identity. The legacy of that suffering, she says, was 'a mantle of memory with distinctive texture and weight'. She recalls the clear lesson that accompanied it: 'My family's and community's lesson was simple: remember our suffering, our victimization, and the deaths of so many. Be our witness.'

In her theological work, Keshgegian took up the ethical and theological challenge to bear witness to this experience. Her Christian feminist political theology challenged the complicity of Christian theology in an oppressive amnesia. In her writing she remembered what many were inclined to ignore, and she explored ways in which facing these painful truths could be transformative and liberating. By this time, I was working in Belfast for the Irish School of Ecumenics, Trinity College Dublin. The issues Keshgegian was raising had an immediate relevance to my work. A course I taught on 'When the Fighting Stops: Trauma and Recovery' was a steep learning curve on the impact of the conflict in Northern Ireland. Keshgegian's work on bearing witness and redemptive memory gave insight into the traumas and painful memories that were still to be addressed there. It also showed how hard this work would be.

Since the turn of the century, the field of trauma theology has grown significantly. The works of Serene Jones, Shelly Rambo and other feminist pioneers demonstrate the value of bringing theology and trauma studies into close conversation. The potential of this theology to generate new theological reflection is beyond question. The chapters which follow are characterized by courageous attention to bear witness to lived experience and speak honestly about trauma in its different forms. This is never an easy task. The volume shows that there are ways to address even the most challenging of subjects with sensitivity and hope.

This volume is an important milestone in the ongoing development of trauma theologies. It enlarges the vision of the field by attention to a fuller spectrum and a wider sense of interdisciplinarity. The chapters will be read and re-read for the range of questions they raise, the wisdom they show and the inspiration they offer for further work.

Notes

1 Karen O'Donnell and Katie Cross (eds), *Feminist Trauma Theologies: Body, Scripture and Church in Critical Perspective* (London: SCM Press, 2020), pp. xviii.

2 'The ordinary response to atrocities is to banish them from consciousness. Certain violations of the social compact are too terrible to utter aloud: this is the meaning of the word *unspeakable*.' Judith Herman, *Trauma and Recovery: The Aftermath of Violence – from Domestic Abuse to Political Terror* (New York: Basic Books, 1992), p. 1.

3 Flora A. Keshgegian, *Redeeming Memories: A Theology of Healing and Transformation* (Nashville, TN: Abingdon Press, 2000).

Introduction

KATIE CROSS AND KAREN O'DONNELL

We could not have predicted, when we began inviting scholars to contribute to this volume, that much of the research and writing they would undertake would happen during a global pandemic of Covid-19. We could not have known that all this reflection on trauma in conversation with theology would take place during what has been widely referred to as an experience of mass trauma. In many ways this has made this research – like so much other academic work – much more difficult. At the same time, it has reaffirmed the profound importance of trauma theology.

While experiences of pain and suffering are an innate part of human life, trauma involves a particular rupturing of biological, physiological and spiritual systems, assumptions and coping strategies. It affects the brain (memory and language in the frontal lobe) and the body (where traumatic memories are stored in the limbic system). Trauma can take many forms, and what is considered traumatic is largely personal, cultural and contextual. Lucy Bond and Stef Craps note that trauma is

> slippery: blurring the boundaries between mind and body, memory and forgetting, speech and silence. It traverses the internal and the external, the private and the public, the individual and the collective. Trauma is dynamic: its parameters are endlessly shifting as it moves across disciplines and institutions, ages and cultures.[1]

What is important to note is that, regardless of context, trauma is a particular form of suffering and anguish that does not go away. For those who experience trauma, its effects are ongoing. The chapters in this volume do not reflect singular 'moments' of trauma. Rather, they reflect more chronic, complex, constant forms, experienced in denials, microaggressions and absences.

Trauma as intersectional

The global experience of the Covid-19 pandemic has also underlined that we are not 'all in this together'. The pandemic has not impacted all people in the same way, nor has any potential trauma experience worked itself out in standard form in people's lives.[2]

In this volume, trauma is presented and understood as 'intersectional'. The concept of intersectionality historically emerged from Black feminist and womanist understandings of interlocking systems of discrimination,[3] culminating in the work of the Black lawyer and civil rights activist Kimberlé Crenshaw,[4] who coined the term. In this collection, it is important to acknowledge our debt to these women of colour. Their labour has created a framework of naming and understanding intersectionality, which allows us to better articulate the ways in which unique experiences of discrimination and marginalization shape trauma. Through a lens of intersectionality, we come to understand that 'multiple oppressions reinforce each other to create new categories of suffering'.[5]

When we first commissioned chapters for this volume, we did so, in part at least, in reflection on the limitations of the first volume we worked on together, *Feminist Trauma Theologies: Body, Scripture and Church in Critical Perspective* (SCM Press, 2020). While we affirm the important work that this volume reflects, we were also conscious, as editors, of what was missing. We felt that we did not reflect enough diversity of perspective in that work. We acted, as so many white feminist scholars have done in the past, in forgetting the intersectionality of experience. This volume is intended to redress that omission, at least to some extent. Here, we have deliberately sought out voices and perspectives that prioritize the experiences of people of colour, non-cisgendered and LGBTQIA+ people, those living in poverty, and those who live with a range of physical and mental health problems. While we have divided the volume into four sections – race, gender and sexuality, poverty, and health – these chapters, intersectional as they are, defy easy categorization. Gender, sexuality, poverty, economics, politics, physical health, mental health, spiritual health, race and ethnicity all weave uneasy and complex webs of relationship and intersection throughout the volume.

In the pursuit of theology and understanding of God, trauma presents a particular set of problems. It implicates discussions of human brokenness, points towards hopelessness, and challenges our understandings of God's all-knowing, all-loving nature. In addition to this, Grace Ji-Sun Kim and Susan Shaw draw attention to the way in which theology has historically maintained hierarchies of power and reproduced systems of oppression. Even progressive and liberatory theologies tend to focus on one form of oppression, without accounting for privilege and attending to the intersections of difference at work.[6] Trauma theology seeks to create spaces for such difficult questions, understanding that the individual lived realities of traumatic experience often do not find easy resolution, or fit into neat categories. Frameworks of intersectionality place similar emphasis on the ways in which discrimination is cumulative and complex. As such, the aims and methods of trauma theology support (and in this volume, uphold) intersectional considerations. In this book, we seek to redress the exclusion of traumatic experience from theological discourse by bearing witness to the pain and anguish of the intersections of traumatic experience.

Bearing witness

Asking questions of God's providence is an innately human activity, particularly when confronted by trauma and suffering. Historically, explanations for suffering (theodicies) have dominated theological responses to what we now know as trauma. While this discourse has sought to defend God's all-loving, all-knowing nature, it has often resulted in answers that shift blame towards the traumatized.[7] It is unsurprising that many theologians default to certain solutions; it is a hopeful action in the face of radical evil and suffering. However, while it is uncomfortable to challenge existing paradigms and admit the mysterious nature of divine providence, doing so creates space for those who are experiencing trauma. Indeed, Shelly Rambo writes that

> trauma forces us beyond a familiar theological paradigm of life and death, and places us, instead, on the razed terrain of what remains. Trauma presses theologians to seek new language to express God's relationship to the world. This is not a new task. In fact, it is the perennial work of theology. Amid the claims about redemption and new life, there must be theologians who testify to the undertow, to witness the pull of death in the tenuous territory of the aftermath.[8]

In this volume, we suggest that in responding to trauma, we must begin by *bearing witness* to it. All of us bear witness every day to one another's stories and experiences, whether in verbal or written form. However, in the study of psychological trauma, we are required to 'witness to horrible events'.[9] This involves actively hearing, listening to, and holding space for others to communicate what has happened to them. In her autobiography *Dust Tracks on a Road*, the African American author Zora Neale Hurston captures something of the power of witnessing, writing that: 'There is no greater agony than bearing an untold story inside of you.'[10] When we bear witness to one another's trauma, these 'untold stories' are brought to voice. The act of listening and providing validation, and acceptance, can be particularly potent, allowing the traumatized person or group to gain empathy, support and catharsis in sharing their stories.

While *witness* is a term and concept used in psychology,[11] to bear witness to trauma is, as Rambo suggests, to join in a biblically rooted, theologically grounded practice. In her own work, Rambo suggests that traditional Western Christologies view hope and redemption as a linear process from death to resurrection. In doing so, they neglect to attend to the 'middle space' of suffering and trauma, which Rambo relates to Holy Saturday (the day between Christ's crucifixion and resurrection). Focusing on pneumatology and the embodied witness of the Holy Spirit, Rambo suggests that in spaces of trauma, God's love persists through the Spirit's witness to human suffering. It is the same Spirit that empowers us to witness to lingering effects of death, holding on to the love that remains in this 'middle space' of trauma: 'This persistence [of the Spirit], this abiding, is the witness not just to death's remaining but to love's survival.'[12]

In the Christian tradition, the term 'witness' is bound up with evangelism and 'witnessing' to one's faith. However, in this book, we find the possibility for the Church to potentially be a witnessing community, as a body that is able to witness to narratives of trauma. Indeed, this is deeply rooted in the origins of the Christian faith. Those first witnesses to Jesus' resurrection – those first sharers of good news – were themselves witnesses, exposed to the traumatic death of their friend and family member Jesus. The women and the Beloved Disciple who did not abandon Jesus in his death, but rather witnessed his torture and crucifixion, are then the traumatized witnesses to the resurrection. They witness to the lingering effects of Christ's death, even as they know of love's survival.[13]

Bearing witness is not an easy route away from explanation. It does not involve an end to questions of God's presence and intent. Rather, it necessitates an active engagement with the realities of traumatic experience. To bear witness is to come alongside the traumatized, remaining with them, listening, and holding space for their trauma to be heard in all its raging, torrential glory. It is to feel God's presence and God's absence at the same time. It is to hear stories that unsettle, and to view scenes that are profoundly disturbing. It is to realize the very liminal spaces and edges of faith, beyond where we can even imagine them.

The contents of this book

The first section of the volume features essays from five outstanding UK-based scholars of colour. Anthony Reddie examines in his chapter why Black lives still don't matter as he examines the trauma caused by white supremacy, enabled by many Christian churches and exported through Western missionary activities. Drawing Black Liberation Theology into dialogue with the experiences of the Windrush Generation and the Black Lives Matter discourse, Reddie highlights the ongoing nature of this trauma, one that is still not dismantled in our societies. Nuam Hatzaw's work also draws on her experience of being a person of colour in the UK. Exploring her own position as a 'Zomi ethnic woman who was born in

Myanmar, but who was raised and educated in Britain', Hatzaw posits her dual heritage as a form of hybridity which is traumatic. She offers a trauma-informed theology of hybridity that takes seriously the dynamism, rupturing and painful nature of her own hybridity. The theme of taking seriously under-acknowledged forms of trauma is picked up by Selina Stone in her work on the trauma context of early Black Pentecostals. She notes that the 'early Black Pentecostals were a traumatized people, and a recognition of their suffering must be brought to bear on how we interpret their lives and understand their theology'. Trauma becomes, for Stone, a hermeneutic through which to read both the lives and the theology of Azusa Street. She turns her attention then to the construction of a trauma-informed pneumatological discourse that seeks to bring life in its fullness. Jarel Robinson-Brown addresses affect and public emotion for Black men as he considers moments of weeping in both the Gospel of John and Augustine's *Confessions*. In doing so, he argues that publicly owning grief and trauma, with the possibility of embodied masculinities that include tears, is an integral part of Black male life. This theme of weeping resonates with our final chapter in this section, in which Anupama Ranawana examines the weeping Madonnas. From a particularly South Asian perspective, Ranawana highlights the motherist activism that many women undertake in the face of traumatic experiences, and considers the contemporary icon Our Lady of Ferguson in dialogue with Mary the mother of Jesus as mothers who both endure trauma along with their children, but then turn to action in the aftermath.

In the second section of the volume, gender and sexuality are brought into dialogue with trauma theory and trauma theology. Susannah Cornwall joins with Alex Clare-Young and Sara Gillingham in examining the concept of epistemic injustice and its role in exacerbating trauma both for trans people and for those with intersex characteristics. They highlight the particular trauma caused by the denial of the self as a 'first-person knower'. Trauma is both inflicted and exacerbated when 'sex- and gender-variant people are not understood as legitimate knowing and speaking subjects'. This kind of trauma is particularly heightened, they argue, in Christian contexts, where variant identity is frequently called into question. The damage inflicted on the LGBTQIA+ community is further highlighted by Adriaan van Klinken's work with LGBT+ Ugandan refugees. Reflecting with those who fled Uganda after the passing of the infamous Anti-Homosexuality Bill, van Klinken highlights the complicated nature of these trauma experiences, as well as ways of engaging with biblical stories that might offer opportunities for framing the narratives of these experiences and space for post-traumatic remaking. The third chapter in this section comes from Brandy Daniels and Micah Cronin, who consider the ways in which feminist trauma theologies that focus on sexual violence often occlude gendered, particularly transgendered, experiences. Naming this as cissexism, Daniels and Cronin conclude that such a consideration might serve survivors of sexual violence well in their post-traumatic remaking and also argue for a transfeminist trauma theology that has space for *ante*-reparative work that might resist drives towards repair and wholeness while offering space for something new, liberative and imaginative. In this section's final chapter, focused on gender and sexuality specifically, Tyler Brinkman argues that 'a trans*-centred trauma theology ultimately destabilizes linear temporalities, ruptures conceptions of embodiment and identity, and demonstrates the liberative and sanctifying work of the Spirit in breaking open binary oppositions.' Brinkman engages in a constructive proposal that centres the trans* experience and opens up new possibilities within the field of trauma theology. These rich chapters aim to address the relative paucity of work in trauma theology that specifically engages with LGBTQIA+ experiences and considers how these experiences intersect with and complicate experience of trauma and post-traumatic remaking.

Our third turn in this volume is towards the body. Again, the body and the embodied nature of trauma experiences are relevant to all of the chapters within this volume and so the chapters within this section specifically pick up characteristics of health in relation to trauma. Claire Williams offers a moving, personal account of attending a charismatic church as an autistic person. She frames her own experience as a 'peculiar trauma' and argues that the non-normative body-mind disrupts definitions of trauma. For Williams, this experience highlights a range of theological questions regarding silence, shame and damage that require trauma-informed theological responses. Margaret Kamitsuka examines the peculiar phenomena of pro-life foetal memorialization and the apparent determination of those promoting these rituals to *cause* trauma to those who have abortions. Abortion and reproductive loss should be seen as two sides of the same coin, Kamitsuka argues, as she complicates and disrupts any easy binaries between these two ways in which pregnancies might come to an end. What enables life in the midst of death? This is the question taken up by M. Cooper Minister in response to their experiences of both cancer and the Covid-19 pandemic. Minister offers a twelve-step guide to resurrection as a way of imagining the process of post-traumatic (or even mid-traumatic?) remaking. Drawing on the work of theologians such as Shelly Rambo and Karen Bray, as well as the late Marcella Althaus-Reid, Minister articulates a possible path to resurrection that does justice to the experience of trauma without negating the experience of death. Finally, in this section, Catherine Williams turns our attention to the ways in which Christian spiritual direction needs to become trauma-informed. Williams argues that spiritual directors are ever more likely to encounter trauma survivors in their ministry and so appropriate responses to those who are traumatized within spiritual direction are essential. Drawing this discussion into the long-standing practices of Ignatian spirituality, she offers guidance and a model for contemporary spiritual directors that centres the body of the trauma survivor and enables gentle ways of drawing them into life.

The final section of this volume focuses on trauma theology in relation to experiences of poverty. Chris Shannahan draws on his extensive and groundbreaking 'Life on the Breadline' research regarding Christian engagement with UK poverty in the age of austerity. Shannahan considers the collective experience of trauma in the devastating 2017 fire that engulfed Grenfell Tower in London, killing 72 people, as one that reflects the intersectional violence of poverty in contemporary Britain. Collective trauma then provides the framework for his exploration of political theology and liberation theology in dialogue with poverty. The collective nature of trauma is similarly considered in Cláudio Carvalhaes' chapter. Carvalhaes expands our attention into a global context as he reflects on his opportunity to listen to poor people across four continents and to 'turn their stories into prayers, songs, poems and rituals'. He highlights the legacies of colonialism as a form of trauma and violence and the ways in which such colonial dynamics are still fully alive in our times. The process of decolonialization is a process of post-traumatic remaking. Carvalhaes brings these collectively traumatized voices into our midst as he offers trauma-informed prayers and rituals for today. Finally, CL Wren Radford draws on their work with Poverty Truth groups in Glasgow and Greater Manchester, as they consider responses to traumatic testimonies in the public sphere. Highlighting the ways public and theological spaces shape our reception of traumatic testimonies, Radford encourages theologians to challenge those circumstances in which 'the circulation of affect reproduces rather than challenges inequalities'. What good is just telling stories, if there is no ethical imperative to act that goes alongside them?

Final thoughts

This volume reflects the fast-paced way in which theology, alongside other disciplines, is progressing in its approaches to and engagement with trauma. In the two years since the publication of our previous volume, there has been significant development in problematizing and disrupting comfortable and seemingly settled accounts of trauma. In particular, postcolonial work on trauma theory has disrupted some of the neat categories of trauma.[14] Most significantly, it has forced a re-evaluation of the primacy of the articulated narrative of trauma by the trauma survivor. While trauma narratives were already accepted as partial, iterative, and unstable in their recollections, postcolonial work in this area has revealed the Western, Enlightenment-influenced assumptions that underline this drive towards 'telling the story', offering alongside such narratives modes of meaning-making that are more embodied, open-ended and creative.

This is cause for cautious hope. With these movements, more space is being created for the traumatized to be heard. In the scope of this volume, we cannot hope to address every form and experience of trauma. As such, we present this collection as part of the incomplete and ongoing task of trauma theology, to better understand the ways that trauma challenges and shapes our understandings of oppression, of suffering, of faith, and of God. The work continues ...

Notes

1 Lucy Bond and Stef Craps, *Trauma* (London and New York: Routledge, 2020), p. 5.

2 Richard Blundell, Monica Costa Dias, Robert Joyce and Xiaowei Xu, 'Covid-19 and Inequalities', *Fiscal Studies* 41, 2 (2020), pp. 291–319.

3 For example, the American abolitionist and activist Sojourner Truth, whose 1851 speech at the Ohio Women's Rights Convention (later named 'Ain't I A Woman?') addresses issues of both race and gender. There are several written versions of this speech. See *Anti-slavery Bugle*, 21 June 1851, *Chronicling America: Historic American Newspapers*, Library of Congress: https://chroniclingamerica. loc.gov/lccn/sn83035487/1851-06-21/ed-1/seq-4/, accessed 14.12.2021. Another example is the Combahee River Collective, an Afrocentric Black feminist lesbian socialist organization operating in Boston (MA) circa 1974–80. This group developed the Combahee River Statement, which pointed to the ways in which the White feminist movement and Civil Rights Movement did not address the specific needs of Black lesbian women. The statement referred to 'interlocking oppression' and 'identity politics', issues later built on by Kimberlé Crenshaw in her work on intersectionality. See The Combahee River Statement: www.blackpast. org/african-american-history/combahee-river-collective-statement-1977/, accessed 14.12.2021. For an in-depth exposition of the Collective, its statement and the impact of Black feminism on the development of activist response (including the Black Lives Matter movement), see Keeanga Yamahtta-Taylor, *How We Get Free: Black Feminism and the Combahee River Collective* (Chicago, IL: Haymarket Books, 2017). Indeed, the terminology of 'Black feminism' has not been static. The Black American activist and author Alice Walker coined the term 'womanist' in her 1979 short story 'Coming Apart' and referred to it again in her 1983 book *In Search of Our Mothers' Gardens: Womanist Prose* (San Diego, CA: Harcourt Brace Jovanovich, 1983). For Walker, 'womanist' refers to a 'black feminist or feminist of color' and has its etymological roots in the Black folk expression, 'acting womanish'. See Justine Tally, 'Why "womanism"? The Genesis of a New Word and What It Means', *Revista de filología de la Universidad de La Laguna* 5 (1986), pp. 205–22. Another key womanist work is bell hooks, *Ain't I A Woman: Black Woman and Feminism* (London: Pluto Press, 1987), which explores the combination of racism and sexism during slavery and its ongoing impact on Black women. Womanist theology emerged to analyse the impact of class, race and gender in the context of theology, ethics and biblical study. It developed at Union Seminary (NY) in the 1980s in response to the inadequacies of both White feminist and Black male theologies. The foremothers of womanist theology include Jacquelyn Grant, Katie Cannon, Renita Weems, Emilie Townes, Delores Williams and Kelly Brown Douglas.

4 Kimberlé Crenshaw, 'Mapping the Margins: Intersectionality, Identity Politics, and Violence against Women of Color', *Stanford Law Review* 46, 6 (1991), pp. 1241–99.

5 Yamahtta-Taylor, *How We Get Free*, p. 3.

6 Grace Ji-Sun Kim and Susan M. Shaw, *Intersectional Theology: An Introductory Guide* (Minneapolis, MN: Augsburg Fortress Publishers, 2018), pp. xiii–xv.

7 See Nick Trakakis, 'Theodicy: The Solution to the Problem of Evil, or Part of the Problem?', *Sophia* 47 (2008), p. 161 (for an exploration of the problematic aspects of theodicy); John Swinton, *Raging with Compassion: Pastoral Responses to the Problem of Evil* (London: SCM Press, 2018), p. 12 (theodicy is here described as both 'theologically questionable' and 'pastorally dangerous'); and Katie Cross, *The Sunday Assembly and Theologies of Suffering* (London: Routledge, 2020), pp. 15–29 (for an overview of the 'dangers' of traditional Augustinian and Irenaean theodicies and explanations for human suffering that have stemmed from these).

8 Shelly Rambo, *Spirit and Trauma: A Theology of Remaining* (Louisville, KY: Westminster John Knox Press, 2010), p. 14.

9 Judith Herman, *Trauma and Recovery: The Aftermath of Violence, from Domestic Abuse to Political Terror* (New York: Basic Books, 2015), p. 7.

10 Zora Neale Hurston, *Dust Tracks on a Road: An Autobiography* (New York: Arno Press, 1969), pp. 220–1.

11 Darryl Stephens, 'Bearing Witness as Social Action: Religious Ethics and Trauma-Informed Response', *Trauma Care* 1, 1 (2021), pp. 49–63.

12 Rambo, *Spirit and Trauma*, p. 160.

13 For a fuller account of this see Karen O'Donnell, 'Surviving Trauma at the Foot of the Cross' in *When Did We See You Naked? Jesus as a Victim of Sexual Abuse*, ed. Jayme R. Reaves, David Tombs and Rocío Figueroa (London: SCM Press, 2021), pp. 260–77.

14 See, for example, Stef Craps, *Postcolonial Witnessing: Trauma Out of Bounds* (Basingstoke and New York: Palgrave Macmillan, 2012).

How to Read this Volume

KATIE CROSS AND KAREN O'DONNELL

We are acutely aware of the powerful descriptions and expositions within this volume. While this collection makes for difficult reading, we think that it contains some vitally important themes and experiences that must be witnessed to. We invite readers to take care when engaging with this book, and would particularly like to draw attention to the following content warnings:

- Racism and xenophobia
- Death
- Bodily harm
- Abortion
- Reproductive loss
- Homophobia
- Cancer

In providing these content warnings, we want to encourage our readers to find ways of engaging with this text that help them to flourish. Some tentative suggestions are included below.

Self-care practices

In our previous volume, we drew attention to importance of self-care practices when reading about trauma. In the context of reading and consuming literature about trauma, self-care involves consciously and deliberately taking actions of self-preservation that contribute to well-being. These actions may vary and will, to some extent, be individual to each reader. This might include reading one chapter at a time and taking some time away from the volume in-between. You might choose to develop journaling or creative practices to work through the themes in this book and express some of the intense emotions that may arise from reading it. It may help to read the volume with someone else, so that you can support one another and talk about the various chapters. If anything in this volume causes you severe distress, we encourage you to seek help by accessing local support and crisis lines. Please take care when reading.

Reading in community

We suggest that this volume is one that is best read in community. The Black feminist, civil rights activist and writer Audre Lorde reminds us that 'there is no such thing as a single-issue struggle because we do not live single-issue lives.'[1] Intersectionality pays particular attention to the ways our lives are shaped by interlocking issues. We inhabit multiple communities and spheres of experience. Further, ideas of intersectionality historically arose through the radical action of Black feminists, who often formed collective organizations and groups. It was the community-based work of the Combahee River Collective, for example, that introduced early terminology of intersectionality. The Combahee River Statement referred to the importance of 'community which allows us to continue our struggle and work'.[2] Finally, in order to bear witness, we need others to hear, understand and share in our experiences of trauma.

Reading in community may be as simple as reading with one other person. Alternatively, you may like to set up an intersectional reading group, with the opportunity to share your experiences with others and hear their perspectives on various chapters. There is much advice on how to run a reading group like this online, but we would suggest the following starting points for your consideration:

- Before getting started, decide on the aim of your group. What will you be focusing on? Will you read beyond this collection?
- Pay attention to different perspectives. Make sure to include a variety of voices in your group.
- Plan dates for sessions and decide on specific readings ahead of time to establish momentum.
- Design opening questions so that everyone is able to share their thoughts early in the session.
- Set some ground rules for group discussion. (You may choose to consider these in your first meeting.)
- Consider the accessibility needs of your participants. Is it better to meet online or in person? If you are meeting in person, consider physical access needs (including but not limited to parking, level entrances, wheelchair accessibility, lifts or elevators, nearby restroom facilities, tactile signage).

How to be an intersectional reader: A non-exhaustive list

- Diversify your readings. Seek out different perspectives and experiences.
- Pay attention to history. Engage in background reading, particularly Black feminist and womanist texts upon which intersectional theories are built. Some suggestions for these are included in note 3 on page 8.
- Consider your privilege. Think about the way your social identities (race, class, gender identity, sexuality) play into this. Reflect on how these impact the discrimination that you do or do not experience.
- Make space for others. Consider whether you are the right person to comment on or speak to an issue. Centre stories and actions on those with lived experiences of a particular situation.
- Listen. Hear and honour the experiences of others and listen carefully to these.
- Learn. Do not rely on marginalized groups for education, as this requires a lot of emotional labour. Be willing to research and learn for yourself.
- Be mindful of your language in discussions. As language evolves away from describing a single identity or experience, avoid terminology that is exclusionary or offensive to marginalized communities. Recognize and correct your use of such terms and accept criticism when this is pointed out to you. We are all responsible for holding others to account when we hear such language being used.

Notes

1 Audre Lorde, 'Learning from the 1960s', www.blackpast.org/african-american-history/1982-audre-lorde-learning-60s/, accessed 14.12.2021.

2 The Combahee River Statement, www.blackpast.org/african-american-history/combahee-river-collective-statement-1977/, accessed 14.12.2021.

SECTION ONE

Raced Reflections on Trauma Theology

Why Black Lives Still Don't Matter

ANTHONY REDDIE

The roots of Black existential struggle

I will start this chapter by saying a few words about myself. Like my all-time hero James H. Cone, I believe all theology to be some form of autobiography[1] (i.e. what theologians say and write about tells you more about them and their social location and formative influences than it does about the God they are seeking to discuss in their work). I am part of a wider community. The mass migratory movement of Black people from Africa and the Caribbean in the years following the end of the Second World War is termed the 'Windrush'. This migratory movement commenced with the arrival of 492 Caribbean people at Tilbury docks on the SS *Empire Windrush* on 22 June 1948.

I was born in Bradford, West Yorkshire, to Jamaican parents who came to this country from the Caribbean in the late 1950s. As such, I am a second-generation Black Caribbean British subject. I was born into and nurtured within the Christian faith from the Wesleyan Methodist tradition, in a large Central Hall in the city of Bradford. I ply my trade as a Black Liberation Theologian and a decolonial educator within Oxford University but have lived in Birmingham for the past 30-plus years. I am also a part-time research fellow and an Extraordinary Professor of Theological Ethics with the University of South Africa.

I have shared these bare details of my life with you because it is my firm belief that all knowledge, and the writing that emerges from it, is embodied. By this, I mean there is always a relationship between the experiences that have shaped one's life and the resulting ideas and theories that emerge in any subsequent writing. Namely, that all knowledge and truth is contextual; all intellectual insights emerge from and are shaped by specific and particular times and spaces.

Many of the enduring values in my life can be traced back to my formative years growing up in a Black Christian home but living within a predominantly white working-class, trade-union and Independent Labour Party stronghold of East Bowling. In this context, Nonconformism, trade unions and Labour party politics went hand in hand. I am named after Tony Benn. My father was an active trade unionist in the 32 years he lived in the UK before he returned to Jamaica when he took early retirement in 1991 due to ill health.

While my formative years were largely pleasant and affirming, what could not be disguised about our existence was the persistent reality of racism that affected the lives of all non-white people in the city of Bradford. I would argue that the consistent and persistent challenge that has faced Black people of Christian faith in Britain has been that of trying to get 'white Christianity' to give expression to a non-racist articulation of the gospel, when juxtaposed with the wider indices of racism in the nation. The former should be different from the latter, but far too often the two are synonymous; that is, the nomenclature of 'Christian' has often meant nothing when differentiating the agency of white people in terms of their proclivity to resist racism and white supremacy, within the context of white Christianity.[2]

The existence of racism in Britain today and in many parts of the so-called developed West, as we speak, is testament to the continuance of an underlying Eurocentric Judeo-Christian framework that has invariably caricatured Africans as 'less than' and 'the other' and often placed white Euro-Americans as the apex of human civilization. The notion that human beings can be categorized into a fixed set of identities, which characterize human potential and capability – often effected in notions of morality and ethics – can be traced back to the first four centuries of the 'Common Era' (CE). It was during this epoch that negative connotations pertaining to Black people as the 'other' begin to surface in Christian thinking.[3]

The scourge of racism in Britain is nothing new for Black people. As Robert Beckford has demonstrated, one can chart a genealogy of racism in European intellectual thought that has exerted a disproportionately negative hold on the life experiences of Black people.[4] Scholars such as Emmanuel Eze have shown the extent to which the allegedly enlightened thinking of such 'luminaries' as David Hume and Immanuel Kant was infected with the stain of white supremacist thought.[5] The construction of the binary of Blackness (as bestial and less than) and Whiteness (as the personification of goodness and the opposite of Blackness) is a product of modernity.[6]

The chief legacy of transatlantic slavery was the unleashing of the rampageous and ravenous animal that is racism. The construction of racialized notions of fixed identity and restricted perspectives on Black human selfhood were the dangerous offspring of the chattel slavery of the 'Black' Atlantic.[7] The outworking of an immutable hierarchical manipulation of humanity did not disappear when the Act to abolish the British slave trade was passed in 1807. The Act brought the making of slaves to an end but racism, the notion of white supremacist norms, most certainly did not end.[8]

Diasporan African Christianity has had to wrestle with the privations of slavery and colonialism. Diasporan Africans have lived for hundreds of years with the continued effects and ongoing trauma of the epoch of slavery. The Maafa (this is a Swahili term relating to the African holocaust) remains a site for deep-seated trauma within diasporan Africans, to which Black pastoral theology and pastoral care have needed to respond.[9] This pastoral response, what Cedric Johnson calls 'Soul Care', which has its equivalents in other pastoral theology texts written by Black people of African descent,[10] seeks to attend to the deep-seated psychological malaise arising from the epoch of slavery. Delroy Hall, who is Britain's leading Black pastoral theologian, has undertaken work exploring the pastoral needs of African Caribbean people as they seek to make sense of their liminal experience living in postcolonial Britain.[11] Black pastoral and practical theologians have sought to offer some form of amelioration for the suffering experienced by Black and working-class poor across the USA and in other parts of the African Diaspora, helping Christian communities to deal with the most deleterious of experiences related to the toxic machinations of neoliberal, global capitalism. These respective theological approaches of Black practical-pastoral theologians provide an important, prophetic diagnosis of the wider environmental milieu in which the Church is immersed. As the old adage states, it is not sufficient to be in the noble cause of rescuing people from drowning in a river if one is not concerned with those who are deliberately throwing them into the water further upstream.

The impact of neoliberal economics and capitalism under the aegis of the 'global economy' have continued the long travails facing Black peoples across the world.[12] In using the phrase 'global economy', I am concerned with the interconnected means by which countries undertake their economic activity. This can be seen in terms of how multi- and transnational companies operate. Quite often the activities of multinational corporations take advantage of being located within large global markets, where they seek to maximize their profits, using the framework of technological capitalism.[13]

The global economy emerged in the nineteenth century, but perhaps came into its own in the last century. In the twenty-first century it is now commonplace. In fact, it is so much a part of the economic landscape that it is hard for us to remember a time when people did not trade across national boundaries, or that companies did not belong to, or have their primary allegiance to, any one country. The national boundaries of so-called sovereign nations have been ignored and are now often overrun by multinational companies whose primary commitment is making profit for their shareholders.[14]

This chapter will critique the role of white Christianity in the transatlantic slave trade. I am arguing that there existed (and continues to this day) an underlying framework that enabled many Christian churches to construct an ideology based upon an incipient, racist theology that assisted them in supporting Black chattel slavery, which was unhindered by any faith in God. The outworking of this historical phenomenon is one that has seen the rise and development of Black liberation theology and Black Lives Matter, as religio-political forms of riposte to the continued existence of white supremacy.

The impact of Christianity on Black suffering

To understand the churches' role in slavery you have to go back to the period of European expansion around the time of the Crusades and the violent conflict with African (Black) Moors (Muslims), which leads to the intensifying of ideas around Christianity = Europe (Christendom) = White versus Non-Christians = Africa (Barbarians) = Black. Black people become the other.[15] This is exacerbated by the fact that white Christianity is a violent religion. It is based upon a form of 'Closed Monotheism'; that is, the Christian God is a jealous and competitive God that will not tolerate rivals or the 'other' that worships such God(s).[16] This can be seen in a number of Hebrew Bible texts, in which a 'competitive' God instructs the people of Israel to commit genocide on others who inhabit the 'Promised Land'.[17]

When you combine problematic tropes around Blackness with white exceptionalist forms of hermeneutics, linked to white European notions of manifest destiny, you have the ingredients for a toxic residue of epistemology that sees Black people as 'the problem'.[18] This ethic of white mastery over those who are deemed 'the other' becomes the basis on which the roots of a colonially inspired capitalism are at play, in which Blackness becomes the demonized other that has to be conquered, subdued and economically exploited. Effectively, Black people become removed from the body politic of 'civilized Europe' of Whiteness.[19] Our exploitation becomes even more egregious when it is then allied to notions of biblical sanction and the belief that Black subservience is decreed by God's very self. In the pre-modern era when epistemological power lay largely in ecclesial hands, the ability to determine the other as less than and a part of an inferior part of God's natural hierarchy, is what enables white Europeans to create an ethic of mastery and control over Black bodies.[20]

The tensions between religion, faith, ethnicity and nationality are then exploited by means of 'specious' biblical interpretation; the main text that resolved the issue of justifying the enslavement of Africans within a Christian framework came from Genesis 9.18–25 – The Curse of Ham. Noah punishes his son Ham by cursing his own grandson Canaan (the son of Ham), condemning him and all his descendants to slavery.[21]

Since there was a widely perpetuated belief that Africans/dark-skinned peoples were the descendants of Ham, this so-called 'curse of Ham' was used as biblical evidence that the enslavement of African people was actually willed and sanctioned by God. There was also a similar but less well-known argument based on the biblical story of Cain and Abel (Gen.

4.8–16), where the 'mark of Cain', punishment for the murder of his brother, is interpreted as representing Black skin. Again, people of African origin are somehow identified as cursed by God for some past wrong. Here, any notions of blame are removed from the slave owners since it can be said that the condition in which the Africans find themselves as slaves is due to the sins their ancestors have committed in the past, for which God is punishing them. Their Black skin is seen as proof of their sinful condition. Proponents of the Atlantic slave trade constructed such wild and fantastical forms of eisegesis in support of slavery, because of the presence of pre-existing views of Africans as 'other' and as being 'cursed by God'.[22]

The charge to 'Christianize' enslaved Africans is undertaken on a number of biblical and theological terms. There is a dichotomy between the body and the soul. This dualism is a particular outworking of Pauline theology. Salvation is achieved solely by faith in Jesus Christ. In the theological construction of Paul, salvation is not dependent on how you act or behave, but largely in terms of what you believe (i.e. faith in Jesus).[23]

This means that if you are a Christian slave owner, you can have faith in Christ and still own slaves, as God is only interested in your soul, which is preserved through faith in Jesus. Your actions on earth are another matter, however. For the enslaved Africans, faith in this same Jesus guaranteed salvation in heaven but not material freedom here on earth for the same reason as that given for the justification of the actions of slave masters. In the theological construction of slave-holding economies, Africans could be saved. Given that this underlying framework of European superiority still held sway, however, even when both Black and white were members of the same religious code (the body of Christ), it is no surprise that even when the slave trade was abolished and later slavery itself, Europeans continued to oppress Africans. It is interesting to note that the 'Dash for Africa' in the mid-nineteenth century came soon after slavery was finally abolished in the British Empire.[24]

The psychological damage arising from Western Missionary Christianity

African American scholars such as Molefi Kete Asante estimate that upwards of 50 million African people were transported between Africa and the Americas over a 400-year period.[25] Inherent within that Black, transatlantic movement of forced migration and labour was a form of biased, racialized teaching that asserted the inferiority and subhuman nature of the Black self.[26] This form of anti-Black teaching was one of the most pernicious aspects of Western Missionary Christianity. The continued struggles of Black people in Britain that arise from the era of slavery can be seen in the overarching material poverty and marginalization of Black people across the world.[27]

Anthony Pinn has undertaken detailed work investigating the dialectic of the existential, material realities of Black bodies and the phenomenon that is Christianity.[28] In *Terror and Triumph*, Pinn rehearses the contested and troubled relationship between white slave-holding Christianity and Black bodies, outlining the levels of demonization and virulent denigration that provided the essential backdrop to transatlantic chattel slavery.[29] Outlining the apparent ease and the complicity with which Christianity colluded with the epistemological frameworks that underpinned the machinery of slavery, Pinn writes:

> In short, Scripture required that English Christians begin their thinking on Africans with an understanding that Africans had the same creator. Yet they were at least physically and culturally different, and this difference had to be accounted for. As we shall see, a sense of shared creation did not prohibit a ranking within the created order, one in which Africans were much lower than Europeans.[30]

The sense of a deep prevailing anti-Black sentiment replete with notions of Greek antiquity[31] and practised within Western (particularly English) Missionary Christianity was given added piquancy in the deliberate attempt to use the developments of early Christian theology as a means of reinforcing the essentially depraved and base status of the Black body.[32]

Kelly Brown Douglas demonstrates how a particular outworking of Pauline, Platonized-influenced theology (one that downplays the concrete materiality of the body in favour of the abstract and the spirit) was used as a means of demonizing Black bodies.[33] She writes:

> Accordingly, it is platonized Christianity that gives rise to Christian participation in contemptible acts and attacks against human bodies, like those against Black bodies. Not only does platonized Christianity provide a foundation for easily disregarding certain bodies, but it also allows for the demonization of those persons who have been sexualised.[34]

One can amplify the prevailing sense of an incipient anti-Black strain within the corporate edifice of Western Missionary Christianity when one considers the ways in which Black Christianity itself has imbibed the strictures against the Black body in their own corporate operations of religiosity. Anthony Pinn, drawing on a similar analysis of Platonized, Pauline theology, argues that Black Christianity (largely in the USA, but I would argue the same exists in the UK also) has imbibed the prevalent suspicion surrounding the Black body. It has taught many Black Christians to remain at best indifferent to the material needs of the Black body or to seek to transcend its supposed, despised nature; this demonization emerging from the tenets of white Christian slave-holding, thought and practice.[35]

For many diasporan Africans, the search for a positive self-esteem has been found from within the frameworks of the Christian faith. Faith in Christ has provided the conduit by which issues of identity and self-esteem have been explored. This search has been helpful at one level, as the frameworks provided by conversion and an alignment with God in Christ have conferred a new spiritual identity on Black people, but the extent to which this new formulation of the self has affirmed the materiality of one's Blackness is open to doubt.[36]

The wider context of being Black and British

To belong to British society and that of the Church, for a Black person, necessitates a denial of one's self. To be Black is to have one's experiences, history and ongoing reality ignored, disparaged and ridiculed. It is to be rendered an insignificant presence, among the many who are deemed one's betters and superiors.[37] Reflecting upon being a Black person in Britain is to be part of a wider context in which what I know or have felt is of no consequence to the nation or world as a whole. What I know and have felt is dismissed as untrue and without any social, political, cultural or theological consequence. Writers such as Kenneth Leech have discussed extensively the marginalization of the urban poor and their estrangement from the wider society and the Church.[38]

Yet prior to the wholesale migration of Black people from the New Commonwealth, between 1948 and 1965, there is within British history the often-submerged presence of Black people such as Mary Prince,[39] Olaudah Equiano[40] and Ignatius Sancho.[41] Their experiences speak of an existence that is characterized by an indomitable spirit that yearned for freedom and which formed the antecedents for the later struggles of which I have been a part. These pioneering individuals belonged to a community of enslaved Black people who resided at some point in their lives in London, and were key figures in the abolition movement, and yet for the most part they have been written out of British history.[42]

The earliest manifestations of Black Christian faith can be traced to the struggle of enslaved Black peoples in the seventeenth and eighteenth centuries in their fight for emancipation. Black Christianity in Britain has *always* had to respond to the realities of racism. The struggles of these enslaved Black peoples in Britain speak to the corruption and the biased self-serving nature of white Christianity at that time. The pioneering work of such luminaries as Sancho[43] and Prince[44] were valiant attempts to remind the English establishment of the basic tenets of Christianity, which they had so regally exported to their empire throughout this era but failed to practise when applied to Black people.

One of the central arguments of this chapter is that there are additional burdens and pressures that are placed upon people who are not white, living in this country or across the wider contours of the 'new world order'. Feminist and womanist[45] theologians have long spoken about multidimensional oppression; that is, the diverse ways in which social, political, cultural and economic pressures are played out on poor, dispossessed and marginalized objects, coalescing around issues of 'race', ethnicity, gender, sexuality, class and geographic and social location.[46] It is the uniqueness of these challenges that have stymied the voice of the urban, disaffected poor, especially if these people are also Black.

In making a claim to identify with those who are marginalized and oppressed in my context I want to suggest that British society and the so-called first world have found convenient ways of ignoring the claims of those who have been pushed to the margins, and whose presence the corporate whole has identified as being undesirable or even subversive.[47] The noted sociologist Paul Gilroy has been an ardent campaigner and chronicler of the subtle and not so oblique pressures that have been exerted upon minority ethnic people in their attempts to find an accommodating space and place within this island.[48]

It is not my intention to claim a privileged role for Black people as the recipients of the dubious honour of being the 'most oppressed of the oppressed'. This would be a fatuous and inane form of discourse. What I want to assert, however, is that due to a unique set of circumstances, many dating back several hundred years to the birth of slavery, Black people have been the recipients of a pernicious, psychological attack that threatened their very existence as human subjects created in the image of a Supreme Being.

As I have detailed previously, the transatlantic slave trade has given rise to a form of biased racialized teaching that asserted the inferiority and subhuman nature of the Black self.[49] The effects of such biased, self-serving instruction are still being felt – the continuing tendency of Black people to internalize their feelings of inferiority, coupled with an accompanying lack of self-esteem. The internalization of this demonized instruction has led to Black people directing the fire of their repressed and disparaged selves on to their own psyche and that of their peers with whom they share a common ancestry and ethnic identity.[50] This can be seen in the growing incidences of lateral violence, more popularly known as 'Black on Black crime', in inner-city areas in Britain and in the United States.

The Black British pastoral theologian Delroy Hall has written movingly and persuasively on the Windrush Generation in Britain, describing our existence as one of 'existential crucifixion'.[51] Hall argues that diaspora African peoples have endured the horrors of 'Good Friday' and our existential crucifixions at the hands of white hegemony, through the privations of slavery, colonialism and neocolonialism, but the exulting freedom of 'Easter Sunday' has yet to materialize. In effect, diasporan African peoples are still wrestling with an acute sense of being mired in 'Low Saturday' or 'Holy Saturday', stuck in a socio-religious and political form of liminality that speaks to the transformative nature of redemptive suffering that has thus far proved to be anything but redemptive.[52] A number of theologians have explored the theological significance of Holy Saturday and the liminal positionality of those stuck between the promises of Easter Sunday and the visceral pain and terror of Good Friday.[53]

The continued marginalization and suffering of Black people has raised an important, if not seemingly insoluble, theological problem: trying to correlate the agency of an omnipotent God with the ongoing negation of faithful peoples who have repeatedly called on God to end their existential travails, but to no avail. The Windrush Generation have not been able to fathom the mysteries of God's seeming inaction in the face of Black suffering any better than many of the luminaries of Black theology and religious studies in Black religion. I believe, however, that their learned and rehearsed repertoire of religio-cultural African retentive beliefs and practices operated as a bulwark against the avalanche of vituperative rhetoric and racist policies that constantly called into question the mysterious presence of the divine.[54] In effect, where is God when you most need a God to shield you from the mendacious and sometimes vicious operations of white hegemony?[55] For many of the Windrush Generation, the religio-cultural patterns of rehearsed practices of faith and spiritual disciplines played and continue to exert a form of psychological meaning-making that provides coping mechanisms for those mired in the pit of racialized forms of existential despair.[56]

It is in this context that the theological apparatus of dialectical spiritualities of Black Caribbean people in seeking to hold in tension suffering and negation alongside hope and transformation acts as an existential marker against the persuasive Black theodicy critique of William R. Jones.[57] Jones has argued against the dogmatic certainties of God having any particular or special relationship with Black people that is predicated on God's active involvement in Black peoples' lives.[58]

When Caribbean migrants came to Britain in the post-Windrush era they brought with them this legacy of spiritual wisdom from Africa, via the Caribbean. Upon arrival in the UK and encountering the hardships of economic deprivation and systemic racism,[59] what enabled many of them to cope with their experiences of rejection was a direct sense of God being with them; this 'God with them' was seen in the form of the Spirit that offers alternative ways of interpreting one's experience and dealing with the reality of marginalization and oppression.[60]

In short, Black bodies, particularly those of the Black proletariat of the Windrush Generation, represent the alternative constructs for what constitutes Christian normality is Britain. In their evocation of the politics, faith and the theology of difference, they embody a critical resistance ethic to the blandishments of empire and its toxic memory and the neocolonial constructs of imperial Mission Christianity.[61] Prior to the emergence of 'Black Lives Matter', Black people whose socio-religious formation had been shaped by the Christian faith were already in the business of seeking to refute the specious, biblical basis of their suffering.

Black theology – the precursor to Black Lives Matter

Black theology is predicated on the theological construction of people who self-identify and who have been racialized as 'Black'. Black identities, particularly, in Britain have always been diverse and complex. They defy any simplistic ways of categorizing people. The term 'Black' has to be understood within the context of Britain and the tradition of identity politics that emerged in the 1970s. So the term does not simply denote one's epidermis but is rather also a political statement relating to one's sense of politicized marginalization within the contested space that is Britain. That is, being 'Black' is not just about those who are of 'African descent' living in the UK. It also relates to other non-white groups who suffer and experience racism.

Using the term 'Black' is to identify oneself as on the alternative side of the fence in terms of what constitutes notions of being considered acceptable and belonging when juxtaposed with the dominant Eurocentric discourses that dominate the normal ways in which we see and understand what it means to be *authentically British*.[62]

This tradition of political mobilization around the once maligned and socially constructed term 'Black' has its roots in the political left and the rise of coalition politics in the 1970s.[63] While Black theology in Britain has been dominated by Black people of African and Caribbean descent, Asian scholars of the ilk of Inderjit Bhogal,[64] Mukti Barton[65] and Michael Jagessar[66] have made an impressive and much-needed contribution to the development and refining of this theological discipline. In using the term 'Black theology', we mean a radical rethinking of how we conceive of God and Jesus in light of the ongoing suffering and oppression of Black people in a world run and governed by white people. Black theology identifies God revealed in Jesus as committed to liberation and freeing Black people from racism and oppression.

The roots of Black theology arise from lives of enslaved African peoples in the so-called 'New World' of the Americas. Enslaved Africans in the Americas and the Caribbean through their introduction to Christianity by white slave owners latched on to the inherent liberative aspects of the Bible, in particular the decisive intervention of God on the side of the oppressed in the Exodus narrative. In the Exodus narrative God demands that Pharaoh 'let my people go'. So God was not seen as neutral nor distant. The key texts in Black theology remain the early work undertaken by James H. Cone, who is still seen as the founder and the greatest of Black theologians. Cone's early books include *Black Theology and Black Power*, *A Black Theology of Liberation* and *God of the Oppressed*.[67] In all three texts, Cone identifies God with the suffering and humiliation of Black people. When he asserts that God is 'Black' he is identifying God with those who are marginalized and oppressed, for whom the term 'Black' has always been linked with negative connotations and demonic imagery. God in Black theology is the active force that overthrows injustice and releases the captors from their oppression.

Black theology seeks to promote the significance of Black people within the sacred story of God's interaction with humankind (i.e. the Bible) and as a means of promoting ideas of reconciliation and living together in unity, in a world that transcends racism. The late Cain Hope Felder, a famous and respected African American New Testament scholar, in his commentary on the Pentecost narrative, identifies the references to Mesopotamia, Pamphylia, Egypt and parts of Libya near Crete[68] as being places connected with Africa. He states:

> Indeed, the physiognomy of the Elamites of Mesopotamian archaeological reliefs shows them to have been a dark-skinned people with hair of tight curls. The modern academy has unfortunately zealously sought to 'whitewash' all inhabitants of the ancient 'Near East' in the vicinity of the Tigris and the Euphrates rivers.[69]

Felder and others[70] are asserting both a Black presence in and a Black, African-centred form of interpretation for reading the Bible. There is difference at the heart of this story. The people are transformed but their differences – the uniqueness of their identities – do not disappear. Many of these people at the heart of the story are Black, so being Black is important and should not be relegated or downplayed, as being of no consequence or value.[71]

Just as the Incarnation – Jesus' historical presence in the world – shows that being flesh, being human and living in a particular time and space (a context) is important, so too does Pentecost. Pentecost shows that the Holy Spirit does not eradicate our differences; rather, the Spirit celebrates them. But life in the Spirit (i.e. living as Christians) is about being one in Christ, in fellowship with each other; being in community with each other and with Christ can take us beyond (transcend) what it means to be linked to a particular identity – in this case, being Black. The status that is often linked to particular identities (being male or being a Jew for example) are exploded. The Spirit does transcend all this (Gal. 3.28). There is, therefore, a tension between these two differing ways of seeing identity. One, that in Christ the differences around ethnicity or gender are overcome and made irrelevant. But also the counter view that in Christ we come to celebrate those very things as essential parts of who we are. Black theology seeks to look at how we live together as people across our differences of ethnicity and cultures, class, and economic disparities.

Black Lives Matter

The existence of the Black Lives Matter[72] movement is testament to the contested nature of Black existence. As Dwight Hopkins has shown, the nature of recognition of Black humanity by white hegemony is relatively recent and, indeed, is a novel epistemological insight for some white people.[73] The trauma experienced by the Black body can be seen in the towering work of James Cone as he outlines the visceral nature of lynching, a reminder of the existential travails faced by Black people in the United States.[74]

Black and womanist theologians have wrestled with existential challenges of being a Black human being in a world that has often been indifferent (at best) and incredibly unjust (at worst) in its treatment of Black people. In more recent times, increasing focus has been placed on the 'Black body' as a site of epistemological struggle in postmodern Black theological discourse. In making the point of departure the subtextual nature of the Black body and the performative hermeneutics of style, as an alternative vista for a resistance ethic that is replete within Black religion, Pinn has made a major epistemic break in the means by which Black religious scholars seek to understand the very intent of this elemental phenomenon. When I began my doctoral studies in the mid-1990s, the accepted primary goal of Black religious studies, even more so in Black liberation theology, was the necessity of rehabilitating the damage unleashed on the Black psyche by the vicious nature of white supremacy. One of my earliest forays into the fieldwork that would later become my doctorate was to explore the work of Black psychologists as they sought to offer Black children and young people alternative narratives in order to rethink their existential identities in postcolonial Britain.[75]

In terms of the religio-cultural framing of Black people and their existential struggles, it is difficult to overestimate the significance of W. E. B. Du Bois's classic text *The Souls of Black Folk*, first published in 1903. Du Bois detailed a phenomenon he termed 'double consciousness'. In using this term, Du Bois was articulating the psychological struggle at work in the consciousness of African Americans seeking to reconcile two opposing realities at war within the Black psyche.[76] This dialectical struggle was one between competing notions of truth, whether determined by a self-affirming internalized form of subjectivity, what Pinn calls the quest for 'complex subjectivity'[77] (on which greater comment will be made shortly), against which there is an externalized form of negation and objectification. Du Bois's most memorable comment in this book that has, to a great extent, helped to define Black diasporan discourse over the course of the last century, was that the 'the problem of the twentieth century is the problem of the color line'.[78] Du Bois argues that this dialectical struggle, between these two 'unreconciled strivings',[79] has continued to fight its tumultuous struggle within the battlefield of the Black mind.

Pinn's theorizing on the Black body as the site for theological reflection has been an intellectual transformation that has created an alternate vantage point for assessing the agency of Black people. His acute dissection of the machinery of torture and oppression of Black bodies, and its impact on Black subjectivity, is a dramatic scholarly breakthrough.[80]

Pinn's reflections on the transgressive nature of the Black body have opened vistas for later works that have focused on the corporeality of the Black body and its theological significance. One can see this significance in the later developments in womanist theology and ethics, in which womanists such as M. Shawn Copeland[81] and Eboni Marshall Turman,[82] for example, have developed scholarly work reflecting on the intellectual significance of Black women's bodies.

As I have stated previously in this chapter, I believe that to belong to British society and to engage with white Christianity, for a Black person, necessitates at some intuitive level a denial of one's self. To be Black is to have one's experiences, history and ongoing reality ignored, disparaged and ridiculed. It is to be rendered an insignificant presence among the many who are deemed one's betters and superiors. The continued ways in which Black bodies are objectified speaks to the enduring challenge evinced in Black theology, namely, to retain a sense of one's human subjectivity. Pinn reminds us that to be a human subject is to possess the ability of creating meaning through art, culture and science, and to reimagine one's world through the prism of religion that inspires the imagination of the human subject. Subjectivity is the ability to create meaning and be a constructive being in creating and remaking one's world. Objects are acted upon and are named, but subjects name themselves and create internalized meaning, seeking to express agency, self-actualization and transcendence.

Complex subjectivity is the attempt by humans to become more than the simple objectified fixed entity oppressive structures try to make them become. Subjectivity is in contradistinction to being an object. An object has no internal meaning in and of itself. The only meaning it has is that which the owner or possessor of it gives it. Objectification is the process of delimiting the power of a subject and so reducing their agency so that they are in effect reduced to becoming an object. The privations of 'fixed identity', which is the dangerous offspring of objectification, is the imposition of non-changing and unmediated forms of imposed constructions of self on to marginalized and oppressed peoples.

Pinn's notion of complex subjectivity speaks to continued struggles evinced by Black people to proclaim a form of humanity that is not compromised and confined by the limits placed on it by the existence of systemic racism and the dominance of white supremacy.

I would like to remind us of the searing contradiction to diasporan Black life, caught up in two brief descriptions of the Black condition. First, from perhaps the greatest artist of the twentieth century, Louis Armstrong and his 1929 recording of Fats Waller's 'Black and Blue' – the words are as follows:

Cold empty bed, springs hard as lead
Feel like Old Ned, wish I was dead
All my life through, I've been so Black and blue

Even the mouse ran from my house
They laugh at you, and scorn you too
What did I do to be so Black and blue?

I'm white – inside – but that don't help my case
Cause I can't hide what is in my face

How would it end? Ain't got a friend
My only sin is in my skin
What did I do to be so Black and blue?[83]

Slavery is long gone but anti-Black racism has long outlived the institution that helped to breathe it into life. In our contemporary era, the underlying framework of Blackness, which still symbolically is seen as representing the problematic other, finds expression in a white police officer placing his knee on the neck of a Black man and despite the plaintive pleas of 'I can't breathe', the officer remains unmoved and maintains his violent posture until this Black man dies.[84] One cannot understand the futility of this death unless you understand that this is no new phenomenon. White power has viewed Black flesh as disposable for the past 500 years. The reason why Black theology came into being was simply to assert that our lives mattered in an era when we were viewed purely as chattel and objects to be placed on a financial ledger.

And before any one suggests that this is a purely American phenomenon, then let me recall the death of Clinton McCurbin, an African Caribbean man who died of asphyxia at the hands of the police in Wolverhampton on 20 February 1987, having been arrested for using a stolen credit card.[85] Eyewitness accounts spoke of seeing McCurbin gasping for breath as white officers pinned him to the floor and crushed the air out of his body, regardless of the fact that his body had grown limp for several minutes as he lost consciousness. Later that year, despite the cautionary words from my very law-abiding and hyper-religious and respectable parents to focus on my studies (I was in the last year of my degree course in Church History at Birmingham university), I nevertheless travelled to Wolverhampton along with thousands of others to protest the death of Clinton McCurbin.

That was my very first march. No officers were ever charged with his death. The coroner ruled it death by misadventure. Black people across the Midlands protested, sang songs of defiance, we railed with anger, but white power, whether in the shape of the Independent Police Complaints Commission (IPCC), or the coroner, or the media (McCurbin had a criminal record, so presumably he deserved to die), they all had no problem in ignoring our pleas for justice, because in the final analysis, Black bodies and people who inhabit those bodies simply do not matter. Our existential pain at the futility of Black life remained raw, visceral and unheeded by the strictures of white entitlement in Britain.

This brings me to the curious case of the toppling of the statue of Edward Colston in Bristol as part of a Black Lives Matter protest on 7 June 2020. It can be argued that the pulling down or removal of statues has become a distraction against the wider issues of systemic racism that need to be addressed more than the removal of historic artefacts often ignored by most people in their daily activities. And yes, that is correct if the focus is solely on statues in and of themselves. But let us consider first the point of the Black Lives Matter movement. It emerged in order to counter the obvious fact that Black lives do not matter. This is not just a question of economics or materiality; it is also about seemingly 'ephemeral matters' like the impact on our psyche and associated questions of representation and spirituality. The latter attends to the ways in which our ongoing trauma as Black people, many of us the descendants of enslaved peoples, continues to be experienced in postcolonial Britain.

It has been interesting observing the concern of many white Christians for matters of law and order and governance and property with the tearing down of the Colston statue in Bristol. Property and capital have always mattered more to the British than respect and justice for Black people, as the settlement for the ending of slavery demonstrated in 1833. White slave owners were awarded £20 million for giving up their enslaved Africans who were deemed to be chattels.[86] Enslaved Africans and their descendants received nothing.

Black people, many of whom are the descendants of enslaved peoples, have lived in that city with the sight of a statue built in honour of slave trader. It is hard to explain the subterranean existential trauma felt having to witness the sight of a heroic statue built in honour of a slave trader! If one wanted a tangible example of the ways in which the body politic of the nation has always exerted a wanton disregard for Black people and our feelings, then the Colston statue is a classic representative form of state-sanctioned Black negation. Polite petitions to move these and other statues were ignored. Long before a so-called mob tore this one down, activists asked for it to be moved to a museum where those who deliberately wanted to see it could, but saving the rest of us from the ignominy of having the lives of our oppressed ancestors constantly insulted. White authority ignored our claims because Black lives and our resultant feelings do not matter. Black Lives do not matter in the face of white complacency and disregard. Therefore, I find it interesting that following the pulling down of a statue, we had the usual furrowed brow of some white Christians sharing their ethical concern for law and order and the dangers of mob rule.[87]

In 2007, I, along with many others, campaigned for a national monument to mark the epoch of the slave trade and the countless millions who died under the yoke of British slavery. We were peaceful, respectful and went through the usual democratic and representative channels, and first the Labour government under Blair, then the coalition government under Cameron and finally May's government all dismissed our pleas. We were courteous, respectful and restrained; we made our entreaties in a time-honoured and peaceful way. But we were ignored because Black feelings do not matter, because ultimately, Black lives do not matter. We campaigned for an apology for Britain's involvement in the slave trade and Blair gave us a 'deeply sorry' but no apology because the slave trade, sanctioned by greedy white mercantile interests, said it was legal at the time. So no apology and certainly no reparations.

Once again, we were not hectoring or behaving like a mob. We made our arguments (some of us have written books, essays and articles[88]) and it has still made no difference. So we continue to live with the psychological and spiritual damage of witnessing monuments to the people who made billions from peddling the Black flesh of our ancestors, and this is before we even get to the tangible manifestations of economic hardship and the social deprivation facing Black bodies in postcolonial Britain as revealed by Covid-19.

The task of challenging the toxicity of white privilege is necessary if the universality and inclusivity of the Church is to be continually realized. Christian discipleship must continue to work within an ethnic of post-colonial, anti-racism and deconstructive Whiteness. Then, and only then, will catholicity and Christian discipleship begin to express its praxiological intent that has been lacking all these years in postcolonial Britain.

Black people of the Windrush Generation have been loyal to Britain, the so-called 'Mother Country' of empire. Our commitment to British Christianity across all the major denominations has demonstrably exemplified across several centuries, and across the last 70 years of our stay in postcolonial Britain during the Windrush epoch.

Undoubtedly, life in Britain for the Windrush Generation has been one of travail, but it has not been entirely without its benefits and compensations. Many of the second-generation Windrush Generation people, like myself, have prospered and exceeded the dreams of our parents, who came as penniless migrants hoping for a better life in the so-called 'Mother Country'. These successes, however, have come at a heavy cost for the bulk of our numbers and they take no account of the non-material, existential and ontological struggles to be self-determined people whose lives have been imbued with a positive sense belonging within a country that has not always affirmed our presence. For Black people of the Windrush Generation to express gratitude for their lives in Britain, the nation will need to deconstruct its addiction to white privilege and entitlement and recant of the anti-Blackness ethic that is replete within Mission Christianity that has created the template for the corporate notions of Britishness, from which we have often been excluded. One hopes that a new epoch awaits! If racial justice and equity can be generated for Black people, then perhaps my own sense of gratitude for being British and will rise. Maybe then, after a life-time of social, political and cultural negation, I will feel differently about this nation. It is my hope that a new future awaits us all. Time will tell if this is ever going to be realized!

Bibliography

Asante, Molefi Kete, 'Afrocentricity and Culture' in *African Culture: The Rhythms of Unity*, ed. Molefi Kete Asante and Kariamu Welsh Asante, Trenton, NJ: First Africa World Press, 1990.

Ashby Jr, Homer U., *Our Home is Over Jordan: A Black Pastoral Theology*, St. Louis, MO: Chalice Press, 2003.

Bailey, Randall C. and Jacquelyn Grant (eds), *The Recovery of Black Presence: An Interdisciplinary Exploration*, Nashville, TN: Abingdon Press, 1995.

Balasuriya, Tissa, 'Liberation of the Affluent', *Black Theology: An International Journal* 1, 1 (2001), pp. 83–113.

Balthasar, Hans Urs von, *Heart of the World*, Rome: Ignatius Press, 1980.

Barton, Mukti, *Rejection, Resistance and Resurrection*, London: Darton, Longman & Todd, 2005.

Beckford, Robert, *Dread and Pentecostal*, London: SPCK, 2000.

Bhogal, Inderjit S., 'Citizenship' in *Legacy: Anthology in Memory of Jillian Brown*, ed. Anthony G. Reddie, Peterborough: The Methodist Publishing House, 2000, pp. 137–41.

Bhogal, Inderjit S., *On The Hoof: Theology in Transit*, Sheffield: Penistone Publications, 2001.

Butler, Lee H., *Liberating Our Dignity, Saving Our Souls: A New Theory of African American Identity Formation*, St. Louis, MO: Chalice Press, 2006.

Calloway, Jamall A., '"To Struggle Up a Never-Ending Stair": Theodicy and the Failure it Gifts to Black Liberation Theology', *Black Theology: An International Journal* 18, 3 (2020), pp. 223–45.

Carretta, Vincent (ed.), *Letters of the Late Ignatius Sancho, an African*, New York and London: Penguin Books, 1998.

Carretta, Vincent (ed.), *Olaudah Equiano: The Interesting Narrative and other Writings*, New York and London: Penguin Books, 1995.

Cone, James H., *Black Theology and Black Power*, Maryknoll, NY: Orbis Books, 1969/1989.

Cone, James H., *A Black Theology of Liberation*, Maryknoll, NY: Orbis Books, 1970/1990.

Cone, James H., *God of the Oppressed*, Maryknoll, NY: Orbis Books, 1975/2005.

Cone, James H., *My Soul Looks Back*, Maryknoll, NY: Orbis Books, 2000.

Cone, James H., *The Cross and the Lynching Tree*, Maryknoll, NY: Orbis Books, 2011.

Copeland, M. Shawn, *Enfleshing Freedom: Body, Race, and Being*, Minneapolis, MN: Fortress Press, 2009.

Day, Keri, 'Global Economics and U.S. Public Policy: Human Liberation for the Global Poor', *Black Theology: An International Journal* 9, 1 (2011), pp. 9–33.

Douglas, Kelly Brown, *What's Faith Got to Do with It? Black Bodies, Christian Souls*, New York: Orbis Books, 2005.

Du Bois, W. E. B., *The Souls of Black Folk*, New York: Bantam Books, 1989, 1st published in 1903.

Eze, Emmanuel C., *Race and the Enlightenment*, Oxford: Blackwell, 1997.

Felder, Cain Hope (ed.), *Stony The Road We Trod: African American Biblical Interpretation*, Minneapolis, MN: Fortress Press, 1991.

Felder, Cain Hope (ed.), *The African Heritage Study Bible*, Nashville, TN: The James C. Winston Publishing Company, 1993.

Fryer, Peter Fryer, *Staying Power: The History of Black People in Britain*, London: Pluto Press, 2018.

Gilroy, Paul, *There Ain't No Black in the Union Jack*, London: Hutchinson, 1987.

Gilroy, Paul, *The Black Atlantic: Modernity and Double Consciousness*, London: Verso, 1993.

Goatley, David, *Were You There? Godforsakenness in Slave Religion*, New York: Orbis Books, 1996.

Gorringe, T. J., *Furthering Humanity: A Theology of Culture*, Aldershot: Ashgate, 2004.

Goulbourne, Harry, 'Collective Action and Black Politics' in *Black Success: Essays in Racial and Ethnic Studies*, ed. Doreen McCalla, Birmingham: DMee Vision Learning, 2003, pp. 9–38.

Hall, Delroy, 'The Middle Passage as Existential Crucifixion', *Black Theology: An International Journal* 7, 1 (2009), pp. 45–63.

Hall, Delroy W., '"But God meant it for good": Inter-personal conflict in an African Caribbean Pentecostal Congregation – a Pastoral Study', unpublished PhD thesis, University of Birmingham, 2013.

Hood, Robert E., *Begrimed and Black: Christian Traditions on Blacks and Blackness*, Minneapolis, MN: Fortress Press, 1994.

Hopkins, Dwight N., *Heart and Head: Black Theology, Past, Present, and Future*, New York: Palgrave Macmillan, 2002.

Hopkins, Dwight N., *Being Human: 'Race' Culture and Religion*, Minneapolis, MN: Fortress Press, 2005.

Hull, John M., *Towards the Prophetic Church: A Study of Christian Mission*, London: SCM Press, 2014.

Jagessar, Michael N., *Full Life for All: The Work and Theology of Philip A. Potter*, Geneva: WCC Publications, 1998.

Jagessar, Michael N., 'A Brief Con-version: A Caribbean and Black British Postcolonial Scrutiny of Christian Conversion', *Black Theology: An International Journal* 7, 3 (2009), pp. 300–24.

Jagessar, Michael N., *Ethnicity: The Inclusive Church Resource*, London: Darton, Longman & Todd, 2015.

Jagessar, Michael N. and Anthony G. Reddie (eds), *Postcolonial Black British Theology*, Peterborough: Epworth Press, 2007.

James, Winston, 'Migration, Racism and Identity' in *Inside Babylon*, ed. Winston James and Clive Harris, London: Verso, 1993.

Jennings, Willie James, *The Christian Imagination: Theology and the Origins of Race*, New Haven, CT: Yale University Press, 2010.

Jennings, Willie James, *After Whiteness: An Education in Belonging*, Grand Rapids, MI: Eerdmans, 2020.

Johnson, Cedric C., *Race, Religion, and Resilience in the Neo-Liberal Age*, New York: Palgrave Macmillan, 2016.

Johnson, Sylvester A., *The Myth of Ham in Nineteenth-Century American Christianity: Race, Heathens, and the People of God*, New York: Palgrave Macmillan, 2004.

Jones, William R., *Is God a White Racist?*, New York: Beacon Books, 1973.

Leech, Ken, *Struggle in Babylon*, London: Sheldon Press, 1988.

Leech, Ken, *The Eye of the Storm: Spiritual Resources for the Pursuit of Justice*, London: Darton, Longman & Todd, 1992.

Leech, Ken, *Through Our Long Exile*, London: Darton, Longman & Todd, 2001.

Maxime, Jocelyn Emama, 'Identity and Consciousness' in *To Overcome is to Undertake: Report of the First Connexional Conference for Young Black Methodists*, London: The Methodist Church, 1991, pp. 13–24.

Morrison, Doreen, 'Reparations: A Call to fulfil the promise of education made by Baptists to the enslaved and their descendants through the 1835 Negro Education Grant' in *Journeying to Justice: Contributions to the Baptist Tradition Across the Black Atlantic*, ed. Anthony G. Reddie, Wale Hudson-Roberts and Gale Richards, Milton Keynes: Paternoster Press, 2017, pp. 149–66.

Perkinson, James W., *White Theology: Outing Supremacy in Modernity*, New York: Palgrave Macmillan, 2004.

Pinn, Anthony B., *Terror and Triumph: The Nature of Black Religion*, Minneapolis, MN: Fortress Press, 2003.

Pinn, Anthony B. and Dwight N. Hopkins (eds), *Loving the Body: Black Religious Studies and the Erotic*, New York: Palgrave Macmillan, 2004.

Pinn, Anthony B. (ed.), *Black Religion and Aesthetics: Religious Thought and Life in Africa and the African Diaspora*, New York: Palgrave Macmillan, 2009.

Prince, Mary, *The History of Mary Prince, a West Indian Slave. Related by Herself. With a Supplement by the Editor. To Which is Added, the Narrative of Asa-Asa, a Captured African*, London: F. Westley and A. H. Davis, 1831.

Rambo, Shelly, *Spirit and Trauma: A Theology of Remaining*, Louisville, KY: Westminster John Knox Press, 2010.

Ramdin, Ron, *Reimaging Britain: 500 Years of Black and Asian History*, London: Pluto Press, 1999.

Ray, Stephen, 'Contending for the Cross: Black Theology and the Ghosts of Modernity', *Black Theology: An International Journal* 8, 1 (2010), pp. 53–68.

Reddie, Anthony G., *Growing into Hope: Believing and Expecting – Vol. 1*, Peterborough: The Methodist Publishing House, 1998.

Reddie, Anthony G., *Nobodies to Somebodies: A Practical Theology for Education and Liberation*, Peterborough: Epworth Press, 2003.

Reddie, Anthony G., 'A Black Theological Approach to Reconciliation: Responding to the 200th Anniversary of the Abolition of the Slave Trade in Britain', *Black Theology: An International Journal* 5, 2 (July 2007).

Reddie, Anthony G., 'A Dialectical Spirituality of Improvisation: The Ambiguity of Black Engagement with Sacred Texts' in *Black Religion and Aesthetics: Religious Thought and Life in Africa and the African Diaspora*, ed. Anthony B. Pinn, New York: Palgrave Macmillan, 2009, pp. 153–71.

Reddie, Anthony G., *Black Theology, Slavery and Contemporary Christianity: 200 Years and No Apology*, Farnham: Ashgate, 2010.

Reddie, Richard S., *Abolition! The Struggle to Abolish Slavery in the British Colonies*, Oxford: Lion, 2007.

Turman, Eboni Marshall, *Toward a Womanist Ethic of Incarnation: Black Bodies, the Black Church, and the Council of Chalcedon*, New York: Palgrave Macmillan, 2013.

Turner, Carlton, *Overcoming Self-Negation*, Eugene, OR: Pickwick Publications, 2020.

Warrior, Robert Allen, 'A Native American Perspective: Canaanites, Cowboys and Indians' in *Voices from the Margin: Interpreting the Bible in the Third World*, ed. R. S. Sugirtharajah, Maryknoll, NY: Orbis Books, 1997, pp. 277–85.

West, Cornel, *Race Matters*, Boston, MA: Beacon Press, 1993.

Williams, Delores, *Sisters in the Wilderness: The Challenge of Womanist God-Talk*, Maryknoll, NY: Orbis Books, 1993.

Williams, Eric, *Capitalism and Slavery*, London: Andre Deutsch, 1983.

Willis, Lerleen, 'The Pilgrim's Process: Coping with Racism Through Faith', *Black Theology: An International Journal* 4, 2 (2006), pp. 210–32.

Internet Links

'Black Lives Matter', https://blacklivesmatter.com/about/.Fats Waller, Harry Brooks and Andy Razaf, '(What Did I do to be so) Black and Blue'. For details, see https://en.wikipedia.org/wiki/Black_and_Blue_(Fats_Waller_song), accessed 19.1.2021.

'Murder of George Floyd', *Wikipedia*, https://en.wikipedia.org/wiki/Killing_of_George_Floyd, accessed 3.3.2021.

Ethan Shone, 'Columnist recalls incident with "shocking parallels" to George Floyd killing', *HoldtheFrontPage*, www.holdthefrontpage.co.uk/2020/news/deputy-editor-reflects-on-similarities-between-george-floyds-murder-and-an-incident-early-in-his-career/, accessed 3.3.2021.

Notes

1 See James H. Cone, *My Soul Looks Back* (Maryknoll, NY: Orbis Books, 2000).

2 In using the term 'white Christianity', I am talking about people of European extraction and descent, who form the majority of the population of the UK, who believe in the God revealed in Jesus Christ and seek to give expression to the central tenets of the Christian faith in myriad forms of social-cultural practices.

3 See Robert E. Hood, *Begrimed and Black: Christian Traditions on Blacks and Blackness* (Minneapolis, MN: Fortress Press, 1994), pp. 23–43.

4 Robert Beckford, *Dread and Pentecostal* (London: SPCK, 2000), pp. 95–130.

5 See Emmanuel C. Eze, *Race and the Enlightenment* (Oxford: Blackwell, 1997).

6 See James W. Perkinson, *White Theology: Outing Supremacy in Modernity* (New York: Palgrave Macmillan, 2004), pp. 154–84.

7 Dwight N. Hopkins, *Being Human: Race, Culture, and Religion* (Minneapolis, MN: Fortress Press, 2005), pp. 144–60.

8 One of the best texts in this regard from a Christian theological view is

by Richard S. Reddie, *Abolition! The Struggle to Abolish Slavery in the British Colonies* (Oxford: Lion, 2007).

9 Cedric C. Johnson, *Race, Religion, and Resilience in the Neo-Liberal Age* (New York: Palgrave Macmillan, 2016), pp. 101–26.

10 See Lee H. Butler, *Liberating Our Dignity, Saving Our Souls: A New Theory of African American Identity Formation* (St. Louis, MO: Chalice Press, 2006). See also Homer U. Ashby Jr, *Our Home is Over Jordan: A Black Pastoral Theology* (St. Louis, MO: Chalice Press, 2003).

11 See Delroy Hall's doctoral work, which has explored the psychosocial needs of African Caribbeans in Britain and the pastoral implications for this community. Delroy W. Hall, '"But God meant it for good": Inter-personal Conflict in an African Caribbean Pentecostal Congregation – a Pastoral Study', unpublished PhD thesis, University of Birmingham, 2013.

12 See Keri Day, 'Global Economics and U.S. Public Policy: Human Liberation for the Global Poor', *Black Theology: An International Journal* 9, 1 (2011), pp. 9–33.

13 Perhaps the best explanation for this phenomenon in terms of Black and womanist theologies can be found in Keri Day's recent work. See Day, 'Global Economics and U.S. Public Policy'.

14 This issue is addressed with great acuity by the renowned Sri Lankan Liberation theologian Tissa Balasuriya. See Tissa Balasuriya, 'Liberation of the Affluent', *Black Theology: An International Journal* 1, 1 (2001), pp. 83–113.

15 See Hood, *Begrimed and Black*.

16 Kelly Brown Douglas, *What's Faith Got to Do with It? Black Bodies, Christian Souls* (Maryknoll, NY: Orbis Books, 2005).

17 See Exodus 23.20–33 and the list of peoples overthrown in the book of Joshua chapter 12. For a critical rereading of the Exodus narrative, which explores an anti-imperialist, anti-hegemonic hermeneutic, see Robert Allen Warrior, 'A Native American Perspective: Canaanites, Cowboys and Indians' in *Voices from the Margin: Interpreting the Bible in the Third World*, ed. R. S. Sugirtharajah (Maryknoll, NY: Orbis Books, 1997), pp. 277–85.

18 See Stephen Ray, 'Contending for the Cross: Black Theology and the Ghosts of Modernity', *Black Theology: An International Journal* 8, 1 (2010), pp. 53–68.

19 See Willie James Jennings, *After Whiteness: An Education in Belonging* (Grand Rapids, MI: Eerdmans, 2020), pp. 23–156.

20 See Willie James Jennings, *The Christian Imagination: Theology and the Origins of Race* (New Haven, CT: Yale University Press, 2010), pp. 1–10.

21 See Sylvester A. Johnson, *The Myth of Ham in Nineteenth-Century American Christianity: Race, Heathens, and the People of God* (New York: Palgrave Macmillan, 2004).

22 See Brown Douglas, *What's Faith Got to Do with It?*.

23 For a more in-depth analysis on this issue, see Anthony G. Reddie, 'A Black Theological Approach to Reconciliation: Responding to the 200th Anniversary of the Abolition of the Slave Trade in Britain', *Black Theology: An International Journal* 5, 2 (July 2007).

24 See Doreen Morrison, 'Reparations: A Call to fulfil the promise of education made by Baptists to the enslaved and their descendants through the 1835 Negro Education Grant', *Journeying to Justice: Contributions to the Baptist Tradition Across the Black Atlantic*, ed. Anthony G. Reddie, Wale Hudson-Roberts and Gale Richards (Milton Keynes: Paternoster Press, 2017), pp. 149–66.

25 See Molefi Kete Asante, 'Afrocentricity and Culture' in *African Culture: The Rhythms of Unity*, ed. Molefi Kete Asante and Kariamu Welsh Asante (Trenton, NJ: First Africa World Press, 1990).

26 See Eric Williams, *Capitalism and Slavery* (London: Andre Deutsch, 1983).

27 See Dwight N. Hopkins, *Heart and Head: Black Theology, Past, Present, and Future* (New York: Palgrave Macmillan, 2002), pp. 127–54.

28 See Anthony B. Pinn, *Terror and Triumph: The Nature of Black Religion* (Minneapolis, MN: Fortress Press, 2003). See also Anthony B. Pinn and Dwight N. Hopkins (eds), *Loving the Body: Black Religious Studies and the Erotic* (New York: Palgrave Macmillan, 2004) and Anthony B. Pinn (ed.), *Black Religion and Aesthetics: Religious Thought and Life in Africa and the African Diaspora* (New York: Palgrave Macmillan, 2009).

29 Pinn, *Terror and Triumph*, pp. 1–80.

30 Pinn, *Terror and Triumph*, p. 6.

31 This phenomenon and theme has been explored by Robert Hood, *Begrimed and Black*.

32 This idea is taken from Kelly Brown Douglas' excellent study on Black bodies and how they have been policed and controlled within the religious framework of Christianity. See Brown Douglas, *What's Faith Got To Do With It?*.

33 Brown Douglas, *What's Faith Got To Do With It?*, pp. 3–38.

34 Brown Douglas, *What's Faith Got To Do With It?*, p. 37.

35 Anthony Pinn, 'Introduction' in *Loving the Body*, pp. 1–8.

36 My friend and colleague in the Black Theology in Britain Movement, Michael Jagessar, has questioned the extent to which 'Christian conversion' has ever delivered on its intent to provide a wholly new existence and identity for Black people, particularly those of Caribbean descent. He feels that the claims for the new, over and against the old, provide an unhelpful binary between the two modes of being, plus they are usually accompanied by a repudiation of the often folk-orientated, historically developed, religious sensibilities that emerge from the cultures of one's ancestral heritage. See Michael N. Jagessar, 'A Brief Conversion: A Caribbean and Black British Postcolonial Scrutiny of Christian Conversion', *Black Theology: An International Journal* 7, 3 (2009), pp. 300–24.

37 See Anthony G. Reddie, *Growing Into Hope: Believing and Expecting – Vol. 1* (Peterborough: The Methodist Publishing House, 1998), p. 8. This training exercise was constructed (using data from the 1991 census) to assist predominantly white leaders who work with Black children to understand both the context in which Black people live in Britain, and the psychological and emotional affects of being a minority in a white-dominated country. Black people who predominantly live in inner-city areas have divided their existence in this country into areas of familiarity. Black children move interchangeably, from areas of great familiarity (where Black people although a minority are suddenly in the majority) to other situations where they become seemingly insignificant. This pattern has not changed appreciably since the post-war wave of mass African Caribbean migration to this country. This interchangeability of African Caribbean life, which is centred on differing contexts, has given rise to issues of cultural dissonance. This issue is dealt with in greater detail in Anthony G. Reddie, *Nobodies to Somebodies: A Practical Theology for Education and Liberation* (Peterborough: Epworth Press, 2003).

38 Kenneth Leech, *Through Our Long Exile* (London: Darton, Longman & Todd, 2001), pp. 87–135. See also his very influential *Struggle in Babylon* (London:

Sheldon Press, 1988) and *The Eye of the Storm: Spiritual Resources for the Pursuit of Justice* (London: Darton, Longman & Todd, 1992).

39 Mary Prince was a Black slave woman in the nineteenth century who published her autobiography in 1831 detailing her experiences of hardship, struggle and emancipation. Her book was entitled *The History of Mary Prince, a West Indian Slave. Related by Herself. With a Supplement by the Editor. To Which Is Added, the Narrative of Asa-Asa, a Captured African* (London: F. Westley and A. H. Davis, 1831). Her book was a key text in the abolitionary movement of the nineteenth century.

40 See Olaudah Equiano and Vincent Carretta (eds), *The Interesting Narrative and Other Writings* (New York and London: Penguin Books, 1995).

41 See Vincent Caretta (ed.), *Letters of the Late Ignatius Sancho, an African* (New York and London: Penguin Books, 1998).

42 Peter Fryer, *Staying Power: The History of Black People in Britain* (London: Pluto Press, 2018), p. 10.

43 See Caretta, *Letters of the Late Ignatius Sancho, an African.*

44 See Prince, *The History of Mary Prince.*

45 Womanist theology can be seen as a related branch of Black theology. It is an approach to theology that begins with the experience of Black women and women of colour. Womanist theology utilizes the experience of Black women to challenge the tripartite ills of racism, sexism and classism. This discipline is influenced by (Black) feminist thought.

46 See Delores Williams, *Sisters in the Wilderness: The Challenge of Womanist God-Talk* (Maryknoll, NY: Orbis Books, 1993).

47 Winston James, 'Migration, Racism and Identity' in Winston James and Clive Harris (eds), *Inside Babylon* (London: Verso, 1993). Also Ron Ramdin, *Reimaging Britain: 500 Years of Black and Asian History* (London: Pluto Press, 1999), pp. 141–90 and 258–305.

48 Paul Gilroy, *There Ain't No Black in the Union Jack* (London: Hutchinson, 1987). See also Gilroy's *The Black Atlantic: Modernity and Double Consciousness* (London: Verso, 1993).

49 See Williams, *Capitalism and Slavery.*

50 Cornel West, *Race Matters* (Boston, MA: Beacon Press, 1993), pp. 11–15.

51 See Delroy Hall, 'The Middle Passage as Existential Crucifixion', *Black Theology: An International Journal* 7, 1 (2009), pp. 45–63.

52 Hall, 'The Middle Passage as Existential Crucifixion', pp. 46–54.

53 Other theologians have explored the theological significance of 'Holy Saturday' as a liminal space in which the unresolved search for redemption continues. See Shelly Rambo, *Spirit and Trauma: A Theology of Remaining* (Louisville, KY: Westminster John Knox Press, 2010), pp. 45–80. See also Hans Urs von Balthasar, *Heart of the World* (Rome: Ignatius Press, 1980).

54 See Lerleen Willis, 'The Pilgrim's Process: Coping with Racism Through Faith', *Black Theology: An International Journal* 4, 2 (2006), pp. 210–32.

55 See David Goatley, *Were You There? Godforsakenness in Slave Religion* (Maryknoll, NY: Orbis Books, 1996).

56 See Carlton Turner, *Overcoming Self-Negation* (Eugene, OR: Pickwick Publications, 2020), pp. 130–62.

57 See William R. Jones, *Is God a White Racist?* (New York: Beacon Books, 1973).

58 See also Jamall A. Calloway, '"To Struggle Up a Never-Ending Stair": Theodicy and the Failure it Gifts to Black Liberation Theology', *Black Theology: An International Journal* 18, 3 (2020), pp. 223–45.

59 See Mukti Barton, *Rejection, Resistance and Resurrection: Speaking out on Racism in the Church* (London: Darton, Longman & Todd, 2005) for perhaps the best scholarly, first-hand account of Black and Asian peoples' experience of dealing with racism in the Church of England.

60 Anthony G. Reddie, 'A Dialectical Spirituality of Improvisation: The Ambiguity of Black Engagement with Sacred Texts' in Anthony B. Pinn (ed.), *Black Religion and Aesthetics: Religious Thought and Life in Africa and the African Diaspora* (New York: Palgrave Macmillan, 2009), pp. 153–71.

61 In using this term, I am speaking of a historical phenomenon in which there existed (and continues to this day) an interpenetrating relationship between European expansionism, notions of white superiority and the material artefact of the apparatus of empire. This form of Christianity became the conduit for the expansionist paradigms of Eurocentric models of Christianity in which ethnocentric notions of Whiteness gave rise to notions of superiority, manifest destiny and entitlement. For a helpful dissection of this model of Christianity, particularly the British version of it, see T. J. Gorringe, *Furthering Humanity: A Theology of Culture* (Aldershot: Ashgate, 2004). See also John M. Hull, *Towards the Prophetic Church: A Study of Christian Mission* (London: SCM Press, 2014).

62 See Michael N. Jagessar and Anthony G. Reddie (eds), *Postcolonial Black British Theology* (Peterborough: Epworth Press, 2007), pp. xiii–xiv.

63 See Harry Goulbourne, 'Collective Action and Black Politics' in Doreen McCalla (ed.), *Black Success: Essays in Racial And Ethnic Studies* (Birmingham: DMee Vision Learning, 2003), pp. 9–38.

64 See Inderjit S. Bhogal, 'Citizenship' in Anthony G. Reddie (ed.), *Legacy: Anthology in Memory of Jillian Brown* (Peterborough: The Methodist Publishing House, 2000), pp. 137–41 and Inderjit S. Bhogal, *On The Hoof: Theology in Transit* (Sheffield: Penistone Publications, 2001).

65 Barton, *Rejection, Resistance and Resurrection*.

66 Among Michael N. Jagessar's many books, see *Full Life for All: The Work and Theology of Philip A. Potter* (Geneva: WCC Publications, 1998) and *Ethnicity: The Inclusive Church Resource* (London: Darton, Longman & Todd, 2015).

67 See James H. Cone, *Black Theology and Black Power* (Maryknoll, NY: Orbis Books, 1969/1989); *A Black Theology of Liberation* (Maryknoll, NY: Orbis Books, 1970/1990) and *God of the Oppressed* (Maryknoll, NY: Orbis Books, 1975/2005).

68 Acts 2.5–12.

69 Cain Hope Felder (ed.), *The African Heritage Study Bible* (Nashville, TN: The James C. Winston Publishing Company, 1993), pp. 1572.

70 Cain Hope Felder (ed.), *Stony the Road We Trod: African American Biblical Interpretation* (Minneapolis, MN: Fortress Press, 1991). Also, Randall C. Bailey and Jacquelyn Grant (eds), *The Recovery of Black Presence: An Interdisciplinary Exploration* (Nashville, TN: Abingdon Press, 1995).

71 This assertion was the basis of my book *Is God Colour Blind?* (London: SPCK, 2009 and 2020).

72 Black Lives Matter is a global protest movement that came to prominence after the murder of Trayvon Martin in 2013. Although it started in the United States, it has become a global movement protesting against the existence of systemic

racism that impacts on the lives of Black people across the world. For further details see *Black Lives Matter*, https://blacklivesmatter.com/about/.

73 See Dwight N. Hopkins, *Being Human: Race, Culture and Religion* (Minneapolis, MN: Fortress Press, 2005), pp. 118–59.

74 See James H. Cone, *The Cross and the Lynching Tree* (Maryknoll, NY: Orbis Books, 2013).

75 See Jocelyn Emama Maxime, 'Identity and Consciousness' in *To Overcome is to Undertake: Report of the First Connexional Conference for Young Black Methodists* (London: The Methodist Church, 1991), pp. 13–24.

76 See W. E. B. Du Bois, *The Souls of Black Folk* (New York: Bantam Books, 1989, first published in 1903), p. 3.

77 Anthony B. Pinn, *Terror and Triumph: The Nature of Black Religion* (Minneapolis, MN: Fortress Press, 2003), pp. 82–107.

78 Du Bois, *The Souls of Black Folk*, p. xxxi.

79 Du Bois, *The Souls of Black Folk*, p. 3.

80 Pinn, *Terror and Triumph*, pp. 27–77.

81 See M. Shawn Copeland, *Enfleshing Freedom: Body, Race, and Being* (Minneapolis, MN: Fortress Press, 2009).

82 Eboni Marshall Turman, *Toward a Womanist Ethic of Incarnation: Black Bodies, the Black Church, and the Council of Chalcedon* (New York: Palgrave Macmillan, 2013).

83 See '(What did I do to be so) Black and Blue', *Wikipedia*, https://en.wikipedia.org/wiki/Black_and_Blue_(Fats_Waller_song), accessed 19.1.2021.

84 On 25 May 2020, George Floyd, an African American, was 'murdered' by a white policeman who placed his knee on Floyd's neck for 8 minutes and 46 seconds. For further details see the following link: https://en.wikipedia.org/wiki/Killing_of_George_Floyd, accessed 3.03.2021.

85 Press details on Clinton McCurbin's death can be found at the following link: Ethan Shone, 'Columnist recalls incident with "shocking parallels" to George Floyd killing', *HoldtheFrontPage*, www.holdthefrontpage.co.uk/2020/news/deputy-editor-reflects-on-similarities-between-george-floyds-murder-and-an-incident-early-in-his-career/, accessed 3.3.2021.

86 See Richard S. Reddie, *Abolition!*, pp. 200–25.

87 This comment is reflective of the push-back of 'some' white Christians on social media responding to the threat to law and order and property. It is important to acknowledge the many Black Christians who have also shared their disquiet at the dangers of mob rule and the desecration of public monuments. I am forced to acknowledge that there are obvious dangers of untrammelled 'violent' direct action of this sort. My comments are not an absolute endorsement of this action, but a criticism of the complicity of the authorities in the city to side with the blandishments of white supremacy that is exemplified in the maintenance of the statue of Edward Colston in the first place.

88 For an example of a scholarly attempt to address the legacies of slavery, see Anthony G. Reddie, *Black Theology, Slavery and Contemporary Christianity: 200 Years and No Apology* (Farnham: Ashgate, 2010). The book contains essays written by scholars from the UK, the USA, the Caribbean and South Africa, all exploring the legacy of slavery and the lack of 'repair' or reparations for the horrors experienced by Black people in the years since the ending of this vile institution.

2

The Trauma of Hybridity

NUAM HATZAW

Introduction

It is only in recent decades that theologians have begun to seriously consider the topic of hybridity. Although the movement of peoples across territories, societies and cultures has been a feature of modern life for a long while now, theology has been slow to examine the impact of migration and movement on the individual's perception of self. Thus far, theological efforts have focused on exploring theologies of migration, centring on concepts of hospitality, welcome, and the impact of migrants on models of ecclesiology and mission. Despite the received wisdom that migration impacts the way a person understands their own identity, there has been surprisingly little written within theology on the subjective experience of the migrant and their sense of identity and belonging. For some migrants, or for those who come from a second or third generation of migrant families, the concept of 'hybridity' is of resonance. Broadly, hybridity refers to the idea of mixing or mixedness of two or more entities – in this case, cultures and identities. This chapter sets out to theologically examine the topic of hybridity through the lens of trauma. I argue that the few theologians who have written about hybridity have done so without proper interrogation of the full experience. An examination of the works of select Asian American theologians, who are perhaps the most prolific writers on the topic, reveals a tendency to view hybridity in a positive light. This, I argue, is an overly romantic understanding that negates the negative and painful aspects of the hybrid condition. I therefore bring in insights from trauma theory, which I believe can further nuance and sharpen existing theologies of hybridity.

This work is unapologetically personal. I intentionally interweave autobiographical elements throughout the chapter and utilize my own experiences to construct my arguments. The use of autobiography within academic writing is still considered an unorthodox move due to concerns that a personal lens can cloud the objectivity that is considered requisite for 'proper' academic research. While I acknowledge the dangers of navel-gazing and autoethnography that can turn into unhelpful introspection, I nonetheless firmly believe in the merit of including the personal within discussions of hybridity and theology. My explorations into this area of scholarship stem directly from my own experiences of hybridity and in-betweenness and my struggles with how to live out this conflicted identity. Rather than casting doubt on the soundness of the research, I maintain that *not* acknowledging the inherently personal standpoint from which I approach this topic is the more intellectually problematic action. As the theologian Natalie Wigg-Stevenson argues, 'autoethnographers, therefore, use their own personal narrative to avoid the pretension to objective and universal claims and to highlight the frailty of all knowledge production.'[1] In a topic as deeply personal and subjective as hybridity and theology, it is illogical and unwise to assume that any degree of objectivity can be properly maintained – particularly when the researcher herself identifies as hybrid. In writing this chapter then, I purposefully engage with my own experiences in order to reflect upon theologies of hybridity and theologies of trauma.

Writing so personally on a topic comes with one important and necessary acknowledgement that needs to be made. I write as a Zomi[2] ethnic woman who was born in Myanmar, but who was raised and educated in Britain. My experiences of hybridity, my sense of self, and my understandings of trauma and theology are all shaped by factors and forces that intersect to make up who I am – my gender, my sexuality, my ethnicity, my class, education and so on. It is important, therefore, to clarify that I cannot and do not claim to speak for other migrant or in-between women. Their experiences of hybridity might align or differ from my own and I am not claiming my perspective as the sole authority on the matter. The goal is instead to 'unfold narratives intended to compel the reader to a transformative response, not commit the reader to a point of view'.[3] It is my hope that these personal reflections on the subject can contribute to our wider understanding of trauma and hybridity and bring a different voice to the conversation.

My (dis)location

In January 2020, I began what was meant to be eight months of fieldwork in Myanmar. In the weeks and months before leaving, I recall feeling both nervous and excited in equal measure. My family migrated from Myanmar to the UK when I was five years old, and I had only been back a few times since. This would be the first time I had spent any significant length of time in the country of my birth. I was looking forward to reconnecting with my heritage, to learning more about what I had lost and left behind when we moved. Although I had spent most of my life in Britain, there were always parts of British culture and life that my upbringing excluded me from – my family's socio-economic status, my parents' desire, and insistence, that we practised our Zomi culture at home, and my brown skin that marked me out very visibly as 'different'. I was therefore excited and hopeful about the prospect of returning to Myanmar, and finding that sense of belonging that I had been craving my whole life. I had imagined there would be some magical moment while I was there when I would be able to confidently and contently say, 'I'm home, I belong'. Sadly, however, that moment never came. Instead, when I got there, I experienced culture shock. I found myself struggling to adjust to the different rhythms of life, to the unfamiliar foods and the weak coffee, to the heat and the humidity, to the complexities of the language that my untrained ear had never picked up on.

I recall a particular incident that exemplified some of the difficulties I encountered. In late February, nearly one month after I arrived at the first of my field sites, I was invited on a day trip with 20 or 30 of the youth from the local church. The purpose of the trip was socializing and fellowship, so I was also looking forward to spending some time with Zomi people my age. As the day progressed, however, melancholy came over me as I realized something profoundly sad and disorientating. The whole day was spent playing silly games as two competing teams, and a playful atmosphere emerged as participants teased and bragged and joked with each other. Except, through it all, because of my limited Zopau (the Zomi language) I found myself unable to partake in any of the fun or conversation. I realized, as I sat there on the edge, watching everything going on, that my inability to speak the language fluently meant that there was a whole side of my personality that I was unable to express. As I wrote in my journal that day:

When I talk about loss though, I mean the loss of my own unique sense of self, that gets shut down or shut up when I am conversing in something other than my native tongue of English. Being rendered almost-mute in a language that is your only method of communication with those you spend every single day with, is a devastating blow. In English, I can fully express all the facets of my personality – all the good, the bad, and certainly the ugly. Yet in Zopau, I am unable to tell anecdotes in the same captivating(!) manner that I can in English. In Zopau I am unable to make jokes in the same quick-fire way, nor articulate my concerns and worries as delicately or as sensitively as I would in English. I spend most of my days listening in, rather than partaking in the conversation. As you can imagine, that gets lonely very quickly.

It had never occurred to me, not once, that I might feel similarly out of place in Myanmar, among my own people, as I did in the UK. When the Covid-19 pandemic forced me to return to Scotland unexpectedly, I was able to unpack my experiences. With the benefit of hindsight and distance, I came to realize that I did not find the belonging that I sought, that I had no clue about who I was or where I belonged, and that there might not be anywhere at all where I could feel at home. These revelations sent me spiralling and led me to seek counselling. In my fiancé's small, one-bedroom flat, with nothing but a thin wall and a closed door for some semblance of privacy, I spent many hours in front of my laptop talking to a kind woman with a soft voice who listened as I wrestled with these issues. She once asked me, 'Where or when would I feel content?' I could not give her an answer. My sense of self, I discovered, is split between my Zomi heritage and ethnicity and my Western upbringing. I have a foot in both worlds, but I am not fully within either. Instead, I am untethered and dislocated – 'too Asian to be British' and 'too British to be Asian'. I am torn between two worlds, uncomfortable in both, and always searching for belonging.

Hybridity and theology

This state or feeling of being in-between, of being neither fully one thing nor the other, of being a complicated mix of multiple entities, has been referred to by some scholars as 'hybridity'. Like trauma, the term 'hybridity' has a long and muddled history.[4] Perhaps the most well-known usage of the term comes from the postcolonial literary theorist Homi K. Bhabha, who uses hybridity to describe the points of contact, exchange or collision between the colonizer and the colonized.[5] According to Bhabha, a new hybrid creation emerges when the colonizer attempts, and fails, to subsume the colonized into its framework of reference. Being a fusion or mix of both worlds, the hybrid's very existence thereby rejects the essentialism of either pole. Bhabha theorizes that hybridity occurs in the in-between, or 'third space of enunciation'.[6] The third space is a disruptive space filled with creative potential, as it 'initiates new signs of identity and innovative sites of collaboration and contestation'.[7] In this 'cutting edge of translation and negotiation',[8] the hybrid person is a mediator between the two cultures, able to navigate differences due to their location as in-between. Serving as a conduit, the hybrid can traverse between cultures and in so doing, holds much creative and counter-hegemonic potential.

Although theorists within fields such as geography, anthropology and literary studies have been quick to pick up on the concept of hybridity, there has not been much theological engagement with the term. Unsurprisingly, the little that has been written has come from theologians who themselves have dual or multiple heritages. Due to our shared Asian heritage, I limit my discussion in this chapter to the work of Asian American theologians, although it is important to note that other theologians have examined hybridity within their own contexts.[9]

One of the earliest theologians to address hybridity and identity from the Asian American perspective is the Korean American Jung Young Lee. Lee's book *Marginality: The Key to Multicultural Theology*[10] is deeply personal and his theological reflections stem from his own experience of discrimination and prejudice as an Asian migrant in a predominantly white society. Unsurprisingly then, Lee prefers the term 'marginality' to refer to the experience of the Asian American, and names three stages of being within that experience. First is the 'in-between' stage, which is marked by negativity. Of this, Lee writes 'I am situated ambivalently between two worlds – America and Asia – and I absorb the repulsions and attractions or the rejection and acceptance of each. The marginal person has to live in these two worlds, which are not only different but often antagonistic to each other.'[11] Second is the 'in both' stage, where the positive aspects of both cultures are emphasized. This is a self-affirming stage that complements the in-between: 'what I want to stress is my positive perspective of myself as a marginal person. I am in both, in both the world of my ancestors and the world of my residence. In other words, I am both an Asian and an American.'[12] For Lee, the final 'in-beyond' stage is the most crucial. Here, we leave behind the dualism of the previous stages and enter a more mature state of 'new marginality'.[13] Lee argues that although this marginality is difficult to bear, it can nonetheless bring about much-needed balance between those at the centre and those at the margin. He writes: 'Such a balance, which creates harmony, finds a new centre, the authentic centre, which is no longer oppressive but liberative to the people located at the centre or the margin.'[14] He elaborates further:

> To transcend or to live in-beyond does not mean to be free of the two different worlds in which persons exist, but to live in both of them without being bound by either of them. The new marginal person is a liberated person, a person who is truly free, because each is a whole person and able to be fully present in the world.[15]

The in-beyond position, therefore, bestows upon the marginal, or hybrid, person creative and redemptive power, allowing them to transcend artificial barriers and reform both worlds. Like Bhabha, Lee identifies a generative and redemptive nature to the experience of being hybrid.

Other theologians have also adopted Lee's constructive and positive stance. The Vietnamese American Peter C. Phan has spent much of his career writing on issues around migration and Christianity. Phan identifies transnational migrants as occupying a state of 'betwixt-and-between'. While Phan acknowledges that this can be 'a source of much soul-searching and suffering'[16] he is nonetheless optimistic about the potential that this in-between identity holds, saying that it can function as 'an incentive and resource for a creative rethinking of both cultural traditions, the native and the foreign'.[17] Phan argues that although transnational migrants do not fully belong in one culture or the other, 'by the same token however, they belong to both, though not fully.'[18] They are therefore uniquely positioned 'to see more clearly and to appreciate more objectively, both as insiders and outsiders … the strengths as well as the weaknesses of both cultures'.[19] Like Lee, Phan believes that these individuals can contribute significantly to a new culture that is enriched by both worlds. Finally, the feminist theologian Rita Nakashima Brock has written widely on the topic of multiple belonging from her vantage point as an Asian American woman. In her writings, Brock discusses the sense of displacement she felt, moving to the USA as a young child and growing up with a Japanese mother, a white stepfather and a Peruvian biological father. To absolve the confusion over her identity, Brock suggests the term 'interstitial integrity', which refers to 'the places in between, which are real places, like the strong connective tissue between organs in the body that link the parts'.[20] This interstitial integrity denotes multiplicity, fluidity and a refusal to rest in one place while still retaining a paradoxical sense of wholeness. It is 'the monumental task of making meaning out of multiple worlds by refusing to disconnect from any of them, while not pledging allegiance to a singular one'.[21] This is the core of Brock's subjectivity. She writes: 'Interstitial integrity is how I improvise a self, recognizing the diverse cultures and experiences that have made me who I am. It is how I mix a life together from myriads of ingredients.'[22] For Brock, this dwelling in the in-between is a positive experience that enables her to participate in multiple worlds and bring critical insight and consciousness from each one.[23]

We can identify a tendency towards viewing hybridity or in-betweenness as a positive attribute in the works of these Asian American theologians. Hybridity is generally construed as something to be celebrated – a promising sign of a utopian, cosmopolitan future where borders and boundaries fade and we are all free to traverse between worlds and identities. Although they make overtures towards acknowledging the difficulties that hybrid persons might experience, there is nonetheless a general sense that hybridity is a unique and advantageous state of being. This is not an uncommon judgement. Angie Hoogvelt notes that in other fields, hybridity is also 'celebrated and privileged as a kind of superior cultural intelligence owing to the advantage of in-betweeness, the straddling of two cultures and the consequent ability to negotiate the difference'.[24] For these theorists, hybridity is something to be lauded. After all, we can speak multiple languages! We feel at home wherever we go! We can take the best from each culture and create something new! In my experience, however, this is an overly romantic view of hybridity that fails to account for the trauma inherent within hybridity itself. The reality is that norms and values cannot be so easily divorced from the contexts that formed them, nor can we traverse between worlds with ease and grace – instead, each juncture is imbued with pain, and our movements between are always questioned and judged. I caution against viewing hybridity as purely positive, as doing so can overlook just how painful being hybrid can be. In glorifying in-betweenness and border-crossing, these theologies downplay the trauma and pain that can come from being caught in-between. Being able to step between worlds might be an appealing theoretical notion, but the reality more often looks like experiencing rejection wherever you turn. After all, crossing boundaries is easiest when you are already on the margins. With this in mind, I turn now to trauma theory and trauma theology, which I believe can better inform how we theologize about hybridity.

A turn to trauma

Trauma, broadly defined, refers to 'severely disruptive experience that profoundly impacts the self's emotional organisation and perception of the external world'.[25] Normative definitions of trauma associate it with a devastating event, such as domestic or sexual violence, an act of terror or the loss of a loved one. However, recent developments in the field have expanded our understanding of what constitutes trauma and traumatic stressors. Where once the traumatic stressor was generally accepted to be a 'single, extraordinary, catastrophic event',[26] scholars have since argued for a more expansive and wide-ranging definition. This can include larger, invisible or structural stressors which build up over time to create a trauma that is just as devastating in impact as those occurring from singular, catastrophic events. These definitions aim to capture 'the normative, quotidian aspects of trauma in the lives of many oppressed and disempowered persons'[27] and can include racial trauma, oppression-based trauma, intergenerational trauma or complex PTSD. An expanded definition of trauma is helpful to bear in mind when discussing hybridity, as it allows us now to consider experiences such as racism, discrimination, microaggressions, othering, lack of representation and alienation as traumas. Although seemingly banal and occasionally intangible, these experiences can nonetheless be debilitating and have a profound detrimental impact on the psyche of in-between or hybrid people. Indeed, in my own experience, I would venture so far as to say that hybridity is *itself* a traumatic experience.

Having made this provocative statement, I reiterate my earlier disclaimer that I cannot speak for other hybrid persons. Certainly, there are those who sit very comfortably in their in-betweenness and who would, understandably, balk at the idea that their subjectivity is traumatized. I theorize from my perspective and experience alone. It is also important to note here that in drawing upon trauma theory, I am not aiming to medically diagnose myself or others. Instead, I am interested in exploring the connections between trauma theory and my experiences of hybridity to see what arises. The question that motivates me in this personal quest is: how might placing a trauma lens on to the experience of hybridity illuminate existing theologies of hybridity and identity? To that end, I offer three tentative suggestions for how trauma theory might better inform theologies of hybridity. First, trauma theory will bring in a much-needed temporal element that reminds us of the precarity of hybridity. Second, it can teach us to pay appropriate attention to the pain of being in-between and to refrain from glossing over the discomfort and unease. Last, it would reimagine an understanding of healing based on these new insights.

Interruption

Trauma and hybridity are alike in the sense that they are both precarious and unstable conditions. Trauma scholars have long been aware that trauma persists and remanifests. The effects of the traumatic event/s can bleed and continue long after – even more so for insidious and 'everyday' traumas such as racial trauma. Judith Herman, one of the pioneers in trauma studies, writes: 'Long after the danger is past, traumatized people relive the event as though it were continually recurring in the present. They cannot resume the normal course of their lives, for the trauma repeatedly interrupts.'[28] Similarly, Cathy Caruth, in her seminal work *Trauma: Explorations of Memory*, argues that traumatic events return in the form of flashbacks, hallucinations, nightmares and other phenomena. This is because 'the event is not assimilated or experienced fully at the time, but only belatedly, in its repeated *possession* of the one who experiences it.'[29] For Caruth, 'it is not the event itself, but rather the mental experiencing of it, that constitutes the psychological trauma.'[30] The power of the trauma, therefore, lies not in its inability to be processed in the moment, but instead in its unpredictable reoccurrence. The trauma scholars Shoshana Felman and Dori Laub emphasize the nonlinear nature of trauma, writing: 'Trauma survivors live not with memories of the past, but with an event that could not and did not proceed through to its completion, has no ending, attained no closure, and therefore, as far as its survivors are concerned, continues into the present and is current in every respect.'[31] The feminist theologian Serene Jones details the story of Leah, who was unexpectedly triggered during a church service and experienced a reliving of her trauma that threw her into 'an old state of terror and confusion, which she could not stop or control'.[32] Trauma can therefore be viewed as the nexus through which past, present and future collide in a volatile manner; trauma disrupts time. It does not always lie dormant in the past but can instead interrupt and interject itself into the present at unpredictable moments. Its presence lingers long after the event has passed, and it is the reliving and continual manifestation of the trauma that is the locus of pain for the survivor.

This is a helpful insight when we consider theologies of hybridity. Like trauma, hybridity is also unstable and nonlinear. It is not a fixed mode of identity that is frozen in time; rather, it is something that occurs over and over again, consistent only in its dynamism. Nikos Papastergiadis refers to it as 'an energy field of different forces',[33] denoting its dynamic and fluid nature. Hybridity can remanifest or be reshaped over time, and in myriad different ways according to the external forces surrounding it. Hybrid identity is, therefore, 'constructed through a negotiation of difference' where 'the presence of fissures, gaps and contradictions is not necessarily a sign of failure'.[34]

Dominant theologies of hybridity have been too quick to envision an identity that sits still, untouched by forces outside. For Lee and Phan, the in-between person reaches a sense of contentment and then remains in that space between two cultures. While Brock does gesture towards a more fluid understanding with her depiction of moving between worlds, the core of her concept still rests upon a wholeness, or integrity, that connects and spans multiple worlds: 'Integrity has to do with moments of entireness, of having no part taken away or wanting. Integrity is closely related to integration, to acts of connecting many disparate things by holding them together.'[35] The continually constructed nature of hybridity has therefore been overlooked in favour of a portrait of hybridity as a static and fixed state – motionless and defined, unable to be reworked. This contradictory claim to stability and wholeness, to interstitial integrity, is at odds with the realities of living on the margins of worlds. I draw upon my own experiences to illustrate my point. As an Asian woman growing up in the UK, I have become intimately familiar with the feeling of being different from those around me. Most days, my sense of dislocation is something that simmers quietly in the background of my life, like a small ache in your neck that only hurts when you turn your head a certain way but is otherwise manageable, forgettable even. Other times, however, I am affronted by the sheer force of it – like when I was 13 and I had 'chink' and other racist taunts shouted at me every day as I walked home from school. There are also moments when the awareness of my difference, my otherness, comes creeping up on me and I must endure a puzzling period of unease and discomfort before it finally clicks as to why I feel so uncomfortable.

A few years ago, on a cold November day, I attended a training event for successful scholarship holders. We spent the entire day networking and doing various academic exercises and workshops, all of us held hostage by the promise of free wine and refreshments at the end. As the day progressed, I noticed I was feeling more and more uncomfortable and ill at ease. My body was tensing up, my heart felt tight in my chest, I kept shivering, feeling as if something was crawling under my skin. It was not until the final hour that I realized what exactly was making me so anxious – out of the 70 or so people in the room, I was the only non-white person. Out of that entire year's 63-strong cohort of successful award holders, drawn from all over Scotland, I was the only brown person chosen to receive this scholarship. Certainly, I was not the only BAME person qualified; I was merely the only one they picked. The day ended; I drank enough free wine to make up for institutional racism and left.

In sharing my experiences, I am not aiming to 'rank' traumas or draw unhelpful comparisons between traumas such as Leah's and my own experiences of being othered. The two are vastly different events – although it is worth bearing in mind that traumas can intersect and that one's experience of trauma will be confounded and multiplied by factors such as race, gender, class and others. Rather, the point I am making is that moments of rupture can also happen for the hybrid person – in those experiences, I was blindsided by the magnitude of disruption to my carefully curated sense of self. Like trauma, hybridity, or dislocation, or in-betweenness can announce itself in random and unpredictable ways. Societal and cultural forces work in conjunction to influence and shape the subjectivity I occupy. Where one day I might feel 'more' Zomi or more 'Asian', the next day, I might feel more British than I ever have before, depending on the context and situation. Hybridity is therefore not a fixed mode of being that, once reached, remains whole or integral. It is instead precarious and malleable, subject to external forces and influence. Following insights from trauma theory that emphasize its interruptive, volatile nature and the confluence of past, present and future, theologies of hybridity must rediscover the inherent precarious nature of hybridity and pay closer attention to its process and formulation.

This might seem like an overly pessimistic reading – after all, what hope is there for the hybrid if their ontology is constantly contested and unsettled? A dismissal of this reading would be premature, however, as I believe it bears fruit in the long run. If we follow the theologians in prescribing the goal of hybridity as not reaching a belonging that can never be disputed, but rather a sense of peace in the hybridity itself, then seeking the interstitial integrity that Brock identifies is an ultimately hollow pursuit. It is futile so long as it rests on the idea that integrity, once achieved, cannot be shaken. Paradoxically then, to come to terms with one's unstable location is to come to terms with the fact that it might never be stable. We reach interstitial integrity when we acknowledge that our integrity might collapse at any moment. Trauma theory does not shy away from this realization. Trauma occurs and then reoccurs, and each time it interrupts it must be worked on and through. It does not follow logic; it refuses to succumb to reason. Similarly, the acceptance of precarity within theologies of hybridity can be the first step towards stability.

The middle

Second, a trauma-informed theology of hybridity would force us to reckon with exactly that – trauma. If theologies of hybridity and identity are to be helpful, we must do the necessary work of engaging with the pain that is incurred by being caught between multiple worlds. If we categorize the feelings of confusion and the experiences of inhospitality and othering as trauma, then we can begin to acknowledge the pain and ennui that hybrid people might hold. Last summer, my sister told me that she recently concluded that we would never feel truly at home anywhere. We fell silent, the realization muting us for a while as we grappled with what precisely this meant. Phan is certainly correct when he calls this 'soul-searching'. It is demoralizing to spend energy trying to call a place 'home', only to be reminded by internal or external forces that you do not belong. It is angering to see others sit so comfortably in their skin while you wonder if you might ever find peace in yours.

Acknowledging and recognizing this as trauma is an important step that theologies of hybridity have thus far failed to take. All too often, theologians and theorists have been quick to espouse the merits of hybridity and in-betweenness while forgetting the difficulties associated with this subjectivity. Hybridity is viewed as the rejection of 'primordial unity or fixity';[36] it allows us to transcend arbitrary boundaries and divisions such as race, class, gender, sexuality. For Lee, the hybrid person is 'a symbol of a creative nexus that connects different, often antagonistic worlds together'[37] or, in other words, 'a reconciler and wounded healer to the two-category system'.[38] The hybrid person is hailed as the harbinger of a cosmopolitan, utopian future where essentialist markers of identity cease to be of importance and where cultural forms, symbols and histories 'can be appropriated, translated, rehistoricized and read anew'.[39] This is a grand, but ultimately naive, vision. While hybridity can indeed be a generative space, and while some might certainly feel at ease functioning as border-crossers or signposts to a more unified future, for others such as myself, there is still much unease and discomfort in the in-between. Theologies of hybridity must draw lessons from trauma studies and take care not to overlook the trauma within hybridity itself.

The trauma theologian Shelly Rambo's work is a refreshing example of a theology unafraid to wrestle with pain. It offers us an alternative picture of hybridity that is perhaps more in line with the realities of life in the in-between. In her book, *Spirit and Trauma: A Theology of Remaining*, Rambo imagines trauma as 'a crisis of remaining or a crisis of the middle'.[40] Those who have endured trauma dwell in the 'suspended middle territory, between death and life'.[41] Rambo argues that the Christian preoccupation with the death and resurrection of Jesus has meant that we have failed to properly account for Holy Saturday – the difficult middle place between death and life. In so doing, Christians have been complicit in glossing over suffering. Rambo writes:

> The gloss of redemption is, perhaps, the greatest enemy to those who survive trauma; it provides a promise often unaccompanied by forms of life that can deliver on that promise. Life, for many, does not triumph over death. Instead, life persists in the midst of death and death in the midst of life.[42]

A trauma-reading, therefore, leads us to recognize that 'the site of suffering extends to the middle space, which means that theological discourse about trauma must press beyond interpretations of the cross – the death event.'[43] It is in this painful middle territory that we encounter the presence of God – the Spirit that remains. Rambo urges us to give due attention to this middle place, where suffering does not disappear and life does not abound unhindered. Doing so would do justice to trauma survivors who exist at an interstice 'between a radical ending and an impossible beginning'.[44]

Rambo's reconfiguring of the middle is an alternative model that theologies of hybridity would do well to adopt. Like trauma survivors, hybrid individuals also exist in the middle – caught between worlds, identities and affinities. As Rambo has argued, it is important to sit in that middle place and recognize 'a way of being in the depths, a practice of witnessing that senses life arising amid what remains'.[45] A trauma-informed theology of hybridity would therefore centre the traumatic experiences associated with being in-between. By extending the site of suffering to this middle territory, as Rambo advises, we can reconceptualize the middle not as playful hybridity, but perhaps as limbo, or as languishing. This would give due recognition to the pain caused by such destabilizing sentiments and do justice to the lived realities of hybrid individuals, whose daily lives might not reflect the cosmopolitan future that theorists envision. We cannot shy away from sitting in the pain of the middle and, instead, must pay attention to the arduous work that occurs in this space, as hybrid individuals negotiate their sense of self. In seeking to reconcile ourselves, we might be too eager to reach a place of belonging, of interstitial integrity, and forget the trauma within that act of reconciliation. When we rush too eagerly to the resurrection or the resolution of identity, we ignore the wisdom of trauma theory that teaches us that there is no 'clean break from the past, of death behind and life ahead'.[46] We must therefore be sceptical of dominant narratives around hybridity that gloss over the suffering of being caught in the middle. Theology must be willing to dwell on the Holy Saturday of hybridity.

Healing

Last, trauma theory can offer us a new and alternative perception of healing. Trauma scholars do not naively assume that survivors can return to life as it was before the trauma. In many cases, the traumatic events become the marker by which life is now orientated – there is life before the event, and life in the aftermath, now marred by the trauma and its lingering effects. Trauma survivors know that they cannot return to the world as it was before, and instead, must learn new ways of being and living. Hilary Jerome Scarsella writes that 'The process of forging relation in order to reconstruct person-hood in the aftermath of trauma is, thus, not a process of recovery but one of creation. It is a process of making something new in the place of that which has been lost.'[47] Recovery is not a return to the before, but the construction of a new life entirely, remade in the wake of trauma.

In their desire to make peace with their in-betweenness, theologians have neglected to account for the specific ways in which hybridity can play out. Duncan Pedersen makes the important point that trauma is specific: 'What constitutes a "trauma" then is not entirely dependent on the nature of the event but also on the personal meaning assigned and the social interpretation of the event, including responses of the affected person, their family and community, as well as the society at large.'[48] Like trauma, hybridity must also be thought of as a specifically defined experience that cannot and should not be universally applied. When theologians have attempted to come to terms with their hybridity, they have adopted a positive reading of their hybrid condition that might not resonate with every person. Just like trauma survivors cannot create a future where the trauma does not exist, hybrid individuals might also struggle to satisfactorily reconcile their hybridity. The outlook you possess on your hybridity is dependent on your social location. Without wishing to elide the marginalization that theologians such as Lee, Phan and Brock have experienced, I argue that these theologians have been able to come to peace with their in-betweenness in part due to the strength and perseverance of the Asian American community of which they are part. To be sure, the Asian American community has been and continues to be on the margins of US society in many ways. I do not wish to discredit or downplay the sufferings they have experienced.[49] However, I believe that navigating the murky waters of hybridity and belonging is much easier when you travel with others. Lee's vision of the in-beyond marginal person that reconciles binaries, or Brock's interstitial integrity that connects and grounds her, are attractive notions that unfortunately are not helpful to all hybrid persons, particularly those who must struggle with their identity alone. After all, is it not quicker to accept your hybridity when you can turn to others who have successfully navigated those tricky waters before you? Is it not more comforting to search for belonging in the in-between when you are surrounded by others with whom you can journey? As the only member of my Zomi ethnic group currently in Scotland, I live a lonely existence. To continue the metaphor of adventure, the already momentous task of wrestling with my identity is even more difficult when I must be my own commissioner, cartographer and pioneer all at once.

Furthermore, theologies of hybridity have approached this problem of reconciling the dislocated self by searching for peace *within* hybridity. Instead, I believe that it might be more productive, for some individuals, to search for peace *despite* hybridity. This is a subtle but important shift in perspective. The former reading makes the hybridity the object of attention and the very channel through which one can reach a sense of peace and ontological security. However, if we understand hybridity as trauma, we can now view hybridity as a condition that must be negotiated and worked through, or around. Trauma theory is careful to point out that healing does not look like a return to the life before, but rather a new creation or remaking. Hybridity as trauma must also be understood in the same way. Just as we cannot imagine a healing from trauma that is achieved through the trauma itself, we cannot rest our efforts for a reconciled hybrid self solely *within* hybridity. Trauma theory, therefore, indicates an alternative vision of healing or contentment that does not rest upon finding peace within the instability of the hybrid subjectivity. This is particularly important for persons such as myself who might never find a way to be comfortable in my dislocated self. As we have seen, coming to terms with one's dislocation is easier for some than it is for others, and depends heavily on the environment that surrounds us and the social location we occupy. There is also the important fact that although we might have found peace within ourselves, the surrounding society might still hold us at arm's length and question our allegiance. Being one of the first of my ethnic community to grow up in the UK, I have no role models of Zomi-Britishness to turn to. I have no prior idea of what a Zomi-British person looks like, acts like, thinks like. There is no well-trodden path for me to follow, but rather each step I take is the first in a new and unfamiliar, occasionally hostile territory. Trauma theory is therefore very pertinent here as it invokes a new vision of healing that is not predicated on the need to be content in our hybridity or trauma. Scarsella issues us with a powerful warning that we must remember traumatic events as the painful ruptures that they are. This is crucial to the healing and recovering process, for 'when it is forgotten, it repeats'.[50] Naming hybridity as traumatic, rather than as a universally applicable panacea, leads us to a different configuration of healing that might be more beneficial. It sets us upon a path that does not see hybridity as the method and cure to in-between selves, but rather imagines a recovery *despite* the dislocation.

Conclusion

Trauma theory and theologies of hybridity might seem, at first glance, an awkward pairing. Yet in this chapter I hope that I have shown how the two can be brought into fruitful conversation with one another. Theologians have shied away from engaging with the notion of hybridity – an oversight given the proliferation of identities and modes of being in our increasingly interconnected world. It is Asian American theologians who have been the most eager to engage with this concept, yet they have tended to display an overly optimistic reading of the experience of hybridity. While this is certainly an attractive conclusion, it unfortunately fails to capture the full contours of the hybrid condition. Insights from trauma studies are valuable in remedying this romantic vision of hybridity. I have offered three suggestions as to what a trauma-informed theology of hybridity might look like. First, it would recall the precarious nature of hybridity and its ongoing, dynamic nature. Second, it would be alert to the pain and trauma of being caught in-between multiple worlds, and last, it would reimagine a new idea of healing that does not centre hybridity itself as the cure but offers hope despite it.

I wish to end upon this last, hopeful note. Having spent the past few pages opining on the traumatic and distressing nature of being in-between, it might seem contradictory to say that I am nonetheless optimistic about the future of theological thinking on hybridity. But allow me to expand. A foundational idea within trauma studies is the idea of irrepresentability – trauma is so devastating and disruptive an experience that it cannot be represented in language.[51] Words fail us; orthodox writing methods and forms cannot properly articulate the pain, loss, grief and weariness that we feel.[52] This is one concept from trauma theory that I do not believe should be adopted into our theologies of hybridity. Instead, I believe in the opposite. As I have sought to argue throughout this chapter, we must widen our theological understanding of hybridity so that we include those whose experiences of hybridity are primarily that of painful, uncomfortable moments. In so doing, we give space to an alternative perspective on hybridity. Although it is contradictory, the inclusion of this other perspective enriches and livens the discourse. Representation is achieved when people come forward and speak – be it to lend a supportive voice or to offer a different, perhaps critical lens. While trauma scholars might be dubious of the possibility of representing trauma authentically, by contrast, hybridity can become easier and more accurate to represent, at least in theological circles, when we incorporate more voices to the chorus.

Bibliography

Balaev, Michelle, 'Trauma Studies' in *A Companion to Literary Theory*, Blackwell Companions to Literature and Culture, ed. David H. Richter, Chichester: John Wiley & Sons, 2018, pp. 360–71.

Bhabha, Homi K., *The Location of Culture*, 2nd edn, Abingdon: Routledge, 2004.

Bond, Lucy and Stef Craps, *Trauma: The New Critical Idiom*, Abingdon: Routledge, 2020.

Brock, Rita Nakashima, 'Cooking without Recipes: Interstitial Integrity' in *Off the Menu: Asian and Asian North American Women's Religion and Theology*, ed. Rita Nakashima Brock, Jung Ha Kim, Pui-lan Kwok and Seung Ai Yang, Louisville, KY: Westminster John Knox Press, 2007, pp. 125–43.

———, 'Interstitial Integrity: Reflections toward an Asian American Woman's Theology' in *Introduction to Christian Theology: Contemporary North American Perspectives*, ed. Roger A. Badham, Louisville, KY: Westminster John Knox Press, 1998, pp. 183–96.

Brown, Laura S., *Cultural Competence in Trauma Therapy: Beyond the Flashback*, Washington DC: American Psychological Association, 2008.

Caruth, Cathy, *Trauma: Explorations in Memory*, Baltimore, MD: Johns Hopkins University Press, 1995.

Craps, Stef, 'Beyond Eurocentrism: Trauma Theory in the Global Age' in *The Future of Trauma Theory: Contemporary Literary and Cultural Criticism*, ed. Gert Buelens, Sam Durrant and Robert Eaglestone, London: Routledge, 2013, pp. 45–61.

————, *Postcolonial Witnessing: Trauma Out of Bounds*, Basingstoke: Palgrave Macmillan, 2013.

Felman, Shoshana and Dori Laub, *Testimony: Crises of Witnessing in Literature, Psychoanalysis, and History*, New York: Routledge, 1992, http://site.ebrary.com/id/10784330.

Herman, Judith Lewis, *Trauma and Recovery: The Aftermath of Violence, from Domestic Abuse to Political Terror*, New York: Basic Books, 2015.

Hoogvelt, Ankie M. M., *Globalization and the Postcolonial World: The New Political Economy of Development*, Basingstoke: Macmillan, 1997.

Jones, Serene, *Trauma + Grace: Theology in a Ruptured World*, 2nd edn, Louisville, KY: Westminster John Knox Press, 2019.

Lee, Jung Young, *Marginality: The Key to Multicultural Theology*, Minneapolis, MN: Fortress Press, 1995.

Papastergiadis, Nikos, 'Tracing Hybridity in Theory' in *Debating Cultural Hybridity: Multicultural Identities and the Politics of Anti-Racism*, ed. Pnina Werbner and Tariq Modood, 2nd edn, Critique Influence Change 8, London: Zed Books, 2015.

Pedersen, Duncan, 'Rethinking Trauma as a Global Challenge' in *Trauma and Migration: Cultural Factors in the Diagnosis and Treatment of Traumatised Immigrants*, ed. Meryam Schouler-Ocak, Cham, Switzerland: Springer, 2015, pp. 9–31.

Phan, Peter C., *Christianity with an Asian Face: Asian American Theology in the Making*, Maryknoll, NY: Orbis Books, 2003.

Rambo, Shelly, *Spirit and Trauma: A Theology of Remaining*, Louisville, KY: Westminster John Knox Press, 2010.

Scarsella, Hilary Jerome, 'Trauma and Theology: Prospects and Limits in Light of the Cross' in *Trauma and Transcendence: Suffering and the Limits of Theory*, ed. Eric Boynton and Peter Capretto, New York: Fordham University Press, 2018.

Wigg-Stevenson, Natalie, 'You Don't Look Like a Baptist Minister: An Autoethnographic Retrieval of "Women's Experience" as an Analytic Category for Feminist Theology', *Feminist Theology* 25, 2 (January 2017), pp. 182–97, https://doi.org/10.1177/0966735016673261.

Notes

1 Natalie Wigg-Stevenson, 'You Don't Look Like a Baptist Minister: An Autoethnographic Retrieval of "Women's Experience" as an Analytic Category for Feminist Theology', *Feminist Theology* 25, 2 (January 2017), p. 185, https://doi.org/10.1177/0966735016673261, accessed 9.05.2022.

2 The Zomi are a predominantly Christian ethnic minority from Chin State, Myanmar. They have a distinct religious, cultural and linguistic identity that sets them apart from most of Myanmar's population. Decades of state oppression and declining employment prospects have seen migration from Chin State rise significantly in recent years. The Zomi community in the UK is one of the smallest Zomi diasporas, numbering just under 100 individuals.

3 Wigg-Stevenson, 'You Don't Look Like a Baptist Minister', p. 186.

4 The term originated in biology, where it describes the intermingling of different species. It was then used derogatorily within colonial discourse to refer to the

unwanted 'mixed' offspring of miscegenation. The term has since been reclaimed, to a certain degree, within contemporary academic discourse and is now used in a neutral or positive sense to refer to mixedness or the process of mixing.

5 Homi K. Bhabha, *The Location of Culture*, 2nd edn, Routledge Classics (Abingdon: Routledge, 2004).

6 Bhabha, *The Location of Culture*, p. 54.

7 Bhabha, *The Location of Culture*, p. 2.

8 Bhabha, *The Location of Culture*, p. 56.

9 Perhaps the other most significant body of theological work on hybridity comes from Latina/o theologians, who use the term 'mestizaje', first popularized by Virgilio Elizondo. Influential scholars include Ada María Isasi-Díaz and Gloria E. Anzaldúa.

10 Jung Young Lee, *Marginality: The Key to Multicultural Theology* (Minneapolis, MN: Fortress Press, 1995).

11 Lee, *Marginality*, p. 43.

12 Lee, *Marginality*, p. 49.

13 Lee, *Marginality*, p. 60.

14 Lee, *Marginality*, p. 31.

15 Lee, *Marginality*, p. 63.

16 Peter C. Phan, *Christianity with an Asian Face: Asian American Theology in the Making* (Maryknoll, NY: Orbis Books, 2003), p. 9.

17 Phan, *Christianity with an Asian Face*, p. 9.

18 Phan, *Christianity with an Asian Face*, p. 9.

19 Phan, *Christianity with an Asian Face*, p. 9.

20 Rita Nakashima Brock, 'Interstitial Integrity: Reflections toward an Asian American Woman's Theology' in *Introduction to Christian Theology: Contemporary North American Perspectives*, ed. Roger A. Badham (Louisville, KY: Westminster John Knox Press, 1998), p. 190.

21 Brock, 'Interstitial Integrity', p. 190.

22 Rita Nakashima Brock, 'Cooking without Recipes: Interstitial Integrity' in *Off the Menu: Asian and Asian North American Women's Religion and Theology*, ed. Rita Nakashima Brock et al. (Louisville, KY: Westminster John Knox Press, 2007).

23 Brock, 'Interstitial Integrity', p. 190.

24 Ankie M. M. Hoogvelt, *Globalization and the Postcolonial World: The New Political Economy of Development* (Basingstoke: Macmillan, 1997), p. 158.

25 Michelle Balaev, 'Trauma Studies' in *A Companion to Literary Theory*, ed. David H. Richter, Blackwell Companions to Literature and Culture (Chichester: John Wiley & Sons, 2018), p. 360.

26 Stef Craps, 'Beyond Eurocentrism: Trauma Theory in the Global Age' in *The Future of Trauma Theory: Contemporary Literary and Cultural Criticism*, ed. Gert Buelens, Sam Durrant and Robert Eaglestone (London: Routledge, 2013), p. 50.

27 Laura S. Brown, *Cultural Competence in Trauma Therapy: Beyond the Flashback* (Washington DC: American Psychological Association, 2008), p. 18.

28 Judith Lewis Herman, *Trauma and Recovery: The Aftermath of Violence, from Domestic Abuse to Political Terror* (New York: Basic Books, 2015), p. 38.

29 Cathy Caruth, *Trauma: Explorations in Memory* (Baltimore, MD: Johns Hopkins University Press, 1995), p. 4; emphasis original.

30 Lucy Bond and Stef Craps, *Trauma*, The New Critical Idiom (Abingdon: Routledge, 2020), p. 56.

31 Shoshana Felman and Dori Laub, *Testimony: Crises of Witnessing in Literature, Psychoanalysis, and History* (New York: Routledge, 1992), p. 69, http://site.ebrary.com/id/10784330.

32 Serene Jones, *Trauma + Grace: Theology in a Ruptured World*, 2nd edn (Louisville, KY: Westminster John Knox Press, 2019), p. 24.

33 Nikos Papastergiadis, 'Tracing Hybridity in Theory' in *Debating Cultural Hybridity: Multicultural Identities and the Politics of Anti-Racism*, ed. Pnina Werbner and Tariq Modood, 2nd edn, Critique Influence Change 8 (London: Zed Books, 2015), p. 258.

34 Papastergiadis, 'Tracing Hybridity in Theory', p. 258.

35 Brock, 'Interstitial Integrity', p. 190.

36 Bhabha, *The Location of Culture*, p. 55.

37 Lee, *Marginality*, p. 63.

38 Lee, *Marginality*, p. 63.

39 Bhabha, *The Location of Culture*, p. 55.

40 Shelly Rambo, *Spirit and Trauma: A Theology of Remaining* (Louisville, KY: Westminster John Knox Press, 2010), p. 32.

41 Rambo, *Spirit and Trauma*, p. 32.

42 Rambo, *Spirit and Trauma*, p. 176.

43 Rambo, *Spirit and Trauma*, p. 167.

44 Rambo, *Spirit and Trauma*, p. 176.

45 Rambo, *Spirit and Trauma*, p. 181.

46 Rambo, *Spirit and Trauma*, p. 168.

47 Hilary Jerome Scarsella, 'Trauma and Theology: Prospects and Limits in Light of the Cross' in *Trauma and Transcendence: Suffering and the Limits of Theory*, ed. Eric Boynton and Peter Capretto (New York: Fordham University Press, 2018), p. 269.

48 Duncan Pedersen, 'Rethinking Trauma as a Global Challenge' in *Trauma and Migration: Cultural Factors in the Diagnosis and Treatment of Traumatised Immigrants*, ed. Meryam Schouler-Ocak (Cham, Switzerland: Springer, 2015), p. 9.

49 Indeed, anti-Asian hate crimes have risen significantly in the wake of the Covid-19 pandemic and continue to this day. The need for cross-movement and transnational solidarity and activism is greater than before.

50 Scarsella, 'Trauma and Theology: Prospects and Limits in Light of the Cross', p. 262.

51 This stems in part from trauma theory's origins in Holocaust literature, as writers grappled with the momentous task of doing justice to the sheer scale of destruction and malevolence. For a concise history of the foundations of trauma theory, see Bond and Craps, *Trauma*.

52 The idea that experimental and modernist writing forms are best able to capture the disruptive psychic nature of trauma is received wisdom in trauma studies. For a critique of this insistence, see Stef Craps, *Postcolonial Witnessing: Trauma Out of Bounds* (Basingstoke: Palgrave Macmillan, 2013), ch. 3.

3

Spirit for the Oppressed?: Pentecostalism, the Spirit and Black Trauma

SELINA STONE

Introduction

William J. Seymour, an African American man, and the son of freed slaves, is recognized by many historians as the father of Pentecostalism. Arriving in Los Angeles at the invitation of a local Black Holiness church, he led this congregation of mainly working-class and poor Black people in praying for the coming of the Holy Spirit as recorded in the book of Acts. As a result, a revival started that would continue for three and a half years and would capture the attention of the entire world. For these early Pentecostals, encounter with the Holy Spirit is the cornerstone of spirituality and theology, as the writer of *The Apostolic Faith* in September 1906 describes:

> The power of God now has this city agitated as never before. Pentecost has surely come and with it the Bible evidences are following, many being converted and sanctified and filled with the Holy Ghost, speaking in tongues as they did on the day of Pentecost.[1]

Early accounts of these encounters focus on Spirit-baptism (evidenced by speaking in tongues for many Pentecostals), confession and repentance of individual sin and healing of the body. In this sense, Pentecostal theology follows the trajectory set by Wesley's Holiness movement, which placed personal piety and sanctification at the centre of the Christian ethic. The Holy Spirit is believed to fill individual believers directly, which for many of these early Pentecostals is evidenced by speaking in tongues. The Holy Spirit's presence does not only impact upon the spiritual life, but it has implications for the embodied realities of those who are filled. These 'Bible evidences' also included stories of miraculous healings as seen in the same edition of *The Apostolic Faith*. In the September 1906 edition, people are recorded as having eyes healed so that they no longer need glasses; deafness, consumption, lung and heart problems are healed as well as bodily pain.[2] The Holy Spirit is understood to heal the individual body suffering from various kinds of illness.

Yet Azusa Street has come to be known by some scholars as a place of social healing as well as being a context for spiritual revival and miracles. The social and political significance of the revival at Azusa Street, for both the contemporary believers and scholars, was the seeming transcendence of social divisions. One journalist famously writes: 'all classes of people gathered in the temple last night ... there were all ages, sexes, colours, nationalities and previous conditions of servitude.'[3] While the Azusa Street revival began as the gathering of Black Holiness believers from working and lower classes, they were soon joined by white people and Latinx members prompting Frank Bartleman to write that 'the color line' had been 'washed away' at the revival.[4] Therefore, the Azusa Street revival has often been discussed as a moment that represents liberation for Black people and other oppressed racial groups. The leadership of Seymour, the son of Africans who had been enslaved, has been recognized and celebrated as a significant shift in racial power dynamics.[5] The presence of Latinx members at Azusa Street has also been highlighted; many of them were drawn there because of its egalitarian characteristics.[6] Others have noted that revivals were inspired among other marginalized groups such as the Dalits in India, as they heard reports of the supposed breaking down of racial barriers.[7] It can be said that the Azusa Street revival represented a moment of spiritual, social and political significance for Pentecostals but also for the wider Church and the world.

However, though we might recognize Azusa Street as a sign of what was possible in terms of racial unity through the power of the Holy Spirit, in reality the sign did not last. Instead Seymour himself speaks about the 'race war'[8] that took place over the course of several years as some white leaders sought to undermine his leadership at Azusa Street and splits occurred, which amounted to whites enacting racial segregation within Pentecostalism more broadly.[9] Yet the actions of these Pentecostals at Azusa Street is not the primary concern of this chapter; instead we will give our attention to the lives, experiences and beliefs of William Seymour and the African Americans at Azusa Street who were living in the reality of a 'race war' not only in the church but in the nation. While histories of Azusa Street and explorations of Pentecostal theology tend to focus on the spiritual lives of believers and their social interactions, it is the racial trauma of these early Black Pentecostals that is often overlooked.[10] While some have rightly highlighted William Seymour, Jennie Seymour, Charles Mason and other early Black Pentecostals as leaders and trail blazers, insufficient attention has been given to them as whole human beings. The result has been that we celebrate and critique them as religious leaders without giving due recognition to their trauma as men and women who were the descendants of enslaved Africans. In this chapter we will give our attention to the trauma of William Seymour and the African Americans at Azusa Street and the impact this had on their theology, particularly in relation to their understanding of Spirit-baptism and pneumatology. The early Black Pentecostals were a traumatized people, and a recognition of their suffering must be brought to bear on how we interpret their lives and understand their theology.

This chapter comprises three main sections. I will begin by examining Black trauma as a core aspect of Azusa Street's Black Pentecostal life, epitomized in Seymour's sudden death at the Azusa Street Mission at 52 years old. This will include an exploration of the relevance of Post-Traumatic Slave/ry Syndrome (PTSS) as a lens through which to explore the lives of Seymour and the Black believers at Azusa Street. In the second section I will then explore what I call 'traumatized theology' at Azusa Street, arguing that a recognition of Black trauma alongside critiques of Pentecostal as 'colonial theology' allows us to name Black healing and wholeness as a core agenda of decolonization within theology. Finally, I locate the resources for the healing of Black people and the restoration of a truly Pentecostal theology within African traditional spirituality and construct a pneumatology that recognize the wholeness of life and the holistic life given by the Holy Spirit.

Black trauma: Azusa Street's hidden history

Black Azusa Street

Histories of Pentecostalism and discussions of Pentecostal theology have neglected to take seriously the survivor status of William J. Seymour and the African Americans of Azusa Street who lived in the reality of collective trauma. It is noted in biographies of Seymour that he was the son of freed slaves, and historians have also highlighted that Charles H. Mason, who would found the Church of God in Christ, the largest Black Pentecostal denomination in America, was also the descendant of slaves.[11] For many of the African Americans at Azusa Street, they, like Seymour, would have travelled north from the southern states of America, where they or their parents had been enslaved. They were people who had lived in or with the reality of slavery and had seen emancipation yet continued to endure white supremacist violence – both interpersonal and systemic – as James M. Shopshire explains:

> During the same period that the Holiness-Pentecostal movements were developing into explicit currents of belief and practice, physical slavery of Black persons in America ended, the Reconstruction was phased away from any positive meaning for the Black populace, Jim Crowism came into existence, disenfranchisement of the Black minority was perfected, and racist ideology supportive of 'separate but equal' institutions in the society was given ultimate expression by the Supreme Court.[12]

The Black members of Azusa Street were not simply facing the same challenges that many poor white people were experiencing at the time. If Pentecostalism in general could be categorized as a spiritual movement among the 'disinherited' – those who were in general 'economically, socially, culturally and even physically displaced and deprived'[13] – then Black Pentecostals represented the oppressed among the oppressed.

For some, naming this social and political context reinforces the narrative that Pentecostalism was powerful because it allowed those living in oppressive circumstances to experience liberation – even momentarily – while caught up in the throes of the revival service.[14] According to this perspective, exemplified by Robert Mapes Anderson in *Vision of the Disinherited*: 'The poorer, the more dislocated and despised, the more marginal and highly mobile such people are in the social order, the more extreme will be their ecstatic response.'[15] From this vantage point, the focus of Black Pentecostals on personal holiness and spiritual ecstasy would amount to an attempt for those without much control in their wider social and political lives to exert some agency over their bodies and social lives.[16] Others might add that the charismatic vibrancy of Pentecostal worship allowed Black Pentecostals to experience the liberation of their African heritage, retained through the oppressions of slavery.[17] The popularity of the 'ring shout', of dancing, shouting and singing, would itself have represented a deep sense of individual freedom within the church service, which they would not have experienced elsewhere.[18] Black men and women were recognized as leaders in Pentecostal churches at times while their dignity was overlooked in the wider society. None of these arguments should be underestimated in terms of their relevance to exploring what Pentecostalism meant to Black believers at Azusa Street and in its earliest days.

However, despite all these potential benefits of Pentecostalism for the Black person's life, for William Seymour the end of his life was marked with the signs of trauma and deep grief. Seymour died suddenly of a heart attack on 28 September 1922, aged 52, while dictating a letter at the Azusa Street Mission.[19] As Douglas J. Nelson, a historian of Pentecostalism and Seymour's life writes:

> His followers believe he has died of a broken heart. They erect a headstone engraved with eloquent simplicity: 'Our Pastor.' His passing is unnoticed by any known newspaper religious or secular ... He is buried in a plain California redwood box but soon someone donates enough to provide for the more expensive vault coffin.[20]

Seymour's funeral was attended by around 200 mainly Black people, the majority of whom desired to share testimonies of the impact of his ministry on their own lives.[21] Nelson surmises that Seymour's broken heart was due to the 'crushing disappointment' he felt as the Pentecostal movement moved further away from the vision of the Spirit's work that the movement exhibited from 1906 to 1909, and instead gave in to racial and ideological splits.[22] Specifically, in Nelson's words, the movement can be interpreted as having 'denied its own roots by accepting white American racial attitudes' that drove Seymour to such despair.[23] Seymour carried his anguish so visibly that those in his congregation noticed it. He was known as a pastor first and foremost, as one who cared for and led the congregation. He is considered to be the father of a global movement, yet his death passed by hardly noticed or recognized by those beyond his immediate circle. He had a poor Black man's funeral, and his life was celebrated primarily by Black people, and they are the ones who laid him to rest.

Seymour's heartbreak and his sudden death can be understood – I argue – as representing the grief, heartbreak and death experiences shared by Black Pentecostals and Black people across the board in America at this time. Like Seymour, the wider group of Black Pentecostals and Black Americans overall carried within their bodies the anguish and pain of life in a society marked by white supremacy and the dehumanization of Black life. They were overrepresented among the poorest and the most disadvantaged in socio-economic terms and politically. They were victimized by racism and lived at the risk of sudden death, deaths that went unrecognized and often unreported. So how might we understand the trauma that shaped the experiences of Seymour and the early Black Pentecostals, the broken-hearted ones of the movement and indeed the world?

Post-Traumatic Slave/ry Syndrome and African American life

The term Post-Traumatic Slavery Syndrome (PTSS) was coined by Alvin F. Poussaint and Amy Alexander in *Lay My Burden Down: Suicide and the Mental Health Crisis among African-Americans*.[24] The authors, both of whom have lost brothers to suicide, were concerned with the 'overlooked connections between racial oppression, hopelessness, self-hatred, economics, stress and the patterns of self-destructive behaviour exhibited by some Black Americans'.[25] They are not the first to investigate connections between the trauma of slavery and the contemporary struggles of African Americans,[26] but the formulation of this syndrome is unique to them. Recognizing that the high levels of health problems among African Americans are related somewhat to social factors – namely their overrepresentation among the poorest due to racism and discrimination – they write:

> The persistent presence of racism, despite the significant legal, social and political progress made during the last half of the twentieth century, has created a physiological risk for black people that is virtually unknown to white Americans. We call this posttraumatic slavery syndrome. Specifically, a culture of oppression, the by-product of this nation's development, has taken a tremendous toll on the minds and bodies of black people.[27]

They go on to discuss the increasing levels of Black suicides and the disproportionate numbers of Black people in prisons as concrete signs of Black oppression and PTSS. White medical practitioners, they argue, are often unskilled in recognizing Black mental health issues and the impact of PTSS because of the prevalence of racist stereotypes about Black health and a lack of cultural competence.[28] Poussaint and Alexander name PTSS as a lens through which health disparities between African Americans and Europeans in the USA today might be understood.

Moving beyond the specific issue of Black health in America, Joy DeGruy's *Post Traumatic Slave Syndrome: America's Legacy of Enduring Injury and Healing* outlines the need for a trauma approach to the analysis of African American life as a whole in the wake of slavery.[29] DeGruy begins by describing the enslavement of Africans by Europeans in America as trauma-inducing in myriad ways, one of which was the assault on the will of the enslaved person:

> You [the slave] live in a society that constantly reminds you that you are no different from livestock and in some cases less valuable. When you attempt to express yourself, you are beaten down. When you attempt to protect your loved ones, you are beaten down. You are beaten until you call the cruellest and most vile man you know, 'Master'.[30]

Core to this breaking down of the individual will was the assault on the community through the deliberate destruction of families and kinship bonds. The destruction of African kinship bonds created, in DeGruy's mind, a specific form of relational trauma for enslaved African peoples:

> those brought to these shores had to deal with systematic efforts to destroy the bonds of relationships that held them together, as well as continuing efforts to have them believe themselves to be less than human. The maintenance of healthy and secure relationships is among the most important values within African cultures ... American chattel slavery ... absolutely, categorically destroyed existing relationships and undermined a people's ability to form healthy new ones.[31]

These are merely two examples of what DeGruy argues comprised the trauma of enslaved Africans, trauma which in her estimation has been passed down generationally through to African Americans in contemporary society. Though she admits that proving this empirically is a challenge,[32] she draws on scholarship by others who have demonstrated the impacts of the collective trauma of war, genocide and enslavement on other communities to make her argument about the impact of slavery on African Americans. PTSS is brought about, according to DeGruy, by 'multi-generational trauma together with continued oppression and absence of opportunity to access the benefits available in a society'.[33] According to DeGruy, PTSS manifests itself in three core ways; 'vacant self-esteem', which is 'the state of believing oneself to have little or no worth'; 'an ever present anger', which 'resides just below [African people's] surface';[34] and 'racist socialisation', through which Africans adopt white European standards of beauty and culture as superior to their own.[35] These controversial conclusions are not supported by evidence beyond anecdote in DeGruy's work, but the critical analysis provided by Shari Renée Hicks in her unpublished PhD thesis provides the literature context and support for DeGruy's theory as well as outlining alternative perspectives.[36] While it might be problematic for us to attempt to read DeGruy's thesis into the lives of early Black Pentecostals, her work is useful to us in that it argues that we take seriously the ongoing impact of slavery for descendants of those who were enslaved. We may not be able to locate the 'vacant self-esteem', 'every present anger' or 'racist socialisation' in Seymour's words or in the accounts of Azusa Street's history, but it can be assumed on the basis of DeGruy's work and the trauma studies she depends on,[37] that as the son of enslaved Africans, Seymour along with many other Black Pentecostals fell within the category of the traumatized African person DeGruy and Poussaint and Alexander speak of in their works. The question remains: if the trauma of African Americans is inevitable or at least highly probable in the light of the history of slavery in America, then how might we attend to Black trauma in our discussions of the spirituality and theology of Black people? It is to this question that we will now turn in the rest of this chapter as we discuss Black trauma and traumatized theology in Pentecostalism.

Black Azusa Street's trauma and traumatized theology

The persistent trauma of Seymour's life that remained with him until death – and may even have had a role in causing his premature death as Nelson has suggested[38] – provokes a very important question about the nature of Pentecostalism and Pentecostal theology. While Pentecostal spirituality and theology is often spoken of as holistic because of its concern for bodily healing, it is limited, as we have seen, when it comes to the healing of Black (traumatized) life. Despite the retention of certain African spiritual practices that emphasized embodiment, healing and spiritual freedom, Seymour and the Black Pentecostals at Azusa Street were not healed and liberated in a holistic manner. It is for this reason that Pentecostalism and Pentecostal theology from its earliest days until now has been considered to be consistent with colonial norms that undermine and oppose the cause of Black liberation. Pentecostals have been lambasted for the limitations of their world view and theological emphases, which seem unable or unwilling to dismantle structural injustices within their own churches, or in the wider world, the principal of these being white supremacy and racism. However, I will argue in this section that the adoption of 'colonial' theology and spiritual practices over and against liberating theologies and spiritualities should be recognized as a trauma response. The 'colonial' theology of Azusa Street should be understood as 'traumatized' theology that was retained and passed on generationally from the time of slavery.

Colonialism, trauma and Pentecostal Christianity

Pentecostalism has typically been considered to be sectarian and otherworldly, disengaged from the realities of human life and particularly from struggle and oppression. Pentecostals have faced virulent criticism for their escapist theology, especially in relation to their eschatology, which has been concerned with departure rather than working for transformation. They have been lambasted for their 'otherworldliness', which has been considered impractical for the concerns of the present life. This is unfair in some sense, as there were instances of Pentecostal leaders critically reflecting on politics and caring charitably for the poor even from the earliest days.[39] However, overall it is true that the overarching concern of early Pentecostals was attaining their own sanctification, converting people to their faith and anticipating the second coming of Jesus. The *Apostolic Faith* newspaper sent out by Azusa Street from 1906 is replete with testimonies of healing, conversion and ministry around the world but the matters of social and political life are entirely absent. In *The Doctrines and Discipline of the Azusa Street Mission*, Seymour 'affectionately admonish[es]' believers 'to keep themselves pure from this great evil' (slavery) and 'to seek its extirpation by all lawful and Christian means',[40] reflecting his own familiarity with the Black Christianity that recognized the dignity of Black people.[41] However, he retains suspicion of the place of politics within religious contexts, evident in his banning of any political conversation at Azusa Street.[42]

For some, Seymour's refusal to engage with political reality could be considered to be directly connected to the colonial reality under which many Africans lived, including those Black Pentecostals who had survived slavery or were living with generational trauma. Under colonialism and slavery, Christian theology and spirituality was deformed by white supremacy and anti-Blackness into a religion that undermined Black life and especially social and political liberation. To speak of 'colonial theology' is to name this kind of Christianity that was developed for the primary purpose of keeping colonized and enslaved peoples in their position of subservience. Crucially, colonial Christianity is understood to have involved focusing colonized and enslaved peoples on personal piety and hopes for heaven rather than expecting or working towards social and political change on earth in the present, as Estrelda Alexander explains:

> Masters were more interested in religious indoctrination as a civilizing measure for the temporal sphere than in evangelism that offered salvation

and made the [en]slave[d person] a spiritual brother or sister with an equal stake in eternal reality. In almost every sermon they attempted to entice slaves to patiently and humbly abide their present, God-ordained lot to ensure their future betterment, but such tactics did little to assuage emotional and spiritual angst over the present misery of the slave existence.[43]

Many colonized and enslaved peoples were aware of the distortions of colonial Christianity and retained the liberating faith they had discovered themselves. However, these colonial forms of Christianity, in which one is encouraged to be patient and humble in the face of structural oppression rather than seeking to transform it as a core to one's Christian life and encounter with God, remain present today among Pentecostals and many others. African peoples themselves may well have imbibed some of these colonial forms of Christianity and passed them on generationally, and these colonial forms of Christianity have continued to appeal to African believers throughout the generations.

While it is important to highlight what could be understood as colonial elements of Pentecostal theology, to speak of colonialism is not simply to discuss a political and economic reality in the abstract, but to name a system that has destroyed and irretrievably harmed human beings and their communities. Speaking of colonialism and colonial theology without speaking about Black trauma and 'traumatized theology' centres the oppressors, the powers and the systems of the colonizer, rather than the humanity of those who were and are victimized. Recognizing the trauma of Black Pentecostals is an act of rehumanizing those whose lives and dignity have been contested through oppression and violence. Carlton Turner exemplifies the need to name the traumatic impact of colonialism on African people in the Caribbean in his work *Overcoming Self-Negation*. Exploring the 'deep inner conflict' of African peoples in the wake of colonization he writes:

> African culture and religiocultural retentions are still othered. But this time, it is done so by African Caribbeans themselves. The colonial mind-set has been entrenched, the rules of the plantation have become normative.[44]

While Turner focuses on spiritual embodied practices, the principle remains the same for this discussion; the entrenching of the 'colonial mind-set' relates to theology as well as the spiritual practice. Black trauma due to colonialism and slavery means that the will and perspectives of the colonial masters were imbibed by Africans, while they disowned their own. We see here evidence of the 'vacant self-esteem' and 'racist socialisation' that DeGruy explores in her PTSS theory.[45] Black trauma must not be subsumed in the word 'colonial' in reference to theology, it must be named and made explicit. Analysis of the impact of colonial Christianity involves exploring not only how the *rules* of the plantation become normative for colonized peoples, but also how – for the sake of our discussion – the *theology* of the plantation becomes normative. Viewing early Black Pentecostals not simply as previously colonized or enslaved people who imbibed colonial or white theology, but as human beings traumatized by slavery who thus developed 'traumatized theology', should impact upon how we critique Black Pentecostalism and the approaches we might take to addressing its inadequacies.

If we take a trauma approach to exploring Pentecostal theology, then we might recognize, as Hicks has outlined in her work, that the adoption of a coping strategy rooted in escapism as opposed to a strategy that seeks to face and address the painful realties of one's social and political life can be understood as a form of trauma response.[46] While scholars like Poussaint and Alexander have argued that for some African Americans, escapism may involve the excessive use of drugs or alcohol or disproportionate levels of suicide, for early Pentecostals, a revival service in which one experiences being 'taken over' by the Spirit may have offered a holy alternative. The Black Pentecostal reluctance (and even refusal) to engage with the realities of social and political life can therefore be understood as a theological and religious example of what DeGruy describes as the response of traumatized Africans who 'adapted their attitudes and behaviours in order to simply survive'.[47] While during enslavement, a focus on the spiritual above the social and political may have enabled the enslaved African to cope with their oppression, the continuation of such 'adapted [theological] attitudes' now limits Africans in subsequent generations who have a greater potential for human flourishing as Black people who are not 'living under the threat of the master's whip'.[48] The colonial norms that were rooted in Western dualisms which prioritized the spiritual over the embodied in its fullest sense – social and political as well as metaphysical – inhibited a holistic understanding of the Spirit and the gospel that would have brought life to all aspects of human experience. Instead, Seymour and those who followed him were hampered by spiritual chains, even while tangible ones were no longer present and preventing them from true liberation. The individualized, pietistic theological emphasis limited believers to seek the powerful healing work of the Holy Spirit in relation to the individual body alone. Pentecostals did not seek the power of the Spirit in relation to the healing of Black trauma and the overturning of white supremacy that undermined Black life within the church and beyond.

The Spirit and Pentecostal racism

While Seymour and other early Pentecostals may have sought to avoid politics in order to focus on higher spiritual concerns, politics – and particularly the trauma of their political experience as Black people in America – could not be avoided even within the church. White racism and exposure to colonial forms of Christianity were inevitable for Black Pentecostal believers. Seymour himself had been taught theology by Charles Parham, who was a white supremacist who demonized Black spirituality and did not even allow Seymour to sit inside his Kansas classroom.[49] Pentecostal theology and spirituality was formed within and by white Christians from Europe and America whose white Christianity was oppressive directly and indirectly to Black life. Seymour had attended various white and inter-racial churches, many of which still discriminated against Black people in certain ways, and though he often found them discouraging and left, he would have undoubtedly been influenced by their teaching and emphasis on individual spiritual renewal.[50] Evangelical revivals that took place in Wales in 1904 and Oslo in 1905 set a precedent for Azusa Street, with their leaders exchanging letters with one another sharing testimonies of what was taking place and discussing the guidelines they might follow.[51] Seymour and the leaders of Azusa Street took a similar form and theological focus on baptism in the Spirit, confession and repentance from personal sin, speaking in tongues and miracles. While the multiracial aspect of Azusa Street was celebrated as unique in comparison to other revivals, the politics of race was also a unique burden for Azusa Street, which revivalists were ill-equipped to address.

It is important to state that for Pentecostals, as Steven Land has stated: 'spirituality is the fundament of theology'.[52] This means that to discuss traumatized theology, for Pentecostals, is to examine how trauma impacts upon spirituality (encounter with God), not simply on doctrine (beliefs about God). An exploration of 'traumatized pneumatology' specifically, must therefore involve discussions of Spirit-baptism and particularly the ways understandings of Spirit-baptism have also been traumatized, which we will undertake in this section.

We have already seen the early accounts of the Azusa Street revival in which the Spirit is understood to heal the individual body and empower individuals to speak in tongues and exercise other spiritual gifts. Spirit-baptism was the central feature of Pentecostal spiritual life, as Seymour explains:

> The baptism in the Holy Ghost and fire means to be flooded with the love of God and power for service, and a love for the truth as it is in God's word. So when we receive it we have the same signs to follow as the disciples received on the day of Pentecost. For the Holy Spirit gives us a sound mind, faith, love and power ...[53]

However, the significance of baptism in the Spirit was more than this suggests on the surface; Spirit-baptism had significant social effects as those who were dehumanized and ostracized in wider society experienced divine empowerment and felt, in tangible ways, the closeness of God through the Holy Spirit. Spirit-baptism was also an inclusive experience that transcended gender binaries, divisions based on status or the limitations attached to age. Children, women and men could all be filled by the Holy Spirit, and the fact that women were baptized in the Spirit as well as men, convinced leaders to allow them to preach despite the biblical precedents that led others to prevent women from preaching. All people regardless of age, race, gender or status were encouraged to offer prophetic words gifted by the Spirit in a world where some would have been denied full participation in social and political life or in other churches.

Despite this potential for a revolutionary pneumatology that would have transformed the lives and community of these early Pentecostals, the impact of ongoing trauma is seen most starkly in the promotion of a pneumatology that is restricted from transforming unjust social orders within and beyond the Christian community. Parham embodies the hypocrisy of white supremacist Christianity, offering spiritual leadership while simultaneously condemning Black Pentecostal spirituality as animalistic and denouncing Azusa Street's racial mixing.[54] Parham is known for promulgating the belief that speaking in tongues was the sole evidence required that one was baptized in the Spirit. This idea has been recognized by many as the cornerstone of Pentecostal theology, but in reality it was contested even in the earliest days. Seymour and others recognized speaking in tongues as one of several acceptable signs of baptism in the Spirit. Seymour for example also emphasized 'wisdom, power, truth and holiness'[55] as the work of the Spirit in the believer, and highlighted the need to pursue the fruits of the Spirit as recorded in Galatians 5.22–23.[56] This expanded vision of baptism in Holy Spirit drew more of a person's life into the life of the Spirit and also drew the life of the community into the work of the Spirit. However, in practice, this understanding of the Spirit's work was insufficient for addressing the trauma of Black believers at Azusa Street, because it was too easily spiritualized and individualized. Without there being clear and irrefutable theology of the Spirit that dealt with matters of justice – for example by naming what love meant in a context where white supremacy was rife – revivals came and went and racial trauma remained. While Pentecostals were all believed to be filled with the Holy Spirit's power, the Spirit was rendered powerless within Pentecostal imagination and in Pentecostal community life when faced with the problems of racism and the need for Black healing in the light of racial trauma.

In search of Black healing: African spirituality and Black pneumatology

In *The Apostolic Faith*, the early Pentecostals exhibited a clear understanding that the presence of the Holy Spirit was evidenced in miraculous healings of the body. As the writer of the September 1906 edition notes:

Through Jesus, we are entitled to health and sanctification of soul and body ... Jesus prayed that the Father would keep us from evil, which means sickness and all the works of the devil. All sickness is the work of Satan, and we have just as much right to look to Jesus for the health of those bodies as for the saving and sanctifying of our souls.[57]

However, for the Black Pentecostals of Azusa Street, the health of 'soul and body' depended on more than the assurance of salvation or momentary ecstasy of the revival service; it demanded the healing of racial trauma. Black Pentecostals were not, as I have argued, simply naive believers held captive by colonial theology and spiritual norms from which they needed liberation; they were representative of a traumatized people exhibiting a traumatized theology, both of which are in need of holistic healing. Where might the resources for healing be located? By looking to Pentecostalism's African heritage, we find a holistic understanding of healing and spirituality which I suggest can aid Pentecostal theology and particularly its understanding of the Spirit as a healing presence.

Scholars have often sought to emphasize the African roots of Pentecostalism particularly to ensure that Pentecostal history is not whitewashed as histories often are when told from white Western perspectives. However, the Africanness of Pentecostalism can be emphasized to the point that we neglect to attend to what has been lost for Africans transported as slaves from Africa to America, and for Africans in diaspora more broadly. Though we might marvel at the development of Black folk religion and the retention of particular African spiritual norms despite slavery and the removal from Africa, it is important to name what has been lost in order to know what might be reclaimed. In the case of Pentecostalism, I argue that the loss of African philosophies of healing that integrated spirituality with all other aspects of human well-being and recognized the importance of community for human wellness meant that healing at Azusa Street was dominated by Western emphases on the individual body and a focus on spiritual well-being. African philosophies of healing that recognize human wholeness as related to the harmony within the whole person, harmony within the context of community (spiritual, ancestral and embodied) and harmony with creation offers a source of healing for Black traumatized life that acts as a corrective to Pentecostal theology, which continues to exhibit traumatized features. It is within this context that a Black pneumatology which is liberated from the strictures of white theological dualistic frameworks might offer life in its fullness to those living with the racial trauma that is the result of white supremacist violence.

Black healing in African traditional spirituality

For the Yoruba of contemporary Nigeria, healing and well-being are recognized as being dependent on various factors including a person's physicality, their emotional and mental health, their spirituality (including relating well to God almighty (Olúdumarè), other deities and the ancestors) and their social relationships.[58] Since well-being is interconnected with all aspects of a person's life and experience, then sickness or illness of any kind can be understood to be the result of disorder in any of these dynamics, including a disharmony with the natural world.[59] Traditional healers in Yoruba tradition therefore take a multifaceted approach to healing, as Mary Adekson explains:

> Traditional healers are held in high regard because of their ability to exploit the forces of nature and make contact with the spirit world. Healers vary in terms of their power to heal. They are generally viewed as holistic, because of their ability to serve as a priest-physician-psychologist. They perform religious functions of healing and therapeutic duties concurrently, when there is need for it.[60]

This philosophy of human well-being that depends upon life in all areas, stands in stark contrast with the idea of healing promoted at Azusa Street. For the early Black Pentecostals, healing by the Holy Spirit is understood to relate solely to the individual body and to spiritual health, with some temporary relief for the emotions or mind. What is missing from Azusa Street's pneumatological vision of healing is the addressing of social sicknesses that undermined the health of the community as a whole. Particularly in the case of Azusa Street, this would have meant a vision of healing that would have addressed the legacy and ongoing reality of white supremacist violence and the racial trauma that ensued. Where the traditional Yoruba healers recognize that healing must be 'community-oriented' in order to be effective for African people,[61] the Pentecostal understanding at Azusa Street and in Pentecostalism beyond Azusa Street has an individual emphasis. The Spirit is present to heal the individual body within Pentecostal imagination, not the body of the church.

Towards a Black pneumatology

In undertaking this historical theological task, we must recognize that these traumatized theologies remain present in contemporary Pentecostal life. It is also evident that within charismatic congregations and traditions that would not adopt the title 'Pentecostal', the emphasis on the Holy Spirit and on healing so often neglects the systemic and structural sources of individual pain and suffering. What we gain from the Yoruba tradition are the resources to heal Pentecostal theology from its Western and colonial trauma, in order that Black traumatized lives might find healing and flourishing. It is within this African imagination that we might better speak of the same 'Spirit who raised Jesus from the dead' who now 'give[s] life' to the 'mortal bodies' of Black believers,[62] through healing and restoration that is holistic. If we take our lead from African philosophy and not the individualized notions of Western philosophy, then we might come to several crucial conclusions about what it means for Black life to be filled with 'the same spirit who raised Christ from the dead'. First, in the 'same spirit' we find that the Holy Spirit connects Christ's resurrected body with the Black bodies that live in the midst of life and death, living with the ongoing trauma of a racist world. In this great mystery, they find an eternal bond with Christ who also suffered within his body at the hands of evil men. Second, for the Black traumatized life to be filled with the Spirit who also raised Christ, is for them to know in a very particular way that the promised resurrected life will also come to them and that death will not have the final say. It is a reminder that God is on the side of those victimized by systems and structures that mete out violence, and that they have been defeated and shamed by Christ himself. Third, to recognize the Spirit as one who 'gives life' is to recognize not only that the Spirit heals and sustains the individual body, but that the Spirit gives life back to the person as they are connected to the bonds of love in their communities that attend to their emotional and mental health, as they draw again on the traditions and wisdom of their ancestors, and as they are drawn in to the ever-loving presence of their creator.

It is in this holistic vision of Spirit-given life and of the healing power of the Spirit that Pentecostal theology and pneumatology more broadly may contribute to Black healing, Black life and Black flourishing. This vision does not permit racism or white supremacy to remain prominent among the Spirit-baptized; it demands that the sickness born out of the idolizing of Whiteness be healed in hearts and communities. Such a vision does not permit believers to retain a vision of spiritual revival that simply touches the individual heart in relation to God; it imagines true revival to involve a revolution of the social order and the commitment of the saints to the new order of the kingdom where the last are first.

Bibliography

Adekson, Mary, *The Yoruba Traditional Healers of Nigeria*, New York: Taylor & Francis Group, 2004.

Alexander, Estrelda Y., *Black Fire: One Hundred Years of African American Pentecostalism*, Downers Grove, IL: IVP Press, 2011.

Anderson, Robert Mapes, *Vision of the Disinherited*, Oxford: Oxford University Press, 1979.

Bartleman, Frank, *How Pentecost Came to Los Angeles*, Los Angeles, 1925.

Brogdon, Lewis, 'African American Pentecostalism' in *Handbook of Pentecostal Christianity*, ed. Adam Stewart, DeKalb, IL: Northern Illinois University Press, 2012.

Conn, Charles, *Like a Mighty Army: A History of the Church of God*, Cleveland, OH: Pathway Press, 1977.

DeGruy, Joy, *Post Traumatic Slavery Syndrome: America's Legacy of Enduring Injury and Healing*, Portland, OR: Joy DeGruy Publications, 2005.

Espinosa, Gastón, *Latino Pentecostals in America: Faith and Politics in Action*, Cambridge, MA: Harvard University Press, 2014.

Harris, Antipas L., 'Black Folk Religion in Black Holiness Pentecostalism', *Journal of Pentecostal Theology* 28, 1 (2019), pp. 103–22.

Hicks, Shari Renée, 'A Critical Analysis of Post Traumatic Slave Syndrome: A Multigenerational Legacy of Slavery', PhD dissertation, California Institute of Integral Studies, 2015.

Hollenweger, Walter J., *Pentecostalism: Origins and Developments Worldwide*, Peabody: Hendrickson Publishers, 1997.

Jacobsen, Douglas (ed.), *Reader in Pentecostal Theology: Voices from the First Generation*, Bloomington, IN: Indiana University Press, 2006.

Land, Steven J., *Pentecostal Spirituality: A Passion for the Kingdom*, Sheffield: Sheffield Academic Press, 1997.

MacRobert, Iain, *The Black Roots and White Racism of Early Pentecostalism in the USA*, London: Macmillan Press, 1988.

Malcolmson, Keith, *Pentecostal Pioneers Remembered: British and Irish Pioneers of Pentecost*, Maitland, FL: Xulon Press, 2008.

Nelson, Douglas J., 'For Such a Time as This: The Story of Bishop William J. Seymour and the Azusa Street Revival', PhD dissertation, University of Birmingham, 1981.

Pipkin, Brian K. and Jay Beaman (eds), *Early Pentecostals on Nonviolence and Social Justice: A Reader*, Eugene, OR: Wipf & Stock, 2016.

Poussaint, Alvin F. and Amy Alexander, *Lay My Burden Down: Suicide and the Mental Health Crisis among African Americans*, Boston, MA: Beacon Press, 2000.

Seymour, William J., *The Doctrines and Discipline of the Azusa Street Apostolic Faith Mission*, Joplin, MO: Christian Life Books, 1915.

Shapiro, Stephen and Barnard Philip, 'Pentecostalism and the Protolanguage of Racial Equality' in *Pentecostal Modernism: Lovecraft, Los Angeles and World-Systems Culture*, London: Bloomsbury Academic, 2017.

Shopshire, James M., 'A Socio-historical Characterisation of the Black Pentecostal Movement', PhD dissertation, Northwestern University, 1975.

Thomas, V. V., *Dalit Pentecostalism: Spirituality of the Empowered Poor*, Bangalore: Asian Trading Corporation, 2008.

Vontress, C. E., 'Traditional Healing in Africa: Implications for Cross-Cultural Counseling', *Journal of Counseling and Development* 70, 1 (September–October 1991), pp. 242–9.

White, Calvin, *The Rise to Respectability: Race, Religion, and the Church of God in Christ*, Fayetteville, AR: University of Arkansas Press, 2011.

'How Holy Roller Gets Religion', *Los Angeles Herald*, 10 September 1906, www.newspapers.com/clip/9295061/how-holy-roller-gets-religion-9101906/, accessed 29.10.2020.

The Apostolic Faith, Los Angeles, CA: The Azusa Street Apostolic Faith Mission, AG Consortium of Pentecostal Archives Online, 1906–1908.

Notes

1 'Pentecost has come' in *The Apostolic Faith*, Los Angeles: The Azusa Street Apostolic Faith Mission, 1906, p. 1.

2 'Pentecost has come', pp. 1–2.

3 Anon, 'How Holy Roller Gets Religion', *Los Angeles Herald*, 10 September 1906, p. 7.

4 Frank Bartleman, *How Pentecost came to Los Angeles* (Los Angeles, 1925), p. 54.

5 Stephen Shapiro and Barnard Philip, 'Pentecostalism and the Protolanguage of Racial Equality' in *Pentecostal Modernism: Lovecraft, Los Angeles and World-Systems Culture* (London: Bloomsbury Academic, 2017), p. 65.

6 Gaston Espinosa, *Latino Pentecostals in America: Faith and Politics in Action* (Cambridge: Harvard University Press, 2014), p. 58.

7 V. V. Thomas, *Dalit Pentecostalism: Spirituality of the Empowered Poor* (Bangalore: Asian Trading Corporation, 2008), p. 2.

8 William J. Seymour, *The Doctrines and Discipline of the Azusa Street Mission* (Joplin, MO: Christian Life Books, 2015), p. 30.

9 Seymour, *The Doctrines and Discipline*, p. 30; Iain MacRobert, *The Black Roots and White Racism of Early Pentecostalism in the USA* (London: Macmillan Press, 1988), pp. 60–3; Estrelda Alexander, *Black Fire: One Hundred Years of African American Pentecostalism* (Downers Grove, IL: IVP Academic, 2011), pp. 137–58.

10 For works that name the oppressions faced by Seymour and Black Pentecostals in their historical and theological analysis of the movement, see Douglas J. Nelson, 'For Such a Time as This: The Story of Bishop William J. Seymour and the Azusa Street Revival', PhD dissertation, University of Birmingham (1981), pp. 29–30 and 150–7; Alexander, *Black Fire*, pp. 36–44; Antipas L. Harris, 'Black Folk Religion in Black Holiness Pentecostalism', *Journal of Pentecostal Theology* 28, 1 (2019), pp. 103–22; Lewis Brogdon, 'African American Pentecostalism' in *Handbook of Pentecostal Christianity*, ed. Adam Stewart (DeKalb, IL: Northern Illinois University Press, 2012), pp. 20–3; Walter Hollenweger, *Pentecostalism: Origins and Developments Worldwide* (Peabody, MA: Hendrickson Publishers, 1997), p. 20.

11 Calvin White, *The Rise to Respectability: Race, Religion, and the Church of God in Christ* (Fayetteville, AR: University of Arkansas Press, 2011), p. 16; Nelson, 'For Such a Time as This', p. 243; Alexander, *Black Fire*, p. 111.

12 James M. Shopshire, 'A Socio-historical Characterisation of the Black Pentecostal Movement' (PhD dissertation, Northwestern University, 1975), pp. 3–4.

13 Robert Mapes Anderson, *Vision of the Disinherited* (Oxford: Oxford University Press, 1979), p. 136.

14 Anderson, *Vision of the Disinherited*, pp. 11–12 and 230–1.

15 Anderson, *Vision of the Disinherited*, p. 231.

16 Anderson, *Vision of the Disinherited*, p. 231.

17 Alexander, *Black Fire*, pp. 44–9.

18 Brogdon, 'African American Pentecostalism', pp. 20–1.

19 Nelson, 'For Such a Time as This', p. 43.

20 Nelson, 'For Such a Time as This', p. 43.

21 Nelson, 'For Such a Time as This', p. 270.

22 Nelson, 'For Such a Time as This', p. 271.

23 Nelson, 'For Such a Time as This', p. 271.

24 Alvin F. Poussaint and Amy Alexander, *Lay My Burden Down: Suicide and the Mental Health Crisis among African Americans* (Boston, MA: Beacon Press, 2000).

25 Poussaint and Alexander, *Lay My Burden Down*, p. 12.

26 Poussaint and Alexander highlight the following works as precursors to their own: E. Franklin Frazier, *The Negro Family in the United States* (Chicago, IL: University of Chicago Press, 1939); Amos N. Wilson, *The Falsification of Afrikan Consciousness: Eurocentric History, Psychiatry and the Politics of White Supremacy* (New York: Afrikan World Infosystems, 1993); Na'im Akbar, *Breaking the Chains of Psychological Slavery* (Tallahassee, FL: Mind Productions & Associates, 1996); Brenda L. Richardson and Brenda Wade, *What Mama Couldn't Tell Us About Love: Healing the Emotional Legacy of Racism by Celebrating Our Light* (New York: HarperCollins, 1999).

27 Poussaint and Alexander, *Lay My Burden Down*, p. 15.

28 Poussaint and Alexander, *Lay My Burden Down*, pp. 16–17.

29 Joy DeGruy, *Post Traumatic Slavery Syndrome: America's Legacy of Enduring Injury and Healing* (Portland, OR: Joy DeGruy Publications, 2005), p. 100.

30 DeGruy, *Post Traumatic Slavery Syndrome*, p. 100.

31 DeGruy, *Post Traumatic Slavery Syndrome*, p. 100.

32 DeGruy, *Post Traumatic Slavery Syndrome*, p. 104.

33 DeGruy, *Post Traumatic Slavery Syndrome*, p. 105.

34 DeGruy, *Post Traumatic Slavery Syndrome*, p. 115.

35 DeGruy, *Post Traumatic Slavery Syndrome*, p. 117.

36 Shari Renée Hicks, 'A Critical Analysis of Post Traumatic Slave Syndrome: A Multigenerational Legacy of Slavery' (PhD dissertation, California Institute of Integral Studies, 2015), pp. 116–75. Hicks outlines three alternative theories for analysing the link between slavery and African American contemporary life, including the idea that 'African Americans do not have a syndrome but are symptomatic of the oppressive and dominating White society's sociopathy and psychopathy', pp. 177–81; that 'rather than suffering from a psychological syndrome or disturbance, African Americans are simply coping with the harsh realities of historical subjugation and continuous oppression through escapism', pp. 181–4; and the position Hicks takes that focuses on resiliency in Africans despite slavery, as seen in the retention of traditional African beliefs, self-affirming spirituality and self-love, pp. 184–90.

37 DeGruy draws on K. O'Brian, 'The Uncounted Casualties of War: Epigenetics and Transference of PTSD Symptoms among Children and Grandchildren of Vietnam Veterans in Australia', Centre for Social Change/School of Management (Queensland University of Technology, 2007) and Y. Danieli, *International Handbook of Multigenerational Legacies of Trauma* (New York, Plenum Press, 1980).

38 Nelson, 'For Such a Time as This', p. 271.

39 Charles Conn, *Like a Mighty Army: A History of the Church of God* (Cleveland, OH: Pathway Press, 1977), p. 153; Brian K. Pipkin and Jay Beaman (eds),

Early Pentecostals on Nonviolence and Social Justice: A Reader (Wipf & Stock, 2016), pp. 2–5, 6–16 and 38–9; Douglas Jacobsen (ed.), *Reader in Pentecostal Theology: Voices from the First Generation* (Bloomington, IN: Indiana University Press, 2006), pp. 201–2 and 267.

40 Seymour, *The Doctrines and Discipline*, p. 125.

41 Nelson, 'For Such a Time as This', pp. 157–8.

42 Seymour, *The Doctrines and Discipline*, p. 38.

43 Alexander, *Black Fire*, p. 38.

44 Carlton Turner, *Overcoming Self-Negation: The Church and Junkanoo in Contemporary Bahamian Society* (Eugene, OR: Pickwick Publications, 2020), p. 4.

45 DeGruy, *Post Traumatic Slavery Syndrome*, pp. 108, 117.

46 Hicks, 'A Critical Analysis of Post Traumatic Slave Syndrome', pp. 181–4.

47 DeGruy, *Post Traumatic Slavery Syndrome*, p. 9.

48 DeGruy, *Post Traumatic Slavery Syndrome*, p. 9.

49 Nelson, 'For Such a Time as This', p. 35.

50 Nelson, 'For Such a Time as This', p. 161.

51 Keith Malcolmson, *Pentecostal Pioneers Remembered: British and Irish Pioneers of Pentecost* (Maitland, FL: Xulon Press, 2008), pp. 81–2 and 107.

52 Steven J. Land, *Pentecostal Spirituality: A Passion for the Kingdom* (Sheffield: Sheffield Academic Press, 1997), p. 183.

53 Seymour, *The Doctrine and Disciplines*, p. 43.

54 Alexander, *Black Fire*, p. 138.

55 Seymour, *The Doctrine and Disciplines*, p. 82. 56 'But the fruit of the Spirit is love, joy, peace, forbearance, kindness, goodness, faithfulness, gentleness and self-control' (NIVUK).

57 'Salvation and Healing' in *The Apostolic Faith* (December 1906).

58 Mary Adekson, *The Yoruba Traditional Healers of Nigeria* (New York: Taylor & Francis Group, 2004), pp. 69, 106.

59 Adekson, *The Yoruba Traditional Healers of Nigeria*, pp. 86 and 91.

60 Adekson, *The Yoruba Traditional Healers of Nigeria*, p. 21, citing Vontress, 'Traditional Healing in Africa'.

61 Adekson, *The Yoruba Traditional Healers of Nigeria*, p. 100.

62 Romans 8.11 (NIVUK).

4

Weeping Wounds: Queer Blacksculinity, Trauma and Grief

J. A. ROBINSON-BROWN

Boyhood, Blacksculinity and being

One of the earliest memories of my father is of the both of us walking down Kilburn High Road. I was no more than nine years old, and riddled with a youthful anxiety as this was 'one of our days out' during which I would be picked up from whichever family member or friend was caring for me, and duly returned after my father had fulfilled his duties. On this particular day, however, something, perhaps the busyness of the street, caused me to reach out for my father's hand, placing mine in his – not something the rest of life had provided much opportunity for, and not something I remember ever doing before. I did not know then that that would be both the first and final time. As soon as I placed my hand in his, he thrust mine away with the words, 'Don't do that! That's gay – only battymen do that!' Thus began a reframing not only of our relationship, but my own understanding of Black manhood and Black masculinity. As we entered Argos, I recalled seeing the myriad children, particularly young white boys, holding the hands of older men – perhaps their father's? What rendered these boys visible to me was the trauma of this event – a trauma that expresses itself initially in comparison, a comparison that is rooted not only in gender but also in race. Like many young Black men, growing up in environments where masculine resilience carried a degree of weight, I became aware that, as Guvna B notes, 'My parents brought me up to be the way they believed boys should be and by this, I mean to be proud, strong, robust enough to hold myself together, and manly enough never to cry.'[1] As I began to grow older, I internalized many of the cues received from the older Black men around me, such that my manners, language and dress were moderated by these cues. Eventually, understanding myself as queer meant that I became more determined to do what was necessary to be considered an acceptable Black male. Eventually I understood that there was a certain degree of stigma attached to being seen as a queer Black male, queer not only in terms of sexuality, but also in terms of gender, and queer too within our heteronormative British Jamaican culture – that the showing of emotion meant that one was viewed as less male than others, and by extension less authentically Black. As Anthony Lemelle and Juan Battle note, the 'Stigma associated with homophobia and homosexuality helps us to understand that in everyday and face-to-face interactions, Black masculinity is unique in the management of identity.'[2] To be Black and male is to have your behaviour and your identity restricted and defined by a number of external factors, and it is the hegemonic understanding of masculinity and the hegemonic notions of Blackness that lies particularly heavily upon those who are Black and queer.

This management of identity works itself out in a number of ways within Queer Blacksculinity – the combined result of masculinity and Blackness and queer identity, such that while I understood myself to be the 'man of the house' and knew this to mean a particular thing, it was something that I equally knew I could never attain once I had accepted my homosexuality. Unlike the other men around me, I had little or no interest sexually in women and therefore already found myself positioned beyond what is perceived as the true Black male. Professor Dwight McBride has written that 'The image of the Black man as protector, progenitor, and defender of the race [suggests] that to be a representative race man, one must be heterosexual.'[3] When one finds oneself in such a position, the choices are to maintain the act that allows us as individuals to feel somewhat safe and accepted in heteronormative circles, or to 'refuse to perform a heteronormative drag show',[4] as Professor Emilie Townes puts it.

All of this, the power with which our discourse around race and gender in relation to Black men constitutes a normative discourse in which the Black man is unemotional, unfeeling and unbreakable, cause not only trauma but grief. Added to this, such normative discourse perpetuates the idea that the Black man is heterosexual and cisgendered, pushing the trauma into images that constitute normative conceptualizations of love and romance – such that Black men are conditioned not only in how they must give love, but how they must receive it. Any grief or trauma experienced by Black men who are also trans or queer comes with a sense of already being unseen and unheard, such that when that grief is made public the cost to such emotional honesty can come at a cost heterosexual cisgendered Black men do not carry. Even when the public wounds of Black men are being acknowledged, it is important to note that Black trans men in their life and death have their grief, vulnerability and pain elided and negated. In their article on how the brutal murder of George Floyd was publicly marked, Melz Owusu writes about how George Floyd's name was more prominent than Tony McDade's. Melz made the point that Tony:

was routinely misgendered in the press in what can only be described as a further plunging in of the sharp bullet that took his life. Had social media not rallied behind Tony, the erasure of his transness would have gone unnoticed. I often wonder how many of my trans siblings are denied their humanity and identity just as much in death, as they are in life.[5]

In considering whose tears we do not see, and whose pain we do not hear of, it is important to remember that even in spaces within which Black men feel safe, there are particular groups within the diversity of Black men who are particularly vulnerable or susceptible to trauma.

When thinking about the term 'Black male vulnerability', used frequently in the work of Tommy J. Curry, there are those who are vulnerable to heteronormative discourse and hegemonic constructs of the masculine in a particular way. Defining Black male vulnerability, Curry says:

> *Black male vulnerability* is the term I use to capture the disadvantages that Black males endure compared with other groups; the erasure of Black males' actual lived experience from theory; and the violence and death Black males suffer in society. The term is not meant simply to express the material disadvantages Black males face due to incarceration, unemployment, police brutality, homicide, domestic and sexual abuse throughout society, or their victimhood. The term is also meant to express the vulnerable condition – the sheer fungibility – of the Black male as a living terror able to be killed, raped, or dehumanized at any moment, given the disposition of those who encounter him. Black male vulnerability is an attempt to capture the Black male's perpetual susceptibility to the will of others, how he has no resistance to the imposition of others' fears and anxieties on him.[6]

This vulnerability is seen particularly among those Black men who are not cisgendered.

Returning to Melz Owusu: 'What it means to be a Black cisgender man in the Western world has been conceptualized for years – what it means to be a Black trans man/masculine person is an experience many are not ready to acknowledge, and thus are not ready to protect.'[7] In all our thinking, it is important to think as broadly and inclusively about masculinity as possible.

Peter Levine notes that:

> When touched with a feeling of pain, the ordinary person laments ... becomes distraught ... contracts ... so he feels two pains ... just as if they were to shoot a man with an arrow and, right afterward, were to shoot him with another ... so that he would feel the pains of two arrows ... Trauma sufferers are so frightened of their bodily sensations that they recoil from feeling them. It is as though they believe that by feeling them they will be destroyed or, at the very least, make things worse.[8]

According to Levine's analysis, one of the effects of trauma is that it causes us to be fearful of our bodies – the effects of this on Black men who are queer can manifest itself in the deepest of ruptures, such that a bodyphobia rooted not only in what our cultures tell us is acceptable but also what our religious traditions teach us, can mean we feel deeply the 'two arrows' of pain that become apparent as we manifest queer Black masculine identities. As Durryle Brooks notes, those who are Black and queer have often been left out of the discourse on race: 'Black queer sexuality has historically often been left out of the conversation on race. Black queer sexuality has been marked as deviant, a deviation from the norm and assumed way of being – Black and heterosexual, which has led to the marginalization of Black queer experiences.'[9]

In this chapter, as I explore the story of the raising of Lazarus and moments when weeping, grief or tears are significant in Augustine of Hippo's *Confessions*, I want to consider how the presence of weeping Black men in both the Gospel of John and Augustine's *Confessions* gestures towards a reconceptualization of love and public emotion for Black men. Whether at the epicentre of the Roman Empire, or in the current season of the Black Lives Matter movement:

> Re-conceptualizing love in the context of oppression becomes a critical component for addressing and redressing the ways in which hetero-normativity and racism shape how some Black queer folks conceptualize love and the impacts that it has on their overall well-being. Re-conceptualizing love becomes an intervention unto itself, as it requires folks to explore and reexamine past trauma and to explicitly think about healing and their journey toward completeness and wholeness.[10]

When Joseph Beam remarked in 1986 that 'Black men loving Black men is the revolutionary act',[11] he spoke out of a context in which the Black queer body was, as it continues to be,[12] under threat. Writing at the height of the AIDS crisis, Beam writes against institutional neglect in Philadelphia, cultural violence and the potent stigmatization of Black LGBTQ+ people. Like so many writing at his time, writing served as an antidote to the multivalent and relentless forces of death which thrived in a world that did not want to see queer Black bodies nor hear the depth of their trauma and grief. Such trauma was not only unwelcome, but was characterized as unmanly, feminine and un-African. It was a trauma and grief that was known to many but witnessed by few. To be Black and male was to be un-suffering, unfeeling, to have a resilience that meant the weight of life did not hinder and the hardness of life did not hurt. What, we might ask, is so revolutionary about Black men loving themselves in and through the flesh of the other? What is so revolutionary about public Black male grief? Yet in a time when love and death walk hand in hand, Black queer love and vulnerability was both necessary and inevitable – what is revolutionary about Black queer love? Everything.

Beam's words, his viewing of his own loving as revolutionary, flow from the histories with which Black masculinity is burdened. To love is to transgress, to transgress the borders of one's own body, to give voice to one's own desire and to name in oneself a longing – the need for love, which can only be met through and with the 'other'. To love is to be both disturbed and disarmed; it summons us to maturity but a maturity that is arrived at only through a vulnerability which for the Black man can be a vulnerability that one is taught may lead to death. To speak of Black queer love as a gesture towards thinking through grief and trauma is an attempt to perceive of male-to-male love as the apex of Black masculine vulnerability. This love, however, needn't have a sexual connotation. The vulnerability that makes Black male grief and trauma expressible is a vulnerability that can be witnessed in the love a Black male has for younger Black males, whether siblings, cousins or offspring. To perceive of Joseph Beam's remark that 'Black men loving Black men is the revolutionary act' within the limits of the sexual is to prove the very ways in which Black male love is defined by the Black male body being viewed as sexual and erotic. I am curious to explore what happens to our understandings of Blackness, masculinity and grief when we consider the public grief, the public love displayed by Jesus in relationship to his friend Lazarus. Does the public grief shown by Jesus in John's Gospel offer us a paradigm for reconceiving the acceptability of Black male emotion in relation to death and trauma?

In all of this, it is important to recognize what is referred to in the work of Darius Bost as the 'politics of discretion'. Such politics demand of Black men who are not heteronormative the discretion of their gender and sexual identities not only within white spaces but also within Black communities where the importance of economic survival and cultural belonging are fundamental. Black queer men often faced, and continue to face, cultural and political exclusion, and the management of trauma and grief are not excluded from the politics of discretion. The politics of discretion inevitably led to a crisis of truth, particularly in the AIDS epidemic. In 1988, on 27 December, three days before his 34th birthday, Joseph Beam died. The cause of his death was recorded as AIDS, and he had kept his diagnosis a secret until his death. None of his friends know how he died, although suicide and a drugs overdose[13] were suspected beyond the 'official' story. Beam's body was discovered in a state of advanced decomposition; he had given voice through his journalism, activism and editorial work to so many, but he died in a state of silence and mystery. Bost notes in relation to Beam's story that his 'dying in silence, especially as a leader of a movement to end the silence around Black gay men's lives, reveals how the public efforts of Black gay artists and activists to transform their social worlds could not always alleviate their individual psychic pain'.[14]

The Queer studies scholar John Champagne reflects on a speech given by Essex Hemphill in 1990, during which he broke down in tears. Champagne writes of 'a politics of tears, a politics that assures the validity of its produced explanation by appealing to some kind of "authentic," unique, and (thus) uninterrogatable "human" emotion or experience'.[15] Many people were bewildered by Hemphill's tears at the OutWrite conference on the theme 'AIDS and the Responsibility of the Writer', but what is unavoidable is that the moment, only a few years after Beam's death, resurrects emotion within him that manifests itself as a weeping wound. On the same moment, the Black queer studies scholar E. Patrick Johnson asks: 'What is the significance of a Black man crying in public?' Whether Hemphill, Jesus or Augustine – Black men crying in public marks moments when what is unspeakable is made manifest in the act of tears. Cathy Caruth writes about 'how traumatic experiences disrupt history and memory. She argues that the psychological impact of extremely violent events produces fissures and gaps in the narratives of the traumatized, thereby rendering certain aspects of the traumatic past as unrepresentable and unspeakable.'[16] In moments of the unspeakable, it seems that tears, very often, do the work that speech cannot complete.

The impact of trauma on us in our earliest stages very likely informs the ways in which we navigate our place in the world as Black men, and as queer Black men in particular. Reflecting on what 'manhood' means, the Black Gay African American writer James Baldwin suggests that 'we all exist, after all, and crucially, in the eye of the beholder. We all react to and, to whatever extent, become what that eye sees. This judgement begins in the eyes of one's parents (the crucial, the definitive, the all-but-everlasting judgement), and so we move, in the vast and claustrophobic gallery of Others, on up or down the line, to the eye of one's enemy or one's friend or one's lover.'[17] Not only is it important to recognize how the judgement we receive from the gaze of others informs how we see ourselves, but it is important too to recognize that our own judgements impact how we understand masculinity and sexuality, and how we articulate our own understandings of trauma and grief. We need, then, in all our reflections here, to recognize that the 'meanings of masculinity and femininity vary from one society/culture to another, within any society/culture over time, within each individual over time, and, perhaps most important, among different individuals in one group at one point in time.'[18]

The one time God wept: weeping wounds

In discussing the story of the resurrection of Lazarus, what I explore is whether Jesus' body, when read as male and of colour, reveals to us something of a model for Black masculine expressions of grief and trauma. I seek to unearth how, as a person embodied in a brown male body, Jesus' own experience of grief and trauma in the ancient world might reveal something about Blacksculinity in the modern world – opening up for us connections between Christ's body and other Black male bodies. This story of Lazarus being raised from the dead presents us with a number of issues related to grief, trauma, gender and sexuality. In particular, it is notable that a key feature in this story is premised upon the intimacy between Lazarus and Jesus. The love Jesus has for Lazarus attains a queer quality for us as modern readers gazing back into the ancient world.

In the intimacy between Jesus and his friend, in the very public grief that Jesus embodies, we see that the use of the body in manifesting the grief felt through love is a holy thing, indeed a godly thing. Contrary to the idea 'that the use of one's own body in the act of love is considered a crime against the Holy Ghost',[19] we see that our bodies are made to be the places in which our love for one another is expressed – even when that love is touched by death. For Jesus there is nothing that can get in the way of his love for Lazarus: neither the stone blocking the entrance to his tomb (John 11.38), nor the very stench of death were enough to prevent the love between these two brothers from being rekindled. As James Baldwin said, this was also true of Jesus and Lazarus. Although the quality of love may be different, it stands even in this story that: 'no matter what Saint Paul may thunder, love is where you find it. A man can fall in love with a man: incarceration, torture, fire, and death, and, still more, the threat of these, have not been able to prevent it, and never will.'[20]

The eleventh chapter of John's Gospel contains the story of the death of Lazarus. Not only is the death of Lazarus a story recorded solely in the Gospel of John, but it is the story that in the King James Version of the Bible contains the shortest verse in Scripture: 'Jesus wept'.[21] The narrative containing this moment in the life of Jesus and his closest friends captures moments of grief, trauma and vulnerability. We hear in the beginning that 'a certain man' (John 11.1), Lazarus of Bethany, is ill. Lazarus from the beginning then is placed for us specifically as one positioned in relation to the women who, for the majority of the narrative, appear to be the only ones prepared to mourn him. He belongs in specific relation to Mary and Martha his sister. After being identified with his sisters, Lazarus is identified next with Jesus and the love that Jesus has for him. 'He whom you love is ill' (John 11.3) are the words that give context to Jesus and Lazarus's relationship. And, essentially, Jesus does what many Black men are socialized to do when hearing news that the 'bredrin' they love is dead – Jesus 'fronts it', which is to say, he offers a rebuttal that somewhat negates the violence of the news: 'This illness does not lead to death.' While Jesus is right, his beloved Lazarus will not be dead for ever, the statement of this fact serves as a denial of the pain of the moment. It negates the severity of the reality that Lazarus *is* dead, and whatever should come beyond this moment, Lazarus will *always* have once died.

Eventually, Lazarus becomes a shared relation: 'Our friend Lazarus has fallen asleep' (John 11.11); and in some ways Jesus could be seen to be distancing himself from the group-grief of his friends when he says, 'I am going there to awaken him' (John 11.11). Jesus, as the male in this situation, is the one to whom the responsibility of vindication falls, not just as Saviour but as male. In verse 14, Jesus appears to state the shocking truth but he does so unmoved, according to the writer of the Gospel: 'Then Jesus told them plainly, "Lazarus is dead" (John 11.14). This news is not warmly received, as Jesus now points out not only the obvious but the apparently undoable. He is accused twice:

'Lord, if you had been here, my brother would not have died' (John 11.21).

'Lord, if you had been here, my brother would not have died' (John 11.32).

It is Jesus witnessing the grief of his friends that disturbs his spirit (11.33) and that leads him to ask where his friend Lazarus is buried. And it is the being invited to see Lazarus's grave that causes Jesus to weep. The term used to define Jesus' weeping is 'εδακρυσεν' (edakrusen), which finds its root in 'δακρύω' (dakruo), both of which are clear in the quality that the tears Jesus sheds are properly defined not simply as crying, but more accurately as 'weeping', as a grief felt deeply and profoundly. The act of Jesus weeping can of course be interpreted in a number of ways. The two most potent perhaps are, first, that Jesus' weeping acts as a signifier of his humanity in the sense that it is a human thing to weep and a point of recognition that in Christ God had taken flesh as a full human being. In weeping, Jesus shows that his body is capable of doing what our own bodies do, and that his appearance as a human being was no illusion but that he was one with real bodily functions. The weeping of Jesus can also, however, be seen as a paradoxical image to that of his divine power. Why does Jesus weep when surely, as God, he knows that he has the power to have prevented Lazarus's death, and the power too to put what has gone wrong right?

Witnessing the tears of Jesus, his bearing of his own emotional wound allows others to know and understand not only what is going on within him, but also helps them to understand that Jesus' love for Lazarus was real: 'See how he loved him!' (John 11.36). Jesus' friendship with Lazarus is one defined not just by relational intimacy, but by Christ's love for this other man. Yet those who see Jesus weep cannot help but criticize him: 'Could not he who opened the eyes of the blind man have kept this man from dying?' (John 11.37).

Lazarus becomes an icon of what the love of Christ can bring to birth for all whom Christ calls out of death and captivity. Lazarus dines at the table with Jesus as all those set free from death's power taste and see the eucharistic Christ on earth and in heaven. Christ is wounded in his grief, which leads him not just to feel inwardly the pain of death, but such pain that leads to the outward expression of weeping. Jesus and Lazarus's friendship to us appears queer. It is a relationship between two Black bodies shaped and defined by masculinity but most accurately shaped by love and vulner-ability.

Both John 11.33 and 11.38 show that Jesus is troubled by this experience on a number of levels, with a kind of grief that manifests itself distinctly. In John 11.33 we read that Jesus 'was deeply moved' 'ενεβριμήσατο' (ene-brimesato) and in John 11.38 again that he found himself 'being deeply moved' 'εμβριμώμενος' (embrimomenos); both of these have a quality not only of being moved, but of a raging anger too. The Jesus we see in this scene therefore reveals to us that Jesus:

> is not the majestic, unmoved Lord but rather the one with the passion who knows and shares in the anguish of the brother and sister. The fact that Jesus weeps and that he is moved in spirit and troubled contrasts remarkably with the dominant culture. That is not the way of power, and it is scarcely the way among those who intend to maintain firm so-cial control. But in this scene Jesus is engaged not in social control but in dismantling the power of death, and he does so by submitting himself to the pain and grief present in the situation, the very pain and grief that the dominant society must deny.[22]

In a society where pain is denied and where grief is left unacknowledged, it is those who have already taught their bodies to deny its natural configura-tions who suffer the most. bell hooks, in her book on masculinity and love, offers her reflection built upon a man she knew in her childhood, and the effect of witnessing him weeping. She writes:

> Men cannot speak their pain in patriarchal culture. Boys learn this in early childhood. As a girl, I was awed by a man in my church, a deacon, who would stand before the congregation and speak his love for the divine spirit. Often in the midst of his testimony he would begin to weep, sobbing tears into a big white handkerchief. The girls and boys who witnessed his tears were embarrassed for him, for in their eyes he was showing himself to be weak. When he wept, the men who stood beside him turned their eyes away. They were ashamed to see a man express intense feeling.[23]

Black men been 'fronting' from day: Blacksculinity in antiquity

The Black writer, poet and educator JJ Bola, in his book *Mask Off: Mascu-linity Redefined*, described the first time that he ever saw his father cry. This incident was notable, not only for its impact on him, but more so because of its rarity. His father held what it meant to be a man for him, in the way in which for many Black men, whether role models or otherwise, can be the people who shape for us what Black manhood means, looks like, and is. Bola recalls how the experience of seeing his father crying left him, not uneasy or troubled, but rather 'in shock', having 'been told to be strong and not to cry all my childhood, [now] the one person who I saw as the ultimate source of strength was in tears in front of me'.[24] For Bola, witnessing his father's tears was the beginning of the undoing of his concept of Black masculinity. Not only did the experience mark the unravelling of what Bola perceived as the ultimate source of strength located in his father's lack of public emotion, but it pushes him to believe that – in order to become a real man – he now needed to grow even stronger than his father so that 'no one would ever see me cry; no one would ever see my weakness.'[25]

In crying openly, Bola's father loses his masculine credentials to a certain degree in the sight of his son. His father's tears, rather than telling him something powerful about his father's embodied reality, speaks to him of a vulnerability that has transgressed the bounds of acceptability. The son realizes that his father is not quite who we had been led to believe he was, and the image of his father must be reconsidered now in Bola's young mind. While Bola does not tell us what the origin of his father's tears were, he does reference how many of his male friends do not feel comfortable with such levels of vulnerability, and how some among his friends have not cried in many years even at the death of relatives, during tragic moments or at the end of romantic relationships. It seems in the witnessing of his father's tears, in his father's bearing of his own wounds before his son, that Bola is able to assess the unusual nature of his friends' lack of tears around him. His father's witnessing to his own pain, then, is precisely that which allows Bola to reassess his and his friends' masculinity – to notice the absence of tears in spaces other than that shared with his weeping father.

Judith Butler, in her book *Gender Trouble*, says that 'gender is an identity tenuously constructed in time ... through a *stylized repetition of acts*.'[26] The performative aspect of Blacksculinity, where the performance of gender is tied up with the performativity of race, means that the absence of tears is a fundamental part of the performance. Wherever the lack of tears is held as a mark of manliness in areas committed to toxic notions of masculinity, such a lack of tears operates as a means by which cultural membership of Black masculinity is maintained. It is through one's lack of tears, through one's hard exterior that an individual retains their credibility within spaces that understand Black manhood to be founded on the emotional resilience (or emotional absence) of Black men. From antiquity to the present day, for Black men to not cry is to show one's membership card at the gateway into a culture where masculinity means that a person is always unmoved by trauma or grief. It is here that so many Black men find themselves, gazing into the fold in which our uncles, brothers, friends and even lovers sit. The price of the ticket is the denial of what our Black male bodies tell us when they experience pain and trauma, grief and woundedness. Black masculinity in a sense is always performative, because it operates as the alternative to the dominant default of white men.

In Book Nine of Augustine's *Confessions*, we see in this fourth-century work how Augustine's North African masculinity in relation to the grief of his mother manifests through the control of Augustine's tears, and those of his son. On the ninth day of his mother Monica's illness, aged 56, Monica dies and her son Augustine writes:

> I closed her eyes and an overwhelming grief welled into my heart and was about to flow forth in floods of tears. But at the same time under a powerful act of mental control my eyes held back the flood and dried it up. The inward struggle put me into great agony. Then when she breathed her last, the boy Adeodatus cried out in sorrow and was pressed by all of us to be silent.[27]

Augustine, while feeling the depth of his wound at the passing of his mother, holds back his tears using the total powers of his mind in order to do so. And he expresses how, although successful, the effort to not cry 'put me into great agony'. Augustine's lack of tears is driven not solely by understandings of masculinity, but by theological imperatives too. To cry is to imply sorrow, and, as Augustine says: 'my mother's dying meant neither that her state was miserable nor that she was suffering extinction.'[28] Yet such a belief in the safety of Monica's soul did not allow his heart to rest. Not only does Augustine find that his language is shaped by what is deemed acceptable to those around him ('I discussed subjects fitting for the occasion'[29]), but he notes how their engagement with his shallow speech fails to allow him to be honest about the deep pain he felt: 'They listened to me intently and supposed me to have no feeling of grief.'[30] Of course, Augustine is in this encounter putting up a front, he is 'holding back the torrent of sadness' and he boasts that as bad as he felt, he did not 'burst into tears'[31] nor 'even at those prayers did I weep'.[32] So difficult was the struggle to keep his tears from flowing that Augustine says 'I was inwardly oppressed with sadness.'[33] The one person in the setting who has not been conditioned enough to prevent his grief from finding its voice is Augustine's son, Adeodatus, who cries out in sorrow and is silenced by those around him. Silencing Adeodatus clearly took some time however, as Augustine continues to tell us that 'After the boy's tears had been checked, Evodius took up the psalter and began to chant the psalm.'[34]

Augustine's maternal grief causes him to respond in a different way from how he responds to other types of loss. Earlier in the Confessions in Book Four he writes in relation to the death of an unnamed friend, about whom he articulates how everything begins to speak to him of death, grief and loss. Augustine enters a 'strange world of unhappiness',[35] a world in which all that he once shared with his dear friend has now, in his friend's absence, been 'transformed into a cruel torment'.[36] For Augustine, the grief is so deep that he admits openly not only to his tears but says that 'weeping had replaced my friend'.[37] In all of this, while Augustine appears to be approaching the possibility of moving beyond his pain in saying that 'all that belongs to the past, and with time my wound is less painful',[38] he is clearly still wrestling deeply with his weeping wound. He ponders whether grief in its groaning, weeping, sighing and mourning is the only way to pick the sweet fruit of life. It is in his weeping here that Augustine says he found rest in his bitterness.[39] And yet he goes on to reveal that there is no respite for him: 'when my weeping stopped, my soul felt burdened by a vast load of misery.'[40] Augustine, unlike so many Black men in particular contexts today, manages to articulate so profoundly his grief and its effects on him on losing his friend: 'The reason why that grief had penetrated me so easily and deeply was that I had poured out my soul on the sand by loving a person sure to die as if he would never die.'[41]

It is hard not to wonder what happened to the Augustine who, earlier in the *Confessions*, was so willing to shed tears publicly. Rowan Williams says that, for Augustine: 'Tears become a consolation of sorts.' And yet despite this fact, 'Augustine leaves the site of his bereavement to avoid his memories.'[42] Yet I still want to ask: How over the years was he shaped into the sturdy, almost unbreakable man who watches his mother die without shedding tears, and who silences his son, a vision now, it seems, of Augustine's younger self? Did the brutality of life harden Augustine, or was he so worn out by the grief for his friend that by the death of his mother he simply had no more tears to shed? Judith Herman says that:

> Traumatic events call into question basic human relationships. They breach the attachments of family, friendship, love, and community. They shatter the construction of the self that is formed and sustained in relation to others. They undermine the belief systems that give meaning to human experience. They violate the victim's faith in a natural or divine order and cast the victim into a state of existential crisis.[43]

Augustine I suspect is not so dissimilar to Black men of today – shaped by trauma, and conditioned by the surrounding culture that, as Baldwin said so eloquently, causes us to shape ourselves according to the gaze of others. Perhaps we, like Augustine, are shaped too by the gaze not of the world alone, but also of God. Black men exist in a world in which 'Many of the tropes surrounding Black masculinity rely for effect on a savage heterosexualism',[44] and the words so often used to describe the Black male evoke images of the thuggish, hard, innately savage, dominant, strong, beastly and unbreakable. They contrast the ideas that relate to the tender, loving, romantic, fragile, vulnerable, hurting, human, passionate and caring. Breaking free from these multifarious descriptions of Black men is the work of deconstruction, the work of a lifetime – but it is also the work that Christ and Augustine seem to gesture towards. As both Jesus and Augustine weep for us, they appear queer to us who in peering back are perhaps surprised by their emotion. Howard Thurman understands that it is our bodies that provide us with the safest place of dwelling, the place in which we are able to be most fully ourselves: 'The body is a man's intimate dwelling place; it is his domain as nothing else can ever be. It is coextensive with himself. If for any reason whatsoever a man is alienated in his own body either by shame, outrage, or brutality, his sense of community within himself is rendered difficult, if not impossible.'[45] In all instances wherein the Black male body finds itself with weeping wounds, it must find images, examples, others who model the kind of body it seeks to become – it is in exploring the above characters as possible examples of those who publicly own their grief and trauma that I have attempted to demonstrate the existence of Black and Brown men who have embodied a queer space in the notion of masculinity. Whether Jesus, Augustine, Beam or Baldwin – all reveal how masculinity in every age is more than one hegemonic thing, that tears and grief constitute an integral part of Black male life, and that it is only in naming what one may otherwise hide, that we embody freedom.

Bibliography

Baldwin, James, *James Baldwin Collected Essays*, ed. Toni Morrison, New York: Library of America, 1998.

Beam, Joseph, 'Caring For Each Other' *Black/Out* 1, 1 (1986), p. 9.

Bola, J. J., *Mask Off: Masculinity Redefined*, London: Pluto Press, 2019.

Bost, Darius, *Evidence of Being: The Black Gay Cultural Renaissance and the Politics of Violence*, Chicago, IL: University of Chicago Press, 2018.

Brooks, Durryle N., 'Moving from Trauma to Healing: Black Queer Cultural Workers' Experiences and Discourses of Love', PhD dissertation, University of Massachusetts Amherst, 2017.

Brueggemann, Walter, *The Prophetic Imagination*, Minneapolis, MN: Fortress Press, 2018.

Butler, Judith, *Gender Trouble: Feminism and the Subversion of Identity*, New York and London: Routledge, 1990.

Champagne, John, *Ethics of Marginality: A New Approach to Gay Studies*, Minneapolis, MN: University of Minnesota Press, 1995.

Curry, Tommy J., *The Man-Not: Race, Class, Genre, and the Dilemmas of Black Manhood*, Philadelphia, PA: Temple University Press, 2017.

Guvna B, 'How to Be a Proper Man', *The Church Times*, 19 February 2021, www.churchtimes.co.uk/articles/2021/19-february/features/features/guvna-b-how-to-be-a-proper-man, accessed 21.2.2022.

Hoffman, Rose Marie, John A. Hattie and L. DiAnne Borders, 'Personal Definitions of Masculinity and Femininity as an Aspect of Gender Self-Concept', *The Journal of Humanistic Counseling, Education and Development* 44, 1 (2005), pp. 66–83.

hooks, bell, *The Will to Change: Men, Masculinity, and Love*, New York: Atria Books, 2004.

Lemelle, Anthony J. and Juan Battle, 'Black Masculinity Matters in Attitudes toward Gay Males', *Journal of Homosexuality* 47, 1 (2004), pp. 39–51.

Levine, Peter A., *In an Unspoken Voice: How the Body Releases Trauma and Restores Goodness*, Berkeley, CA: North Atlantic Books, 2012.

Saint Augustine, *Confessions*, ed. Henry Chadwick, Oxford: Oxford University Press, 1991.

Thurman, Howard, *Howard Thurman: Essential Writings*, ed. Luther J. Smith, New York: Orbis Books, 2006.

Townes, Emilie, 'Thin Human Imagination: Searching for Grace on the Rim Bones of Nothingness', University of Warwick: SST, 2019.

Williams, Rowan, *On Augustine*, London: Bloomsbury Publishing, 2016.

Notes

1 Guvna B, 'How to be a Proper Man', *The Church Times*, 19 February 2021, p. 18.

2 Anthony J. Lemelle, Jr and Juan Battle, 'Black Masculinity Matters in Attitudes Toward Gay Males', *Journal of Homosexuality* 47, 1 (2004).

3 Lemelle and Battle, 'Black Masculinity Matters'.

4 Emilie Townes, 'Thin Human Imagination: Searching For Grace On The Rim Bones Of Nothingness' (Society for the Study of Theology, 2021), p. 9.

5 Melz Owusu, 'Black Trans People are Disrespected in Life and Barely Acknowledged in Death – Our Lives Matter Too', *The Independent*, 2 June 2020, www.independent.co.uk/voices/george-floyd-black-lives-matter-racism-tony-mcdade-transgender-a9544131.html, accessed 21.2.2022.

6 Tommy J. Curry, *The Man-Not: Race, Class, Genre, And the Dilemmas of Black Manhood* (Philadelphia, PA: Temple University Press, 2017), p. 29.

7 Owusu, 'Black Trans People are Disrespected in Life'.

8 Peter A. Levine, *In an Unspoken Voice* (Berkeley, CA: North Atlantic Books, 2010), pp. 817–19.

9 Durryle N. Brooks, 'Moving from Trauma to Healing: Black Queer Cultural Workers' Experiences and Discourses of Love' (PhD dissertation, University of Massachusetts Amherst, 2017), https://scholarworks.umass.edu/dissertations_2/944, p. 25, accessed 21.2.2022.

10 Brooks, 'Moving from Trauma to Healing', p. 79.

11 Joseph Beam, 'Caring for Each Other', *Black/Out* 1, 1 (1986), p. 9.

12 Josh Milton, 'Black LGBT+ Youth Hit Hardest by COVID-19 Mental Health Crisis, Reveals Devastating Study', *Pink News*, 22 February 2021, www.pinknews.co.uk/2021/02/22/black-lgbt-youth-covid-19-mental-health-just-like-us/, accessed 10.5.2021.

13 Darius Bost, *Evidence of Being: The Black Gay Cultural Renaissance and the Politics of Violence* (Chicago, IL: University of Chicago Press, 2019), p. 58.

14 Bost, *Evidence of Being*, p. 58.

15 Champagne, John, *Ethics of Marginality: A New Approach to Gay Studies* (Minneapolis, MN: University of Minnesota Press, 1995), p. 59. Hemphill's speech became the introduction to Joseph Beam's work *Brother to Brother* (1991).

16 Bost, *Evidence of Being*, p. 58.

17 James Baldwin, 'Freaks and the American Ideal of Manhood' in *Baldwin: Collected Essays*, ed. Toni Morrison (New York: Library of America, 1998), p. 817.

18 Rose Marie Hoffman, John A. Hattie and L. DiAnne Borders, 'Personal Definitions of Masculinity and Femininity as an Aspect of Gender Self-Concept', *Journal of Humanistic Counseling, Education and Development* 44, 1 (Spring 2005), www.researchgate.net/publication/264781155_Personal_Definitions_of_Masculinity_and_Femininity_as_an_Aspect_of_Gender_Self-Concept, accessed 21.2.2022.

19 James Baldwin, *The Devil Finds Work* (New York: Vintage, 1976), p. 33.

20 Baldwin, *The Devil Finds Work*, p. 54.

21 In the NRSV this verse is: 'Jesus began to weep.'

22 Walter Brueggemann, *The Prophetic Imagination* (Minneapolis, MN: Fortress Press, 2018), p. 92.

23 bell hooks, *The Will to Change: Men, Masculinity and Love* (New York: Atria Books, 2004), p. 135.

24 JJ Bola, *Mask Off: Masculinity Redefined* (London: Pluto Press, 2019), p. 14.

25 Bola, *Mask Off*, p. 14.

26 Judith Butler, *Gender Trouble: Feminism and the Subversion of Identity* (New York and London: Routledge, 1990), p. 140; emphasis original.

27 Henry Chadwick (ed.), *Saint Augustine Confessions* (Oxford: Oxford University Press, 1991), p. 174.

28 Chadwick, *Saint Augustine Confessions*.

29 Chadwick, *Saint Augustine Confessions*, p. 175.

30 Chadwick, *Saint Augustine Confessions*, p. 175.

31 Chadwick, *Saint Augustine Confessions*, p. 175.

32 Chadwick, *Saint Augustine Confessions*, p. 175.

33 Chadwick, *Saint Augustine Confessions*, p. 175.

34 Chadwick, *Saint Augustine Confessions*, p. 175.

35 Chadwick, *Saint Augustine Confessions*, p. 57.

36 Chadwick, *Saint Augustine Confessions*, p. 57.

37 Chadwick, *Saint Augustine Confessions*, p. 58.

38 Chadwick, *Saint Augustine Confessions*, p. 58.

39 Chadwick, *Saint Augustine Confessions*, p. 58.

40 Chadwick, *Saint Augustine Confessions*, pp. 59–60.

41 Chadwick, *Saint Augustine Confessions*, p. 60.

42 Rowan Williams, *On Augustine* (London: Bloomsbury, 2016), p. 5.

43 Judith Herman, *Trauma and Recovery* (New York: Basic Books, 1997), p. 51.

44 Tommy J. Curry, *The Man-Not: Race, Class, Genre, and the Dilemmas of Black Manhood* (Philadelphia, PA: Temple University Press, 2017), p. 195.

45 Luther E. Smith Jr (ed.), *Howard Thurman: Essential Writings* (New York: Orbis Books, 2006), p. 143.

5

The Madonnas Weep: Weeping, Collective Trauma and Emancipatory Transformations

ANUPAMA RANAWANA

Hear my cry, O God;
listen to my prayer.
From the end of the earth I call to you,
when my heart is faint. (Psalm 61.1–2)

All is mourning. Yet mourning and weeping is action. Mourning and weeping is prayer, and in its rising anger it is also healing. This chapter is about collective trauma and the outpouring of trauma into action. By positioning itself in this way, the chapter looks at the action of weeping as a form of public theology, asking how weeping provides an architecture for decolonizing, indeed for *demythologizing* theological thinking on trauma. This chapter extends a consideration begun in 2016, inspired by the icon of *Our Lady, Mother of Ferguson and all those Killed by Gun Violence*.[1] This icon is drawn as weeping, but it is an icon that takes action or inspires us to take action not only for the deaths of Black men and women killed by gun violence in the United States, but also for the social death all around her. I consider this image of the Madonna not only as one mother alone, but of all mothers enjoined to her in their suffering.

Crucified Mother,
Sorrowful Mother,
Mournful Mother,
Afflicted Mother,
Forsaken Mother,
Desolate Mother,
Mother bereaved of thy Son,
Mother pierced by a sword,
Mother overwhelmed by grief,

Mother filled with anguish,
Mother crucified in thy heart,
Mother most sad,
Fount of tears,
Mass of suffering,
Mirror of patience.[2]
(Litany of the *Mater Dolorosa*)

In this chapter, I attempt to examine trauma within a particular context, and how trauma can translate into motherist action. Here I call attention to social movements that are challenging racial and systemic inequality, such as the mothers of the Black Lives Matter movement, the mothers, grandmothers, aunts, wives and sisters searching for the disappeared in Sri Lanka, the Four Mothers in Israel, Kashmiri women's activism against the authoritarian Hindu state, and the Argentinian Grandmothers of the Plaza de Mayo. The chapter focuses in particular on the case of Sri Lanka. I discuss the protest actions and movements of the Sinhala Buddhist Mothers' Front, as well as the current mobilizations of Tamil women seeking justice for their children missing in the aftermath of the Sri Lankan civil war, to consider the relationship between trauma, collective action and what this may mean for a theology of weeping, from acts of grief that occur in public spaces. There is a ritual activity to this weeping, a kind of public sacramentality as the trauma that these women remain in is made vivid, in which we are all called to, in a way, participate, to become 'stuck' to the sadness in their hearts. What we see also here is that the impossibility of returning to one's old self has caused these women to remake motherhood. This outpouring into public struggle also underscores much of what Asian theologies refer to in terms of a theology of struggle that can and does become liberative, of what becomes tested in the struggle.[3] So too Septemmy Lakawa,[4] looking at aftermath friendships in situations of religious violence notes that aftermath rituals were part of creating markers of healing. I would argue that the public act of mourning and calling for justice is, for the women I discuss in this article, a form of aftermath ritual. That is, protest as a form of truth telling and witnessing, repeated over and over again, in silence or in clamour, much like a mourning ritual.

Considering trauma contextually

It is difficult to name trauma and define it, as the experience of trauma can be and is incredibly diverse and connected to each individual and contextual experience. Karen O'Donnell,[5] noting this, says that if we approach the varying definitions via a synthetic view, what we can understand is that trauma is, first and foremost, rupture. Such rupture occurs in terms of bodily integrity, in the shattering of time and in the loss of cognition and language.[6] Shelly Rambo[7] would agree. She draws on the definition that trauma refers to a place in which the ability to integrate pain, loss and suffering into one's life becomes stuck. The traumatic response then is one in which those shields and systems that allow us to be able to recover from and process harm break down. The person cannot return to who they were before as a radical break has occurred between the old person and the new one. The theology of trauma, rightly, rejects traditional formulations on suffering and the acceptance of suffering and interrogates them, seeking to interpret the impact that trauma has. As Rambo further teaches us, the experience of trauma dismantles certain theological notions, especially the idea of theology as a 'fixer'.[8] Rather, trauma theology emphasizes truth telling, wound tending and witnessing to suffering.

What is the truth telling and witnessing that we see in certain contexts? A subjective interpretation is argued to be key to understanding how the event or issue is perceived.[9] The 'telling' of what is experienced, what is broken, what is suffered will also be articulated according to context and perception. Rupture too, perhaps, can take on different understandings. The theologian Andrew Sung Park,[10] reflecting on the Korean concept of 'han' as trauma explains this as a situation that is historical and collective. He notes that we can see han as sentiments of anger and sadness that have become stuck to the heart. Park sees the causes of this han in the communities he focuses on as structural. Hence, such trauma is related to the oppressions caused by the global economy, by patriarchy and by cultural discrimination. In the novel A Passage North,[11] as another example, the protagonist watches his grandmother's caretaker, a woman who has experienced the traumatic loss of her two sons, as she drifts into a kind of ghost world, watching television for hours without the sound on, forgetting the care of her hair and her cultural habits of hygiene. The novel is set in post-war Sri Lanka, a context in which we encounter several different instances of traumas due not only to the long civil war, but instances of insurrection, oppression of minorities, climate events and human rights violations. Added to this also may well be the trauma of belonging. As Susan Abraham argues, postcolonial nations also have the experience of 'originary trauma', where independence from the colonial power continued in terms of the trauma of 'becoming' a nation.[12] Abraham looks primarily at India and Pakistan to make her case that modern nations emerged in a bloodbath. Within the same region, Sri Lanka too experienced the trauma of colonization and postcolonization,[13] and many of the political violences in the immediate independence context are connected to this process of 'becoming'.[14] Few Sri Lankan families will have escaped some form of trauma or another. Much of this trauma is experienced within the collective.

Contemporary studies on trauma in Sri Lanka discuss, primarily, the effect of the thirty-year war, as well as the Boxing Day Tsunami. Pushpa Kanagaratnam, Joanna Anneke Rummens and Brenda TonerVA's examination of war trauma in the Sri Lankan Tamil diaspora in Canada noted how this manifested at both the interpersonal and collective level.[15] Daya Somasundaram's wide-ranging studies of the experience of women in the North of Sri Lanka also notes the importance of the collective.[16] Somasundaram underscores that due to the non-Western collectivist nature of Sri Lankan culture, the individual's embeddedness in the family means that the traumatic events are often experienced as part of the large family unit, as family and community are part of the self.[17] This is not to romanticize the family or the community but to also underline how borders are broken and remade in the process of collectively experienced trauma, of collective weeping, shall we say.

It is important to note that in these studies, there is recognition that many of these communities underwent multiple traumas. This is not only in relation to a collective manifestation of the experience of trauma, but also the fact that trauma in such a context is not linked to any one event. As Sonya Andermahr, among others, argues, the idea of 'one overwhelming event' can be a Eurocentric model of trauma.[18] Rather, it can be inter-generational, historical, and/or a series of events of extreme violence. As an example, during fieldwork I undertook in 2018 to study women entrepreneurs in post-war Sri Lanka, I often spoke to women who had been multiply displaced due to the civil war or extreme climate events, who were also bearing the scars of the oppression of being women, lower caste, as well as from a minority community in the country. Further to this, many had also lost children or partners during the war and were faced with rebuilding their lives often at an older age. As such, that experience of rupture can also occur multiple times, perhaps so much so that any aspect of the original self or the original community can be lost. I wonder if this 'lostness' is perhaps why there is an outpouring into the motherist action I discuss below.

The first contemplation: reading the icon with Asian feminist liberation theology

I want to turn back to the icon for just a moment. The icon invites us to pray, to meditate. The icon invites us all to weep. Our first movement towards the decolonial transformation of hearts and minds must be in the weeping. The icon expresses the Madonna standing at the foot of the cross, not waiting meekly but weeping and angry and inspiring action and reflection. The icon invites us to this weeping, to, as aforementioned, take on the anguish of this social death, weeping for what has happened and our own complicity in fostering this reality. On the cross, the Son experienced all the anguish and trauma of the world, and so did his mother. She, as the very embodiment of humanity, of flesh and blood, a pedestrian woman of the people.[19] Indeed, this is Pope Paul VI's Mary:

Who 'stands out among the poor and humble of the Lord', a woman of strength, who experienced poverty and suffering, flight and exile (cf. Mt. 2:13–23) ... the disciple who works for that justice which sets free the oppressed and for that charity which assists the needy; but above all, the disciple who is the active witness of that love which builds up Christ in people's hearts.[20]

By reading the icon in this way, I am not only referring to Paul VI's modern Mary, but also reading the icon using the lens of Asian, particularly Asian feminist, liberation theology. As Kwok Pui-lan has told us, for Asian feminist theologians, the emergence of feminist awareness is closely linked to personal history and the suffering in their own lives and the suffering they see in context.[21] Asian women also are the other in their own society and are therefore writing with an intense awareness of the suffering of those who are marginalized when engaged in the struggle for liberation.[22] As Namsoon Kang[23] and Pauline Chakkalakal[24] have both noted, there is also a strong link between the differing social movements of the 1970s and 1980s and the emergence of Asian feminist thinking. Such theologizing also received a significant boost from political organizing in the Third World, specifically in the fight against exploitative development, as well as the emergence of Third World theology itself. Asian feminist theology began when Asian women gathered to discuss the Bible and their faith in the contexts of their own lives and Asian realities. In the 1970s and 1980s, Asian Christian women organized theological networks, convened ecumenical conferences and began to publish academically.[25]

I anchor this particular reading of the icon to the Mary understood by the Indonesian feminist theologian Marianne Katoppo. Katoppo, a theologian of the EATWOT,[26] rejected the 'meek' Mary as a feudalist, capitalist Mary by suggesting a different way of understanding submission.[27] Submission here is not the abject submission of a slave who has no choice, but the 'creative' submission of the fully liberated human being, who, not being subject to any other human being, is then free to serve God.[28] She leads an autonomous life, not a derived life. Mary of the Magnificat is sensitive to social injustices that take place in her times and is ready to restore human beings as *imago Dei*. Thinking with a social-justice reading of the Magnificat, as well as an understanding of the cultural goddesses of ancient Africa, India, China and Polynesia, Katoppo reminds us that Mary's excellence derives from her motherhood.[29] Katoppo is also drawing from an Indonesian understanding of the importance of the Mother, not so much as 'my personal mother', but as all-embracing communal motherhood.[30] This motherhood, which is not simply her virginhood, argues Katoppo, is a powerful way to liberate woman and to see the importance of Mary in the context of love and self-giving, as the pre-eminent model of humanity, 'growing into the full image of God'.[31]

This 'creative' Mother whose work is to share in the mission of bringing the good news of salvation to the world is a model not only for woman but also for man.[32] In making this argument, Katoppo is underscoring the arguments of Asian feminist theology that see Mary as a woman of faith who actively and freely responds to God's invitation, a 'self-defining woman' who announces the end of the patriarchal order, a liberated woman who embodies the good news in the proclamation of the Magnificat.[33] Tissa Balasuriya,[34] in his work on Mary and liberation agrees, pointing to the importance of the Annunciation, where Mary would come to know the suffering that she and her child would have to undergo. Although possibly 'terrified by such an extraordinary vocation',[35] Mary agrees to taking on motherhood, thus interrupting any narrative of docility but agreeing to carry out the divine plan of redemption.[36] Joseph Cheah notes: 'Clearly, there is nothing domesticated or pietistic about this Mary. She is the woman who embodies the gospel in her proclamation of the Magnificat.'[37]

Thus, this Mother is the new human being 'receptive before God who calls him/her to be *imago Dei*'.[38] Through Mary's motherhood, women in a special way, argues Katoppo, personify the oppressed. The creative reception of Mary's motherhood, importantly, makes her the truly liberated and full human being – whose activity in the world is marked by compassion and the work towards redemption. This, it could be argued, then, in terms of creative submission, is what it means to be a true disciple. Hisako Kinukawa, in noting the fleeing of the male disciples at the persecution of Jesus, extends this creativity also to Mary and the women disciples who follow their leader to the very end.

However, it is important to reiterate that the discussion of motherhood in Asian feminist theology is not only about submission and receptivity, but, as we can see in what has been articulated by Katoppo, Kang and Chakkalakal, it is also the importance of what is poured forth. It is due to this that in Asian feminist theology, there is great stress also on the Motherhood of God. Katoppo stresses the importance of including Mother in the triune Godhead because it is only with a mother's womb that a family propagates. She writes vividly of sitting in an endarkened church and re-experiencing the womb in order to illustrate this. The Asian hope for the succession of the family is akin to an eschatological vision. Katoppo tells us that:

> we should see the great emphasis which the people of Asia place on the continuation of family life, and the Asian outlook on salvation, closely related as it is to the experience of life in the mother's womb.[39]

Reading Mary in this way, one can argue that Mary's suffering as a mother at the foot of the cross pours out into the world as part of the creative activity of redemption, Mary as *co-liberator*. Although the icon may have her hands raised up, that it is in the position of the *orans* indicates prayerful, creative activity – a motherhood that stands alongside suffering and demands action. This is political motherhood.

Motherist action: the open wounds of 'childless motherhood'

Motherist activity, it is understood,[40] is very much focused on the politicization of motherhood, a creative motherhood. Motherist movements, of course, mobilize women to act based on their identity as mothers, and encompass a wide political spectrum, from environmental movements to anti-militarist, anti-colonial, anti-racist political actions as well as nationalist and racist mobilizations.[41] There is, of course, contestation as to whether such movements are feminist, with some feminist scholars[42] seeing such mobilization as essentialist or entirely conservative. However, as Sanam Anderlini argues, there is a breaking of social barriers – a kind of reclamation that occurs by using motherhood as a political tool that could (and has been) positioned as feminist.[43] Simona Sharoni notes the importance of how motherhood is used subversively by motherist movements, to argue for the hybrid feminist nature of such mobilization, but agrees that there may be some such activists who would refuse the feminist label.[44] What is important for this chapter, however, are the ways in which motherhood is 'recreated' and poured into activity, especially via the open demonstration of public grief and anger, of transcendent sorrow, that comes forth from the trauma experienced by the mothers within the movement, of their now childless motherhood, as well as their imagination of the traumas their children would have experienced.

One of the most significant motherist movements within our modern imagination is that of the Mothers of the Plaza de Mayo in Argentina. These women used the concept of a traditionally understood motherhood, parlaying the 'work' of motherhood – that is, suffering, irrationality, self-sacrifice, passivity and powerlessness to call attention to their disappeared children who had been either kidnapped or killed by the Argentine junta. As Mabel Bellucci notes in her study of Nora Cortiñas and her journey of 'childless motherhood', the Mothers began as a self-convened and diverse, even diffuse, movement of women who were simply asking to see their children alive and who, by doing so, generated a different form of political consciousness through collective action and transformed the classic values associated with politics and motherhood.[45]

Thus, women began coming out of their homes and into public life, opening the way for new forms of civic participation.[46] In doing so, they force a reckoning with motherhood, making it not biological activity but political concept. As Diana Taylor and colleagues argue, this transformation was a key action to underscore that 'mere' motherhood was not enough; it was necessary to politicize motherhood, to pour out the suffering experienced into activity.[47]

This tactic is not solely one used in Argentina or Israel either, as Anwar Mhajne and Crystal Whetstone have highlighted: in countries like Egypt and Sri Lanka as well,[48] motherist movements position themselves to take on patriarchal discourses on 'respectable' femininity and maternal identities in order to resist the state. Similarly, Judith Stevenson's study of Tswana women's political activity notes how the African National Congress focused on a traditional idea of motherhood, appealing to the mothers who mostly populated the societies.[49] However, when, during the 1980s, feminist contextual theology began to articulate a challenge to patriarchal Christianity, one could see how the discourses and ideologies of womanhood and motherhood coalesced. Black women identified a space wherein they were able to reclaim their traditional roles as public decision-makers, leaders and actors, as well as mothers.[50]

Malathi de Alwis, who spent many decades studying women's activism – particularly the work of the Mothers' Front – in Sri Lanka, also talks about the importance of such reclamation.[51] For de Alwis, as well as other chroniclers of women's activism in Sri Lanka, among the most significant moments in the 1980s, 1990s and later 2010s was the collective mobilization of maternalism in opposition to the brutality of the state.[52] Indeed, Sri Lankan women have historically organized, across ethnicity and religion, at different points in time, largely anchored to what has been termed as the 'relational respectability' of motherhood.[53] In the South of Sri Lanka, a Mothers' Front emerged following the second socialist insurrection in Sri Lanka and were a group of women demanding to know the truth about the disappearances of their young sons and daughters who had been part of the socialist movement. These women, de Alwis notes, transgressed the codes of respectability and domesticity that govern a woman's presence in the public sphere through their public deployment of tears and curses.[54] De Alwis and Chulani Kodikara[55] point out the importance of this weeping, this wailing, for there is nothing more damning or powerful in South Asian cultures than the authenticity of open grief and anger, the public performance of maternalized suffering. De Alwis found that the double power of this open emotion acted not only as protest per se, but also as a way of inciting protest.[56] Kodikara finds this particularly interesting, as she notes that many of these women were themselves not political activists or organizers, but from low-income, trading and working-class families with no previous history of participation in the political sphere, not even in village-level political committees.[57] They did, however, receive political assistance from the leading opposition, whose female leader at the time appealed to them by casting herself also as a mother who 'sorrowed and wept'.[58]

In the north and east of the country, the Jaffna Mothers' Front formed in July 1984, years before their southern counterpart organized to protest the mass arrest of Tamil youth by the Sri Lankan state.[59] In the east, protestors symbolically took their 'rice pounders' out on to the streets with them, to symbolize the link between the home and the space of the protest. Some 30 years later, another group of women (mostly mothers and grandmothers, but also sisters and wives) are again lobbying the Sri Lankan state to search for their missing.[60] Since 2017, these women have organized roadside demonstrations across the island, as their response to the constant failure of the state to provide answers to the whereabouts of their missing or disappeared children.[61] These mothers and grandmothers sit on the road, holding the photos of their loved ones, sometimes in loud, but often in mute, appeal.

> They quietly handed us the photos: a young man sitting on a motor-cycle, a family of five posed at a child's birthday party, a toddler with her slightly older brother playing in their yard. One woman cried bitterly as she explained that she had told the story of her loss so many times and nothing ever changed.[62]

The protests are full of pain, heartbreak and disappointment, with grief and trauma visibly being poured out into the powerful activity of demanding justice. Standing in solidarity with one of these protests, as the women sat silently on a roundabout holding up the pictures of their children, I was struck again by the power of what was being said in this 'childless motherhood'. Indeed, for these women in particular, who are Tamil speakers attempting to parlay with a state that, for decades, has also suppressed the language rights of minorities, the silent grief displayed unrelentingly in the public sphere becomes overwhelmingly powerful.

> By appealing for a return to the 'natural' order of family and motherhood these women were openly embracing patriarchal stereotypes that primarily defined them through familial/domestic subject positions such as wife and mother. However, by accepting this responsibility to nurture and preserve life, which is also valorized by the state, they revealed the ultimate transgression is the state as well for it was denying women the opportunities for mothering through a refusal to acknowledge life by resorting to clandestine tactics of 'disappearance'.[63]

These subversions of respectability politics centred around motherhood and religion. By these displays of grief, anger and cursing, by openly showing the wounds of motherhood (especially in contexts where religion and women's roles as the foundation of the family rigidly structure the lives of women), motherhood can and has been utilized as a powerful tool for political mobilization and contestation.

Demythologizing suffering

The multiple ruptures experienced by these women, outputs the idea of motherhood so it is no longer relegated to the home, or to the physical presence of the child, but is an outpouring of creative action, of work towards justice and liberation. Looking at photographs and reels of these protests, in standing alongside a protest, I consider Mary, standing at the foot of the cross, swinging between rage and grief, experiencing trauma as a mother losing her Son, and also, as mothers do, experiencing the trauma that he too was undergoing. This Son, a political prisoner, made to suffer torture and death at the hands of an imperial state. Mary of the icon, her hands raised in the *orans*, which, reading the icon through the lens of Asian feminist theology, as well as in the images of mothers searching for their children, becomes not just hands raised in prayer, but hands raised in the demand for justice. Katoppo's Mary, the fully liberated human, transforming into a figure of action, not mute acceptance or acquiescence to redemptive suffering. It is not to share in the redemptive suffering of Christ in such a way that points to an eschatological end, a time that *is* to come. The creative activity of pouring motherhood out into the world centres a liberation theology *of demanding justice now*, of envisioning the just kingdom in the present moment, of resisting the death-creating structures of state oppression, of waiting for some historical end. Suffering is not mysterious. Even the Son, on the cross, dies and experiences trauma publicly, calling attention to the brutality of the dominant forces of the state. It is the perfect act of protest.

Relating the protests of the mothers as they are, as they have been chronicled by scholars, and in seeing the active Mary standing alongside these movements, what is striking here is the work that is done not to be victims of trauma or oppression by the military state, but the ways in which motherhood is leveraged as resistance to systemic injustice, to subvert norms and traditions. Refusing to be dehumanized as 'mere mothers', these movements, this creative motherhood, works to 'rehumanize' injustices. Sister Dr Rasika Pieris, who studied the activity of war widows in Sri Lanka, agrees, noting that such activity calls the attention of us as theologians and ministers to the importance of how such movements work to become creative in overcoming suffering and trauma so that it becomes enjoined to struggle, a struggle to build a better society.[64] What occurs in these movements, and also in the understanding of Mary's creative motherhood, is the redirection of dominant measures of control, a journey that refuses meekness and silence and insists on transformation. This is the underscoring point of the ways in which liberation, and the activity of the full liberated human Mary, are intimately tied to the Mary who declares the Magnificat, who works for the common goal of all: liberation.

Thinking in this way about liberation, how can we perhaps reinscribe a little the litany of the *Mater Dolorosa*? I take up my rosary, I say my prayer, and I add to it:

Mother in rage
Mother who searches
Mother who is relentless
Mother who liberates.

Bibliography

'Social Realities of Rural Women in the Conflict Region', Food and Agricultural Organization of the United Nations, 1996, www.fao.org/3/ag114e/AG114E07.htm, accessed 22.2.2022.

Abraham, Susan, 'Traumas of Belonging: Imagined Communities of Nation, Religion, and Gender in Modernity' in *Post-Traumatic Public Theology*, ed. Stephanie N. Arel and Shelly Rambo, Cham: Springer International Publishing, 2016, pp. 267–90.

Anderlini, Sanam Naraghi, *Women Building Peace: What They Do, Why It Matters*, Boulder, CO: Lynne Rienner Publishers, 2007.

Andermahr, Sonya, '"Decolonizing Trauma Studies: Trauma and Postcolonialism" – Introduction', *Humanities* 4, 4 (2015), pp. 500–5.

Anonymous, 'Rosary of our Mother of Sorrows' in *Devotion to the Sorrowful Mother*, Ashland, NC: TAN Books, 2002.

Arudpragasam, Anuk, *A Passage North*, London: Granta, 2021.

Balasuriya, Tissa, *Mary and Human Liberation*, Colombo, Sri Lanka: Centre for Society & Religion, 1997.

Bellucci, Mabel, 'Childless Motherhood: Interview with Nora Cortiñas, a Mother of the Plaza de Mayo, Argentina', *Reproductive Health Matters* 7, 13 (1999), pp. 83–8.

Chakkalakal, Pauline, 'Asian Women Reshaping Theology: Challenges and Hopes', *Feminist Theology* 9, 27 (May 2001), pp. 21–35, https://doi.org/10.1177/096673500100002703, accessed 22.2.2022.

Cheah, Joseph, 'Asian Women's Mariology in Christological Context', *Marian Studies* 46, 9 (1995), pp. 71–88.

Chung Hyun Kyung, *Struggle to be the Sun Again: Introducing Asian Women's Theology*, Maryknoll, NY: Orbis Books, 1990, p. 37.

Cronin-Furman, Kate and Roxani Krystalli, 'The Things They Carry: Victims' Documentation of Forced Disappearance in Colombia and Sri Lanka', *European Journal of International Relations* 27, 1 (March 2021), pp. 79–101.

de Alwis, Malathi, 'Motherhood as a Space of Protest: Women's Political Participation in Contemporary Sri Lanka' in *Women in Peace Politics*, ed. Paula Bannerjee, New Delhi: Sage, 2008, pp. 152–74.

de Alwis, Malathi, 'Maternalist Politics in Sri Lanka: A Historical Anthropology of its Conditions of Possibility', PhD dissertation, University of Columbia, 1998.

de Mel, Neloufer, *Women and the Nation's Narrative: Gender and Nationalism in Twentieth Century Sri Lanka*, Lanham, MD: Rowman & Littlefield, 2001.

Doox, Mar, *Our Lady, Mother of Ferguson and all those Killed by Gun Violence*, acrylic paint and collage, 2016.

Ecumenical Association of Third World Theologians, Virginia Fabella and Sergio Torres (eds), *Irruption of the Third World: Challenge to Theology: Papers from the Fifth International Conference of the Ecumenical Association of Third World Theologians, August 17–29, 1981, New Delhi, India*, Maryknoll, NY: Orbis Books, 1983.

Foster, Yolanda, 'The Long Shadow of Disappearances in Sri Lanka', *Norwegian Human Rights Fund*, 2018, https://nhrf.no/article/2018/the-long-shadow-of-disappearances-in-sri-lanka, accessed 22.2.2022.

Howe, Sara, 'The Madres de La Plaza de Mayo: Asserting Motherhood; Rejecting Feminism?', *Journal of International Women's Studies* 7, 3 (2006), pp. 43–50.

Parameswaran, Siva, 'Sri Lanka: Tamil Mothers Appeal to Sinhalese to Help Tracing the Disappeared', *JDS*, 4 June 2020, www.jdslanka.org/index.php/news-features/human-rights/953-sri-lanka-tamil-mothers-appeal-to-sinhalese-to-help-tracing-the-disappeared, accessed 22.2.2022.

Jetter, Alexis, Annelise Orleck and Diana Taylor (eds), *The Politics of Motherhood: Activist Voices from Left to Right*, Hanover, NH: Dartmouth College: University Press of New England, 1997.

Jongeling, M. C., 'Indonesian Theologians on Women–Men Relationships in Church and Society', *Exchange* 16, 2 (1987), pp. 49–67.

Kanagaratnam, Pushpa, Joanna Anneke Rummens and Brenda TonerVA, '"We Are All Alive … But Dead": Cultural Meanings of War Trauma in the Tamil Diaspora and Implications for Service Delivery', *SAGE Open* (October 2020).

Kang, Namsoon, 'Re-constructing Asian Feminist Theology: Toward Glocal Feminist Theology in an Era of NeoEmpire(s)' in *Christianity in Asia*, ed. Sebastian Kim, Cambridge: University of Cambridge Press, 2008.

Katoppo, Marianne, *Compassionate and Free: An Asian Woman's Theology*, Eugene, OR: Wipf & Stock, 2001, pp. 16–17.

Kodikara, Chulani, *30 Years Later: Reading the Southern Mothers' Front with Malathi de Alwis – Chulani Kodikara – SSA Sri Lanka*, 2021, http://ssalanka.org/30-years-later-reading-southern-mothers-front-malathi-de-alwis-chulani-kodikara/, accessed 22.2.2022.

Krishna, Sankaran, *Postcolonial Insecurities: India, Sri Lanka, and the Question of Nationhood*, Borderlines, vol. 15, Minneapolis, MN: University of Minnesota Press, 1999.

Kwok, Pui-lan, *Introducing Asian Feminist Theology*, Sheffield: Sheffield Academic, 2000.

Lakawa, Septemmy E., 'Aftermath Friendship: An Indonesian Feminist Theological Perspective on Trauma and Interreligious Peace', *International Journal of Asian Christianity* 4, 2 (2021), pp. 236–47.

Mhajne, Anwar and Crystal Whetstone, 'The Use of Political Motherhood in Egypt's Arab Spring Uprising and Aftermath', *International Feminist Journal of Politics* 20, 1 (2018), pp. 54–68.

O'Donnell, Karen, *Broken Bodies: The Eucharist, Mary and the Body in Trauma Theology*, London: SCM Press, 2019.

Park, Andrew Sung, *The Wounded Heart of God: The Asian Concept of Han and the Christian Doctrine of Sin*, Nashville, TN: Abingdon Press, 1993.

Paul VI, *To honour Mary: apostolic exhortation Marialis cultus of His Holiness Paul VI to all bishops in peace and communion with the Apostolic See for the right ordering and development of devotion to the Blessed Virgin Mary* [translated from the Latin] Vatican Polyglot Press; London: Catholic Truth Society, 1974.

Pieris, Rasika, 'Widowhood and Religious Perception', *International Journal of Asian Christianity* 1, 2 (2018), pp. 307–28.

Rambo, Shelly, *Spirit and Trauma: A Theology of Remaining*, Louisville, KY: Westminster John Knox Press, 2010.

Rambo, Shelly, 'How Christian Theology and Practice are being Shaped by Trauma Studies: Talking about God in the Face of Wounds that won't go Away', *The*

Christian Century, 1 November 2019, www.christiancentury.org/article/critical-essay/how-christian-theology-and-practice-are-being-shaped-trauma-studies, accessed 22.2.2022.

Ranawana, A., 'Why I went to the Woods in the First Place: The Voices of Asian Feminist Liberation' in *Asian Liberation Theology*, ed. Mario I. Aguilar et al., Berlin: De Gruyter, 2022.

Riaz, Ali, Zobaida Nasreen and Fahmida Zaman (eds), *Political Violence in South Asia*, London, New York: Routledge, Taylor & Francis Group, 2019.

Sharoni, Simona, 'Motherhood and the Politics of Women's Resistance: Israeli Women Organizing for Peace' in *The Politics of Motherhood: Activist Voices from Left to Right*, ed. Alexis Jetter, Annelise Orleck and Diana Taylor, Hanover, NH: University Press of New England, 1997, pp. 144–60.

Somasundaram, Daya and Sambasivamoorthy Sivayokan, 'Rebuilding Community Resilience in a Post-War Context: Developing Insight and Recommendations – a Qualitative Study in Northern Sri Lanka', *International Journal of Mental Health Systems* 7, 1 (2013), p. 3.

Somasundaram, Daya, 'Collective Trauma in Northern Sri Lanka: A Qualitative Psychosocial-Ecological Study', *International Journal of Mental Health Systems* 1, 1 (2007), p. 5.

Stevenson, Judith, '"The Mamas Were Ripe": Ideologies of Motherhood and Public Resistance in a South African Township', *Feminist Formations* 23, 2 (2011), pp. 132–63.

Whetsone, Crystal and Anwar Mhajne, 'Troubling Conception of Motherhood: State Feminism and Political Agency of Women in the Global South' in *Troubling Motherhood: Maternality in Global Politics*, ed. Lucy B. Hall, Anna L. Weissman and Laura J. Shepherd, Oxford: Oxford University Press, 2020.

Whetstone, Crystal, 'Is the Motherist Approach More Helpful in Obtaining Women's Rights than a Feminist Approach? A Comparative Study of Lebanon and Liberia', MA thesis, Wright State University, 2013.

Notes

1 Mar Doox, *Our Lady, Mother of Ferguson and all those Killed by Gun Violence*, 2016, acrylic paint and collage.

2 Anonymous, 'Rosary of our Mother of Sorrows' in *Devotion to the Sorrowful Mother* (Ashland, NC: TAN Books, 2002).

3 Ecumenical Association of Third World Theologians, Virginia Fabella and Sergio Torres (eds), *Irruption of the Third World: Challenge to Theology: Papers from the Fifth International Conference of the Ecumenical Association of Third World Theologians, August 17–29, 1981, New Delhi, India* (Maryknoll, NY: Orbis Books, 1983).

4 Septemmy E. Lakawa, 'Aftermath Friendship: An Indonesian Feminist Theological Perspective on Trauma and Interreligious Peace', *International Journal of Asian Christianity* 4, 2 (2021), pp. 236–47, https://doi.org/10.1163/25424246-04020006.

5 Karen O'Donnell, *Broken Bodies: The Eucharist, Mary and the Body in Trauma Theology* (London: SCM Press, 2019).

6 O'Donnell, *Broken Bodies*, e-book format (no pagination).

7 Shelly Rambo, *Spirit and Trauma: A Theology of Remaining* (Louisville, KY: Westminster John Knox Press, 2010).

8 Shelly Rambo, 'How Christian Theology and Practice are being Shaped by Trauma Studies: Talking about God in the Face of Wounds that won't go Away', *The Christian Century*, 1 November 2019, www.christiancentury.org/article/crit ical-essay/how-christian-theology-and-practice-are-being-shaped-trauma-studies, accessed 22.2.2022.

9 Pushpa Kanagaratnam, Joanna Anneke Rummens and Brenda TonerVA, '"We Are All Alive … But Dead": Cultural Meanings of War Trauma in the Tamil Diaspora and Implications for Service Delivery', *SAGE Open* (October 2020), https://doi.org/10.1177/2158244020963563.

10 Andrew Sung Park, *The Wounded Heart of God: The Asian Concept of Han and the Christian Doctrine of Sin* (Nashville, TN: Abingdon Press, 1993).

11 Anuk Arudpragasam, *A Passage North* (London: Granta, 2021).

12 Susan Abraham, 'Traumas of Belonging: Imagined Communities of Nation, Religion, and Gender in Modernity' in *Post-Traumatic Public Theology*, ed. Stephanie N. Arel and Shelly Rambo (Cham: Springer International Publishing, 2016), pp. 267–90, https://doi.org/10.1007/978-3-319-40660-2_13, accessed 22.2.2022.

13 Ali Riaz, Zobaida Nasreen and Fahmida Zaman (eds), *Political Violence in South Asia* (London, New York: Routledge, Taylor & Francis Group, 2019).

14 Sankaran Krishna, *Postcolonial Insecurities: India, Sri Lanka, and the Question of Nationhood*, Borderlines, vol. 15 (Minneapolis, MN: University of Minnesota Press, 1999).

15 Kanagaratnam et al., '"We Are All Alive … But Dead"'.

16 Daya Somasundaram, 'Collective Trauma in Northern Sri Lanka: A Qualitative Psychosocial-Ecological Study', *International Journal of Mental Health Systems* 1, 1 (2007), p. 5, https://doi.org/10.1186/1752-4458-1-5, accessed 22.2.2022.

17 Daya Somasundaram and Sambasivamoorthy Sivayokan, 'Rebuilding Community Resilience in a Post-War Context: Developing Insight and Recommendations – a Qualitative Study in Northern Sri Lanka', *International Journal of Mental Health Systems* 7, 1 (2013), p. 3, https://doi.org/10.1186/1752-4458-7-3, accessed 22.2.2022.

18 Sonya Andermahr, '"Decolonizing Trauma Studies: Trauma and Postcolonialism" – Introduction', *Humanities* 4, 4 (2015), pp. 500–5, https://doi.org/10.3390/h4040500, accessed 22.2.2022.

19 Tissa Balasuriya, *Mary and Human Liberation* (Colombo, Sri Lanka: Centre for Society & Religion, 1997).

20 Pope Paul VI, *To honour Mary: apostolic exhortation Marialis cultus of His Holiness Paul VI to all bishops in peace and communion with the Apostolic See for the right ordering and development of devotion to the Blessed Virgin Mary* (London: Catholic Truth Society, 1974).

21 Kwok Pui-lan, *Introducing Asian Feminist Theology* (Sheffield: Sheffield Academic, 2000).

22 Chung Hyun Kyung, *Struggle to be the Sun Again: Introducing Asian Women's Theology* (Maryknoll, NY: Orbis Books, 1990), p. 37.

23 Namsoon Kang, 'Re-constructing Asian Feminist Theology: Toward Glocal Feminist Theology in an Era of NeoEmpire(s)' in *Christianity in Asia*, ed. Sebastian Kim (Cambridge: University of Cambridge Press, 2008).

24 Pauline Chakkalakal, 'Asian Women Reshaping Theology: Challenges and

Hopes', *Feminist Theology* 9, 27 (May 2001), pp. 21–35, https://doi.org/10.1177/096673500100002703, accessed 22.2.2022.

25 A. Ranawana, 'Why I went to the Woods in the First Place: The Voices of Asian Feminist Liberation' in *Asian Liberation Theology*, ed. Mario I. Aguilar et al. (Berlin: De Gruyter, 2022).

26 Ecumenical Association of Third World Theologians. A significant moment in the early years of the EATWOT were feminist theologians' arguments to have their voice and experience taken seriously and be fully accepted in the organization, an 'irruption within an irruption'. This signalled a deepening awareness for some and a blossoming awareness for others and was the beginning of a feminist theology of liberation manifesting itself. Katoppo's particular irruption was seen as key here.

27 Marianne Katoppo, *Compassionate and Free: An Asian Woman's Theology* (Eugene, OR: Wipf & Stock, 2001), pp. 16–17.

28 Katoppo, *Compassionate and Free*, pp. 16–17.

29 Katoppo, *Compassionate and Free*, p. 18.

30 M. C. Jongeling, 'Indonesian Theologians on Women–Men Relationships in Church and Society', *Exchange* 16, 2 (1987), pp. 49–67, https://doi.org/10.1163/157254387X00134, accessed 22.2.2022.

31 Katoppo, *Compassionate and Free*, p. 22.

32 Katoppo, *Compassionate and Free*, p. 23.

33 Joseph Cheah, 'Asian Women's Mariology in Christological Context', *Marian Studies* 46, 9 (1995).

34 Balasuriya, *Mary and Human Liberation*, p. 18.

35 Balasuriya, *Mary and Human Liberation*, p. 13.

36 It is important to clarify here that other theologies – especially those from the Third World – do take up the discussions on Mariology, as well as the Godhead with regards to liberation and salvation, in terms of understanding the fully liberated human. I work here with Asian feminist theologies as this particular case is from Asia, and also because of the very outright statement of Asian feminist theology that it stands with and speaks directly of and alongside the suffering of women telling stories with the goal of reclaiming 'women as subjects with their own thoughts, feelings and voice, and, in particular, the work of Asian feminist theologians to reclaim and interrupt the traditional narratives of the family within Asian culture, but also within theology'. For example, Katoppo's forthright declaration that an all-male Trinity is an entirely oppressive construct.

37 Cheah, Asian Women's Mariology, p. 18.

38 Katoppo, *Compassionate and Free*, p. 23.

39 Katoppo, *Compassionate and Free*, p. 83.

40 Crystal Whetstone, 'Is the Motherist Approach More Helpful in Obtaining Women's Rights than a Feminist Approach? A Comparative Study of Lebanon and Liberia' (MA thesis, Wright State University, 2013), https://corescholar.libraries.wright.edu/etd_all/785/, accessed 22.2.2022.

41 Crystal Whetsone and Anwar Mhajne, 'Troubling Conception of Motherhood: State Feminism and Political Agency of Women in the Global South' in *Troubling Motherhood: Maternality in Global Politics*, ed. Lucy B. Hall, Anna L. Weissman and Laura J. Shepherd (Oxford: Oxford University Press, 2020).

42 Sara Howe, 'The Madres de La Plaza de Mayo: Asserting Motherhood; Rejecting Feminism?', *Journal of International Women's Studies* 7, 3 (2006), pp. 43–50.

43 Sanam Naraghi Anderlini, *Women Building Peace: What They Do, Why It Matters* (Boulder, CO: Lynne Rienner Publishers, 2007).

44 Simona Sharoni, 'Motherhood and the Politics of Women's Resistance: Israeli Women Organizing for Peace' in *The Politics of Motherhood: Activist Voices from Left to Right*, ed. Alexis Jetter, Annelise Orleck and Diana Taylor (Hanover, NH: University Press of New England, 1997), pp. 144–60.

45 Mabel Bellucci, 'Childless Motherhood: Interview with Nora Cortiñas, a Mother of the Plaza de Mayo, Argentina', *Reproductive Health Matters* 7, 13 (1999), pp. 83–8, www.jstor.org/stable/3775707, accessed 22.2.2022.

46 Bellucci, 'Childless Motherhood', p. 85.

47 Alexis Jetter, Annelise Orleck and Diana Taylor (eds), *The Politics of Motherhood: Activist Voices from Left to Right* (Hanover, NH: Dartmouth College: University Press of New England, 1997).

48 Anwar Mhajne and Crystal Whetstone, 'The Use of Political Motherhood in Egypt's Arab Spring Uprising and Aftermath', *International Feminist Journal of Politics* 20, 1 (2018), pp. 54–68, https://doi.org/10.1080/14616742.2017.1371624, accessed 22.2.2022.

49 Judith Stevenson, '"The Mamas Were Ripe": Ideologies of Motherhood and Public Resistance in a South African Township', *Feminist Formations* 23, 2 (2011), pp. 132–63, www.jstor.org/stable/41301660, accessed 22.2.2022.

50 Stevenson, '"The Mamas were Ripe"'.

51 Malathi de Alwis, 'Motherhood as a Space of Protest: Women's Political Participation in Contemporary Sri Lanka' in *Women in Peace Politics,* ed. Paula Bannerjee (New Delhi: Sage, 2008), pp. 152–74.

52 Neloufer de Mel, *Women and the Nation's Narrative: Gender and Nationalism in Twentieth-century Sri Lanka* (Lanham, MD: Rowman & Littlefield, 2001).

53 de Alwis, 'Motherhood as a Space of Protest'.

54 Malathi de Alwis, *Maternalist Politics in Sri Lanka: A Historical Anthropology of its Conditions of Possibility* (PhD dissertation, University of Columbia, 1998).

55 Chulani Kodikara, *30 Years Later: Reading the Southern Mothers' Front with Malathi de Alwis – Chulani Kodikara – SSA Sri Lanka* (2021), http://ssalanka.org/30-years-later-reading-southern-mothers-front-malathi-de-alwis-chulani-kodikara/, accessed 22.2.2022.

56 de Alwis, 'Motherhood as a Space of Protest'.

57 Kodikara, *30 Years Later: Reading the Southern Mothers' Front*.

58 Kodikara, *30 Years Later: Reading the Southern Mothers' Front*.

59 FAO, 'Social Realities of Rural Women in the Conflict Region' (1996), www.fao.org/3/ag114e/AG114E07.htm, accessed 22.2.2022, and also Yolanda Foster, 'The Long Shadow of Disappearances in Sri Lanka', *Norwegian Human Rights Fund* (2018), https://nhrf.no/article/2018/the-long-shadow-of-disappearances-in-sri-lanka, accessed 22.2.2022.

60 Siva Parameswaran, 'Sri Lanka: Tamil Mothers Appeal to Sinhalese to Help Tracing the Disappeared', *JDS Lanka*, 4 June 2020, www.jdslanka.org/index.php/news-features/human-rights/953-sri-lanka-tamil-mothers-appeal-to-sinhalese-to-help-tracing-the-disappeared, accessed 22.2.2022.

61 Kate Cronin-Furman and Roxani Krystalli, 'The Things They Carry: Victims' Documentation of Forced Disappearance in Colombia and Sri Lanka', *European Journal of International Relations* 27, 1 (March 2021), pp. 79–101.

62 Cronin-Furman and Krystalli, 'The Things They Carry'.

63 de Alwis, 'Motherhood as a Space of Protest', p. 14.

64 Rasika Pieris, 'Widowhood and Religious Perception', *International Journal of Asian Christianity* 1, 2 (2018), pp. 307–28, https://doi.org/10.1163/25424246-00102008, accessed 22.2.2022.

Gender and Sexuality in Dialogue with Trauma Theology

6

Epistemic Injustice Exacerbating Trauma in Christian Theological Treatments of Trans People and People with Intersex Characteristics

SUSANNAH CORNWALL, ALEX CLARE-YOUNG AND SARA GILLINGHAM

Introduction

In this chapter we focus on the trauma caused to trans people, and people with intersex characteristics, by theological and church responses that do not accord them autonomy and legitimacy as 'first-person knowers'. Attention to trauma in theologies of the last two decades has moved beyond war and conflict as vectors of traumatization and moral injury, noting how trauma continues to affect bodies experiencing sexual abuse and rape, reproductive loss, natural disasters and terrorist events. The Covid-19 pandemic has catalysed further work, especially on how churches could help their local communities through trauma when people could not gather, clergy could not conduct in-person funerals, and many established coping strategies were unavailable.[1]

In the intersex activism movement's mid-1990s early days, testimonies about intersex medical treatment made clear that many individuals had experienced such interventions as traumatic. On top of the trauma of invasive non-consensual medical treatment itself, many commentators noted trauma caused by secrecy and lies, having learned that they had been misled (or simply not told) by their doctors and parents about the nature of their conditions.[2] More recently, trauma has continued to be an important lens through which intersex characteristics are figured in legal texts, notably via the recognition of non-consensual medical interventions as human rights violations and forms of torture.[3]

Many trans and gender-diverse people also experience trauma in connection with their bodies and identities, whether prompted by gender dysphoria (trauma connected with the physical body itself or social perceptions of oneself) or by literal and conceptual violence inflicted via social and medical treatment. Risk factors for trans people include trans-specific hate crime (such as rape and sexual assault, non-sexual physical violence, and murder),[4] emotional abuse by relatives, self-harm, inadequate access to appropriate healthcare, and institutional discrimination.[5] Trauma as a result of victimization is common among trans people,[6] and many suffer from minority stress.[7]

In both cases, despite their evident differences, we suggest here that trauma is inflicted and exacerbated when sex- and gender-variant people are not understood as legitimate knowing and speaking subjects. As we discuss below, Miranda Fricker's concept of epistemic injustice[8] has been built upon by those, such as Talia Mae Bettcher,[9] who show that first-person authority is frequently undermined in contexts where sex- and gender-variant people are assumed not to be reliable judges or arbiters of their own realities.

Foundational work on theology and trauma includes that by Shelly Rambo, who points to the importance of Christian communities' witnessing to the reality of the horror of suffering, abiding with those who are traumatized, rather than jumping ahead to a triumphalist resurrection story;[10] Dirk Lange, who reminds readers that proper reflection on trauma cannot be an optional add-on for a tradition that has violent, traumatizing events at the heart of its doctrine and continues to commemorate them in liturgy;[11] and Jennifer Beste, who interrogates the implications of trauma theory for theologies of grace and human free will, noting that trauma can entirely disrupt individuals' agency and capacity to respond in relationships, and that Christianity must therefore have a robust account of ameliorative neighbour-love at its heart.[12] Jennifer Baldwin[13] and Meg Warner et al.[14] have woven theologically rich accounts of trauma into their practitioner-facing resources for those working therapeutically, in churches and beyond, with trauma survivors. Karen O'Donnell and Katie Cross showcase work by both established and emerging scholars on feminist trauma theologies, with attention on domestic abuse/intimate partner violence, violent crime and the dually traumatizing and therapeutic potential of church communities.[15]

Trauma is, these accounts show, profoundly embodied. It entails 'a specific and automatic collection of physiological responses to an event, which are triggered when an individual's or community's adaptive capacity is overwhelmed'.[16] Trauma that arises because of responses to bodily difference – as for trans people and people with intersex characteristics – is therefore particularly potent. In this chapter we suggest that this trauma may be heightened even further in religious contexts where the truth about physical embodiment and identity is said to rest outside individual experience, but in ways that call only variant identity into question and do not adequately disrupt the contingent and contested nature of all identity.

Conservative Christian theologies of sex and gender have tended to erase diversity, inflicting epistemic injustice by claims rooted in the assumption that sex- and gender-variant people's identities rest in peculiarly unreliable knowledge.

Sex and gender diversity and epistemic injustice

One irony of the early corrective surgery paradigm for intersex characteristics is that most medics who promoted its protocols believed that by doing so they would eliminate psychosocial trauma resulting from growing up with an unusual body. However, as is now well attested, 'The surgical treatments and the secrecy surrounding them may have actually amplified difficulties they intended to solve. In some cases, rather than eliminating trauma, they may have unintentionally created it.'[17] Iain Morland suggests that the project of medically assigning gender to children with intersex characteristics has trauma as an inevitable concomitant, because it hastens a process of gender development that should have been allowed to unfold over time. Thus, he holds, 'traumatization has happened not by omission but by design.'[18]

Doctors have often claimed intersex patients who experienced interventions as traumatizing 'were the disgruntled minority, the few who suffered bad outcomes'.[19] Consequently, those who protested against their treatment were frequently dismissed or erased. Arlene Baratz and Katrina Karkazis suggest that speaking about one's treatment might in itself be retraumatizing if it forces one to relive one's pain, as well as inviting further trauma via social stigma. Thus, they hold, the relatively few publicly vocal protestors at medical protocols for the treatment of people with intersex characteristics 'may not be the bad outcomes, as they have so often been characterized, but the better outcomes because they have somehow healed enough to share their pain without threat of dissolution'.[20] Narratives by intersex survivors have, they hold, showed a capacity to adapt and grow even in the face of trauma and ongoing struggle.

We note here the importance of distinguishing between experience that may entail suffering but is nonetheless primarily experienced as ameliorative (retelling one's story, and being listened to and validated); experience that entails trauma (retelling one's story, but being challenged by hearers as to its truth and accuracy); and experience that is retraumatizing. Sara Gillingham comments further on these distinctions below.

Trans people and epistemic injustice

Trans people frequently experience transphobia and repudiation. Repudiation occurs via multiple systems that assume a binary model of gender; particularly relevant here is the contention that trans people are repudiated when they are not considered the primary experts on their own lives.[21] Repudiation is opposed to theologies emphasizing the importance of mutual recognition, and the endorsement of full personhood, through social communication.[22] Repudiation may, therefore, be experienced as denial of trans people's very personhood. Injustice is done when someone is not recognized as a legitimate speaking subject and allowed to self-define.

For the philosopher Talia Mae Bettcher, first-person authority is part of a set of social and philosophical understandings of the credence we tend to give certain claims. It is not *impossible* for someone to be mistaken about a belief about themselves, but without compelling evidence to the contrary, we tend give weight to what people tell us and to assume that they 'retain some epistemic authority'[23] due to the privileged first-person knowledge they have about themselves.

By contrast, in many theological treatments of both trans people and people with intersex characteristics, others' assessments of what these persons' bodies and identities mean and signify are privileged over their own. Conservative evangelical Christian writings on trans people tend to claim that trans people's self-identification denies 'the biological realities that the Creator has embedded into every cell in our bodies'[24] and reject any notion that 'a person's self-awareness is different than and more important than [their] physical body'.[25] Such theologies often assume that, by definition, all who experience trans or gender-variant identity are mentally ill (despite the fact that the International Statistical Classification of Diseases and Related Health Problems no longer classifies gender incongruence as a mental health disorder), and their self-assessment therefore unreliable. In other words, in these accounts, trans people cannot be granted first-person authority, trusted to know the truth about themselves. Trans identity is, for many conservative evangelicals, in itself a signal that something has gone wrong with someone's self-knowledge, because people who *really* know themselves understand that healthy gender identity cannot be at odds with physical sex. There is little evidence here of trans people's first-person authority, but plenty of appeal to first-person authority by the authors – albeit camouflaged behind claims that this is simply God's plan, what the Bible says, and not up for debate.

Thus, trans people's first-person authority is undermined by basic denial of their authenticity.[26] This chimes with Miranda Fricker's account of 'testimonial injustice', wherein someone's speech is predetermined as dubious or dismissible because an aspect of their identity renders them an unreliable witness. Such judgement in advance, holds Fricker, injures and wrongs people epistemically, as knowers.[27] Trans people whose testimony, including their self-understanding, is deemed in advance to be suspect *because* they are trans are therefore, we suggest, left in an unwinnable situation.

Trauma, epistemic injustice and communities of faith

How far do communities of faith have potential to be therapeutic sites for those trans people, and people with intersex characteristics, who have experienced the trauma of (and/or the exacerbation of suffering caused by) such epistemic violence? Some clearly find involvement with religion to affirm their worth, as research from contexts including Britain and Germany shows.[28] Based on research with people with intersex characteristics in Australia, Stephen Kerry remarks:

> If, as the intersex literature suggests, intersex individuals are comparing their experiences with mainstream discourses of sexual abuse … it is of little surprise that intersex individuals are also turning to methods of coping that are also found within mainstream communities. That intersex individuals are not alone in their trauma marks intersex as yet another site of human suffering that may drive people to religiosity for (among other things) 'answers'.[29]

However, where communities of faith hold theological anthropologies and doctrinal claims that are non-affirming of trans people or those with intersex characteristics, further spiritual damage may be done beyond even the social trauma that many already experience. Theological anthropologies grounded in the assumption that God intended biological sex to be solely binary and dimorphic in nature, and that healthy gender identity may only 'match' biological sex (for trans people) or the gender pragmatically assigned (for people with intersex characteristics), inflict harm. They have been used to tell sex- and gender-variant people, implicitly and explicitly, that they, their bodies and identities, are particularly compelling evidence of a spiritual fall, and further from God's intent than those of non-trans (cisgender) and non-intersex (endosex) people.[30] Trans identity and variant sex characteristics have been held up as particular instances of creation gone wrong, to be redeemed at the eschaton.[31]

Such characterizations may be particularly excluding and traumatizing because they cut right to the heart of someone's personhood. Variant sex characteristics and trans identity are not a matter of choice but concern a person's very ontology. The message that these unchosen aspects of the self are particularly marked by sin therefore communicates that there is something wrong with an individual's substantial being. Where trans people and people with intersex characteristics have hoped to find messages of acceptance and love in churches and are instead met with suspicion, their social trauma is repeated and exacerbated spiritually.

Furthermore, argues Rob Clucas, the specific microaggressions trans people face within some religious institutions, like inadequate recognition of themselves and their relationships, may exacerbate their psychological distress.[32] Building on work by Nadal, Skolnik and Wong,[33] Clucas identifies microaggressive triggers, including denial that transphobia exists; endorsement of solely-binary and gender-normative behaviour and identity; and systemic and environmental factors (such as, in the Church of England, the fact that clergy may conscientiously opt out of presiding at marriages where one partner has transitioned gender, and faith-based exemptions from the Equality Act 2010, which mean religious groups may lawfully discriminate against people who have the protected characteristic of gender reassignment), leading to institutional hostility to trans people.

As the experiences of some sex- and gender-variant Christians make clear, attempts to 'include' them in church discussions about sex and gender may be traumatizing or retraumatizing if there is not adequate recognition that conversations on church 'turf' – whether literal or conceptual – may be triggering.[34] The act of 'inviting someone in' to a church discussion can be traumatizing for them if the church seeks to retain the power to set the terms of the conversation, or police participants' tone. In work on trauma and restorative justice, Stephanie Arel suggests there are likely to be continued barriers to truly transformative practice when restorative justice efforts take place within prisons, since, she holds, especially in the US context, these are frequently sites of disempowerment, diminishment and shame.[35] Churches and prisons are clearly not the same, but churches' power structures and dynamics may also hinder attempts at reconciliation. Church authorities might have what Arel calls 'affective responsibility';[36] that is, the responsibility to be aware of how the affective power of the space they curate and control is likely to impact on the emotional and spiritual state of those 'invited in'. Even where conversations are well meant, they might reinscribe inequality, especially where there is little acknowledgement that even if everyone in the conversation is ostensibly equal, they have not been equally traumatized and that the outcomes of the conversations are therefore unlikely to impact equally on their future experiences. Furthermore, as Sara Ahmed remarks:

> When something is wearing, you do not always feel worn down. Feeling worn down can be a retrospective realization that you have been or are being worn down. It might be that in order to inhabit certain spaces we have to block recognition of just how wearing they are: when the feeling catches us, it might be at the point when it is just too much. You are shattered.[37]

Living with moral injury

Moral injury occurs when someone's sense of their own grasp on the rightness of the world is disrupted.[38] This can happen in wartime when people witness or are made to enact violence, but might also occur, for example, when someone they had considered a moral exemplar is shown to be anything but, or indeed when something happens to disturb their capacity to believe that other people are generally trustworthy. In the cases we have been discussing, churches have not always admitted how they have perpetuated and reinscribed trauma on trans people and those with intersex characteristics – even when they were attempting to include them. We are not suggesting that churches should not take seriously the reality of sex- and gender-diverse people's lives and testimonies. Yet discussions in which churches continue to hold all the power to direct and manage the conversation can be problematic.

This is the case even where churches are trying to atone for former inadequate responses to sex- and gender-diverse people, since the latter groups may carry with them the ongoing effects of their earlier treatment. Eleonore Stump holds that, in order to be a sufficient response to the reality of the depth of suffering and alienation, Christian atonement theory needs to take seriously and deal adequately with the reality of both human guilt and human shame; existing atonement theories do not do this because they do not give adequate weight to the power of divine love.[39] Churches have not yet, we suggest here, adequately recognized their own culpability in inflicting shame on intersex and trans people, leading to intersex and trans people's diminution[40] and perpetuating moral injury – as Alex's and Sara's own stories show. It is to these that we turn next.

Alex's story

As a transmasculine person, I have experienced trauma that I feel it is important for theologians and church bodies to understand. These traumas include sexual violence and repudiation/rejection by churches and members thereof, by family and friends, and by medical bodies.

I am a survivor of sexual violence. In 2009, as I was beginning to explore my gender identity, I was raped by a 'Christian' man. This was preceded by the statement, 'I will show you how to be a real woman.' I have since reflected upon the theological grounding of this statement. This man had been taught, by both church and society, that people are either male or female and that femaleness is defined by sexual biology, function and role.

Surviving sexual violence is, of course, traumatic. I feel, however, that the repudiation and rejection of my identity by many is a trauma that continues to affect me even more greatly. When I was 15, I was asked to leave a church because I had begun to express my gender nonconformity.

My rejection by that church was predicated on an assumption that I was attracted to people of the same gender, and a lack of understanding of my gender nonconformity. As an ordained minister, I am aware that there are churches that will not allow me to lead worship, and who reject my calling, due to my gender identity. I regularly read articles by theologians repudiating my identity. I also receive hate mail, suggesting that I am leading my congregations astray and am a danger to Christians. These letters often state that I am not a real Christian. My religious identity is rejected alongside my gender identity.

When I began to disclose my gender identity, many friends rejected me. Further, I had a period of familial rejection. All of the friends that I lost identified as Christian. My parents were influenced by Christian theology and, even more greatly, by the opinions of church members. As such, I believe that the rejection of my identity by family and friends had a theological root. My parents have since come to accept my gender identity through facilitated conversations over a prolonged period. If churches were equipped to support the families and friends of trans people, perhaps our experiences would be very different.

Repudiation and rejection also occur when trans people dare to tell our stories or attempt to participate in ecclesial conversations about trans people. When I took part in the construction of the Church of England's *Living in Love and Faith* resources,[41] I expected to be part of some difficult conversations, which I am very able to contribute to as a theologian, minister and facilitator. I did not expect to be the target of misgendering, hate speech and threats coordinated by a Christian charity and viewed by tens of thousands. This traumatic experience has been largely ignored by the denomination concerned. There is a clear need for further conversations around safeguarding trans people from trauma when we participate in ecclesial processes.

Finally, I have suffered repudiation by medical professionals, always on the basis of faith. When I first came out as trans to a male doctor, he insisted on examining my genitalia. He then 'explained' to me that I had female genitalia and, therefore, my 'God-given' gender was female. Later, a gender identity specialist suggested that I could not be trans, as it was not in keeping with my Christian faith. This delayed my transition by several years. Later still, a nurse refused to administer my testosterone injections, citing her faith as the reason.

I strongly feel that the Church has a role in my trauma, both in initial cause, and in the duty to respond. I wish, I suspect in vain, that churches and theologians would cease to assert that 'God made man and woman' and that only dimorphic male and female sexes and genders exist. This assertion is at the root of all of the trauma that I have suffered within and outside the Church. This assertion is theologically and scientifically inaccurate, is propagated mainly by the Church, and infects cultures, societies, families and individuals.

The Church has a responsibility to respond to our trauma. First, I feel that church bodies should publicly apologize for incorrect theological understandings of personhood, specifically relating to sex and gender, and for the harm that they have directly and indirectly caused. Second, churches should take seriously their duties of pastoral care to trans members and their families. This could involve churches receiving training on gender identity, so that they can offer pastoral care to trans people who have experienced trauma, and to families and friends who are wrestling with a loved one's transition. Finally, churches should reconsider safeguarding policies and practices so that they attend to trans experiences of trauma.

Sara's story

I was born with intersex traits, which I also describe as variations in sex characteristics. I underwent surgery twice, at the age of two and then at 11. I was not told of the true nature of that surgery, although I can remember the outpatient visits, the examinations in front of medical students, and being in hospital for the second round of surgery.

It is hard to say if it was the surgery in itself that left me with lifelong symptoms of trauma and depression to manage, or whether it was the secrecy. I was always aware there was something 'different' about me, which left me unhealthily shy and introverted, which in turn led to bullying at school and an inability to socialize. It was not until I was 43 that I eventually demanded a copy of my GP medical records, after which I truly understood all that had happened to me.

My faith has always been important, and I have been either a practising Methodist or Anglican much of my life. I always found comfort in reading the Bible, revisiting particular passages that assisted me (2 Corinthians 4.8; Romans 5.1–5). Just as Susannah Cornwall[42] and Stephanie Budwey[43] have observed in other Christians with intersex characteristics, my faith affirmed my sense of worth.

There are many reasons I am so passionate about telling this story in church. One is simply that church is largely made up of families, and I am conscious the stigma and embarrassment is still felt by children with intersex traits and their parents and I may be in a position to alleviate some of that. There are those among our congregations who are suffering in silence and are sometimes being retraumatized like myself through ill-considered comments and preaching.

In recent years I have been working to raise awareness of intersex in the Church of England. I knew there would be lack of knowledge, even some embarrassment, but I had not expected a concerted effort to label me as 'disordered'. My own experience is too often dismissed and framed by others as representing creation gone wrong.[44] My telling of my story has on occasions been rejected and I have experienced having rumours spread that

I was really a man with malicious intent. It has been both wearing[45] and on occasions retraumatizing.[46]

Telling my story to supportive individuals and groups does reignite some difficult memories, which can be cathartic on a good day but then cause suffering on another. What is retraumatizing is that when I tell my story, while I may well be listened to, I am then challenged as to the validity of my experience. To give one example, when I was invited to speak at a church, it was felt appropriate by the organizers to invite someone else to give an alternative perspective on my personal experience that I was going to share. In this case they had in mind a conservative surgeon who performed surgery on children who had not been made in what he perceived to be the way God intended. (I need to underline that I am fully supportive of children opting for surgery when they are old enough to give informed consent, or where there is a medical emergency.) This was unexpected and traumatic for me and resulted in a serious episode of depression. It took many months to recover. The Church remains totally oblivious to the consequences of some of its actions, as it fails to listen to those outside its usual circle of senior clergy and theologians. The continued discussions within the Church around intersex are very much a cerebral exercise, where we are analysed and spoken about by others. I am cognizant that not all trauma is instantaneous and the continual flow of comment and literature labelling people like myself as disordered as a result of the Fall[47] has a long-term impact on our sense of being. This repeated message, which often is delivered in a patronizing tone of pity, does induce trauma. The continual patronization is particularly insidious, undermining any sense I may have of first-person authority.[48] Sometimes trauma is not instantaneous, but manifests itself after a prolonged period of what may be described as suffering. Being worn down, as described by Sara Ahmed,[49] and the re-emergence of trauma, are intertwined.

The Church needs to recognize the harm it causes in its misplaced desire for unity, which countenances all views that remain within the Church while ignoring views of those who have either left or do not feel welcome to join. The reality is that the current approach is one of epistemic violence. I often hide from church in all its forms, as it too often makes the task of managing episodes of depression, anxiety, flashbacks and panic attacks harder, and I can often manage these symptoms more successfully away from church. The education of clergy and congregations is vital, in order to provide the spiritual support and fellowship needed to create a space for healing. Listening to and validation of people's experiences is essential in building a church of love where the most vulnerable are able to recover from their trauma.[50] All church denominations have been found wanting when intersex Christians have suffered and been retraumatized by ill-considered comments and preaching. Safeguarding policy and training has failed in the past in protecting the most vulnerable adults and children, for fear of upsetting the strong voices. It is encounter that changes hearts and minds, alongside education. Encounter will only happen where there are affirming and safe spaces in which people with intersex traits and their families are given the confidence to share their stories. Epistemic violence will be never-ending if this is a cerebral exercise, rather than one of bodily encounter.

This brings me finally to the Church of England and its discussions on relationships, identity and sexuality entitled *Living in Love and Faith*. I contributed to the video resources by sharing a snippet of my experience of church, challenging people to think about how they relate to others different from themselves. On the one hand it is a pivotal moment, a positive one, the first time that the Church has nationally shared the story of someone with intersex traits. However, the other side is that I have found the material being used flippantly and used to harm others, with the Church being shown wanton when it comes to expressing pastoral concern and safeguarding those most vulnerable in the process. Again, I am having to leave the Church to heal the wounds the Church reopens, as we see a church in a never-ending cycle of discernment, prayer and inaction.

Discussion

There are good reasons to be wary of assumptions that the lives of trans people, and those with intersex characteristics, are inherently or inevitably marked by dysphoria and tragedy. David Valentine, for example, has notably argued that increased identification of trans identity with experiences of trauma, violence and threat is 'useful … for activism'[51] as focus for community organization, but diminishes diverse trans narratives that do not assume harm or paint all trans people as victims.[52] Indeed, some of the most generative theological responses to the trauma suffered by trans people and those with intersex characteristics come about via working transformatively with pain: not denying or suppressing it, nor engaging in overly heroic narratives of overcoming it, but rather starting from a place of its reality and then working to show how its existence becomes the occasion for new epiphanies. Elsewhere one of us, Alex Clare-Young, states: 'Being human is messy, complex and transformational … Our bodies are miracles, works of art, astounding creations, and should be treated as such.'[53] For Clare-Young, as a non-binary trans Christian, transformation is an active, agential work of reframing their embodiment. This does not mean denying the existence of pain, but rather doing justice to their experience holistically.[54]

This has implications for the ways in which sex- and gender-diverse people's difference and specificity are framed in church contexts. Rachel Mann, a Church of England priest, describes her experiences of being a 'public' trans person in the church and the sacrifices attached to being part of a group of people whose legitimacy is often questioned. Despite the difficulty, Mann holds that 'it is possible to experience this odd, potentially paradoxical place' as gift and well as cost.[55] Certain experiences that create vulnerability for those understood as insider-outsiders to the church teeter, she suggests, on a knife-edge between being horrific and wounding, or mediating grace. She is quick to note that in recognizing this reality she is 'not attempting to make a virtue out of trauma'.[56] Rather, she holds, the experience of being one of those whose existence is understood as liminal, or what she terms 'interstitial', is an experience of dwelling with Christ, whose own existence challenges norms and binaries, and that as such, reminders of one's precarity 'can – in the midst of much trauma – draw one close to the company of the Living God'.[57]

But despite all this, in Heather Love's words, 'Sometimes damage is just damage.'[58] As we have shown throughout this chapter, well-meant actions of church communities to discuss questions pertaining to trans and intersex people can themselves injure. A tendency to 'invite in' people from 'outside' to speak as 'experts' on their experiences can, even while well intended, expose them to scrutiny and retraumatization that institutions have not always been equipped (or for which they have not always taken responsibility) to help them manage. Building on Robin James's work on resilience and melancholy,[59] Karen Bray shows that in situations of 'inclusion', the problem is often assumed to be with the person 'invited in' for being insufficiently resilient to deal with the conversation, rather than with the situation into which they have been brought: 'Those who cannot bounce back are not considered resilient, but rather toxic. Those who cannot flee their damaged situations have no worth ... Inclusion is conditioned on exercising the right kind of resilience: making the right kind of choices out of one's damage.'[60]

What, then, *can* mitigate the moral injury caused when a trusted person or institution perpetuates harm? If moral injury has come about as a result of betrayal by a moral authority, its reparation will surely include humility and repentance on the part of the former moral authority. Yet institutions should be attuned to the fact that their own 'processing' of the impacts of their former practices is not always best done in the presence of those who have been injured by them. This is exacerbated when alongside a church's attempts to make reparations there are concerns to protect itself, carry out damage limitation on its bruised reputation, and so on.

Further work is needed to devise alternative modes of learning for churches with regard to trans people and those with intersex characteristics. Briefly, however, we recommend that these should centre on listening processes that: enable sex- and gender-variant people to explicate their trauma; enable researchers to examine the causes of trans and intersex people's trauma and their links to theology; facilitate engaged collaborative research projects in which researchers and those with lived experience contribute as equal partners; and have the resources and support they need to lead to meaningful change, in theology, praxis, pastoral care, safeguarding practices, and beyond.

A range of contributions point to the importance of churches providing space for healing via allowing trauma to be expressed and 'held', both in the practice of liturgy and the invocation of broader community practices – though, as they acknowledge, this is not an unproblematic process, especially when churches themselves have perpetrated or enabled traumatic events.[61] Indeed, it is hard for churches to hear that what seem like neutral or actively positive practices such as traumatized people's participation in communal worship can themselves be retraumatizing.[62] Often, trauma, having 'overwhelmed' the body's usual mechanisms for coping and resilience, is presented as challenge to integration, with the possibility of reintegration, 'restoring trust and connections',[63] held out as the hope. But survivors may feel that these kinds of accounts do not do enough to acknowledge that ongoing 'apartness' from church communities may be a necessary response, and an important affirmation of their agency to walk away.

Conclusion

It is perhaps too easy for institutions to believe that if traumatized people are now able to speak and be present there, then the trauma (and the institution's own responsibility for perpetuating it) cannot have been as overwhelming as all that. But what seem like abstract or academic issues for some undertaking 'dialogue' on the part of churches are intimate, deeply personal realities for some invited to contribute. The emotional and spiritual toll on the latter group is likely to be far greater than on those who can simply treat the question as an interesting debate. Those traumatized people who do choose to disclose their experiences may relive their trauma in doing so.

Furthermore, if, as they share their stories, they express anger, fear or indignation at what happened, they may find themselves labelled 'difficult', 'troublemakers' or insufficiently 'rational' or 'resilient'.[64] Rachel Mann describes her experience of being present for conversations at the General Synod where speakers proceeded as though trans people were not there and were entirely other to what was happening: 'I was caught in the double-bind: speak up and risk being coded as a troublemaker and as an issue, or stay silent and allow others to speak as if we, trans people, are an issue or an embarrassing complication.'[65] Tone policing does not adequately acknowledge that the calm, detached way in which some interlocutors may be able to approach discussions of abjected identities is not evidence of their greater virtue or rationality, but a function of the privilege that comes from being able to walk away.

As we have shown throughout this chapter, conversations about sex and gender diversity in faith communities should never start from a position of expecting trans people, and people with intersex characteristics, to justify their existence, nor to engage in apologetics-inflected processes that make them objects of others' sympathy. The capacity of sex- and gender-diverse people to know God and know themselves is no more inherently flawed or limited than that of those whose sex and gender go unremarked. Trauma created by stigmatizing theologies and inadequate pastoral responses is real and long-lasting, and all those who pronounce on the theological and anthropological significance of gender and sex should be aware that their implications for trans and intersex people are great.

Bibliography

Ahmed, Sara, *Living a Feminist Life*, Durham, NC: Duke University Press, 2017.

Archbishops' Council (Church of England), *Living in Love and Faith: Christian Teaching and Learning about Identity, Sexuality, Relationships and Marriage*, London: Church House Publishing, 2020.

Arel, Stephanie, 'Examining Restorative Justice: Theology, Traumatic Narratives, and Affective Responsibility' in *Post-Traumatic Public Theology*, ed. Stephanie Arel and Shelly Rambo, Cham: Palgrave Macmillan, 2016, pp. 173–91.

Ashworth, Pat, 'Self-Care Training is Put Online for Clergy Traumatised by Coronavirus', *Church Times*, 26 June 2020, www.churchtimes.co.uk/articles/2020/26-june/news/uk/self-care-training-is-put-online-for-clergy-traumatised-by-coronavirus, accessed 22.2.2022.

Baldwin, Jennifer, *Trauma-Sensitive Theology: Thinking Theologically in the Era of Trauma*, Eugene, OR: Cascade, 2018.

Baratz, Arlene and Katrina Karkazis, 'Cris de Coeur and the Moral Imperative to Listen to and Learn From Intersex People', *Narrative Inquiry in Bioethics* 5, 2 (2015), pp. 127–32.

Beste, Jennifer, *God and the Victim: Traumatic Intrusions on Grace and Freedom*, Oxford: Oxford University Press, 2007.

Bettcher, Talia Mae, 'Trans Identities and First-Person Authority' in *You've Changed: Sex Reassignment and Personal Identity*, ed. Laurie Shrage, Oxford: Oxford University Press, 2009, pp. 98–120.

Bray, Karen, *Grave Attending*, New York: Fordham University Press, 2020.

Brock, Rita Nakashima and Gabriella Lettini, *Soul Repair: Recovering from Moral Injury After War*, Boston, MA: Beacon Press, 2012.

Budwey, Stephanie, '"God is the Creator of All Life and the Energy of this World": German Intersex Christians' Reflection on the Image of God and Being Created in God's Image', *Theology and Sexuality* 24, 2 (2018), pp. 85–97.

Burk, Denny, 'Training our Kids in a Transgender World' in *Designed for Joy: How the Gospel Impacts Men and Woman, Identity and Practice*, ed. Owen Strachan and Jonathan Parnell, Wheaton, IL: Crossway, 2015, pp. 89–98.

Burk, Denny, 'The Transgender Test' in *Beauty, Order, and Mystery: A Christian Vision of Human Sexuality*, ed. Todd Wilson and Gerald Hiestand, Downers Grove, IL: InterVarsity Press, 2018, pp. 87–99.

Carpenter, Morgan, 'The Human Rights of Intersex People: Addressing Harmful Practices and Rhetoric of Change', *Reproductive Health Matters* 24, 47 (2016), pp. 74–84.

Clare-Young, Alex, *Transgender. Christian. Human.*, Glasgow: Wild Goose Publications, 2019.

Clare-Young, Alex, 'Living in Love and Faith? The Construction of Contemporary Texts of Terror', *Theology and Sexuality* 27, 2–3 (2021), pp. 115–36.

Clucas, Rob, 'Trans People and the Church of England: Disadvantage and Micro-aggressions', *Modern Believing* 58, 4 (2017), pp. 321–42.

Congregation for Catholic Education, '"Male and Female He Created Them": Towards a Path of Dialogue on the Question of Gender Theory in Education', 2019, www.educatio.va/content/dam/cec/Documenti/19_0997_INGLESE.pdf, accessed 22.2.2022.

Cornwall, Susannah, 'British Intersex Christians' Accounts of Intersex Identity, Christian Identity and Church Experience', *Practical Theology* 6, 2 (2013), pp. 220–36.

Cornwall, Susannah, 'Telling Stories About Intersex and Christianity: Saying Too Much or Not Saying Enough?', *Theology* 117, 1 (2014), pp. 24–33.

Council on Biblical Manhood and Womanhood, 'Nashville Statement', 2017, https://cbmw.org/nashville-statement/, accessed 22.2.2022.

Diocese of Sydney (Anglican Church of Australia), 'Doctrine Statement on Gender Identity', 22 October 2019, www.sds.asn.au/sites/default/files/Doctrine Statement on Gender Identity .docx.pdf?doc_id=NDM4NzA=, accessed 22.2.2022.

Drescher, Kent, Jason Nieuwsma and Pamela Swales, 'Morality and Moral Injury: Insights from Theology and Health Science', *Reflective Practice: Formation and Supervision in Ministry* 33 (2013), pp. 50–61.

Fausto-Sterling, Anne, *Sexing the Body: Gender Politics and the Construction of Sexuality*, New York: Basic Books, 2000.

Fricker, Miranda, *Epistemic Injustice: Power and the Ethics of Knowing*, Oxford: Oxford University Press, 2007.

Hollinger, Dennis, *The Meaning of Sex: Christian Ethics and the Moral Life*, Grand Rapids, MI: Baker Academic, 2009.

Human Rights Campaign, 'Violence Against the Transgender Community in 2019', *Human Rights Campaign*, 2019, www.hrc.org/resources/violence-against-the-transgender-community-in-2019, accessed 22.2.2022.

James, Robin, *Resilience and Melancholy*, Alresford: Zero Books, 2015.

Jones, Serene, *Trauma and Grace: Theology in a Ruptured World*, Louisville, KY: Westminster John Knox Press, 2009.

Kerry, Stephen, 'Intersex Individuals' Religiosity and their Journey to Wellbeing', *Journal of Gender Studies* 18, 3 (2009), pp. 277–85.

Kessler, Suzanne, *Lessons from the Intersexed*, New Brunswick, NJ: Rutgers University Press, 1998.

Lange, Dirk, *Trauma Recalled: Liturgy, Disruption, and Theology*, Minneapolis, MN: Augsburg Fortress, 2009.

Lev, Arlene Istar, 'Intersexuality in the Family: An Unacknowledged Trauma', *Journal of Gay and Lesbian Psychotherapy* 10, 2 (2006), pp. 27–56.

Love, Heather, *Feeling Backward: Loss and the Politics of Queer History*, Cambridge, MA: Harvard University Press, 2007.

McFadyen, Alistair, *The Call to Personhood: A Christian Theory of the Individual in Social Relationships*, Cambridge: Cambridge University Press, 1990.

McLemore, Kevin, 'A Minority Stress Perspective on Transgender Individuals' Experiences with Misgendering', *Stigma and Health* 3, 1 (2018), pp. 53–64.

Mann, Rachel, *Dazzling Darkness: Gender, Sexuality, Illness and God* (2nd edn), Glasgow: Wild Goose Resource Group, 2020.

Méndez, Juan, 'Report of the Special Rapporteur on Torture and Other Cruel, Inhuman or Degrading Treatment or Punishment', United Nations General Assembly, 1 February 2013, www.ohchr.org/Documents/HRBodies/HRCouncil/Regular Session/Session22/A.HRC.22.53_English.pdf, accessed 22.2.2022.

Mizock, Lauren and Thomas Lewis, 'Trauma in Transgender Populations: Risk, Resilience, and Clinical Care', *Journal of Emotional Abuse* 8, 3 (2008), pp. 335–54.

Monro, Surya, Daniela Crocetti and Tray Yeadon-Lee, 'Intersex/Variations of Sex Characteristics and DSD Citizenship in the UK, Italy and Switzerland', *Citizenship Studies* 23, 8 (2019), pp. 780–97.

Moreno, Angela, 'In Amerika They Call Us Hermaphrodites' in *Intersex in the Age of Ethics*, ed. Alice Dreger, Hagerstown, MD: University Publishing Group, 1999, pp. 137–9.

Morland, Iain, 'Intersex Treatment and the Promise of Trauma' in *Gender and the Science of Difference: Cultural Politics of Contemporary Science and Medicine*, ed. Jill Fisher, New Brunswick, NJ: Rutgers University Press, 2011, pp. 147–63.

Morris, Esther, 'The Self I Will Never Know', *New Internationalist* 364 (2004), pp. 25–7.

Nadal, Kevin, Avy Skolnik and Yinglee Wong, 'Interpersonal and Systemic Microaggressions Toward Transgender People: Implications for Counseling', *Journal of LGBT Issues in Counseling* 6, 1 (2012), pp. 55–82.

O'Donnell, Karen, *Broken Bodies: The Eucharist, Mary, and the Body in Trauma Theology*, London: SCM Press, 2018.

O'Donnell, Karen and Katie Cross (eds), *Feminist Trauma Theologies: Body, Scripture and Church in Critical Perspective*, London: SCM Press, 2020.

Pantalone, David, Sarah Valentine and Jillian Shipherd, 'Working with Survivors of Trauma in the Sexual Minority and Transgender and Gender Nonconforming Populations' in *Handbook of Sexual Orientation and Gender Diversity in Counseling and Psychotherapy*, ed. Kurt DeBord, Ann Fischer, Kathleen Bieschke and Ruperto Perez, Washington DC: American Psychological Association, 2017, pp. 183–211.

Pikramenou, Nikoletta, *Intersex Rights: Living Between Sexes*, Cham: Springer, 2019.

Preves, Sharon, *Intersex and Identity: The Contested Self*, New Brunswick, NJ: Rutgers University Press, 2003.

Rambo, Shelly, *Spirit and Trauma: A Theology of Remaining*, Louisville, KY: Westminster John Knox Press, 2010.

Rambo, Shelly, 'Introduction' in *Post-Traumatic Public Theology*, ed. Stephanie Arel and Shelly Rambo, Cham: Palgrave Macmillan, 2016, pp. 1–21.

Shay, Jonathan, 'Moral Injury', *Psychoanalytic Psychology* 31, 2 (2014), pp. 182–91.

Shelley, Christopher, *Transpeople: Repudiation, Trauma, Healing*, Toronto: University of Toronto Press, 2008.

Stump, Eleonore, *Atonement*, Oxford: Oxford University Press, 2018.

Swinton, John, *Dementia: Living in the Memories of God*, Grand Rapids, MI: Eerdmans, 2012.

Valentine, David, '"The Calculus of Pain": Violence, Anthropological Ethics, and the Category Transgender', *Ethnos* 68, 1 (2003), pp. 27–48.

van Ommen, Armand Léon, 'Remembering for Healing: Liturgical Communities of Reconciliation Provide Space for Trauma' in *Trauma and Lived Religion: Transcending the Ordinary*, ed. R. Ruard Ganzevoort and Srdjan Sremac, Cham: Palgrave Macmillan, 2019, pp. 203–23.

Walker, Andrew, *God and the Transgender Debate: What Does the Bible Actually Say About Gender Identity?* Epsom: The Good Book Company, 2017.

Warner, Megan, Christopher Southgate, Carla Grosch-Miller and Hilary Ison (eds), *Tragedies and Christian Congregations: The Practical Theology of Trauma*, Abingdon: Routledge, 2020.

Yarhouse, Mark, *Understanding Gender Dysphoria: Navigating Transgender Issues in a Changing Culture*, Downers Grove, IL: InterVarsity Press, 2015.

Notes

1 Pat Ashworth, 'Self-Care Training is Put Online for Clergy Traumatised by Coronavirus', *Church Times*, 26 June 2020, www.churchtimes.co.uk/articles/2020/26-june/news/uk/self-care-training-is-put-online-for-clergy-traumatised-by-coronavirus, accessed 22.2.2022; Megan Warner, Christopher Southgate, Carla Grosch-Miller and Hilary Ison (eds), *Tragedies and Christian Congregations: The Practical Theology of Trauma* (Abingdon: Routledge, 2020).

2 Suzanne Kessler, *Lessons from the Intersexed* (New Brunswick, NJ: Rutgers University Press, 1998); Angela Moreno, 'In Amerika They Call Us Hermaphrodites' in *Intersex in the Age of Ethics*, ed. Alice Dreger (Hagerstown, MD: University Publishing Group, 1999), pp. 137–9; Anne Fausto-Sterling, *Sexing the Body: Gender Politics and the Construction of Sexuality* (New York: Basic Books, 2000); Sharon Preves, *Intersex and Identity: The Contested Self* (New Brunswick, NJ: Rutgers University Press, 2003); Esther Morris, 'The Self I Will Never Know', *New Internationalist* 364 (2004), pp. 25–7.

3 Juan Méndez, 'Report of the Special Rapporteur on Torture and Other Cruel, Inhuman or Degrading Treatment or Punishment', *United Nations General Assembly*, 1 February 2013, www.ohchr.org/Documents/HRBodies/HRCouncil/RegularSession/Session22/A.HRC.22.53_English.pdf, accessed 22.2.2022; Morgan Carpenter, 'The Human Rights of Intersex People: Addressing Harmful Practices and Rhetoric of Change', *Reproductive Health Matters* 24, 47 (2016), pp. 74–84; Surya Monro, Daniela Crocetti and Tray Yeadon-Lee, 'Intersex/Variations of Sex Characteristics and DSD Citizenship in the UK, Italy and Switzerland', *Citizenship Studies* 23, 8 (2018), pp. 780–97; Nikoletta Pikramenou, *Intersex Rights: Living Between Sexes*, Cham: Springer, 2019.

4 Human Rights Campaign, 'Violence Against the Transgender Community in 2019', *Human Rights Campaign*, 2019, https://www.hrc.org/resources/violence-against-the-transgender-community-in-2019, accessed 22.2.2022.

5 Lauren Mizock and Thomas Lewis, 'Trauma in Transgender Populations: Risk, Resilience, and Clinical Care', *Journal of Emotional Abuse* 8, 3 (2008), pp. 335–54.

6 David Pantalone, Sarah Valentine and Jillian Shipherd, 'Working with Survivors of Trauma in the Sexual Minority and Transgender and Gender Nonconforming Populations' in *Handbook of Sexual Orientation and Gender Diversity in*

Counseling and Psychotherapy, ed. Kurt DeBord, Ann Fischer, Kathleen Bieschke and Ruperto Perez (Washington DC: American Psychological Association, 2017), pp. 183–211.

7 Kevin McLemore, 'A Minority Stress Perspective on Transgender Individuals' Experiences with Misgendering', *Stigma and Health* 3, 1 (2018), pp. 53–64.

8 Miranda Fricker, *Epistemic Injustice: Power and the Ethics of Knowing* (Oxford: Oxford University Press, 2007).

9 Talia Mae Bettcher, 'Trans Identities and First-Person Authority' in *You've Changed: Sex Reassignment and Personal Identity*, ed. Laurie Shrage (Oxford: Oxford University Press, 2009), pp. 98–120.

10 Shelly Rambo, *Spirit and Trauma: A Theology of Remaining* (Louisville, KY: Westminster John Knox Press, 2010).

11 Dirk Lange, *Trauma Recalled: Liturgy, Disruption, and Theology* (Minneapolis, MN: Augsburg Fortress, 2009).

12 Jennifer Beste, *God and the Victim: Traumatic Intrusions on Grace and Freedom* (Oxford: Oxford University Press, 2007).

13 Jennifer Baldwin, *Trauma-Sensitive Theology: Thinking Theologically in the Era of Trauma* (Eugene, OR: Cascade, 2018).

14 Warner et al., *Tragedies and Christian Congregations*.

15 Karen O'Donnell and Katie Cross (eds), *Feminist Trauma Theologies: Body, Scripture and Church in Critical Perspective* (London: SCM Press, 2020).

16 Warner et al., *Tragedies and Christian Congregations*, p. 1.

17 Arlene Istar Lev, 'Intersexuality in the Family: An Unacknowledged Trauma', *Journal of Gay and Lesbian Psychotherapy* 10, 2 (2006), pp. 27–56, here pp. 33–4.

18 Iain Morland, 'Intersex Treatment and the Promise of Trauma' in *Gender and the Science of Difference: Cultural Politics of Contemporary Science and Medicine*, ed. Jill Fisher (New Brunswick, NJ: Rutgers University Press, 2011), pp. 147–63, here p. 158.

19 Arlene Baratz and Katrina Karkazis, 'Cris de Coeur and the Moral Imperative to Listen to and Learn From Intersex People', *Narrative Inquiry in Bioethics* 5, 2 (2015), pp. 127–32, here p. 127.

20 Baratz and Karkazis, 'Cris de Coeur', pp. 128–9.

21 Christopher Shelley, *Transpeople: Repudiation, Trauma, Healing* (Toronto: University of Toronto Press, 2008), pp. 3–4.

22 Alistair McFadyen, *The Call to Personhood: A Christian Theory of the Individual in Social Relationships* (Cambridge: Cambridge University Press, 1990). See also the work of scholars of disability and intellectual impairment who note the importance of being known by God even where one is not capable of knowing or being known by others, e.g. John Swinton, *Dementia: Living in the Memories of God* (Grand Rapids, MI: Eerdmans, 2012).

23 Bettcher, 'Trans Identities and First-Person Authority', p. 100.

24 Denny Burk, 'Training our Kids in a Transgender World' in *Designed for Joy: How the Gospel Impacts Men and Woman, Identity and Practice*, ed. Owen Strachan and Jonathan Parnell (Wheaton, IL: Crossway, 2015), pp. 89–98, here p. 91.

25 Andrew Walker, *God and the Transgender Debate: What Does the Bible Actually Say About Gender Identity?* (Epsom: The Good Book Company, 2017), p. 25.

26 Bettcher, 'Trans Identities and First-Person Authority', p. 105.

27 Fricker, *Epistemic Injustice*, p. 20.

28 Susannah Cornwall, 'British Intersex Christians' Accounts of Intersex Identity, Christian Identity and Church Experience', *Practical Theology* 6, 2 (2013), pp. 220–36; Susannah Cornwall, 'Telling Stories About Intersex and Christianity: Saying Too Much or Not Saying Enough?', *Theology* 117, 1 (2014), pp. 24–33; Stephanie Budwey, '"God is the Creator of All Life and the Energy of this World": German Intersex Christians' Reflection on the Image of God and Being Created in God's Image', *Theology and Sexuality* 24, 2 (2018), pp. 85–97.

29 Stephen Kerry, 'Intersex Individuals' Religiosity and their Journey to Wellbeing', *Journal of Gender Studies* 18, 3 (2018), pp. 277–85, here p. 281.

30 Dennis Hollinger, *The Meaning of Sex: Christian Ethics and the Moral Life* (Grand Rapids, MI: Baker Academic, 2009), p. 84; Mark Yarhouse, *Understanding Gender Dysphoria: Navigating Transgender Issues in a Changing Culture* (Downers Grove, IL: InterVarsity Press, 2015); Walker, *God and the Transgender Debate*; Council on Biblical Manhood and Womanhood, Nashville Statement (2017), https://cbmw.org/nashville-statement/; Denny Burk, 'The Transgender Test' in *Beauty, Order, and Mystery: A Christian Vision of Human Sexuality*, ed. Todd Wilson and Gerald Hiestand (Downers Grove, IL: InterVarsity Press, 2018), pp. 87–99; Congregation for Catholic Education, '"Male and Female He Created Them": Towards a Path of Dialogue on the Question of Gender Theory in Education', 2019, www.educatio.va/content/dam/cec/Documenti/19_0997_INGLESE. pdf.

31 Diocese of Sydney (Anglican Church of Australia), 'Doctrine Statement on Gender Identity', 22 October 2019, https://www.sds.asn.au/sites/default/files/Doc trine Statement on Gender Identity .docx.pdf?doc_id=NDM4NzA=.

32 Rob Clucas, 'Trans People and the Church of England: Disadvantage and Microaggressions', *Modern Believing* 58, 4 (2017), pp. 321–42.

33 Kevin Nadal, Avy Skolnik and Yinglee Wong, 'Interpersonal and Systemic Microaggressions Toward Transgender People: Implications for Counseling', *Journal of LGBT Issues in Counseling* 6, 1 (2012), pp. 55–82.

34 Alex Clare-Young, 'Living in Love and Faith? The Construction of Contemporary Texts of Terror', *Theology and Sexuality* 27, 2–3 (2021), pp. 115–36.

35 Stephanie Arel, 'Examining Restorative Justice: Theology, Traumatic Narratives, and Affective Responsibility' in *Post-Traumatic Public Theology*, ed. Stephanie Arel and Shelly Rambo (Cham: Palgrave Macmillan, 2016), pp. 173–91, here p. 186.

36 Arel, 'Examining Restorative Justice'.

37 Sara Ahmed, *Living a Feminist Life* (Durham, NC: Duke University Press, 2017), p. 164.

38 Rita Nakashima Brock and Gabriella Lettini, *Soul Repair: Recovering from Moral Injury After War* (Boston, MA: Beacon Press, 2012); Kent Drescher, Jason Nieuwsma and Pamela Swales, 'Morality and Moral Injury: Insights from Theology and Health Science', *Reflective Practice: Formation and Supervision in Ministry* 33 (2013), pp. 50–61; Jonathan Shay, 'Moral Injury', *Psychoanalytic Psychology* 31, 2 (2014), pp. 182–91.

39 Eleonore Stump, *Atonement* (Oxford: Oxford University Press, 2018), p. 340.

40 See Stump, *Atonement*, p. 345.

41 This project has produced a suite of resources, including a book plus a website containing videos, podcasts, annotated bibliographies, academic background

papers and a study guide for groups. See Archbishops' Council (Church of England), *Living in Love and Faith: Christian Teaching and Learning about Identity, Sexuality, Relationships and Marriage* (London: Church House Publishing, 2020). See also Clare-Young, 'Living in Love and Faith?'.

42 Cornwall, 'British Intersex Christians' Accounts'; Cornwall, 'Telling Stories'.

43 Budwey, '"God is the Creator of All Life"'.

44 See Congregation for Catholic Education, '"Male and Female He Created Them"'; Diocese of Sydney, 'Doctrine Statement on Gender Identity'.

45 Ahmed, *Living a Feminist Life*.

46 Baratz and Karkazis, 'Cris de Coeur'.

47 Hollinger, *The Meaning of Sex*, p. 84; Diocese of Sydney, 'Doctrine Statement on Gender Identity'.

48 Bettcher, 'Trans Identities and First-Person Authority'.

49 Ahmed, *Living a Feminist Life*.

50 Karen O'Donnell, *Broken Bodies: The Eucharist, Mary, and the Body in Trauma Theology* (London: SCM Press, 2018), p. 11.

51 David Valentine, '"The Calculus of Pain": Violence, Anthropological Ethics, and the Category Transgender', *Ethnos* 68, 1 (2003), pp. 27–48, here p. 29.

52 Valentine, '"The Calculus of Pain"', pp. 31–2.

53 Alex Clare-Young, *Transgender. Christian. Human.* (Glasgow: Wild Goose Publications, 2019), p. 71.

54 Clare-Young, *Transgender. Christian. Human.*, p. 28.

55 Rachel Mann, *Dazzling Darkness: Gender, Sexuality, Illness and God*, 2nd edn (Glasgow: Wild Goose Publications, 2020), p. 161.

56 Mann, *Dazzling Darkness*, p. 161.

57 Mann, *Dazzling Darkness*, p. 161.

58 Heather Love, *Feeling Backward: Loss and the Politics of Queer History* (Cambridge, MA: Harvard University Press, 2007), p. 27.

59 Robin James, *Resilience and Melancholy* (Alresford: Zero Books, 2015).

60 Karen Bray, *Grave Attending* (New York: Fordham University Press, 2020), p. 52.

61 Armand Léon van Ommen, 'Remembering for Healing: Liturgical Communities of Reconciliation Provide Space for Trauma' in *Trauma and Lived Religion: Transcending the Ordinary*, ed. R. Ruard Ganzevoort and Srdjan Sremac (Cham: Palgrave Macmillan, 2019), pp. 203–23; Warner et al., *Tragedies and Christian Congregations*.

62 Serene Jones, *Trauma + Grace: Theology in a Ruptured World* (Louisville, KY: Westminster John Knox Press, 2009), pp. 3ff.

63 Shelly Rambo, 'Introduction' in *Post-Traumatic Public Theology*, ed. Stephanie Arel and Shelly Rambo (Cham: Palgrave Macmillan, 2016), pp. 1–21, here p. 4.

64 Bray, *Grave Attending*, p. 52.

65 Mann, *Dazzling Darkness*, p. 161.

7

'We Shall Not Be Eaten by Any Lions': Healing Ugandan Queer Trauma through Creative Contextual Bible Study

ADRIAAN VAN KLINKEN

Introduction: 'My mum didn't even look at me'

I had met Tigan the year before, while I was reconnecting with the Nature Network, a community-based organization of Ugandan LGBT+[1] refugees based in Nairobi, Kenya, to develop the project of which this chapter is an outcome and in which he became deeply involved. From our first encounter, I had been impressed by him, not just by his handsome looks that were accentuated by gorgeous dreadlocks, but by the demeanour with which he carried himself. Here was a young man, in his mid-twenties, soft-spoken but confident, a little introvert but with natural warmth; a beautiful smile on his face but with a melancholic air surrounding him. He kind of intrigued me. As we interacted more and worked together in planning for the project, we developed trust and friendship. About a year later, in September 2019, he was one of the first participants volunteering for a life-story interview. I had the privilege to get an intimate insight into his life experiences as he shared about growing up as a young gay man in Uganda and ending up as a refugee in Kenya.

In the interview, there was one part where his voice became particularly thin, while he was trying to control the emotions swelling up in his throat. Tigan had elaborated at length how his boss, after finding out incidentally about his sexuality, had started blackmailing him: forcing him to sleep with him, while refusing to pay him the salary he owed and threatening to disclose his sexuality to his father, whom the boss was friends with. After months of being in this situation, which caused him sleepless nights and made him lose weight, Tigan had finally taken the step to no longer go back to work and ignore the phone calls of his boss. Yet one dramatic night, when he arrived home he found his boss seated with his father. Quickly receding into his bedroom, his mother soon knocked on the door asking him to come back to the living room. As he walked in, he could tell from his parents' faces that they knew the secret about their son. It is at this moment in the interview that Tigan became emotional. He recounted how his father shouted accusations at him, beat him, and told him to leave the house. However, what upset Tigan the most while he narrated his story is the memory of how his mother let him down. In slightly different versions he repeated the same phrase four times: 'She did not look at me'. In Tigan's own words:

> What really hurt me so very bad was the fact that my mum said nothing to me; she didn't look at me at all. And I had a very good relationship with mum. Even when I was younger, my mum used to stand in for me every time my dad was like, 'He has to do this and that.' She was always like, 'This is my son, let him rest.' But this time, she didn't look at me or say anything. I wanted her to say something, even if it was hateful, but she didn't. My dad was like, 'Pack your bags and leave, you're not going to stay here any longer; at least I've given you education, go hustle on your own, you're not staying in this house with those behaviours of yours.' ... I left that night. Still when I was leaving, I looked at my mum: she was seated at the dining table, she was putting her head down, as if she was too embarrassed to look in my eyes. I looked at her, but she didn't look at me; then I left. I stood at the door waiting for her, and my dad was like, 'Leave! No one is going to be on your side.'[2]

After leaving the house, Tigan stayed with a friend for some time, and then decided to move to Kenya, where he registered as a refugee and entered the process with UNHCR for resettlement to a third country on a different continent. Five years later, at the time of telling his story, Tigan is still stuck in Kenya, struggling to survive while awaiting the outcome of the notoriously slow resettlement process.

Tigan's story is a deeply moving account of the abuse he faced from his boss, and the rejection he experienced from his parents, simply because of his sexuality. His experience is far from unique. Many other refugees participating in the project related similar experiences of harassment, violence, exclusion and rejection. Tigan's story of being expelled from home can be read at another level, as a metaphor for Ugandan LGBT+ persons being rejected by, and expelled from, the country they call home. Especially in the time following the passing of Uganda's infamous Anti-Homosexuality Bill (AHB, late 2013/early 2014), many LGBT+ Ugandans could no longer see a future for themselves in the country, with hundreds moving to neighbouring Kenya as refugees. The initial draft of the AHB, introduced in 2009, included a death-penalty clause for 'aggravated homosexuality'. Although this clause – after international outcry – had been removed from the version that in December 2013 passed through parliament, the Bill created and reinforced a socio-political climate in which homosexuality had become deeply politicized. Indeed, it was in the aftermath of the passing of the AHB that Tigan found himself in the situation narrated above. The assumption of the AHB and the discourse around it was that homosexuality is against Ugandan culture, religion and tradition.[3] Mama Uganda, so to say, refused to look her queer children in the eyes while political and religious leaders in the country introduced a body politic that de facto excluded sexual and gender minorities from the body of the nation.

Multiple, everyday and long-term trauma of Ugandan LGBT+ refugees

In this chapter, I conceptualize trauma with the help of feminist and queer, as well as postcolonial theories of trauma. From feminist and queer studies, I take the notion of what Ann Cvetkovich describes as 'the everyday life of trauma', in which trauma is not so much a specific and discrete event but is 'everyday and ongoing'.[4] This does not mean that specific events cannot be significant, but that they are embedded in, and illustrative of, deeper-rooted and socially embedded cultures and histories of trauma. Thus, in relation to the focus of this chapter, the introduction and passing of the AHB in Uganda can be seen as an event, but not in an isolated sense. The Bill was part of a social and political context in which homosexuality had become deeply politicized – a politicization that already severely impacted the everyday lives of LGBT+ persons and communities long before the Bill was signed into law in February 2014, and which continued to impact them after the Anti-Homosexuality Act was nullified by the Ugandan Constitutional Court six months later. As one of the participants captured the multiplicity and encompassing nature of the trauma refugees have experienced, 'We have gone through a lot of trauma because of our parents, religion, and culture.'[5] And the trauma continued to multiply in Kenya, because life as a refugee – with no right to work, and with very little economic support from refugee agencies – is incredibly hard. Many of the refugees participating in this project narrated experiences of struggling to navigate the refugee bureaucracy, being expelled from their accommodation by queer-phobic landlords, being harassed by the police, suffering abuse and violence in the community, and engaging in sex work as a means of survival, at the risk of contracting HIV and other sexually transmittable diseases. Tigan captured their day-to-day reality with an understatement: 'It's not like heaven here.'

Postcolonial theories have sought to decolonize the concept of trauma by also problematizing the notion of trauma as individual and an event, and instead foregrounding the collective, sustained, long-term and ongoing nature of trauma embedded in colonial and neocolonial experiences.[6] Trauma, from that perspective, is seen as generational and as foundational to social memory and national history. The latter notion is particularly relevant to understanding the politics of homosexuality in contemporary Uganda, which is shaped by a long history of colonial and postcolonial trauma. As the political scientist Rahul Rao puts it, the response of 'the homophobic Ugandan state' to queer difference (exemplified by the Anti-Homosexuality Act) reveals 'the structure of a grammar forged ... through the ruptures of colonization, decolonization, civil war, structural adjustment, and HIV/AIDS'.[7] This may hold true for the politics of homosexuality in many other postcolonial African countries too. Yet even more so in Uganda, where the early encounter with European colonialism and missionary Christianity resulted in a traumatic historic event: the killing of over 20 young male converts who used to serve as pages in the royal court, on the order of Kabaka Mwanga II, the ruler of the Buganda kingdom. The reason for their killing was later associated with the king's allegedly homosexual tendencies, to which the pages after their conversion would have refused to give in, thus inciting his anger; the pages were later sanctified as martyrs by the Catholic and Anglican Churches. Thus, as Rao captures it, 'The story of the "Ugandan martyrs", or at least this version of it, places an instance of thwarted same-sex intimacy at the heart of what is essentially the founding myth of both the Ugandan state and Ugandan Christianity.'[8] Indeed, the memory of the Ugandan martyrs was directly invoked in the discourse around the Anti-Homosexuality Bill. This discourse reflected postcolonial trauma as the Bill was framed by its supporters as a symbol of Ugandan sovereignty vis-à-vis the West, which was trying to impose its own liberal-secular values on to an independent African nation. Like the martyrs had resisted the king's 'immoral' lusts, so Uganda should now resist Western pressures and instead defend its own culture. Gay activists, including some of our participants, on the other hand, referred to the same story to argue that if the Buganda king practised homosexuality, the popular argument that homosexuality is against Ugandan traditions does not hold up. Thus, they invoked this memory to address the trauma of their being denied Ugandan cultural citizenship, and in order to claim belonging.

The focus of the present chapter is, however, not so much on culture but on religion, specifically Christianity and its sacred Scripture, the Bible, as another key site of contested claims of belonging, experiences of trauma and quests for healing.

Bible, life storytelling and performative arts

This chapter is based on a project in which I collaborated with my colleague Johanna Stiebert, and in which we worked with a community-based organization of Ugandan LGBT+ refugees called the Nature Network. Based in Matasia, at the far outskirts of the Nairobi metropole, the Nature Network is a self-help and empowerment group, mostly consisting of gay men and trans women, through which refugees have organized themselves to provide basic necessities such as shelter and food, but also engage in advocacy with UNHCR and other refugee agencies and undertake health-awareness education relating to malaria, HIV and, most recently, Covid-19. In this project, which took place in 2019 and early 2020, we explored the intersections of Ugandan LGBT+ life stories and selected Bible stories, through a process of life storytelling combined with contextual and creative Bible study. A full account of the methodology and findings can be found in the monograph that has come out of the project.[9] Here, I will briefly outline three methodological considerations specifically relevant to the question of the healing of queer trauma.

The Bible was introduced in most parts of sub-Saharan Africa in the era of European colonization and mission. It came as a 'tool of imperialism', but as the biblical scholar Gerald West has demonstrated in his book, *The Stolen Bible*, through a long and complex reception process it has been widely appropriated and has become 'a people's Bible' and even an 'African icon'.[10] The contemporary African context has been described by the feminist biblical scholar Musa Dube as a 'multilayered context of traumatic experiences' of African communities, and African women in particular – the interconnected traumas of colonialism and neocolonialism, violent conflict, political struggle, social and economic inequalities, patriarchy, gender-based violence, HIV and AIDS and so on.[11] In this context, African women theologians have actively engaged in the quest of reading the Bible for healing:

> African women's biblical hermeneutics share in the political agenda of addressing various challenges that confront them and their communities as a whole, and the quest for liberation from oppressive conditions ... The agenda of African women's biblical hermeneutics is to contribute towards building healing and healed communities in their countries and the world as a whole. Healing here describes a process of being resilient against all forms of oppression confronting groups and individuals that may be carried out on the basis of race, ethnicity, class, religion, gender, sexuality, age, dis/ability, and health, among others.[12]

This commitment to reading the Bible for healing of multilayered and ongoing trauma has taken different methodological forms. Most relevant for the purpose of this chapter are storytelling methods, building on the rich traditions of storytelling in African cultures, and the method of reading with and from non-academic readers, in order to decentre academic and elitist interpretations and instead to privilege grassroots, liberatory and emancipatory ways of interpreting biblical texts.[13]

In the same way as African women have had to reclaim the Bible from colonial and patriarchal Christianity, and appropriate it in their quest for liberation, justice and healing, LGBT+ persons and communities on the continent have to reclaim the Bible from dominant heteronormative and queer-phobic interpretations in their own quest for the healing of queer trauma. Some work has been done recently on the role of the Bible in the politics of homosexuality in Africa, and on LGBT+ affirming interpretations.[14] Adding to this, our project adopted a method of 'reading with' LGBT+ communities, in this case specifically the community of Ugandan LGBT+ refugees, providing a space for them to read the Bible from the perspective of their own life experiences.[15] To that aim, we also conceived of this space as a storytelling space, in a twofold way. First, a space for the telling of participants' life stories, inspired by feminist, postcolonial and queer activism and scholarship adopting autobiographical storytelling as a method for marginalized groups to recover and perform agency.[16] Second, a space for inter-reading their own life experiences vis-à-vis biblical stories – which for participants are sacred, as they come from a book they consider Holy Scripture – and for subsequently creating a new story, which can be described as a sacred queer story. The sacred story from the Bible is appropriated by, and retold through, the experience of queer trauma and the quest for liberation and healing. As such, in the words of the anthropologist Michael Jackson, in the context of this project storytelling became 'a form of restorative praxis – of sharing one's experiences with others, of finding common ground, of coming out of the closet, of restoring one's place in the public sphere'.[17]

In the process of retelling the Bible story in a contemporary context and from the perspective of participants' life experiences, we adopted creative methods of community-based theatre, with participants enacting the story in a drama play. This is inspired by recent scholarship on art and trauma in Africa, which emphasizes the important role that various forms of creative art – visual arts, literature, film, theatre and so on – can play in 'working through trauma, and ultimately enabling forgiveness, reconciliation and healing'.[18] This is as relevant in societies coming to terms with histories of social and political violence, such as post-apartheid South Africa and post-genocide Rwanda, as it is for communities that have been particularly affected by multilayered trauma, such as women who have experienced sexual and gender-based violence, LGBT+ people who have experienced various forms of queer-phobic violence, and refugee communities who have experienced profound displacement and disorientation. In our project, Ugandan LGBT+ refugees engaged in performative art, playing out the retellings of the Bible stories. The creative and collective process of reading their experiences into the biblical text, transforming the biblical text into a story about themselves, and enacting this new story, opened up a space in which they could work through trauma and engage in a restorative and healing praxis.

The Daniel story as an interface

In the first stage of the project, where we undertook life-story interviews, we asked participants about their favourite story in the Bible.[19] Two of them, independently of each other, mentioned the story of Daniel in the lions' den. The book of Daniel is part of the Old Testament (or Hebrew Bible), and narrates the story of Daniel, a young man from Jerusalem in Judah, who has been taken into captivity in Babylon, Persia, after the Babylonian king had successfully besieged Jerusalem and defeated the king of Judah. Daniel is one of the young men who, on the basis of their intellect and handsome looks, are selected to be trained in the royal court. Much of the book is about how he and his companions try to navigate their new environment while maintaining their faith in the God of Israel and following Jewish religious laws. Daniel excels and is appointed by King Darius to one of the highest offices in the country, as one of three regional governors. His political rivals are jealous and set up a trap, persuading Darius to sign a decree prohibiting any citizen from worshipping anyone but the king himself. They then report Daniel for praying to his God, and the king has no choice but to throw him in the lions' den. Thanks to the protection of an angel sent by God, Daniel survives the lions' den and is restored to his position. His accusers are thrown into the lions' den instead, and King Darius rules that from then on, everyone in his kingdom should worship the God of Daniel.

The book of Daniel has been interpreted by scholars through the lens of psychological and spiritual trauma as a text that reflects and processes the 'historical events of war, destruction and exile that traumatized the Jewish people'.[20] Most likely unaware of these academic interpretations, the two just-mentioned participants did refer to Daniel in the lions' den not only as their favourite Bible story, but as a story they recognized themselves in as LGBT+ refugees. When the story was subsequently selected to use in a contextual and creative Bible study session, participants collectively explored the moments of recognition and identification. They read and retold it from their own perspective, which turned out to be very productive because, as one group member put it, 'Daniel's story is a backdrop against which we can see many of our life experiences.' Virtually all participants automatically identified themselves with the character of Daniel in the story. The identifications were multiple. Daniel's living in exile mapped on to their situation as refugees, having left their home country and having to navigate and adjust to the circumstances in a foreign land. Daniel being intelligent and successful in his career was sometimes related to their past situation in Uganda, for instance by the participant who referred to himself as being 'of good standing' by virtue of his family background and level of education; others related it to the situation in Kenya where some participants, in spite of the hardship, felt they had become relatively successful, for instance as activists and community organizers; yet for others it was aspirational, as they expressed the hope to become successful professionally after being resettled in a third country. Daniel's commitment to his faith in spite of the pressure was interpreted as him 'staying true to who he was', which participants applied to their own commitment to owning a sexual and gender identity that puts them at odds with society and comes at a risk. Daniel's fellow governors plotting against him also offered a moment of recognition, as the governors were identified with politicians and clergy who are pushing the anti-homosexual tendencies in Uganda, as well as with community leaders, family members and relatives perpetuating queer-phobic hatred and violence. The experience of becoming the victim of a newly imposed law and being persecuted on the basis of it provided participants with another basis for identifying with Daniel, and they quickly associated the decree signed by King Darius with the Ugandan Anti-Homosexuality Bill that had been passed through the Ugandan parliament and had been signed into law by President Museveni. Several of these points are captured in the following reflection by one of the participants, a young trans woman called Tina:

> Daniel in the story became the victim of the new law. … Let me take you back to 2014 when the President of Uganda signed the Bill. We LGBTI became the victims. We started advocating for our rights. We stood for our rights. No matter what, we stood for our rights. We do not just come out to pretend; it is who we are, it is our nature. The same applies to Daniel. Daniel also stood by what he knew best and this is shown when he believes he was serving a living God and refused to serve any other being. This applies to us. We have to be true to ourselves. No matter what comes out, we have to be true to what we are. To Daniel God was natural, and for us to be who we are is our natural way so we have to stand by it.[21]

Clearly, the story of Daniel serves as a rich interface offering participants multiple and overlapping points of identification. In this process of engaging, appropriating and retelling the story, it was in particular the lions' den that became the focal point of recognition, as it metaphorically mapped on participants' experiences of trauma. Daniel's liberation from this place of life-threatening danger reinforced the hope and faith of participants that God will come to their rescue too.

The lions' den as a metaphor of trauma

Most participants spatially associated the lions' den with Uganda, the home country they had left behind in search for safety, but it was also associated with Kenya, the country where they had sought refuge but continued to experience hardship. The drama play that resulted from the creative Bible study offered a political re-retelling of the Bible story in contemporary Uganda.[22] It centred around the passing of the Anti-Homosexuality Bill, which was at the heart of what has been described as the 'Uganda homophobia spectacle'.[23] King Darius became President Museveni (who in the play has the First Lady seated next to him, dressed in a regal robe while the president wears a crown, as if they are monarchs). The governors and advisers to the king became members of the cabinet, MPs and religious leaders persuading an initially reluctant president to sign the AHB into law. Daniel became an LGBT+ rights activist who also was an adviser to the president, but whose minority opinion was shouted down by the other advisers, and who is arrested and thrown into prison soon after the passing of the AHB. The decision of the group to centre the play around the passing of the AHB was not just inspired by the obvious association of the decree in the Bible story with the AHB, but also by the very real impact that the Bill, and its surrounding socio-political climate, had had on the lives of participants. As one of them, Doreen, recounted:

> So, beginning school in January 2014, people came back from the Christmas holiday, and they were all thinking about this topic, 'the Gay Bill' that had been passed. Everyone came back with a story to tell: 'In my village two were beaten...'; 'in our church, two were beaten...'; 'in our home, this happened...'; 'when we were going to our Christmas function, this happened to some gay person...' I felt that guilt all the time, every time I would hear that: I felt that they were talking about me, because you relate to the situation, you feel like it's you. It was tormenting me... So, I failed to continue with school.[24]

Not only did Doreen quit school, she also experienced increasing pressure from her family. Referring to local media publishing highly sensitized reports about 'the threat' of gay people in Uganda, and publishing lists of 'top homosexuals', she recalled:

> Pictures from the gay community started being put in the tabloids. You'd find coverage in the newspapers, online, on TV stations. All the time, everything and everyone was talking about that and it became the atmosphere we were in. So you'd find yourself in one day, having three or four members of your family telling you, 'Uhh, you're so weird, you behave the same way as those people behave.' You know? And for me, I had lived my whole life trying to escape that kind of attention.[25]

It was in this environment that Doreen and many other LGBT+ Ugandans decided that the climate had become too toxic and the pressure too much, feeling no other option but to escape. Uganda, to them, had become like a lions' den, with their own parents and siblings, classmates and community members acting like lions attacking them in the form of everyday abuse, harassment and violence. Some participants associated the lions with the police, narrating their experiences of being persecuted and arrested, spending days if not weeks in police cells without formal charges being made, being subjected to humiliating anal examination or otherwise being physically tortured.

Having fled from Uganda, and finding themselves now in Kenya, participants were quick to admit that life there was far from easy either and they agreed that Kenya too could be seen as a lions' den. In particular the Kakuma refugee camp was mentioned in this regard – an official UNHCR-run camp in the north-western part of Kenya, it houses tens of thousands of refugees, mostly from Somalia and South Sudan. Several participants had spent some time there and recalled their traumatic experiences: added to overcrowded accommodation and semi-desert-like weather conditions, as LGBT+ people they experienced aggression and harassment from queer-phobic fellow refugees, camp guards and police officers. Although participants agreed that the Nairobi urban area was a much better place to live, especially thanks to the work of community-based organizations such as the Nature Network that provide shelter and support, each of them had their own stories about the challenges and hardship they experienced there too. As one of them, Sulah, simply put it, 'Yeah, the lions' den is also in Kenya because it is an environment you are not used to and yet you find yourself in here and have to manage.'[26] These words capture the trauma of being a refugee in a foreign land, which is as much about navigating very practical but real challenges – linguistic, cultural, social and economic – as about the existential experience of displacement, disorientation and alienation that comes with it. One participant, Shamuran, tellingly described his situation by invoking the biblical story of the expulsion from the Garden of Eden (Genesis 2—3): 'I feel connected to Adam and Eve. Like them, I was living in the garden of heaven, that's my home, but after my parents found out that I'm gay, which they believe to be evil, I was chased away.'[27] Most literally this quotation illustrates the point made by Jackson, about refugee stories that 'typically juxtapose nightmarish recollections of flight and nostalgic images of Paradise Lost'.[28] Yet in this case it is not so much the flight itself but the tough life as a refugee that is juxtaposed to childhood and youth memories of home. The trauma is ongoing, indeed.

Clearly, participants mapped their life experiences as LGBT+ refugees in many different ways on to the Bible story, which illustrates the multiplicity of trauma that the lions' den came to represent. However, they recognized themselves in the story, not just because of their own traumatic experiences, but also because the story mapped on to their experiences of, and hope for, liberation and healing.

Daniel's story as a source of hope and healing

Daniel survived the lions' den, according to the Bible story, thanks to the intervention of an angel sent by God, after which the king released him from the den and restored him to his position of authority. This good ending of the story (for Daniel at least, not for his rivals who had schemed against him and who ended up in the lions' den instead, together with their families) was interpreted by participants in two ways: partly they related it to their own experiences of survival and liberation, and partly it reinforced their hope for future deliverance. One might say that as much as their trauma is everyday and ongoing, so is their healing and liberation – with both experiences running alongside each other because trauma and healing coexist rather than the latter simply succeeding the former.

Where Uganda was associated with the lions' den, the escape from Uganda into the relative safety of Kenya was seen as one way in which their own experience as refugees mapped on to the story of Daniel's rescue. And where Kenya was also identified as a possible lions' den, especially by participants who had spent time in the Kakuma camp, the experience of now living in 'better off' Nairobi and participating in self-help community empowerment groups, was also related to Daniel's liberation. As Tigan, who first mentioned the Daniel story as his favourite Bible story, reflected:

> Like Daniel, we have survived a lot, and we are still around, we are surviving, we didn't die when we went through persecution, blackmailing, sex work, and now we are here. There used to be a time I needed someone to talk to, but right now there are people who come to me and be like, 'Tigan, I need to talk to you, this and this is happening, I have got some issues.' And then I can advise them. I feel like we haven't been eaten yet. And I don't think we shall be eaten by any lions. Daniel was protected, you can imagine. And I feel like there's a very big ray of hope; I know we are still going through it all, but there's a very big ray of hope.[29]

This rich quotation contains multiple relevant elements. Tigan reads his own transformation, from a refugee who needed help from others to someone who is now a community leader himself, into Daniel's transformation from being an exile to being in a position of power. He further reads his experiences of surviving the hardship he and other refugees have faced, both back home in Uganda and in Kenya, into Daniel's experience of 'not being eaten', and the Bible story reinforces his hope – or call it faith – that 'we shall not be eaten' at all. He acknowledges that 'we are still going through it' – the lions' den is still real, trauma is everyday and ongoing – yet the story inspires him to imagine a different future, not just of survival but of prosperity:

The homophobic people in Uganda, our families – I don't hate my family at all, because they don't know, they are ignorant about it all – they threw us into the lions' den. But by the time they will come to check on us, we shall be prosperous, we shall still be here, we shall be alive, because God loves us.[30]

The story of Daniel's rescue from the lions' den was related by quite a number of participants to their possible future resettlement in a third country, for which they were in the process with UNHCR. The following account, from Isaac, is illustrative here:

Personally the best rescue mission is when you're given the opportunity to leave the lions' den. It feels like one day waking up and being resettled to a country where you are given another chance to breathe, maybe to get married and have a family together. Also to have a second chance in life to smile, because we are always happy but internally there is always fear because we are still in the lions' den. But one day you wake up and they say you're being resettled to a particular country where there is protection, there are laws that protect you and allow you to have a private life that is enjoyable; and maybe for those who are interested in politics also to engage in law-making and law implementation. So for me seeing Daniel leave the den, I can say even me at one point I will be out.[31]

The resettlement process is rather slow – many participants have seen their cases in the pipeline for years – and the outcome remains uncertain. There have been numerous incidents of LGBT+ refugees protesting at the premises of UNHCR against the draining process and the lack of economic support. In a drama early in 2020, one refugee committed suicide by hanging himself in front of the UNHCR office in Nairobi. In spite of this, one participant, Tina, identified the UN body responsible for their well-being and for managing their resettlement with the angel in the Bible story:

Even when governments have disowned us, for the UNHCR we are still their people, they see us as human beings. If it were not for the UNHCR we would not have been here. The Kenyan government would not have allowed us. Even when the government says they do not want us, the UNHCR advocates for us.[32]

Most participants, however, did not pay too much attention to the role of the angel in the story, and instead directly focused on God as the intervening actor coming to Daniel's rescue. They applied that to themselves, testifying how they had experienced God's support in past situations of adversity, and expressing faith that God would continue to sustain them and come to their rescue again. As Sulah put it:

The story showed me that no matter what challenges we go through, God will see us through. There is always a light at the end of the tunnel. We have been challenged but at the end of the day, God will see us through. We are just having some blows ... They call them difficult times of life, but at the end of the day you will push through, God will see you through.[33]

The belief that God will help them through whatever challenges they face is reinforced by the work that virtually all participants have had to do in reimagining God. As the Ghanaian theologian Mercy Oduyoye points out, 'Re-imagining God is an exercise that all African Christians have been forced to go through.'[34] She makes this comment in relation to the history of European imperialism and missionary Christianity, which imposed a white and patriarchal concept of God that African Christians, and in particular women, needed to deconstruct and reimagine. The point is perhaps even truer for African LGBT+ Christians in contemporary society, as many churches are explicitly perpetuating the (equally European colonial) idea that queer sexuality – 'sodomy' – is an abomination, thus instilling feelings of inferiority and guilt in the people concerned. Working through, and overcoming such feelings, several participants testified to have rediscovered God as a God of acceptance and love – not despite, but in recognition of, their sexuality because it is part of how God created them. As Chris put it:

God knew us, God oriented us before even those [queer-phobic] people knew us, before even my parents, before even my mother, before even anyone knew me... God knew that this one was going to be a gay ... an LGBTI ... No matter what they do, no matter what they say, God will come and rescue us.[35]

What, then, is the nature of God's intervention?

In the drama play, Daniel the gay activist is rescued from prison after the president nullifies the AHB. This somewhat mirrors events in Uganda where the Anti-Homosexuality Act was nullified by the Constitutional Court, six months after it had been passed through parliament. When Daniel is released, he shouts, 'God has helped me', while his fellow LGBT+ activists rejoice and celebrate his liberation. This happy ending of the play does not neatly map on to developments in Uganda where also after the formal nullification of the Act, LGBT+ people continued to suffer from stigmatization, marginalization, harassment and violence, and where the threat of a revised AHB being introduced remains real. Of course, participants were aware of this, otherwise they would not have been refugees in Kenya. However, writing the script of the play enabled them to rewrite history, and performing the play enabled them to inhabit this alternative possibility. It is one illustration of how storytelling as a creative process can offer a space for healing.

Interestingly, God is not prominently present in the drama play. The voice of God is only heard at the beginning and at the end of the play. At the beginning, a deep, dark voice recites the words, 'I am God. I am a living

God. I am omnipresent. I am a merciful God. I am love'; at the end, the same voice concludes, 'I am a living God. I rule for ever. My power will not come to an end. I save and rescue. I saved Daniel from prison.' Perhaps this format – God as a voice-over in the play – illustrates how participants experience the reality of God in their lives: present in the background as a supporting and comforting force rather than as a directly intervening power. This is further illustrated in the video recording of the drama play, where the editor (who had been a participant in the whole process) added a Buganda gospel song under the footage of Daniel in prison. The lyrics are translated as: 'Let's not easily forget that he [God] feels whatever we feel. God never tries us beyond what we can do or manage.'

Conclusion

This chapter has built on traditions in African religious and theological scholarship that engage the Bible as a resource for addressing and healing trauma. Where African women's biblical hermeneutics have appropriated the Bible specifically in relation to women's experiences of trauma, this chapter has widened the scope and potential of this methodology, applying it to LGBT+ communities and their trauma as a result of social and political anti-queer attitudes and aggression. In particular, the story of Daniel in the lions' den has proved to be a rich interface to explore and narrate the experiences of multiple, everyday and ongoing trauma of Ugandan LGBT+ refugees, as well as their experiences of liberation and healing. The book of Daniel being a story about psychological and spiritual trauma, it appeared to offer multiple opportunities for participants to recognize themselves in and identify with. However, there is an abundance of other stories in the Bible that have great potential in this regard. For instance, as part of the same project, we also used the story of Jesus and the 'woman caught in adultery' (John 8.1–11), which turned out to be particularly productive for exploring the trauma of stigmatization and community violence.[36] Especially in societies where the Bible is widely known and is held in high esteem because of its status as sacred Scripture, such as in many parts of Africa, methods of creative and contextual Bible study through storytelling and drama, such as used here, have a great potential for engendering healing of trauma. As mentioned earlier, neither trauma nor healing should be considered as an event. They are everyday and ongoing, and often coexist alongside each other. Part of the healing that participants in this project experienced was through the move of reclaiming the Bible – a book that is often used against them, but that they now discovered is actually about them and their lives, and maps on to their challenges and struggles but also their quest for survival and liberation. As the two community leaders who served as research assistants, and who had facilitated the Bible study session, reflected afterwards:

The session allowed us to like the Bible again. There were remarks from some who said they did not know the Old Testament had something that could relate to them. But the session allowed us to think deeply about the different causes of divisions among people which most times are based on prejudice and unfounded conclusions. The community needs sessions like these ones about the Bible and other religious books. Participants found hope and strength. They were able to turn around and find meaning from the Scriptures often used for preaching hate about them. They left knowing that there are rays of hope, opportunities for transformation and movers into their lives.[37]

This process of reclaiming the Bible, combined with creative storytelling methods, was clearly perceived as affirming and empowering, and thus healing. As Jackson suggests, 'Re-presenting traumatic events as a story is a kind of redemption, for one both subverts the power of the original events to determine one's experience of them, and one moves beyond the self into what Buber calls an essential-we relationship.'[38] The point made here may hold particular truth in relation to biblical stories and other sacred Scripture, as it allows for the mapping of stories of divine redemption on to the lives of those reading themselves into it and appropriating it. As one of the participants, Chris, concluded after the session about Daniel in the lions' den: 'Yes this story inspires so much. God loves all of us. The Bible strengthens you to have that faith.'[39]

Finally, writing about women's readings of the Bible in a quest for healing, Musa Dube has commented: 'If African churches and communities are spaces where some members are silenced, then they deny themselves the ministry of healing and birthing hope from persistent traumatic processes.'[40] As much as this applies to the silencing of women, it applies to the silencing of LGBT+ people. Not only do these churches and communities deny themselves the ministry of engendering healing from trauma, they also deny themselves the opportunity to learn from the grassroots narrative theologies of survival and redemption, or simply, theologies of life powerfully captured in these words of faith: 'We shall not be eaten by any lions.' Anyone watching the drama play, 'Daniel in the homophobic Lion's Den', can witness how these theologies are embodied and lived in the midst of ongoing trauma and the quest for healing.

Acknowledgement

This publication is an output of the project 'Tales of Sexuality and Faith: The Ugandan LGBT Refugees Life Story Project', funded by the British Academy and The Leverhulme Trust (award SRG1819\190405). In this project I collaborated with Johanna Stiebert (University of Leeds) as co-investigator, and with Hudson Fredrick and Sebyala Brian from the Nature Network (Matasia, Nairobi, Kenya) as local research coordinators. I am grateful to them for the very stimulating collaboration, and to all participants for sharing their stories and contributing to the process of creative and contextual Bible study.

Bibliography

Bisschoff, Lizelle and Stefanie van de Peer, 'Representing the Unrepresentable' in *Art and Trauma in Africa: Representations of Reconciliation in Music, Visual Arts, Literature and Film*, ed. Lizelle Bisschoff and Stefanie van de Peer, London: I. B. Tauris, 2013, pp. 3–27.

Cvetkovich, Ann, *An Archive of Feelings: Trauma, Sexuality, and Lesbian Public Cultures*, Durham, NC: Duke University Press, 2003.

Dube, Musa W., 'Introduction' in *Other Ways of Reading: African Women and the Bible*, ed. Musa W. Dube, Atlanta, GA: Society of Biblical Literature, 2001, pp. 1–19.

Dube, Musa W., 'The Cry of Rachel: African Women's Reading of the Bible for Healing' in *The Healing of Memories: African Christian Responses to Politically Induced Trauma*, ed. Mohamed Girma, Lanham, MD: Lexington Books, 2018, pp. 115–35.

Edmondson, Laura, *Performing Trauma in Central Africa: Shadows of Empire*, Bloomington, IN: Indiana University Press, 2018.

Gabel, Stewart, 'The Book of Daniel: Trauma, Faith, and the Resurrection of the Dead', *Trauma and Memory* 4, 2 (2016), pp. 67–81.

Gunda, Masiiwa Ragies and Jim Naughton (eds), *On Sexuality and Scripture: Essays, Bible Studies, and Personal Reflections by the Chicago Consultation, the Ujamaa Centre, and Their Friends*, New York: Church Publishing, 2017.

Kintu, Deborah, *The Ugandan Morality Crusade: The Brutal Campaign against Homosexuality and Pornography under Yoweri Museveni*, Jefferson, NC: McFarland & Co., 2018.

Marnell, John, *Seeking Sanctuary: Stories of Sexuality, Faith and Migration*, Johannesburg: Wits University Press, 2021.

Mikya, Kenne, 'The Media, the Tabloid, and the Uganda Homophobia Spectacle' in *Queer African Reader*, ed. Sokari Ekine and Hakima Abbas, Dakar: Pambazuka Press, 2013, pp. 141–54.

Oduyoye, Mercy, *Introducing African Women's Theology*, Cleveland, OH: The Pilgrim Press, 2001.

Stone-Mediatore, Shari, *Reading Across Borders: Storytelling and Knowledges of Resistance*, New York: Palgrave Macmillan, 2003.

van Klinken, Adriaan and Tom Muyunga-Mukasa, '"Accused of a Sodomy Act": Bible, Queer Poetry and African Narrative Hermeneutics', *Journal for Interdisciplinary Biblical Studies* 2, 2 (2021), pp. 25–46.

van Klinken, Adriaan and Johanna Stiebert, with Sebyala Brian and Fredrick Hudson, *Sacred Queer Stories: Ugandan LGBTQ+ Refugee Lives and the Bible*, Suffolk: James Currey, 2021.

West, Gerald O., *The Academy of the Poor: Towards a Dialogical Reading of the Bible*, Sheffield: Continuum, 1999.

West, Gerald O., *The Stolen Bible: From Tool of Imperialism to African Icon*, Leiden: Brill, 2016.

Notes

1 Lesbian, Gay, Bisexual, Transgender and related communities.

2 Interview with Tigan, Nairobi, 15 September 2019. For the full version of Tigan's story, see Adriaan van Klinken and Johanna Stiebert, with Sebyala Brian and Fredrick Hudson, *Sacred Queer Stories: Ugandan LGBTQ+ Refugee Lives and the Bible* (Suffolk: James Currey, 2021), pp. 41–51.

3 See Deborah Kintu, *The Ugandan Morality Crusade: The Brutal Campaign against Homosexuality and Pornography under Yoweri Museveni* (Jefferson, NC: McFarland & Co., 2018).

4 Ann Cvetkovich, *An Archive of Feelings: Trauma, Sexuality, and Lesbian Public Cultures* (Durham, NC: Duke University Press, 2003), p. 33.

5 Interview with Raymond Brian, Nairobi, 15 September 2019.

6 Michael Rothberg, 'Decolonizing Trauma Studies: A Response', *Studies in the Novel* 40, 1/2 (2008), pp. 224–34; Abigail Ward, 'Introduction' in *Postcolonial Traumas: Memory, Narrative, Resistance*, ed. Abigail Ward (New York: Palgrave Macmillan, 2015), pp. 1–13.

7 Rahul Rao, *Out of Time: The Queer Politics of Postcoloniality* (New York: Oxford University Press, 2020), p. 215.

8 Rao, *Out of Time*, p. 55.

9 See van Klinken et al., *Sacred Queer Stories*. Our methodology was broadly inspired by Contextual Bible Study methods as developed at the Ujaama Centre of the University of KwaZulu-Natal, South Africa, which we adapted to include creative life-story telling and community-based theatre methods.

10 Gerald West, *The Stolen Bible: From Tool of Imperialism to African Icon* (Leiden: Brill, 2016).

11 Musa W. Dube, 'The Cry of Rachel: African Women's Reading of the Bible for Healing' in *The Healing of Memories: African Christian Responses to Politically Induced Trauma*, ed. Mohamed Girma (Lanham, MD: Lexington Books, 2018), p. 117.

12 Dube, 'The Cry of Rachel', p. 115.

13 Musa W. Dube, 'Introduction' in *Other Ways of Reading: African Women and the Bible*, ed. Musa W. Dube (Atlanta, GA: Society of Biblical Literature, 2001), pp. 3–10.

14 For example, see Masiiwa Ragies Gunda and Jim Naughton (eds), *On Sexuality and Scripture: Essays, Bible Studies, and Personal Reflections by the Chicago Consultation, the Ujamaa Centre, and Their Friends* (New York: Church Publishing, 2017).

15 Inspired by Gerald O. West, *The Academy of the Poor: Towards a Dialogical Reading of the Bible* (Sheffield: Continuum, 1999).

16 Shari Stone-Mediatore, *Reading Across Borders: Storytelling and Knowledges of Resistance* (New York: Palgrave Macmillan, 2003). For an example in a contemporary African queer context, see John Marnell, *Seeking Sanctuary: Stories of Sexuality, Faith and Migration* (Johannesburg: Wits University Press, 2021).

17 Michael Jackson, *The Politics of Storytelling: Variations on a Theme by Hannah Arendt* (Copenhagen: Museum Tusculanum Press, 2013), p. 23.

18 Lizelle Bisschoff and Stefanie van de Peer, 'Representing the Unrepresentable' in *Art and Trauma in Africa: Representations of Reconciliation in Music, Visual Arts, Literature and Film*, ed. Lizelle Bisschoff and Stefanie van de Peer (London:

I. B. Tauris, 2013), p. 6. Also see Laura Edmondson, *Performing Trauma in Central Africa: Shadows of Empire* (Bloomington, IN: Indiana University Press, 2018).

19 In addition to Johanna Stiebert and myself, interviews were also conducted by our two local research coordinators, Hudson Fredrick and Sebyala Brian. Interviewees are referred to by their names and pronouns of preference.

20 Stewart Gabel, 'The Book of Daniel: Trauma, Faith, and the Resurrection of the Dead', *Trauma and Memory* 4, 2 (2016), p. 67.

21 Interview with Tina, Nairobi, 15 January 2010.

22 The drama play was performed and video recorded and can be watched on YouTube. See The Nature Network, 'Daniel in the homophobic Lion's Den', *YouTube*, 24 January 2020, www.youtube.com/watch?v=-oj9xq6xX8c&t=745s, accessed 8.9.2021.

23 Kenne Mikya, 'The Media, the Tabloid, and the Uganda Homophobia Spectacle' in *Queer African Reader*, ed. Sokari Ekine and Hakima Abbas (Dakar: Pambazuka Press, 2013), pp. 141–54.

24 Interview with Doreen, Nairobi, 21 September 2019.

25 Interview with Doreen.

26 Interview with Sulah, Nairobi, 15 January 2020.

27 Interview with Shamuran, Nairobi, 22 September 2019.

28 Jackson, *The Politics of Storytelling*, p. 103.

29 Interview with Tigan, Nairobi, 15 September 2019.

30 Interview with Tigan.

31 Interview with Isaac, Nairobi, 15 January 2020.

32 Interview with Tina, Nairobi, 15 January 2020.

33 Interview with Sulah, Nairobi, 15 January 2020.

34 Mercy Oduyoye, *Introducing African Women's Theology* (Cleveland, OH: The Pilgrim Press, 2001), p. 39.

35 Interview with Chris, Nairobi, 15 January 2020.

36 See Adriaan van Klinken and Tom Muyunga-Mukasa, '"Accused of a Sodomy Act": Bible, Queer Poetry and African Narrative Hermeneutics', *Journal for Interdisciplinary Biblical Studies* 2, 2 (2021), pp. 25–46.

37 Hudson Fredrick and Sebyala Brian, reflective report, February 2020.

38 Jackson, *The Politics of Storytelling*, p. 73.

39 Interview with Chris, Nairobi, 15 January 2020.

40 Dube, 'The Cry of Rachel', p. 130.

8

Un(en)titled? Cissexism, Masculinity and Sexual Violence: Towards a Transfeminist Theological Hermeneutic Beyond Repair

BRANDY DANIELS AND MICAH CRONIN

Late summer of 2018, an article ran in *The New York Times* with the headline: 'What Happens to #MeToo When a Feminist is the Accused?'. The splashy headline in the form of a provocative, and curious, question brought to light a story that had been unfolding for almost a year (or, depending on when you start the timeline, well over a year) – Avital Ronell, a renowned professor of German and Comparative Literature at New York University, was found responsible for sexually harassing a former graduate student, Nimrod Reitman. *Reported* incidents of sexual harassment by a professor to a graduate student are, tragically, too common to be the occasion of a feature or even story in *The New York Times* (even as they are exceedingly rare in proportion to the number of incidents of sexual harassment of students by professors as a whole).[1] This story stood out, though. The scholarly stature of Ronell certainly contributed, as did the inverted gender power dynamics at play. But two things really made this story a news story. The first 'alleged twist', as *The Atlantic* put it, had to do with further complexities in the power dynamics and identity politics at play in the case.[2] Not only was the perpetrator a female and the victim a male, but Ronell identifies as a lesbian and Reitman, as a gay man. What do we make of the gay man who was sexually harassed by a lesbian? Is such a thing even *possible*?

The second aspect of this case that played a key role in its garnering national popular media attention had to do with the showing of support for Ronell among her peers – particularly the support by feminist theorists. A group of renowned scholars had crafted a letter to the president and provost of NYU in support of Ronell, expressing their 'profound and enduring admiration for Professor Ronell whose mentorship of students has been no less than remarkable over many years. We deplore the damage that this legal proceeding causes her', they continue, explaining that they 'seek to register in clear terms [their] objection to any judgement against her'.[3] First among the signatories was the esteemed feminist theorist Judith Butler, whose work has taken seriously the often subtle and overlooked violence effected by the productive functions of power.[4] The fact that Butler, whose work has consistently and capaciously probed the analytics around 'whose lives are considered valuable, whose lives are mourned, and whose lives are considered ungrievable' was not only a signatory but presumably spearheaded the letter of support despite admitting to 'hav[ing] no access to the confidential dossier' of the harassment charges, shocked and dismayed many, particularly those doing feminist scholarship around sexual violence and trauma.[5]

This painful and problematic story and its particularities are not the subject of this chapter, and are largely beyond the scope of it. We begin with this case, however, because many of the questions and themes it raises are, and point to, questions and themes that this chapter aims to illuminate and engage. Who is recognized as victims/survivors of sexual violence, and who is not? What are the factors that delimit that (un)recognizability, and what is the impact of it on those who are not recognized – how do our hermeneutical lenses, our epistemic frames, engender further trauma for the marginalized of the marginalized? And moreover, how does that unrecognizability not only harm those who have experienced the trauma of sexual violence, but also harm the very scholarship that aims to better understand, address and minimize/decrease (and ultimately/in an ideal world, utterly eliminate) sexual violence and the trauma that such violence engenders?

In this chapter, we consider how feminist scholarship that focuses on sexual violence – and, importantly, feminist trauma theologies that do so – either explicitly or implicitly focus on female survivors of (presumptively cis) male violence. While this is an understandable, and indeed valuable, focus, we explore the impacts of the significant occlusion of (trans)gender difference in that focus and analysis – an occlusion that we identify and name, following Julia Serano, as cissexism – both on (trans) male survivors of sexual violence, and on the analytical and liberative aims of feminist trauma studies and theologies. From there, we turn to the queer theorist and theologian Kent Brintnall's exploration of 'the male-body-in-pain as redemptive figure' as constructive resources for a trans feminist trauma theology.[6] Placing Brintnall in conversation with Serano's identification and critique of cissexism, we argue that a hermeneutic that decentres hegemonic masculinity is pivotal for a robust, trans feminist trauma theology, and suggest a turn to trans masculine experiences of sexual violence as a crucial lens.

While the focus of this chapter is largely methodological – critically examining and constructively (re)considering the nature and scope of feminist scholarship and trauma theologies surrounding sexual violence vis-à-vis transmasculine experiences – we conclude by reflecting not only on what this methodological intervention is in service of (the reduction of trauma), but also how it might be of service to and for survivors of sexual violence.

We consider the post-traumatic possibilities of a hermeneutic of subjugated masculinities. Building on Brintnall, we begin to consider the post-traumatic potential of an *ante*-reparative transfeminist trauma theology, one in which subjugated masculinity is beyond repair. This potential, we argue, while beyond repair, also paradoxically opens up liberative possibilities towards post-traumatic flourishing.

What do we make of the raped trans man?

What do we make of the raped trans man? This essay considers this question. Wrapped up in this question, though, are a range of both explicit and implicit presuppositions: that trans men are raped, that this violence has occurred to a degree that we can and/or should make something of it, and finally, that we have not quite yet made something of it – at least not enough of a something.

The troubling tale of Avital Ronnell (or, rather, the tragic tale of Nimrod Reitman?), as noted above, is instructive, as it highlights theory's – and *theorists'* – limits and failures when the context falls or moves outside the field of recognition. We began with it for that reason, despite the fact that the context, a gay cis man who was the victim of extensive sexual harassment that at times may have moved into the territory of assault, differs from that of our inquiry, the raped trans man.

While contextually distinctive, there are also overlaps – not only threads that serve as bridges, but ways in which the contexts are entangled at points: threads of gender, norms of masculinity, the genders and sexualities that are read as constituting a threat to masculinity, and so on. These threads, among others, and their entanglements, are what constitute the unrecognizability of these categories of victims/survivors.

It was actually this shared unrecognizability, these entanglements across and between contexts, that incited this collaborative inquiry. Given our shared academic interests and shared justice commitments, we occasionally share and discuss relevant news stories via text. A *Chronicle of Higher Ed* story about Ronnell's return to NYU after her year-long suspension was shared in our text thread. Following a lengthy rant from Brandy about the inadequacies of the Title IX process, Micah then reflected briefly on another difficult and underexplored aspect of sexual harassment and violence, the reality of (queer and/or trans) survivors.[7] 'When I was younger,' he wrote, 'I had the idea that transitioning, and blending in as a cis man, would keep me safe from this sort of thing. It has not.' Micah went on to talk about other trans men in his orbits who have had similar experiences, and mused that such experiences seem to occur not despite, but perhaps *because* of, the trans and queer performance of masculinity. 'Feminism and theology haven't given me the tools to understand that', he noted. This chapter is our attempt, then, to wrestle with and reckon with these concerns Micah expressed, and we hope, to begin to identify and/or build such tools for better understanding and response.

So to return to, and begin to parse out, the question and its presuppositions: *What do we make of the raped trans man?* While frequently unrecognized, the reality of sexual violence against trans men is very real. Statistics documenting transgender people's experience of sexual violence indicate shockingly high levels of sexual assault and abuse. According to the US Department of Justice's Office for Victims of Crimes, nearly 50 per cent of transgender people are sexually abused or assaulted at some point in their lives, and some reports estimate that transgender survivors may experience rates of sexual assault up to 66 per cent, often coupled with physical assaults or abuse.[8]

The impact of sexual violence on transgender people is significant, and has led to higher rates of homelessness and incarceration as well as educational and economic disparities – all of which makes transgender individuals more susceptible to further sexual violence.[9] Sexual violence has been identified as one of the major contributing factors to the astoundingly high rate of suicidality among transgender individuals – 41 per cent of trans people have reported attempting suicide (for comparison, less than two per cent of the general population has attempted suicide), and of that 41 per cent, 64 per cent had reported surviving sexual assault.[10]

But – again – what, in particular, do we make of the raped trans *man?* In a fair number of the studies that have explored sexual violence against transgender people, gender identity was not part of the data collected or analysed. Of those studies that do take gender identity into consideration, many of them point to only slightly higher rates of sexual violence among trans women.[11] And one recent national (US) study showed that that trans men were actually *more* likely to be survivors of adult sexual assault (31 per cent) than trans women (28 per cent).[12]

Given the tragedies and the trauma that these statistics represent and point to, we should indeed make *something* of the raped trans man. By this, we (the authors of this chapter) mean that, to and for and with regards to the trans men who are victimized by sexual violence, there should be some level of acknowledgement, attention and response – by society as a whole, by feminist scholars who contend with and address sexual violence and, notably, by feminist theorists and theologians who contend with and address sexual violence as it relates to and in conversation with theories and experiences of trauma.

Yet the literature that addresses trans men's experiences of sexual violence is notably sparse. The emerging and still very nascent analysis on *why* this is the case is, well, nascent; it is complex, and it is by no means singular. Some have emphasized how the prevalence of male *perpetrators* of sexual violence has occluded attention to male victims – an occlusion that, while understandable to most, is problematic for some, and for others, is at least somewhat justified.[13] Others have pointed to the alarming rates of hate crimes against trans people, especially hate crimes that result in death. Given that trans women (and particularly trans women of colour) are far more at risk of physical violence and murder than trans men or gender non-binary people, attention within trans studies and to the trans community has understandably been focused there first, as a matter of urgency.[14] Others still have considered how men's experience of sexual violence has been controversial, as, at least to some extent, 'struggles over framings and knowledge feed into antifeminist movements and masculinist politics around issues of intimate partner violence'.[15] Trans men, by this account, carry a kind of privilege (dependent on their level of passing) that must be acknowledged, and, at the same time, their experiences problematically get subsumed into dominant narratives despite their differences.[16]

Attempting any kind of comprehensive picture of the reasons for this lack is beyond the scope of this chapter. Rather, we aim to identify and illuminate just *a* reason, one 'why' amid many: the distinct form of prejudice and discrimination that Julia Serano identifies as cissexism.[17] Homing in on this 'why', one that is multiple and complex in its own right, we highlight its delimiting impact on feminist trauma theology, loosely sketch a potential alternative hermeneutic of subjugated masculinities, and consider the *ante*-reparative impact of this revised hermeneutic on, and of, trans men who have survived sexual violence.

Cissexism, sexual violence and feminist theologies

While (feminist) literature on sexual violence among trans men is notably sparse overall, within feminist theologies, it is nearly non-existent. The prevailing norm within feminist scholarship on sexual violence, and particularly in feminist trauma theologies addressing sexual violence, is an emphasis on (presumably, but not solely, cisgender) female victims/survivors of (presumably, but not solely, cisgender) male perpetrators. We offer just one very brief and particularly relevant example, found in *Feminist Trauma Theologies: Body, Scripture and Church in Critical Perspective*, the volume that precedes, and shares editors with, this one. In the Introduction, when outlining the organization of the volume, as is customary, Karen O'Donnell and Katie Cross explain that it is divided into sections on methods in feminist trauma theologies, on violence against women, on Christian communities and trauma, and on the modes of post-traumatic remaking with which the trauma survivor might engage. Woven in as a parenthetical, after naming the second section on violence against women, O'Donnell and Cross note that 'interestingly, almost all of the chapters could have gone into this section.'[18] *Feminist Trauma Theologies*, an important and rich text that makes significant contributions to the field and to the lives of those who have endured trauma, is emblematic of feminist trauma theologies in its emphasis on violence against women.

Given that nearly one in five women experience sexual assault at some points in their lives, compared to around one in 33 men, and given that over 97 per cent of the perpetrators are male, this emphasis within the literature is not only understandable but justified.[19] But what presumptions and norms might underlie or inadvertently develop from this emphasis within the field? And (how) do those undergirding presumptions and norms and inadvertent developments work to not only obscure other survivors of sexual violence, but actually bolster harmful logics that contribute to patriarchy and thus to sexual violence?

Feminist scholarship has long identified patriarchy as a, if not the, key factor in and feature of sexual violence, highlighting the cyclical relation between the two – patriarchy empowers and 'justifies' sexual violence, which functions to maintain patriarchy. This relation between patriarchy and sexual violence was a key emphasis of radical 'second wave' feminists in the 1970s and 80s and was bound up with gender roles and norms. The 'expectations the culture cherishes about his gender identity encourages the young male to develop aggressive impulses', Kate Millet writes.[20] Violence and sexual conquest, then, become male traits. This led to the development of the 'rape paradigm', centring on men's sexual violence against women as the foundational threat wielded by misogynistic, patriarchal power.[21] The nearly routine realities of sexual violence and the compounding harassment women experience, are part of a patriarchal system that is founded and fuelled by a structure of violent domination. As Catharine MacKinnon put it starkly: 'Man fucks woman; subject verb object.'[22] Given this reality, radical feminists have argued, it is thus rational and appropriate for women to harbour a basic mistrust of men.[23]

While the rape paradigm has importantly highlighted the pervasiveness of sexual violence, and the logic and operations of violence within a patriarchal system, it has been the subject of a range of critiques and corrections from feminists of colour, poststructuralist and queer perspectives.[24] Feminist scholarship, by including trauma theologies of sexual violence, has responded in turn in many ways, as this volume itself points to. One key critique proffered against this paradigm that has received little attention, particularly in theological literature, is its own reigning cissexism.

In her groundbreaking book, *Whipping Girl: A Transsexual Woman on Sexism and the Scapegoating of Femininity*, Julia Serano describes cissexism as 'the belief that transsexuals' identified genders are inferior to, or less authentic than, those of cissexuals (i.e., people who are not transsexual and who have only ever experienced their subconscious and physical sexes as being aligned)'.[25] A pivotal aspect or feature of cissexism, according to Serano, is cissexual/cisgender privilege – 'the double standard that promotes the idea that transexual genders are distinct from, and less legitimate than, cissexual genders'.[26] This privilege, when uninterrogated and taken for granted, leads to cissexual gender entitlement, and results in a range of cissexist behaviours, policies and norms. Serano outlines a range of impacts of this cissexual privilege and resultant cissexism, one of which is trans-erasure.[27] The impact of cissexism on trans men who are survivors of sexual violence is clear. As Michaela Rogers puts it, in discussing the particular context of intimate partner violence (IPV), the 'literature and evidence-base are largely rooted to a gender paradigm in which IPV predominantly occurs within a cisgendered and heterosexual context; that is, it is a problem of heterosexual male violence against heterosexual females'. As such, she notes, 'trans people are often invisible in official statistics' and in the theories and practices that look to those statistics.[28]

One key feature of cissexism is its presumption that all men are cis men and all masculinities are hegemonic masculinities. Feminist trauma theologies addressing sexual violence of course, and rightfully, highlight the prevalence of sexual violence perpetrated by cis men against women. They also importantly highlight, document and analyse links between hegemonic masculinity and the preservation and exercise of patriarchal power, as evidenced in the rape paradigm and its impact on feminist trauma theologies (and feminist trauma scholarship writ large). However, one of the things that our inquiry *What do we make of the raped trans man?* illuminates is that hegemonic masculinity and the preservation and exercise of patriarchal power is not delimited to violence against women, but that it also impacts and is linked to violence against trans men.[29] Yet there is a lack of attention and analytical precision around the role of *hegemonic* masculinity in patriarchal power and particularly with regards to sexual violence in feminist scholarship and theologies on and of trauma.

The practical theologian Danielle Tumminio Hansen points to this lack of analytical precision in our language and highlights its impact on survivors. In her essay 'Absent a Word: How the Language of Sexual Trauma Keeps Survivors Silent', Tumminio Hansen argues that the words we deploy to describe sexual trauma fail in their ability to represent the scope of the problem, and therefore negatively affect survivors' ability to articulate their experiences and integrate them as they live after the event(s). Among the range of terms that Tumminio Hansen critically interrogates are 'violence against women' and 'gender-based violence'. These terms, she explains, speak to the majority of survivors, but function to exclude in ways that harm already marginalized and traumatized individuals, as not all violence is done to women, nor is all violence undertaken by men.

Moreover, 'gender-based violence', a term that is used as a synonym for 'violence against women' while at the same time purporting a kind of inclusivity, further calcifies the notion that sexual violence is exclusively organized around the (cisgender, heterosexual) male perpetrator and the (cisgender) female victim, while obscuring that calcification under a veil of presumed inclusivity. Experiences that fall outside of that configuration, especially trans and gender nonconforming experiences, are rendered 'linguistically irrelevant'.[30] Though we can clearly see that all genders are prone, to varying degrees, to both perpetrate and suffer sexual violence, our language leaves us without the tools to evaluate, understand and integrate an array of other experiences. Tumminio Hansen illuminates Serano's claims about cissexual privilege, demonstrating how it operates in our language around sexual violence in ways that lead to trans-erasure.

Tumminio Hansen's insight indicates a broader framework of meaning-making surrounding sexual violence that oscillates around masculinity as a gender experience that is self-actualized via the domination of femininity. Such a framework is prone to render transmasculine experiences of sexual victimization as female, or female adjacent. We struggle to understand masculine experiences of suffering and victimization as masculine. Thus we also leave untouched the monopoly cisheterosexual, hegemonic masculinity purports to maintain on masculinity.

With this in mind, we suggest a revision to MacKinnon's formula: ~~men~~ those possessing and enacting hegemonic masculinity fuck ~~women~~ those who do not, those who are perceived possessing and enacting femininity – including but not limited to women (both cis and trans), gay men and trans men; subject verb object. The revision admittedly trades quippiness for clunkiness, but avoids cissexism and, importantly, speaks more adequately to the complexities of patriarchal power dynamics at play.

Or to put it differently, and to begin to turn our inquiry into a task, an imperative even: *We* should *make something of the raped trans man.* Those of us who do feminist trauma theology should do so because it is part of the work that feminist trauma theology aims to do. As O'Donnell and Cross put it in *Feminist Trauma Theologies*, in a passage worth citing at length:

> Feminist trauma theologies can be understood, therefore, as theologies (in plurality) that seek to engage with experiences of trauma (that which overwhelms ordinary human adaptations to life) from a feminist approach that *aims to pay critical attention to questions of power, knowing and representation as well as broader issues of social justice, with an eye to understanding the ways in which patriarchal societal structures both cause trauma and create the environments in which traumas can flourish.*[31]

Not only is sexual violence against trans men a pressing social justice issue, given the rates of occurrence, its impact on health and well-being (particularly the link with suicide rates), and trans-erasure and unrecognizability, but conflating hegemonic masculinity into masculinity writ large, however implicitly, centres it and thus concedes it. This further perpetuates cissexism and, to some degree, and rather paradoxically, patriarchy. While we can and should be critical of how hegemonic masculinity functions in the world, when we centre it we, on some level, affirm its own operational (if not espoused) claim about itself: that authentic masculinity is characterized by (sexual) domination. One way that feminist trauma theologies addressing sexual violence can resist and critically challenge this conflationary matrix is to decentre hegemonic masculinities.

Not All Men? From hegemonic to subjugated masculinity: towards a transfeminist hermeneutic

As the rise of the #MeToo movement spread on social media and millions of women (and some men) shared their experiences of sexual violence, a rather predictable pattern emerged – men would comment in defence, pointing out that *not all men* are sexist, that *not all men* are rapists, *not all men* are misogynists; that most, in fact, are 'good guys'. Feminists, including many men, quickly responded, pointing to the defensiveness of these retorts and how it missed the point, as patriarchal systems and structures operate rather smoothly regardless.[32]

'Toxic masculinity *does* affect all men.'[33] The statement was reason number five of a listicle on '6 Reasons "Not All Men" Misses The Point' published by the popular women's periodical *Bustle*. 'Whether you like it or not,' writes Suzannah Weiss, 'if you are a man who has grown up in the United States or really any Western culture, you have picked up some aspect of toxic masculinity.' Weiss rightly highlights the pervasive and often exceptionally subtle but nevertheless pernicious ways that men have been socialized by and into a toxic masculinity. What Weiss overlooks, however, is the ways in which toxic masculinity also harms men who do not express or embody prototypical, hegemonic masculinities. Yes, toxic masculinity *does* affect all men, though *not all men* in quite the same way – some are socialized by and into it, others are impacted by others' socialization (and, of course, men can occupy both subject positions at different times and in different contexts).[34]

What might it mean and look like, then, to decentre hegemonic, toxic masculinity in ways that do not succumb to cissexism – that do not further marginalize trans men and the violence they experience? What might it mean and look like *theologically*? While hegemonic masculinity is deeply entangled with Christian tradition – embedded within, wielded, defended and reinforced through its history and in the present – subjugated masculinity also has its own rather central place within it, via the crucifixion of Christ and narratives and representations of it.

This is the topic the queer theorist and theologian Kent Brintnall explores in *Ecce Homo: The-Male-Body-in-Pain as Redemptive Figure*. Drawing significantly on and 'collaborat[ing] with' the French theorist Georges Bataille, Brintnall considers how fantasies of excessive and toxic masculinity 'contain the seeds of their own destruction'.[35] Examining a range of arts and texts that feature masculine subjectivity – the Hollywood films *Rambo* and *The Passion of the Christ*, psychoanalytic literature, the photography of Robert Mapplethorpe and the paintings of Francis Bacon – Brintnall considers how they are informed by Christian imagery and narratives of the crucifixion, which is all about 'the brutalization, humiliation, and degradation of a male body'.[36] These texts and visual arts, Brintnall compellingly argues, present possibilities for undoing the 'dominant fiction of masculine power, privilege, and plenitude' through an 'insistence on sacrificial rupture'.[37]

Brintnall's compelling and elegantly crafted argument turns to the crucifixion and the reach of its narrative and imagery as a kind of hermeneutic, mediated through art and text, from which we counter the production and maintenance of the hegemonic masculinity we seek to resist (and, for Brintnall, the production and maintenance of graspable, stable, theological meaning). For instance, Brintnall reflects at length on the vulnerability of the male body that is depicted throughout Bacon's paintings. 'Just as certain Christian discourses command the believer to identify with the crucified body on the cross,' he writes, 'the formal devices of Bacon's paintings compel the viewer to identify with the mutilated body on the canvas.'[38] The male-body-in-pain destabilizes our imagination of masculinity, and leads to 'the possibility of greater intimacy, decency, and generosity between human beings by undoing illusions of self-sufficiency ... that perpetuate alienation, anxiety, and violence'.[39] Brintnall turns to art and text as that which facilitates this hermeneutic shift, but what does this mean for the raped trans man and his experiences?

At the most basic level, Brintnall's insights about the male-body-in-pain further points to the need for scholarship, as well as aesthetic and cultural work, on and by trans men who have experienced sexual violence. The (*ante*)redemptive work that the male-body-in-pain does (more on this *ante-* shortly) – needed work that de(con)structs hegemonic masculinity, dismantling illusions of self-sufficiency and of invulnerability – is, well, *needed*, in and for feminist trauma theologies.

This does not mean turning to the raped trans man as a sacrificial object in and for trauma theology. Feminist trauma theologies have done a great deal of work in critically examining, challenging and working to dismantle traditional atonement models' valorization of self-sacrifice and the ways that valorization has functioned to uphold racial and gender hierarchies.[40] Our proposal here is not for a new self-sacrificial object to replace the old ones that we are still dismantling. Moreover, to do so would also mean succumbing to another impact of cissexism that Serano identifies: trans-objectification.[41] Rather, this means developing and uplifting scholarship and other mediums that bear witness to what the raped trans man has experienced, and that, from there, by such witnessing, work to prevent and delimit further violence and harm. As Brintnall highlights, Bataille's 'call for sacrificial violence, in substitutionary form, is neither homicidal nor suicidal. Just the opposite', he asserts: 'Bataille argues that violent spectacle has the capacity to shatter the very conceptions that cause human beings to injure, destroy, and oppress one another.'[42] Bearing witness to the painful and violent reality and experiences of the raped trans man in our theologies of trauma and in cultural mediums serves both to (begin to) recognize trans men and the sexual violence that many of them experience, and, at the same time, to honour their unrecognizability in a way that opens up possibilities for *ante*-reparative, and post-traumatic, flourishing.

Beyond repair? Towards post-traumatic transfeminist possibilities

With all of this in mind, we return to our initial question: *What do we make of the raped trans man*? We have outlined how the raped trans man has been unrecognized in feminist scholarship on sexual violence; how, due to cissexism and its focus on hegemonic masculinity, he has been unrecognizable. From there, we have argued for attention to move beyond *just* critical analysis of hegemonic masculinity to a consideration of subjugated masculinities. Turning to Brintnall, we have considered the theological possibilities and resources for such an attention and, importantly, for the ethical and socio-political implications of it.

For Brintnall, as for his primary interlocutor Bataille, the figure of the male-body-in-pain is one that reveals the hegemonic figure of toxic masculinity as a fantasy and fiction – 'Behold the figure of a masculine subject incapable of sustaining the fiction of its coherence, uniqueness, and claim to power and privilege', Brintnall writes.[43] But what do we make of the male-body-in-pain not just as they are figured, but as they are, as suffering and, for many, traumatized?

To even begin to adequately address that question is far beyond the scope of this chapter, and demands much more attention and further reflection.[44] Yet we raise it here because we believe that Brintnall's Bataillean lesson on the self-shattering impact that figures of subjugated masculinity have on hegemonic masculinity also hold within it possibility for post-traumatic possibility.

In the postlude of *Ecce Homo*, Brintnall writes:

> The redemptive figure I have invoked – representations of suffering male bodies, metaphors of self-dissolution, Jesus on a cross – work against these desires [for a redemption that secures the self]. This redemption is only ever a risk, a chance at glimpsing oneself in the other across the wound's abyss, a headlong fall of dizzying ecstasy... The redemptive loss of self figured by the male-body-in-pain does not make suffering meritorious or provide an account of its origins; rather, it recognizes pain, violence, and trauma as the givens of human existence and reimagines intersubjective relation and human community in light of them. This redemptive figure does not offer itself as an instrument of healing and transformation but reveals that self-shattering, while traumatic, *is always something more*.[45]

In a vein similar to Brintnall, Brandy has argued elsewhere that 'socio-cultural and theological visions of healing that aim to restore the survivor [of sexual violence] to wholeness are misguided and risk exacerbating the psychic and social pain that follows trauma.'[46] It is our cultural tendency to engage the fantasy that this vision of wholeness offers and is. Within the framework of this fantasy, coherence and meaning-making is linked to the survivor's victimization; in the devastation of traumatic sexual violence, the survivor becomes obligated to strive after healing and wholeness, and perhaps even find healing and wholeness through or on account of their victimization. This whole, healed, coherent self is, in our estimation, that same ideal self which is assumed by cissexism.[47]

So, then, *What do we make of the raped trans man?* On one level, nothing. A transfeminist hermeneutic that foregrounds subjugated masculinity, in our reading, is one that aims to dispossess and rupture, cognisant of the ways in which possession and wholeness are bound up with a patriarchal order and hegemonic masculinity. Yet a transfeminist hermeneutic of subjugated masculinity also locates a constructive edge, something more, within dispossession and rupture.

In making nothing of the *figure* of *the* raped trans man, and in taking seriously his unrecognizability within the current patriarchal order of things, we hope and believe that this opens up post-traumatic ways of being that are not necessarily reparative, as repair presumes a kind of wholeness, but that are, neither, anti-reparative. Rather, they are *ante*-reparative, standing not against, but to the side of a logic of repair, attentive to the ways the subject who experiences the trauma of sexual violence, and the enacted fantasy of dominant masculinity that fuels it, cannot so much be repaired, but that something more, something new, something liberative and imaginative, can be made of and from the shattering.

A hermeneutic of subjugated masculinity opens up space for dismantling the fantasy of hegemonic masculinity that fuels violence, thus leading to a minimization and preventing of further violence and 'the possibility of greater intimacy, decency, and generosity between human beings'.[48] Moreover, in recognizing the unrecognizability of the trauma of the sexual violence that has victimized far too many trans men, a transfeminist hermeneutics of subjugated masculinity frees these men to imagine and act otherwise beyond the too-delimited vision of what masculinity or sexual violence or healing might look like. Brintnall ends *Ecce Homo* by reminding his readers that 'Bataille imagines a space of anguished ecstasy that propels the desiring subject and desired object beyond subjectivity, beyond objectivity, beyond gender, beyond identity. Propelled, through rupture, into fragmentation,' he concludes, 'we find ourselves-by losing ourselves-anew.'[49] We offer that this is not only true for the subject, but for how masculinity as a cultural construct and embodied reality is conceived of and performed, and thus for how our cultures, and our theologies, imagine gender, relations, violence, trauma, and the multiple entanglements between them.

Bibliography

Ableson, Miriam J., 'Dangerous Privilege: Trans Men, Masculinities, and Changing Perceptions', *Sociological Forum* 29, 3 (2014), pp. 549–70.

Aguilar, Stephen J. and Clare Baek, 'Sexual Harassment in Academe is Under-reported, Especially by Students in the Life and Physical Sciences', *PLoS ONE* 15, 2 (2020), pp. 1–18.

Bart, Paulina, 'Rape as a Paradigm of Sexism in Society – Victimization and its Discontents', *Women's Studies International Quarterly* 2 (1979), pp. 347–57.

Biblarz, Timothy J. and Evren Savci, 'Lesbian, Gay, Bisexual, and Transgender Families', *Journal of Marriage and Family* 72, 3 (2010), pp. 480–97.

Black, Michelle C., Kathleen C. Basile, Matthew J. Breiding, Sharon G. Smith, Mikel L. Waters, Melissa T. Merrick, Jieru Chen and Mark R. Stevens, '2010 Summary Report', *The National Intimate Partner and Sexual Violence Survey*, Atlanta, GA: National Center for Injury Prevention and Control, Centers for Disease Control and Prevention, 2011.

Brintnall, Kent L., *Ecce Homo: The Male-Body-In-Pain as Redemptive Figure*, Chicago, IL: University of Chicago Press, 2011.

Butler, Judith, *Gender Trouble: Feminism and the Subversion of Identity*, New York: Routledge, 1999.

Butler, Judith, *Frames of War: When is Life Grievable?*, New York: Verso, 2016.

Cannon, Claire and Frederick Buttell, 'Illusion of Inclusion: The Failure of the Gender Paradigm to account for Intimate Partner Violence in LGBT Relationships', *Partner Abuse* 6, 1 (2015), pp. 65–77.

Connell, Raewyn, 'A Very Straight Gay: Masculinity, Homosexual Experience, and the Dynamics of Gender', *American Sociological Review* 57, 6 (1992), pp. 735–51.

Cook-Daniels, Loree, 'Op-Ed: Trans Men Experience Far More Violence than Most People Assume', *The Advocate*, 23 July 2015, www.advocate.com/commentary/2015/07/23/op-ed-trans-men-experience-far-more-violence-most-people-assume, accessed 22.2.2022.

Daniels, Brandy, 'Sexual Violence and the "End" of Subjectivity: Queer Negativity and a Theopolitics of Refusal' in *Lee Edelman and the Queer Study of Religion*, ed. Kent Brintnall, Rhiannon Graybill and Linn Marie Tonstad, New York: Routledge, forthcoming 2022.

Dworkin, Andrea, *Intercourse*, New York: Free Press, 1987.

FORGE, 'Sexual Violence in the Transgender Community Survey', 2005, unpublished data.

Grant, Jamie M., Lisa A. Mottet and Justin Tanis, 'Injustice at Every Turn: A Report of the National Transgender Discrimination Survey', Washington: National Center for Transgender Equality and National Gay and Lesbian Task Force, 2011, https://transequality.org/sites/default/files/docs/resources/NTDS_Report.pdf, accessed 22.2.2022.

Gluckman, Nell, 'How a Letter Defending Avital Ronell Sparked Confusion and Condemnation', *The Chronicle of Higher Education*, 12 June 2018, www.chronicle.com/article/how-a-letter-defending-avital-ronell-sparked-confusion-and-condemnation/, accessed 6.5.2022.

Gottzén, Lucas, Margunn Bjørn and Floretta Boonzaier, 'What has Masculinity to do with Intimate Partner Violence?' in *Men, Masculinities, and Intimate Partner Violence*, ed. Lucas Gottzén, Margunn Bjørn and Floretta Boonzaier, New York: Routledge, 2021, pp. 1–15.

Halperin, David M. and Trevor Hoppe (eds), *The War on Sex*, Durham, NC: Duke University Press, 2017.

Hansen, Danielle Tumminio, 'Absent a Word: How the Language of Sexual Trauma Keeps Survivors Silent', *Journal of Pastoral Theology* 30, 2 (2020), pp. 136–49.

Harris, Adam and Alia Wong, 'When Academics Defend Colleagues Accused of Harassment', *The Atlantic*, 20 August 2018, www.theatlantic.com/education/archive/2018/08/why-do-academics-defend-colleagues-accused-of-harassment/567553/, accessed 22.2.2022.

Holland, Sharon P., *The Erotic Life of Racism*, Durham, NC: Duke University Press, 2012.

Javaid, Aliraza, 'The Dark Side of Men: The Nature of Masculinity and its Uneasy Relationship with Male Rape', *The Journal of Men's Studies* 23, 3 (2015), pp. 271–92.

Javaid, Aliraza, 'Behind Closed Doors: Hegemonic Masculinities, Romantic Love, and Sexual Violence in Gay Relationships' in *Men, Masculinities, and Intimate Partner Violence*, ed. Lucas Gottzén, Margunn Bjørn and Floretta Boonzaier, New York: Routledge, 2021, pp. 97–111.

Kenagy, Gretchen, 'The Health and Social Service Needs of Transgender People in Philadelphia', *International Journal of Transgenderism* 8, 2/3 (2005), pp. 49–56.

Kenagy, Gretchen and Wendy Beth Bostwick, 'Health and Social Service Needs of Transgendered People in Chicago', *International Journal of Transgenderism* 8, 2/3 (2005), pp. 57–66.

Kipnis, Laura, *Unwanted Advances: Sexual Paranoia Comes to Campus*, New York: Harper Books, 2017.

Leiter, Brian, 'Blaming the Victim is apparently OK when the Accused in a Title IX Proceeding is a Feminist Literary Theorist', *Leiter Reports: A Philosophy Blog*, 10 June 2018, https://leiterreports.typepad.com/blog/2018/06/blaming-the-victim-is-apparently-ok-when-the-accused-is-a-feminist-literary-theorist.html, accessed 22.2.2022.

Lisak, David, Jim Hopper and Pat Song, 'Factors in the Cycle of Violence: Gender Rigidity and Emotional Constriction', *Journal of Traumatic Stress* 9, 4 (1996), pp. 721–43.

MacKinnon, Catherine A., *Toward a Feminist Theory of the State*, Cambridge, MA: Harvard University Press, 1989.

Messner, Michael A., 'Bad Men, Good Men, Bystanders: Who Is the Rapist?', *Gender & Society* 30, 1 (2016), pp. 57–66.

Millett, Kate, *Sexual Politics*, Urbana, IL: University of Illinois Press, 1970.

Morgan, Rachel E. and Grace Kena, 'Criminal Victimization, 2016: Revised', US Department of Justice: Bureau of Justice Statistics, 2016, https://bjs.ojp.gov/content/pub/pdf/cv16.pdf, accessed 22.2.2022.

O'Donnell, Karen and Katie Cross (eds), *Feminist Trauma Theologies: Body, Scripture and Church in Critical Perspective*, London: SCM Press, 2020.

Office for Victims of Crime, 'Responding to Victims of Sexual Assault', US Department of Justice: Office of Justice Programs, June 2014, https://ovc.ojp.gov/sites/g/files/xyckuh226/files/pubs/forge/sexual_notes.html#_edn1, accessed 22.2.2022.

Patterson, Jennifer (ed.), *Queering Sexual Violence: Radical Voices from within the Anti-Violence Movement*, New York: Riverdale Avenue Books, 2016.

Rogers, Michaela, 'Transphobic "Honour"-Based Abuse: A Conceptual Tool', *Sociology* 51, 2 (2016), pp. 225–40.

Rogers, Michaela, 'The Intersection of Cisgenderism and Hate Crime: Learning from Trans People's Narratives', *The Journal of Family Strengths* 17, 2 (2017), pp. 1–25.

Rogers, Michaela, 'Exploring Trans Men's Experiences of Intimate Partner Violence through the Lens of Cisgenderism' in *Men, Masculinities, and Intimate Partner Violence*, ed. Lucas Gottzén, Margunn Bjørn and Floretta Boonzaier, New York: Routledge, 2021.

Scarsella, Hilary Jerome and Stephanie Krehbiel, 'Sexual Violence: Christian Theological Legacies and Responsibilities', *Religion Compass* 13, 9 (2019), pp. 1–13.

Serano, Julia, *Whipping Girl: A Transsexual Woman on Sexism and the Scapegoating of Femininity*, New York: Seal Press, 2007.

Serano, Julia, 'Whipping Girl FAQ on Cissexual, Cisgender, and Cis Privilege', *Whipping Girl*, 25 August 2011, https://juliaserano.blogspot.com/2011/08/whipping-girl-faq-on-cissexual.html, accessed 22.2.2022.

Serano, Julia, 'Cissexism and Cis Privilege Revisited – Part 1: Who Exactly Does "Cis" Refer To?', *Whipping Girl*, 1 October 2014, https://juliaserano.blogspot.com/2014/10/cissexism-and-cis-privilege-revisited.html, accessed 26.05.2022.

Weiss, Suzannah, '6 Reasons "Not All Men" Misses the Point', *Bustle*, 9 July 2016, www.bustle.com/articles/171595-6-reasons-not-all-men-misses-the-point-because-its-derailing-important-conversations, accessed 22.2.2022.

Wiegman, Robyn, *Object Lessons*, Durham, NC: Duke University Press, 2012.

Zimmerman, Jess, 'Not All Men: A Brief History of Every Dude's Favorite Argument', *Time Magazine*, 28 April 2014, https://time.com/79357/not-all-men-a-brief-history-of-every-dudes-favorite-argument/, accessed 22.2.2022.

Notes

1 According to the Justice Department's analysis of violent crime in 2016, nearly 80 per cent of rapes and sexual assaults go unreported. See Rachel E. Morgan and Grace Kena, 'Criminal Victimization, 2016: Revised', US Department of Justice Bureau of Justice Statistics, https://bjs.ojp.gov/content/pub/pdf/cv16.pdf. See also Stephen J. Aguilar and Clare Baek, 'Sexual Harassment in Academe is Underreported, Especially by Students in the Life and Physical Sciences', *PLoS ONE* 15, 2 (2020), pp. 1–18.

2 Adam Harris and Alia Wong, 'When Academics Defend Colleagues Accused of Harassment', *The Atlantic*, 20 August 2018, www.theatlantic.com/education/archive/2018/08/why-do-academics-defend-colleagues-accused-of-harassment/567553/.

3 See Nell Gluckman, 'How a Letter Defending Avital Ronell Sparked Confusion and Condemnation', *The Chronicle of Higher Education*, 12 June 2018, www.chronicle.com/article/how-a-letter-defending-avital-ronell-sparked-confusion-and-condemnation/. For link to letter, see Brian Leiter, 'Blaming the Victim is Apparently OK when the Accused in a Title IX Proceeding is a Feminist Literary Theorist', *Leiter Reports: A Philosophy Blog*, 10 June 2018, https://leiterreports.

typepad.com/blog/2018/06/blaming-the-victim-is-apparently-ok-when-the-accused-is-a-feminist-literary-theorist.html. In the letter, Reitman was rendered a villain, cast as a maligned graduate student determined to mount a 'malicious campaign' against Ronell.

4 In the course of writing this introduction, Brandy revisited the 1999 preface of Butler's *Gender Trouble: Feminism and the Subversion of Identity* (New York: Routledge, 1999), to review her remarks on how 'the naturalized knowledge of gender operates as a preemptive and violent circumscription of reality' (p. xxiii) and how 'it was difficult to bring this [gendered] violence into view precisely because gender was so taken for granted at the same time that it was violently policed' (p. xix). While doing so, she was struck by how, between these two points, Avital Ronell is referenced in passing, and that the reference is rather ... ironic. Asking the reader to take seriously the 'ruses that motor the ostensibly "clear" view' with regards to gender, Butler notes that 'Avital Ronell recalls the moment in which Nixon looked into the eyes of the nation and said, "let me make one thing perfectly clear" and then proceeded to lie' (p. xix).

5 Judith Butler, *Frames of War: When is Life Grievable?* (New York: Verso, 2016), p. 38; Brian Leiter, 'Blaming the Victim is Apparently OK'.

6 See Kent L. Brintnall, *Ecce Homo: The Male-Body-In-Pain as Redemptive Figure* (Chicago, IL: University of Chicago Press, 2011); Julia Serano, *Whipping Girl: A Transsexual Woman on Sexism and the Scapegoating of Femininity* (New York: Seal Press, 2007).

7 Given the collaborative, co-written nature of this chapter, we reserve first-person pronoun usage for its plural form, avoiding the singular 'I'. When one of us is referred to directly, we utilize third-person pronouns. While potentially awkward, it avoids the confusion of needing to clarify which 'I' is speaking in a particular instance.

8 Office for Victims of Crime, 'Responding to Victims of Sexual Assault', June 2014, https://ovc.ojp.gov/sites/g/files/xyckuh226/files/pubs/forge/sexual_notes.html #_edn1. See also FORGE, 'Sexual Violence in the Transgender Community Survey', 2005, unpublished data; Gretchen Kenagy, 'The Health and Social Service Needs of Transgender People in Philadelphia', *International Journal of Transgenderism* 8, 2/3 (2005), pp. 49–56; Gretchen Kenagy and Wendy Beth Bostwick, 'Health and Social Service Needs of Transgendered People in Chicago', *International Journal of Transgenderism* 8, 2/3 (2005), pp. 57–66.

9 See Jaime M. Grant, Lisa A. Mottet and Justin Tanis, 'Injustice at Every Turn: A Report of the National Transgender Discrimination Survey' (Washington: National Center for Transgender Equality and National Gay and Lesbian Task Force, 2011), https://transequality.org/sites/default/files/docs/resources/NTDS_Report.pdf. As 'Injustice at Every Turn' reports, 19 per cent of trans and gender nonconforming people have reported experiencing homelessness due to their gender identity. Fifteen per cent of trans men (vs 26 per cent of trans women) reported being sexually assaulted by residents or staff (55 per cent experienced harassment, and 22 per cent turned away altogether) (p. 118). It is also important to note that 'Injustice at Every Turn' does not report on sexual violence against trans folks as a whole, but in a variety of particular contexts (i.e. homeless shelters, schools, workplace, prison). Moreover, the study only asked about sexual violence that was 'motivated by a person's transgender or gender non-conforming status' (p. 202),

thus potentially excluding data that wasn't directly perceived as, but may well have been, related to the victim's gender identity.

10 See Grant et al., 'Injustice at Every Turn', p. 2, n. 2.

11 See notes 8–9 above.

12 FORGE, 'Sexual Violence in the Transgender Community Survey'. This study also showed that trans men were also more likely to be victims of childhood sexual assault, dating violence, domestic violence and stalking than were trans women. See also Loree Cook-Daniels, 'Op-Ed: Trans Men Experience Far More Violence than Most People Assume', *The Advocate*, 23 July 2015, www.advocate.com/commentary/2015/07/23/op-ed-trans-men-experience-far-more-violence-most-people-assume.

13 See Raewyn Connell, 'A Very Straight Gay: Masculinity, Homosexual Experience, and the Dynamics of Gender', *American Sociological Review* 57, 6 (1992), pp. 735–51; Aliraza Javaid, 'The Dark Side of Men: The Nature of Masculinity and its Uneasy Relationship with Male Rape', *The Journal of Men's Studies* 23, 3 (2015), pp. 271–92; Michael A. Messner, 'Bad Men, Good Men, Bystanders: Who is the Rapist?', *Gender & Society* 30, 1 (2016), pp. 57–66.

14 Cook-Daniels, 'Trans Men Experience Far More Violence than Most People Assume'.

15 Lucas Gottzén, Margunn Bjørn and Floretta Boonzaier, 'What has Masculinity to do with Intimate Partner Violence?' in *Men, Masculinities, and Intimate Partner Violence*, ed. Lucas Gottzén, Margunn Bjørn and Floretta Boonzaier (New York: Routledge, 2021), p. 11 [1–15].

16 Timothy J. Biblarz and Evren Savci, 'Lesbian, Gay, Bisexual, and Transgender Families', *Journal of Marriage and Family* 72, 3 (2010), pp. 480–97; Michaela Rogers, 'Transphobic "Honour"-Based Abuse: A Conceptual Tool', *Sociology* 51, 2 (2016), pp. 225–40; Michaela Rogers, 'The Intersection of Cisgenderism and Hate Crime: Learning from Trans People's Narratives', *The Journal of Family Strengths* 17, 2 (2017), pp. 1–25.

17 See Serano, *Whipping Girl*, p. 12. While the terms cissexism and cisgenderism are often used as synonyms, and cisgenderism is a preferred term for many, we rely on the term cissexism for the same reasons Serano retains it in her work/in revised editions of *Whipping Girl*. Most significantly, because our inquiry considers the experiences and realities of trans *men* in particular, we chose to retain the term cissexism, as we are operating to some degree within a gender binary that critiques of cisgenderism aim to challenge. For more on this, see Serano, 'Cissexism and Cis Privilege Revisited – Part 1: Who Exactly Does "Cis" Refer To?', *Whipping Girl*, 1 October 2014, https://juliaserano.blogspot.com/2014/10/cissexism-and-cis-privilege-revisited.html.

18 Karen O'Donnell and Katie Cross, *Feminist Trauma Theologies: Body, Scripture and Church in Critical Perspective* (London: SCM Press, 2020), p. xxiii.

19 See, for instance, Michelle C. Black et al., '2010 Summary Report', *The National Intimate Partner and Sexual Violence Survey* (Atlanta: National Center for Injury Prevention and Control, Centers for Disease Control and Prevention, 2011); David Lisak, Jim Hopper and Pat Song, 'Factors in the Cycle of Violence: Gender Rigidity and Emotional Constriction', *Journal of Traumatic Stress* 9, 4 (1996), pp. 721–43. According to the latter study, 97 per cent of perpetrators identify as male, and of that 97 per cent, over 98 per cent identify as heterosexual. It is important

to note here that accurately acquiring and assessing data around sexual violence is complex. For more on this, see Laura Kipnis, *Unwanted Advances: Sexual Paranoia Comes to Campus* (New York: Harper Books, 2017), pp. 13, 40ff.

20 Kate Millett, *Sexual Politics* (Urbana, IL: University of Illinois Press, 1970), p. 31.

21 Paulina Bart, 'Rape as a Paradigm of Sexism in Society – Victimization and its Discontents', *Women's Studies International Quarterly* 2 (1979), pp. 347–57.

22 Catharine A. MacKinnon, *Toward a Feminist Theory of the State* (Cambridge, MA: Harvard University Press, 1989), p. 124. Or, as MacKinnon's comrade Andrea Dworkin put it perhaps even more starkly in *Intercourse* (New York: Free Press, 1987), 'violation is a synonym for intercourse' (p. 154).

23 Bart, 'Rape as a Paradigm of Sexism in Society', p. 356.

24 See, for instance, Jennifer Patterson (ed.), *Queering Sexual Violence: Radical Voices from within the Anti-Violence Movement* (New York: Riverdale Avenue Books, 2016); David Halperin and Trevor Hoppe (eds), *The War on Sex* (Durham, NC: Duke University Press, 2017); Sharon Patricia Holland, *The Erotic Life of Racism* (Durham, NC: Duke University Press, 2012); Robyn Wiegman, *Object Lessons* (Durham, NC: Duke University Press, 2012).

25 Serano, *Whipping Girl*, p. 12; see note 17 above. See also Serano, 'Whipping Girl FAQ on Cissexual, Cisgender, and Cis Privilege', *Whipping Girl*, 25 August 2011, https://juliaserano.blogspot.com/2011/08/whipping-girl-faq-on-cissexual. html, accessed 25.2.2022. Serano explains that the term and concept of cissexism is particularly useful as it draws an important analytic distinction from overtly violent forms of transphobia and enables deeper and more specific interrogation and analysis of the ways that many of the acts of discrimination that have been previously lumped under the term 'transphobia' are 'more specifically designed to undermine the legitimacy of trans people's identified genders rather than targeting trans people for breaking oppositional gender norms' (p. 185).

26 Serano, *Whipping Girl*, p. 162

27 See Serano, *Whipping Girl*, pp. 188–90. Other impacts she explores are trans-exclusion, trans-objectification, trans-mystification and trans-interrogation (pp. 185–8).

28 Michaela Rogers, 'Exploring Trans Men's Experiences of Intimate Partner Violence through the Lens of Cisgenderism' in *Men, Masculinities, and Intimate Partner Violence*, p. 112 [112–125]. See also Claire Cannon and Frederick Buttell, 'Illusion of inclusion: The Failure of the Gender Paradigm to Account for Intimate Partner Violence in LGBT Relationships', *Partner Abuse* 6, 1 (2015), pp. 65–77.

29 Other subjugated masculinities, such as gay and bi men, are also subject to a greater risk of violence. See Aliraza Javaid, 'Behind Closed Doors: Hegemonic Masculinities, Romantic Love, and Sexual Violence in Gay Relationships' in *Men, Masculinities, and Intimate Partner Violence*, pp. 97–111.

30 Danielle Tumminio Hansen, 'Absent a Word: How the Language of Sexual Trauma Keeps Survivors Silent', *Journal of Pastoral Theology* 30, 2 (2020), pp. 141–2 [136–149].

31 O'Donnell and Cross, *Feminist Trauma Theologies*, p. xxi; emphasis added.

32 See Jess Zimmerman, 'Not All Men: A Brief History of Every Dude's Favorite Argument', *Time Magazine*, 28 April 2014, https://time.com/79357/not-all-men-a-brief-history-of-every-dudes-favorite-argument/.

33 Suzannah Weiss, '6 Reasons "Not All Men" Misses the Point', *Bustle*, 9 July 2016, www.bustle.com/articles/171595-6-reasons-not-all-men-misses-the-point-because-its-derailing-important-conversations.

34 That being said, there has also been research that has pointed to the ways in which those who experience and express masculinities that are subjugated are susceptible to embracing and performing toxic masculinities for safety and social belonging. See Miriam J. Ableson, 'Dangerous Privilege: Trans Men, Masculinities, and Changing Perceptions', *Sociological Forum* 29, 3 (2014), pp. 549–70.

35 Brintnall, *Ecce Homo*, p. 20.

36 Brintnall, *Ecce Homo*, p. 131.

37 Brintnall, *Ecce Homo*, p. 197. These mediums themselves, Brintnall explains, function sacrificially, compelling 'an encounter with the permeability and incoherence of the self' and thereby leading to 'the possibility of greater intimacy, decency, and generosity between human beings by undoing illusions of self-sufficiency … that perpetuate alienation, anxiety, and violence' (p. 8).

38 Brintnall, *Ecce Homo*, p. 165.

39 Brintnall, *Ecce Homo*, p. 8. Or, as he puts it elsewhere, 'Recognizing shared vulnerabilities, mutual lacerations – and a common capacity for muddling through – challenges systems of differentiation, power, and control. It is difficult to acknowledge one's frailty. But what if we did? What if we lingered in the rain with the battle-scarred Rambo? … What if Christianity cried out "*lama sabachtani*" more frequently than "He is risen"? Might we begin to see, hear, and engage one another differently?' (p. 64).

40 For a helpful summary of this, see section 3.1, Christianity's Complicity: Theology, in Hilary Jerome Scarsella and Stephanie Krehbiel, 'Sexual Violence: Christian Theological Legacies and Responsibilities', *Religion Compass* 13, 9 (2019), pp. 3–5 [1–13]. In his consideration of suffering and triumph via his analysis of *The Passion of the Christ*, Brintnall points out that '[w]hile feminist theologians have rightfully pointed to … how the suffering of Jesus has been relied on to admonish oppressed people to suffer in silence, it may very well be that the doctrine of the resurrection – with its quiet, subterranean, structural influence – has played the largest role in maintaining the illusion of masculinity necessary for the patriarchal denigration of women and womanish men' (*Ecce Homo*, p. 62, n. 95).

41 It is important to note that Brintnall speaks at length to how attentiveness and emphasis differ from fetishization and objectification in Bataille. See *Ecce Homo*, pp. 172–84.

42 Brintnall, *Ecce Homo*, p. 17.

43 Brintnall, *Ecce Homo*, p. 188.

44 We echo what Brintnall writes in the postlude of *Ecce Homo*: 'Found(er)ing redemption on self-shattering and fragmentation raises a number of important ethical and political questions … To treat these questions quickly – and, hence, superficially – in this closing moment would be an act of violence: it would fail to treat them with the seriousness they deserve …' (p. 186).

45 Brintnall, *Ecce Homo*, p. 186; emphasis added.

46 Brandy Daniels, 'Sexual Violence and the "End" of Subjectivity: Queer Negativity and a Theopolitics of Refusal' in *Lee Edelman and the Queer Study of Religion*, ed. Linn Tonstad, Kent Brintnall and Rhiannon Graybill (New York: Routledge, forthcoming 2022).

47 Similarly, Micah's current research considers this dynamic and its manifestations within American evangelicalism. Via pseudo/'reparative' therapies and/or spiritual disciplines, US evangelical Christianity claims to offer wholeness and healing to salve the purported brokenness of queer and trans identities. Such brokenness is typically, and erroneously, connected to childhood sexual abuse and other family system dysfunction as a causative factor for queer and trans identities.

48 Brintnall, *Ecce Homo*, p. 8.

49 Brintnall, *Ecce Homo*, p. 197.

9

Transgressive Bodies: A Constructive Proposal for a Trans*-Centred Trauma Theology

TYLER BRINKMAN

Theologians have only in the last few decades begun to do theology seriously and systematically in light of the fact that we live in 'the age of trauma'.[1] An increasing number of writers have produced books and articles at the intersection of trauma and theology, but it is still a new and burgeoning field. Utilizing the experience of trauma as a theological hermeneutic offers the potential for new insights for theologians for all dimensions of both systematic and practical Christian theology. Despite this rise in popularity, there has been little done from the perspective of trans* persons despite their frequent experiences of trauma. In this chapter, trans* will be used as an umbrella term encompassing transgender, genderqueer, non-binary and any other identity that falls outside the typical categories of cis-male and cis-female. The only exception to this will be indigenous communities with their own particular tradition (e.g. American Indian two-spirit; hijra).

This chapter will attempt to construct a trans*-centred trauma theology by utilizing the experiences of trans* persons, insights from queer theology, and psychiatric research. I will argue that a trans*-centred trauma theology ultimately destabilizes linear temporalities, ruptures conceptions of embodiment and identity, and demonstrates the liberative and sanctifying work of the Sprit in breaking open binary oppositions. To do this, I will 1) describe in detail some methodological concerns this chapter will follow, 2) articulate some of the ways in which the experiences and trauma of trans* persons offer challenges and opportunities to theological discourse and reflection, 3) explore the realities of human embodiment and temporality – with particular emphasis on the impact of trauma and somatic memory and how they can inform queer discourses, and 4) develop an apocalyptic pneumatology of identity in light of the experiences of trans* persons.

Methodology

Before I begin in earnest, I want to briefly sketch out a threefold method-ology this chapter will utilize. 1) As a person within the Wesleyan tradition, I want to follow John Wesley's three general rules for his Methodist soci-eties: 'do no harm, to do good, to attend the ordinances of God'.[2] Because this chapter is centred around the traumatic experiences of a deeply margin-alized community, it is necessary to begin with a posture of 'do no harm'. 2) Unlike many theologies of trauma, this chapter will avoid an overreli-ance on psychodynamic theories of trauma, which draw resources from the humanities more so than from contemporary clinical research surrounding trauma. 3) Drawing from insights from postcolonial discourse, I want to call into question the event-based model of trauma as well as the process of 'naturalization' through which deviant sexualities were first established through violence as a tool for colonization. Because of this history, 'Queer studies must examine settler colonialism as a condition of its own work: a queer critique of location, temporality, or belonging that naturalized its relationship to settler colonialism will no longer be considered transgres-sive.'[3] This queering of the 'natural', space, time and belonging will become significant later in this chapter.

Theological sources for trans*-orientated trauma

The existence of trans* persons poses significant challenges and opportun-ities for Christian theology. The experiences of trans* persons as well as their extreme rate of trauma demand a theological response. I will present two primary challenges trans* bodies and trans* folks bring to Christian theology. The first is that of the 'natural'. The second is interpersonal rela-tionality, which can help inform our trinitarian discourse.

'Natural'

The most frequent critique I have seen of the trans* experience is that it is unnatural. The operative logic in this case equates a kind of essential 'naturality' with moral goodness. Deviations outside of what is natural necessarily are only orientated towards death and destruction; deviation from the 'natural' sex/gender binary poses a fundamental rejection of both creation and God Godself.

Trans* persons pose a fundamental threat to this male/female binary opposition by destabilizing what a 'natural' human is.

Transgendered narratives help to ask transgressive questions, such as: Why must a genetic man, when he puts on 'feminine' clothing, suddenly be coded as a woman? Why can't this performance of gender be constructed as male or be understood as a disruptive category of man, or rather, neither?[4]

If human beings are always and absolutely either male or female, then anything outside of those boxes falls outside the scope of humanity. Sally Gross, an intersex individual,

> reports being told by Christian acquaintances that her baptism was not valid since, as she did not fall into either of the categories 'determinately male' or 'determinately female', she also did not fall into the category of 'human', and was therefore not 'the kind of thing' which could have been baptized validly.[5]

Her experience is obviously a quite literal and explicit example of this kind of dehumanizing rhetoric.

These ways of thinking deny the humanity of others and are an extreme form of social rejection, a form of trauma that has been demonstrated through peer-reviewed scientific research. One study utilizing fMRI imaging looked for a connection between social rejection and physical pain. It suggests 'social pain is analogous in its neurocognitive function to physical pain, alerting us when we have sustained injury to our social connections, allowing restorative measures to be taken.'[6] A different study demonstrated that 'social peer rejection should be considered as a traumatic event that has long-term effect on individuals' psychological well-being.'[7] The social exclusions trans* persons often experience are predicated on these theologies, which maintain a 'natural' sex/gender binary. My contention is that these theological perspectives fail two of the basic theological rules I mentioned earlier (i.e. doing good and not doing harm).

The enforcement of 'naturality' is violent, traumatic, and excludes trans* persons. These ontologies of personhood predicated on a 'natural' male/female binary are expanded and create ontologies of sexuality and social structures (i.e. heteropatriarchy, cissexism etc.), which are enforced through systems of biopsychosocial violence. One of the most dramatic examples is the treatment of American Indian two-spirit people. Patrick Cheng recounts how upon encountering them, 'One of the characteristics of Indigenous people that most disturbed the European explorers and missionaries were gender-variant, or Two-Spirit, individuals who took on different roles that differed from their biological sexes.'[8] They were deemed deviant from the natural order of things and, as a result, they were subjected to horrific violence by European colonists – even to the point of being eaten alive by dogs.[9] These violent processes of naturalization are at the heart of both queer and postcolonial studies. Melanie Richter-Montpetit critiques the connection between 'common sense' and the process of naturalization. She explains, '"Common sense" provides frames of intelligibility that make certain practices, identities and desires appear "natural", possible and desirable, to the exclusion of other practices and identities.'[10] Her articulation of 'common sense' is analogous to the presuppositions that undergird a 'natural' sex/gender binary.

Relationality

Trauma studies, postcolonial discourses and trans* bodies all complicate conceptions of relationality. We often think of interpersonal relationships as existing between discrete persons. People *in essence* exist independently of one another. A trans*-centred trauma theology rejects this vision of relationality and points to a landscape of relations in which a person is constituted by their relationships with one's body, others, the world and God. This anthropology is supported by contemporary evidence-based research. Interpersonal Neurobiology (IPNB) is a particularly useful evidence-based framework for conceptualizing personhood. It 'describes human development and functioning as being a product of the relationship between the body, mind and relationships'.[11] It offers insights into the effects of trauma since 'trauma almost invariably involves not being seen, not being mirrored, and not being taken into account.' Instead of atomistic anthropologies, people are only people as they are persons-in-relations; this fact undermines the concept of human essentialism wherein some *thing* is identified as being the source of one's humanity.

This undermining of anthropological essentialism lies at the heart of queer theory in which 'body and identity are not fixed notions, but rather are dynamic and complex concepts'.[12] In the same manner, physical bodies cannot be essentialised, neither can sex or gender. Trans* persons necessitate a re-examination of static notions of gender, sex and sexuality. Beyond these kinds of abstract discourses of sexuality, however, are the concrete lived-out experiences of trans* persons. Many trans* people report that before they come out even their healthy relationships can be a source of pain for them because of a fundamental incongruity between a person's gender identity and their gender-in-relationship. Scott Bader-Saye explains: 'the experience of gender incongruity is more like a socially revealed (and socially determined) fracture in the self ... the potentially graced moment of recognition and desire is not an affirmation but rather a negation.'[13]

To avoid this kind of fracturing they might need to be publicly gender nonconforming and gender transgressive. However, by presenting themselves as themselves, trans* persons make themselves extremely vulnerable to rejection and violence. Social rejection is traumatic in its own right and is experienced by the nervous system as a type of pain.

If Shelly Rambo is right when she says that 'Trauma is the suffering that does not go away',[14] then I think we can safely call this state of being a closeted queer person traumatic. The closet is a place of suffering that does not go away. This causes severe interpersonal impediments since 'we can't be in right relationship to each other if we can't see each other. We can't be fully present in any relationship we're walling off part of ourselves or hiding beneath a mask.'[15] This is a deformed relationality that reduces persons-in-relation into atomized individuals; in short, it is dehumanizing.

If we take seriously this requirement that identity and relationality are inherent because they cannot be essentialized or made static, this should lead us to reconsider the Trinity *ad intra*. How can we reinterpret *una substantia, tres personae* if we can no longer easily affirm either *substantia* or *personae* as ontological categories? While a relatively common area of investigation during the twentieth century, the development of a trans*-centred trauma theology might offer new insights. Many theologians have attempted to ground anthropological differences – including sexual differences – within the relational existence of the Trinity. Theologians have seemingly always been interested, even obsessed, with sexuality and sexual relations. It is taken as a given that they are the primary kind of relationship. Arguably, this ubiquitous privileging is part of that colonizing 'common sense'. There are no reasons why Christian ontologies of relationality must inherently privilege sexual relationships rather than friendships. In my mind, the most common theological assertion driving this impulse to privilege sexual rela-tionality is *creatio ex nihilo*. Because the Trinity *ad intra* is constituted by a mutual relationality of love, we are quick to implicitly (and explicitly) iden-tify creation with an intra-trinitarian eroticism. This is not the only – or even most useful – way to conceptualize relationality within the Godhead. Ultimately I think that, for the sake of theological imagination, we need a multitude of metaphors. If the identity of God is ontologically slippery, how much more must our God-talk be?

A better trinitarian relationality and intimacy is one grounded on friend-ship rather than sexuality. 'Friendship is not a second-tier, perfunctory kind of interaction. Imagine how our lives would be transformed if we took seriously that friendship is the necessary base for every possible relationship',[16] Mihee Kim-Kort explains. Far beyond the merely perfunc-tory, 'Friendship ... is in its postpatriarchal, postheterosexist potential an insight, experience, and concept able to carry us to new heights in theology.'[17] I am particularly drawn towards queerplatonic relationships, a newer term coined only within the last decade in online asexual com-munities. The term:

> indicate[s] a relationship [that] defies the divide between romantic part-nership and 'just' friends. [It also] describe[s] feelings and relationships of either/both a nonromantic or ambiguously-romantic nature, in order to express that they break social norms for platonic relationships.[18]

Friendship is queered by virtue of transgressing the binarism of romance/ friendship. People can experience the heights of human intimacy with others without that intimacy being necessarily sexual. If we can imagine and experience this between human beings, I think it is reasonable to extrapolate to intra-trinitarian relationships; there is no need for sexualized trinitarian imaginations when sexual relationships are not privileged.

Embodiment, memory and relationality in a trans*-centred trauma theology

Trauma is always embodied. There is no disembodied trauma. It occurs when our bodies' abilities to integrate physical sensations, emotions, hormonal stress response and memories are overwhelmed. While trauma is always embodied, its impact often comes in the forms of depersonalization, disembodiment and dissociation. Nothing stands at the intersection of queer theology and trauma studies more than human embodiment; it is where these two often-disconnected theological discourses are integrated. The queer theologian Kim-Kort states simply: 'Queerness begins from the premise that bodies matter. We need our bodies. More than that, we are our bodies ... Queerness doesn't judge, contain, or see our bodies as things to be conquered or mastered ... Queerness sometimes remakes bodies.'[19]

It is for this reason that a primary commitment for a trauma-sensitive theology involves giving priority to the body. This chapter has so far analysed certain themes of embodiment; next it will attempt to explore how actual living (and traumatized) bodies should inform our theological convictions. If we look afresh at bodies, in the light of queer and trauma studies, we might find our 'common sense' theology is ruptured. I will explore two related aspects of embodiment that are particularly important for a queer trauma theology: trauma's effects on a body's somatic memory, and how those effects can help to destabilize our theologies of time.

Somatic memory

Trauma is always and for ever a somatic experience. This is affirmed by theologians and clinicians alike. Karen O'Donnell writes that 'The core of trauma lies in somatic memory.'[20] In clinical and medical studies of traumatic experiences, it has been demonstrated time and again that those traumatic memories are physiologically held in a person's body.[21] This occurs at a level literally neuroanatomically lower than our ability to put into words – particularly if the trauma occurred in early childhood before the linguistic areas of the brain developed. Bessel van der Kolk explains simply, 'All trauma is preverbal.'[22] The neurobiological dimensions of neuroplasticity, the three-tier structure of the brain and the stress hormonal system controlled and activated by the limbic system are all major factors in the biological mechanism of somatic memory.[23]

A comprehensive overview of these neurobiological facts is beyond the scope of this chapter; instead, I want to focus on the *experience* of somatic memory. While there are a wealth of sources on this topic, I will primarily use van der Kolk's *The Body Keeps the Score* due to its significant contemporary influence on trauma studies. Since trauma is an overwhelming of the body's ability to process experiences 'It is enormously difficult to organize one's traumatic experiences into a coherent account'.[24] Typically, when the amygdala registers a potential threat, it will release stress hormones as well as a rapid fire of synaptic activity. This is healthy neurological functioning, and after time those stress hormones and synaptic activity will normalize. However, 'If for some reason the normal response is blocked ... the brain keeps secreting stress chemical, and the brain's electrical circuits continue to fire in vain ... the brain may keep sending signals to the body to escape a threat that no longer exists.'[25] Even after the traumatic experience has ended, van der Kolk explains, you continue 'to organize your life as if the trauma were still going on – unchanged and immutable – as every new encounter or event is contaminated by the past'[26] because the 'amygdala make[s] no distinction between past and present'.[27] While van der Kolk does seem to be primarily utilizing an event-based model of trauma, his reasonings are still consistent with (and perhaps even amplified by) the alternative of a traumatic landscape. If one exists in a landscape of trauma, it must be far more difficult for the body to resolve to a state of healthy functioning.

Somatic memory affects a person's ability to understand their bodyselves. It does this because it 'teaches us that memories and ways of remembering cannot be removed from bodily experience ... bodies, necessarily then, hold the memory of trauma and it is through the body that one can be healed'.[28] A post-traumatic triggering is predicated on the body's connection with some sensation or perception with a past event, and, again, neurobiologically occurs below our ability to verbalize. It often takes significant work for someone to simply identify their post-traumatic triggers. This comes prior to our ability to practise effective coping skills to self-soothe and self-regulate.

> Self-regulation depends on having a *friendly* relationship with your body. Without it you have to rely on external regulation – from medication, drugs like alcohol, constant reassurance, or compulsive compliance with the wishes of others.[29]

The lack of a friendly relationship between the mind and body, and the dependence on externalities for self-regulation, demonstrate a disconnect between a person's mind and body. If our theological anthropology necessitates that our personhood is inherently connected with our physical bodies, then any divide or divorce from a person's body is inherently disordered.

I suggest that the experience of gender dysphoria is also a form of traumatic experience. If we require friendship with our bodies to be appropriately regulated and integrated, this is made extremely difficult or even impossible when our self-identity and bodies are antagonistic to one another. Since this antagonism also disrupts relationships with others, its impact is compounded because it damages one's potential interpersonal support system. What would a person's experience be if their bodyselves are traumatically triggered by their very own bodies? Just like trauma, this occurs on a somatic level below our ability to bring into language.

Destabilizing time

The biopsychosocial reality of somatic memories offers potential insights into how Christians might conceptualize time. Traumatic memories often operate in the form of being triggered, and then the body's memory of that event getting played out as if it were happening all over again. The traumatic event is brought outside of a person's capacity to integrate that trauma into their bodies and personal narratives. It is dislodged in time. Rambo explains:

> [T]ime heals all wounds. Trauma represents an antithesis to this state-ment. In fact, in trauma, distortions in time constitute the wound ... [it] is not a one-time event. Instead, trauma speaks to an event in its excess. The fact that the event was not fully integrated at the time means that some-thing of that event returns at a later time. Its unintegrated nature makes it difficult to locate the suffering in any one place or time.[30]

She goes on to say that: 'The central problem of trauma is that an experi-ence repeats. The past intrudes into the present in such a way that belies clear delineations of time.'[31] Time cannot be essentialized or turned into an easy linearity. No clear demarcation of past, present and future exists. Time itself is queered.

The healing of traumatic memories must then collapse this traumatic atemporality into temporality. Trauma studies indicate, as I have argued, that a person's traumatic disintegration both resituates a person in the experience of eternally present memories and breaks the familiar bonds of interpersonal relationships. Therefore, it is a reasonable theological con-clusion to integrate personal relationality with temporality. One cannot exist relationally outside of time. The work of God in Scripture always takes place within a framework of time; it is not necessarily linear, but God's activity in the world never occurs atemporally. Quite the opposite: in the whole scriptural story – creation, incarnation, resurrection, ascension, eschaton – God, in some ways, acts to restore relationality temporally. Rambo describes Adrienne von Speyr's mystical experiences of hell, noting that 'One does not take on sufferings in hell; one endures what it is to be abandoned.'[32] This abandonment should be likened to the ultimate version of the traumatic effects of depersonalization, derealization, dissociation. It is the disintegration of spatiotemporal persons-in-relation. Healing comes from the reintegration of all those dimensions. And in the same way that traumatic experience can be reintegrated in a survivor's memory and narrative, so too can God reintegrate death's orientation to atemporality. Eugene Rogers writes: 'The Spirit's storied interactions with Christ tell us something about how God enters time, and as human befriends it ... Christ befriends time by becoming human at the conception by the Spirit.'[33] Our salvation, our rescue from hell – is the movement away from the timeless, eternal present experience of death and into the time-full relationality of the Triune God. That the kingdom of God will know no end does not imply any existence outside of time, but rather that the meaningfulness and everlastingness of time will be infinite.

Pneumatology of apocalyptic bodies

For O'Donnell, 'the Body of Christ is a traumatized Body'.[34] Traumatic wounding can come in the form of sexual abuse, physical assault, prolonged separation from caregivers and loved ones, car accidents, medical procedures, forced migration, war, as well as every aspect of human existence. Trauma often seems far more omnipresent than the Spirit of God. In this final section, I want to take the insights regarding the (con)quest for the 'natural', relationality, somatic memory and temporality and develop a pneumatology of embodied apocalyptic trans* identity. To do this I will 1) survey some contemporary literatures and examine how conceptions of trauma can relate to apocalyptic rupturing, 2) describe how trans* experiences demonstrate the body of Christ as queerly apocalyptic and 3) suggest the way in which the Holy Spirit is apocalyptically sanctifying trans* persons.

Trauma and the apocalyptic

Trauma ruptures identity. Since people exist as persons-in-relations, anything that damages those constitutional relationships will inevitably impact their identity. This is not simply the existentialist assertion made by theologians. Van der Kolk writes: 'After trauma the world becomes sharply divided between those who know and those who don't. People who have not shared the traumatic experience cannot be trusted, because they can't understand it.'[35] This has been my experience with others who have histories of trauma; even when they have experienced different traumas, a camaraderie-in-arms mentality often exists among survivors. Speaking as a clinician and theologian, Jennifer Baldwin claims that the 'tragic reality of trauma is that there is no going back. The person you were prior to trauma has changed.'[36] This is fundamental to Rambo's theological project. At the beginning of *Spirit and Trauma* she eloquently says:

> Trauma is described as an encounter with death. This encounter is not, however, a literal death but a way of describing a radical event or events that shatter all that one knows about the world and all the familiar ways of operating with it. A basic disconnection occurs from what one knows to be true and safe in the world. The event comes to be understood as a radical ending past which it is difficult, if not impossible to conceive of life … the event becomes the defining event beyond which little can be conceived. Life takes on a fundamentally different definition.[37]

Trauma constitutionally ruptures and disintegrates persons-in-relations, but in reintegration a person's identity becomes reconfigured. This is a rupture between the already and the not-yet, a rupture of human being and human becoming.

The body of Christ has been ruptured. We are quick to ignore the wounds of Christ. We often talk about the blood of Christ or the death of Christ, but very rarely, in my experience, do we meditate on the woundedness of Christ. Too quickly have Western Christians glossed over the wounds of Christ. The crucifixion and the wounds of Christ are reduced into the competing sports franchises of atonement theories who head into tournament to determine who will be the winner – with their fan base in tow shouting in favour of their team. Rambo states:

> Christian theology is produced by erasing wounds. It sanitizes and purifies. Theology birthed from this wound is dependent on ongoing practices of erasing these origins. It insists on pure beginnings that hover above the soil. And if and when theology hovers above the soil, it denies harm done to bodies on the ground.[38]

A trans*-centred trauma theology must resist any attempt to purify and sanitize. The impulse to sanitize presupposes the logic of eradication and denies the holiness of that which is considered impure.

I am particularly indebted to Shelly Rambo's *Resurrecting Wounds* and the writings of Craig Keen for their influence in shaping my vision of the ruptured body of Christ. Echoing Rambo's articulation that trauma occurs with life's encounter with death, Keen says, 'To understand Jesus Christ one must understand him as the place where forsaken death and holy life concur.'[39] The resurrected Christ appears to Thomas with his wounds intact; his resurrection did not close up his wounds. They were not scabbed over. Skin and flesh are the boundary organ between a person's bodyself and everything else. His skin is opened up. The boundaried body and psychology of God are made porous. Keen beautifully states:

It is because the resurrected Jesus has not 'gotten better' that he is the savior ... It is that forsaken history which is raised, which is transfigured, which is transformed bodily by the Spirit of God. The binary opposition between good and evil – the opposition known so well by Adam – prevails through Good Friday and conquers Jesus there. This is the opposition of health vs. disease, life vs. death, 'without sin' vs. sin, exaltation vs. debasement, master vs. servant, first vs. last, God vs. flesh. In the concurrence of Good Friday and Easter Sunday that binary opposition bursts open like the belly of a dragon slain from within.[40]

The body of Christ is ruptured open. The boundary between God and not-god is not erased, but it is made ambiguous. In Christ's descent into hell, death is brought into the life of intra-trinitarian relations. The binary opposition of life and death were disrupted. The liveliness of life overwhelmed the deadliness of death. This is the meaning of that most queerly named day of the year: Good Friday. Christ's wounds are the means of God's apocalyptic rupturing. Just as in trauma studies, there is no way of reconceiving or restoring a pre-wounded Christ. Such a thing is nonsensical. His wounds are integral to Christ's identity – even retroactively.

Trans* bodies as queerly apocalyptic

Trans* identities similarly disturb the binary oppositions that are taken as a natural given. Named for their transgressive bodies, they threaten the ontologies, theologies and systems that demand the obedience and maintenance of the status quo. By self-identifying as trans*, one ruptures one's bodyself and a new identity is named. The naming for many is quite literal; trans* persons often assume new names and new identities. I am reminded of the many times in Scripture in which people were given new names: Abram to Abraham, Simon to Peter, Saul to Paul. These are just a few among many. Their new names become synonymous with these biblical characters. Very rarely have I heard Abraham primarily referred to as Abram or Peter referred to as Simon. This includes those characters' narratives before they were given a new name. When a trans* person adopts a new name, their previous one becomes a 'deadname'. It refers to an identity that is dead. Perhaps most curious is that trans* folks often wish their chosen name to be used as their name at all times – even prior to transitioning and/or the adoption of their new name. Their deadname is dead for all time. Their trans* identity, in the act of coming out, queers time by rupturing identity temporally. If being gender dysphoric and being in the closet are considered inherently traumatic, healing from that dysphoria must come from integrating their somatic knowledge of their dysphoria into their personal narrative and identities. Their dysphoria exists, just as trauma does, as a kind of somatic timelessness. By bringing one's trans* identity into time (i.e. become embodied), this is the name for the entirety of a person's bodyself – past, present and future. The life of a chosen name is so filled with life that it overwhelms the deadliness of a deadname. To intentionally use a person's deadname is a rejection of a person's identity. Instead, using their chosen name affirms their life and their identity. It embraces the totality of a trans* person as an embodied person-in-relation.

This trans* identity-as-rupturing is based on the simple fact that they transgress gender and sexual norms. Thankfully, the Son 'was wounded for our transgressions ... and by his bruises we are healed' (Isa. 53.5 NRSV). I suggest that Christ being wounded for our transgression is wonderfully good news for those who transgress 'natural' gender and sexual boundaries. These boundaries and binaries are problematized by trans* bodies, and, in this way, they coincide with the liberating work of the Spirit. As I have established above, at the heart of gender dysphoria are antagonisms within persons-in-relation. Another way of putting it is that there is a deficiency of love among a person's constitutive relationships.

Conclusion: an apocalyptic pneumatology for trans* persons

What is needed, then, is an excess of love, which I argue is essentially sanctification, *theosis* and deification. Patrick Cheng argues that 'sanctification is all about our eventual reunion with God (and all creation) so that the barriers that separate us from God (and from creation) are dissolved. This is the restoration of all things.'[41] Craig Keen describes sanctification similarly. He writes: 'Salvation is sanctification. Salvation is the binding of God's creatures to the God who comes unconditionally to them and binds all that God is to all that they are ... Flesh is here made holy because God touches it and it touches God.'[42] Traumatized flesh resists touch; touch can be threatening. Trans* persons might flinch even more because of their antagonistic relationship with their body; to be truly healed, they must find space to love their whole bodyselves.

Thankfully, 'in Christian terms, the Spirit has befriended matter. She has befriended matter for Christ's sake on account of the incarnation.'[43] This offers significant hope for trans* folks – that spirit and matter can be made into friends. They neither must be enemies nor lovers, but in friendship can have the greatest intimacy with one another. The work of the Spirit in restoring all things is the restoration of friendship among all things with God and each other. Those 'natural' boundaries and binary oppositions that prevent and destroy friendships are broken open. Chang states plainly, 'the Holy Spirit collapses our closets and frees us to come out.'[44] The 'closet' is a 'natural' place that maintains its integrity through the maintenance of built walls that enforce and regulate the space which exists between those walls, ensuring its captives remain there. Sanctification, then, necessitates the tearing down of those closeting walls. 'The theosis that the Spirit works, then, is a movement that transgresses the integrity of the creature precisely as the creature participates in the Trinity, i.e., in the Spirit, through the Son, to Father, unfathomable abyss.'[45] Keen concludes his essay when he writes:

> The love of God which transgresses one's integrity 'in a Godward direction' transgresses it again as one's identity is surrendered in and to one's neighbor. It is in this above all that we are most like God in the holy life. Not because we have come to something in ourselves that might be taken as a kind of representation of God. But because by the very energy of God we move beyond ourselves as God has in Christ and in the Spirit. No metaphysical hierarchy can get its hand around this free love.[46]

The sanctifying love of God transgresses 'natural', safe identities through Christ's debasement and human deification. Those immutable boundaries within and among persons-in-relation are not erased so much as made insignificant. This is analogous to how the seemingly safe and natural identity of a trans* person prior to coming out is ruptured and destabilized in the process of identifying as trans*, coming out and adopting a new name. They move away from the identity they have been into the identity they are (and are becoming), and in so doing come to themselves. A person must seek to lose their life in order to find it. A trans* person must seek to destabilize their whole bodyself in order to become who they are. Seen in this light, for trans* folks, transitioning and coming out are more than therapeutic treatments and coping skills. They are means of sanctification and deification.

Bibliography

Aromantics Wiki, 'Queerplatonic', https://aromantic.wikia.org/wiki/Queerplatonic, accessed 19.12.2019.

Bader-Saye, Scott, 'The Transgender Body's Grace', *Journal of the Society of Christian Ethics* 39, 1 (2019), pp. 75–92, https://doi.org/10.5840/jsce2019445.

Baldwin, Jennifer, *Trauma Sensitive Theology: Thinking Theologically in the Era of Trauma*, Eugene, OR: Cascade Books, 2018.

Barber, Charles, 'We Live in the Age of Trauma', *Salon*, 1 May 2013, www.salon.com/2013/05/01/we_live_in_the_age_of_trauma/, accessed 25.2.2022.

Cheng, Patrick S., *Radical Love: Introduction to Queer Theology*, New York: Seabury Books, 2011.

———, *Rainbow Theology: Bridging Race, Sexuality, and Spirit*, New York: Seabury Books, 2013.

Cornwall, Susannah, *Sex and Uncertainty in the Body of Christ: Intersex Conditions and Christian Theology*, London: Routledge, 2010.

Eisenberger, Naomi I., Matthew D. Lieberman and Kipling D. Williams, 'Does Rejection Hurt? An FMRI Study of Social Exclusion', *Science*, 10 October

2003, https://link.galegroup.com/apps/doc/A109958991/HRCA?sid=lms, accessed 25.2.2022.

Hartke, Austen, *Transforming: The Bible and the Lives of Transgender Christians*, Louisville, KY: Westminster John Knox Press, 2018.

Hunt, Mary E., 'Lovingly Lesbian: Toward a Feminist Theology of Friendship' in *Sexuality and the Sacred: Sources for Theological Reflection*, 2nd edn, ed. Kelly Brown Douglas and Marvin Ellison, Louisville, KY: Westminster John Knox Press, 2010.

Integrative Client Counseling Institute, 'What Is Interpersonal Neurobiology (IPNB)?', *Integrative Client Counseling Institute*, https://www.icc.institute/iccm/what-is-interpersonal-neurobiology-ipnb/, accessed 10.2.2019.

Keen, Craig, 'The Transgression of the Integrity of God: Trinity and the Hallowing of the Flesh' in *The Transgression of the Integrity of God: Essays and Addresses*, Eugene, OR: Wipf & Stock, 2012.

Kim-Kort, Mihee, *Outside the Lines: How Embracing Queerness will Transform your Faith*, Minneapolis, MN: Fortress Press, 2018.

Lev-Wiesel, Rachel, Orit Nuttman-Shwartz and Rotem Sternberg, 'Peer Rejection During Adolescence: Psychological Long-Term Effects – A Brief Report', *Journal of Loss and Trauma* 11, 2 (3 April 2006), pp. 131–42, https://doi.org/10.1080/15325020500409200, accessed 25.2.2022.

Méndez Montoya, Angel F., 'Eucharistic Imagination: A Queer Body-Politics', *Modern Theology* 30, 2 (April 2014), pp. 326–39, https://doi.org/10.1111/moth.12099.

Morgensen, Scott Lauria, *Spaces Between Us: Queer Settler Colonialism and Indigenous Decolonization*, Minneapolis, MN: University of Minnesota Press, 2011.

O'Donnell, Karen, *Broken Bodies: The Eucharist, Mary and the Body in Trauma Theology*, London: SCM Press, 2019.

Rambo, Shelly, *Resurrecting Wounds: Living in the Afterlife of Trauma*, reprint edn, Waco, TX: Baylor University Press, 2018.

Rambo, Shelly and Catherine Keller, *Spirit and Trauma: A Theology of Remaining*, Louisville, KY: Westminster John Knox Press, 2010.

Rogers, Eugene F., *After the Spirit*, Grand Rapids, MI: Eerdmans, 2005.

Sheffield, Tricia, 'Performing Jesus: A Queer Counternarrative of Embodied Transgression', *Theology & Sexuality* 14, 3 (May 2008), pp. 233–58, https://doi.org/10.1177/1355835808091421, accessed 25.2.2022.

Sim, Christy Gunter, *Survivor Care: What Religious Professionals Need to Know about Healing Trauma*, Nashville, TN: Wesley's Foundery Books, 2018.

van der Kolk, Bessel, *The Body Keeps the Score: Brain, Mind, and Body in the Healing of Trauma*, reprint edn, New York: Penguin Books, 2015.

Wesley, John, 'Upon Our Lord's Sermon on the Mount V' in *John Wesley's Sermons: An Anthology*, ed. Albert Outler and Richard Heitzenrater, Nashville, TN: Abingdon Press, 1991, pp. 207–21.

Notes

1 Charles Barber, 'We Live in the Age of Trauma', *Salon*, 1 May 2013, www.salon.com/2013/05/01/we_live_in_the_age_of_trauma/, accessed 25.2.2022.

2 John Wesley, 'Upon our Lord's Sermon on the Mount, V' in *John Wesley's Sermons: An Anthology*, ed. Albert Outler and Richard Heitzenrater (Nashville, TN: Abingdon Press, 1991), p. 219.

3 Scott Lauria Morgensen, *Spaces Between Us: Queer Settler Colonialism and Indigenous Decolonization* (Minneapolis, MN: University of Minnesota Press, 2011), p. 26.

4 Tricia Sheffield, 'Performing Jesus: A Queer Counternarrative of Embodied Transgression', *Theology & Sexuality* 14, 3 (May 2008), p. 248, https://doi.org/10.1177/1355835808091421, accessed 25.2.2022.

5 Susannah Cornwall, *Sex and Uncertainty in the Body of Christ: Intersex Conditions and Christian Theology* (London: Routledge, 2014), p. 69.

6 Naomi I. Eisenberger, Matthew D. Lieberman and Kipling D. Williams, 'Does Rejection Hurt? An FMRI Study of Social Exclusion', *Science*, 10 October 2003, https://link.galegroup.com/apps/doc/A109958991/HRCA?sid=lms, accessed 25.2.2022.

7 Rachel Lev-Wiesel, Orit Nuttman-Shwartz and Rotem Sternberg, 'Peer Rejection During Adolescence: Psychological Long-Term Effects – A Brief Report', *Journal of Loss and Trauma* 11, 2 (3 April 2006), https://doi.org/10.1080/15325020500409200, pp. 131–42, p. 139.

8 Patrick S. Cheng, *Rainbow Theology: Bridging Race, Sexuality, and Spirit* (New York: Seabury Books, 2013), p. 73.

9 Morgensen, *Spaces Between Us*, p. 32.

10 Melanie Richter-Montpetit, 'Empire, Desire and Violence: A Queer Transnational Feminist Reading of the Prisoner "Abuse" in Abu Ghraib and the Question of "Gender Equality"', *International Feminist Journal of Politics* 9, 1 (March 2007), p. 41.

11 Integrative Client Counseling Institute, 'What Is Interpersonal Neurobiology (IPNB)?', *Integrative Client Counseling Institute*, www.icc.institute/iccm/what-is-interpersonal-neurobiology-ipnb/, accessed 19.12.2019.

12 Angel F. Méndez Montoya, 'Eucharistic Imagination: A Queer Body-Politics', *Modern Theology* 30, 2 (April 2014), p. 327.

13 Scott Bader-Saye, 'The Transgender Body's Grace', *Journal of the Society of Christian Ethics* 39, 1 (2019), pp. 75–92, p. 86.

14 Shelly Rambo and Catherine Keller, *Spirit and Trauma: A Theology of Remaining* (Louisville, KY: Westminster John Knox Press, 2010), p. 15.

15 Austen Hartke, *Transforming: The Bible and the Lives of Transgender Christians* (Louisville, KY: Westminster John Knox Press, 2018), p. 57.

16 Mihee Kim-Kort, *Outside the Lines: How Embracing Queerness Will Transform Your Faith* (Minneapolis, MN: Fortress Press, 2018), p. 130.

17 Mary E. Hunt, 'Lovingly Lesbian: Toward a Feminist Theology of Friendship' in *Sexuality and the Sacred: Sources for Theological Reflection*, 2nd edn, ed. Kelly Brown Douglas and Marvin Ellison (Louisville, KY: Westminster John Knox Press, 2010), p. 193.

18 'Queerplatonic', Aromantics Wiki, https://aromantic.wikia.org/wiki/Queerplatonic, accessed 12.12.2019.

19 Kim-Kort, *Outside the Lines*, p. 74.

20 Karen O'Donnell, *Broken Bodies: The Eucharist, Mary and the Body in Trauma Theology* (London: SCM Press, 2019), p. 15.

21 Jennifer Baldwin, *Trauma Sensitive Theology: Thinking Theologically in the Era of Trauma* (Eugene, OR: Cascade Books, 2018), p. 39.

22 Bessel van der Kolk, *The Body Keeps the Score: Brain, Mind, and Body in the Healing of Trauma*, reprint edn (New York: Penguin Books, 2015), p. 43.

23 Christy Gunter Sim, *Survivor Care: What Religious Professionals Need to Know about Healing Trauma* (Nashville, TN: Wesley's Foundery Books, 2018), pp. 65–78.

24 van der Kolk, *The Body Keeps the Score*, p. 43.

25 van der Kolk, *The Body Keeps the Score*, p. 54.

26 van der Kolk, *The Body Keeps the Score*, p. 53.

27 van der Kolk, *The Body Keeps the Score*, p. 69.

28 O'Donnell, *Broken Bodies*, p. 12.

29 van der Kolk, *The Body Keeps the Score*, p. 99; emphasis added.

30 Rambo and Keller, *Spirit and Trauma*, p. 19.

31 Rambo and Keller, *Spirit and Trauma*, p. 127.

32 Rambo and Keller, *Spirit and Trauma*, p. 50.

33 Eugene F. Rogers, *After the Spirit* (Grand Rapids, MI: Eerdmans, 2005), p. 205.

34 O'Donnell, *Broken Bodies*, p. 59.

35 van der Kolk, *The Body Keeps the Score*, p. 18.

36 Baldwin, *Trauma Sensitive Theology*, p. 30.

37 Rambo and Keller, *Spirit and Trauma*, p. 6.

38 Rambo and Keller, *Spirit and Trauma*, pp. 76–7.

39 Craig Keen, 'The Transgression of the Integrity of God: The Trinity and the Hallowing of the Flesh', *Wesleyan Theological Journal* 36, 1 (2001), p. 83.

40 Keen, 'The Transgression of the Integrity of God', p. 84.

41 Patrick S. Cheng, *Radical Love: Introduction to Queer Theology* (New York: Seabury Books, 2011), p. 101.

42 Keen, 'The Transgression of the Integrity of God', p. 85.

43 Rogers, *After the Spirit*, p. 58.

44 Cheng, *Radical Love*, p. 103.

45 Keen, 'The Transgression of the Integrity of God', p. 88.

46 Keen, 'The Transgression of the Integrity of God', p. 98.

Trauma Theology and the Whole Body

10

Autism: An Autoethnography
of a Peculiar Trauma

CLAIRE WILLIAMS

> She is speaking to me in the darkness
> but I do not comprehend what she is saying
> She is leading me in the darkness
> but I cannot tell where she is moving
> She is pursuing me in the darkness
> but I cannot discover her purpose.[1]

Introduction

'I am not here today because I want to be. I am terrified.'[2] The words
of Christine Blasey Ford at the Supreme Court Confirmation Committee,
words that have resonance. I resist the drive to write this chapter. Like
Jonah I try to relocate my attention elsewhere, to ignore the imperative to
speak. Writing such a chapter is potentially shame-full – embarrassing and
exposing. Yet the imperative to speak and the cathartic process of speech
compels me.

The speech is further imperilled by the maxim 'If you've met one autistic person, you've met one autistic person'. Despite common diagnostic
criteria, each individual on the autism spectrum encounters autism differently. I write my own testimony of my life, not as a description of life with
an autism diagnosis, for I cannot.[3] I cannot speak of non-verbal autism,
I cannot speak of autism and racial discrimination, I cannot speak of
autism and masculinity.[4] I can, however, chart a course through my own
autoethnography that raises questions and poses challenges that provoke
further reflection upon trauma and autism.[5] Autoethnography is the academic practice of telling stories of the researcher's life. Autoethnography
seeks to understand the personal experience of a researcher in the context
of social and political life. I achieve this via an interaction with charismatic
spirituality, not to denigrate one form of Christian practice over another,

but to find a way through the questions of spirituality, practices and the trauma of otherness and shame in the autistic experience of Christian worship. As one who is committed to this charismatic ecclesiology, I do not merely criticize from the outside but witness this trauma from the position of a hopeful insider. I will describe the experience of encountering charismatic spirituality as an autistic person, I will critically examine it and offer a constructive response. I will attempt to explain the notion of trauma and autism and hope that it will be of value to the wider church community. I offer this to you as a testimony of a life lived peculiarly.

Autism: a peculiar form of trauma

I don't feel quite right as I walk to church on this particular Sunday. I cannot understand this bubble of unwanted emotion but it rests heavy in my chest as I take each step towards Sunday services. I always come to church on a Sunday; it is my habit and my routine, my declaration that it is important to me. I've got my husband alongside me and my children in tow but I've also got this lead weight coming along for the ride, an unwelcome guest who hasn't got a name and hasn't declared intentions.

We approach the doors and are immediately greeted by a number of different voices cheerfully welcoming us. I notice the man smoking outside before he goes in, the bird box stuck above the cigarette bin to stop the birds nesting again in the bin and the disastrous consequences. I spot a lady behaving in a way I don't expect and smell the scent of her unwashed skin. People are with her, chatting and smiling. Good, I think, welcoming, or am I being patronizing, judgemental? I don't know and my mind cascades with thoughts about discrimination and othering; I try not to panic.

I notice a bit of dirt on the floor, the flickering light on the ceiling, the smell of toilet cleaner wafting down the corridor. I notice the lady who always wants to talk to me but I never know why because it is usually a telling off. I notice that my boys look like they aren't going to say good morning to the greeter on the door. I hear the thrum of the bass guitar warming up and the feedback from the sound desk as a teenager takes their eye off the mixing desk. I feel the heat from the sun and worry that I've worn the wrong clothes for that day, that I will be too hot, uncomfortable. I've not even made it in the door yet and my brain clenches at the stimulation and the unwanted guest has settled down – obviously he is staying for the morning. I look about and grab a child's hand, I steer them in through the doors, eyes fixed on their head, remembering to nod and smile at intervals as people say hello. Don't stop me and talk, I think; I want to make it safely to my seat and wait for the service to start – late, I expect. I thought I was going to be OK today, but my voice has frozen, my mind shut down. I am silent. Inside myself. I don't want to be spoken to because I cannot reply.

I sit in my seat and pretend to bow my head and pray. This usually works when the silence comes; the only risk is a particularly brave and somewhat prophetic interruption, wishing to join me in my moment of spiritual encounter. Hopefully those individuals haven't arrived yet, although I know they mean well. I try to think kindly of them. I can't shut out all the chaos around me, the sounds, the wariness I feel as people take seats near me. The shout of my children and the voices of conversations as people meet up after their busy weeks. I centre my thoughts inside myself. My silence permeates my prayer. The walls that are up in my mind stop my thoughts from ascending beyond myself. I want to pray but the attempts hit the wall and bounce back. I cannot reach out; apparently nothing can reach in either. Why is it so hard?

Suddenly the band launches into the start of the first song. We are beginning without an introduction today, the drums pound and the bass guitar slaps down on its strings. The voices of the singers reach out across the auditorium and people leap up from their seats. An exciting start, a loud wave of praise cascades out of their voices as flags are picked up and arms raised. In many ways I am comfortable, despite my surprise at the sudden noise and the fight-or-flight reaction that it triggered. I know what to expect at this point: a few songs, probably louder than I would choose, and I can let it all carry me away. Perhaps the guest will leave.

I am aware of my body, my limbs, my hair. I try to find a way to stand that feels comfortable, not awkward or a bit painful. I seem to settle into it but lose my rhythm when someone near me starts waving a flag. Are they going to hit me? Another person shouts loudly at the back, declaring something, or maybe it is a cry of angst. People gather around them. The fight-or-flight is back, my heart is pounding, the level of activity is unpredictable, loud, staccato, my rhythm has gone. The children are too old now for me to leave the auditorium with them as an excuse. I sit down. I don't care that it looks like I'm not joining in, like I'm sulking. I've removed the limbs, hair and body problem by sitting down. I wish everyone would be quieter. The service carries on. The children leave for their Sunday School and it is quieter as we approach the more reflective time. I still can't reach beyond my own brain. Other people seem to have had prophetic words but none of them are about me. They never are. God can't reach in either, or doesn't want to.

The sermon drones on – it lasts for nearly an hour. I'm really uncomfortable and too hot. I have to decide what to do after the service ends. If I stay in my seat someone will talk to me and my silence is still present. If I go and grab the children from their groups I can walk with purpose and avoid eye contact and therefore conversation. However, that puts me near the tea and coffee area and I will have to talk then. I choose the children and let my husband know I'll do it; he likes talking so he can stay.

After I collect my boys from their various rooms and check they've behaved, remember to thank the leaders because someone once told me nobody does, I walk towards the queue for the coffee. I look at who I'll be next to in the line and panic because they aren't a 'safe' person to talk to, I'll have to try quite hard to find something to say and I haven't had time to plan it. Someone slips in ahead of me and takes up chatting to them, the panic in my chest fades and I decide to face forward to avoid talking to someone behind. I plant a huge grin on my face and ask for a coffee and make use of my bank of small-talk phrases to ask the kind people who are serving about their week and comment upon the hot weather. Successfully negotiated, I turn with my tea and look for the children.

Lots of people are gathered around chatting, sipping, laughing, eating church biscuits. I don't know where to go. My husband is still somewhere else; I wish he was here so I could stand next to him. The boys are racing around in the garden so I can't stand with them. I don't know how to break into a circle. A group of ladies, people I would like to be friends with, are loudly chatting about a planned camping weekend they are going on. Why wasn't I invited? Although I probably wouldn't go even if I had been. I drop my eyes to the floor to avoid someone unexpected talking to me. I recognize my friend's shoes from across the room and realize that she is only standing with her husband and they are both definitely safe. I make a beeline to them and warm up to saying hello. They may be safe but I still have to work out how to start talking, pacing correctly, smiling at the right points, working out what they have said and responding appropriately. She is my dear friend and she must know I'm odd. She is patient with me and her husband launches into questions about my theological studies. I can do this, safe territory. My husband joins me and we continue chatting. Now he is here I can be quiet and just stand.

The knot in my chest relaxes but the unwanted guest just smiles – he isn't going anywhere. The boys start complaining about lunch and we make a move to leave, to walk back home. I cast my mind to the chaos awaiting me there and wonder if my husband will mind if I lie down for a bit this afternoon. I briefly consider that I was supposed to worship and pray this morning. I didn't do either. I expect God is very disappointed in me, if only I could tell what he was thinking. The big black walls in my head appear to take a step towards the centre of my brain. Maybe next Sunday it will be better. The unwelcome guest just smiles – probably not.

Damage, silence and peculiarity

How is this an account of trauma? There is no violence, no immediate threat to life, no sudden encounter with dread or fear. It is an account of a slightly odd, rather peculiar woman who goes about a church service, encountering it as challenging. Yet it is more. Autism is experienced by others, and sometimes by the individual themselves, as peculiar: the gentleman who collects stamps or knows all the numbers of the buses in the local area, the non-verbal child who communicates through grunts and cries, the silent woman who carries a teddy around her local village. The main presentation of autism is peculiarity, a non-normative approach to social life, thinking and sensing the world. The National Autistic Society defines autism as:

> A lifelong developmental disability which affects how people communicate and interact with the world. One in 100 people are on the autism spectrum and there are around 700,000 autistic adults and children in the UK.[6]

Although no definition is sufficient to describe the lived experiences of the 700,000 people in the UK who exist on the spectrum of experience from verbal to non-verbal, intellectually impaired to academically above average, with associated physical or mental conditions, it is meaningful to write about an individual's experience as an example that will provoke more developed conversations and attention to the circumstances of those on the autistic spectrum.

Trauma theology is generous in its encompassing nature. Whereas trauma from a medical or psychological perspective may require a set of particular standards to be met, this is not so for trauma theologians. Marcia Mount Shoop refers to the ability of theologians to 'know it when we see it'.[7] Attendant to this is the requirement of theologians not to diagnose but to describe the conditions that they experience or witness.[8] Trauma is experienced in a multitude of ways but can be broadly understood in ones that are particularly pertinent to autism. Shoop describes non-normative trauma as an 'irritant' to standard definitions. Theology can, however, answer the cry of the non-normative body-mind with acceptance. That which is traumatic to autistic individuals might be peculiar or unusual but it is still defined as trauma. The intersection of autism, trauma and ecclesiology needs careful description and it is to this I will turn now.

Autistic people are more likely to suffer the effects of trauma because they are more vulnerable to external events that are traumatic and caused by other people.[9] Autistic people can encounter events that are violent or are catastrophic interpersonal crises; for example, the ability of a teenage girl to misunderstand a social situation makes her more vulnerable to sexual predators. Research and anecdotal accounts show that the life of an autistic person is fraught with potential for violence to self and the associated trauma that ensues. However, what is not immediately apparent is the potential for this trauma to stem from the church itself. I refer not to those situations when the traumatic violence stems from members of the church – for example in the abominable cases of child abuse – but the church as systematically designed and operating in a way that causes trauma to the autistic person. To make this point requires an understanding of trauma that draws away from individual moments of physical violence and includes relational and chronic trauma. Then I move to an example of one type of church and the specific ways in which their spirituality enacts a relational separation that is traumatic. I make this case via the spirituality of the charismatic church, which has unique capacity to trigger trauma in autistic individuals. However, I do this from a perspective of an insider, one who loves the charismatic church and wishes for it to flourish. I also offer this account as a metaphor that I hope speaks to the wider church rather than just one branch and one type of practice.

Hilary Jerome Scarsella describes trauma as 'a tear, a break, an emptiness'.[10] One that fractures selfhood and destroys relationality. Our personhood is directly related to our ability to be in relationship with others, and trauma occurs when that is limited or impacted. Further to this Scarsella describes the theological understanding of the human's relationship to God. The fracture of this is also trauma: 'When trauma undoes one's ability to sustain particular relations, it does not *lead* to the disintegration of the person; it quite literally *is* the disintegration of the actual parts of that person.'[11]

Trauma, says Shelly Rambo, is an encounter with death. This is not literal death (although it could be a near miss), but the sort of death that shakes the foundations of what is safe and known.[12] In the case of autism, trauma occurs when relationships are fractured and when safety is compromised. This happens in a particular autistic way. Threats to humanity and to safety occur when an individual is exposed to ideas of shame as well as to moments of stark fear. These take place more frequently in the autistic experience, Gordon Gates claims.[13] Chronic invalidation occurs for people with autism because they are frequently misunderstood and stigmatized via their relationships with the world around them. The persistent inability to develop relationships or the continued mis-steps in social communication, the flight-or-fight mechanism that is triggered via sensory processing problems or the sense of existing in a *wrong* way all create trauma for the autistic person. Gates claims that autism is the 'new minority', such is the level of shame and stigma attached to lives of autistic people.[14]

I suggest that this is compounded by the systematizing brain of autism and trauma theology's understanding of memory. Simon Baron-Cohen describes a systematizing mechanism that is predominant in the autistic brain, a desire to follow *if-then* sequencing.[15] *If* I behave inappropriately *then* I will be rejected, for example. The memory of traumatic events has the capacity to retraumatize the individual. Speaking of the impact of the crucifixion narrative on sexual abuse sufferers, Scarsella notes that memory of trauma exists in the nervous system retelling the story of violence again in the present.[16] In autism, the sensory process can be heightened (strong startle reflex, for example), the systematizing brain can be effective and relentless and the potential for triggering trauma therefore is ever present. Relating this to the practices of spirituality is not terribly difficult. The repetitive nature of all spiritual practices has potential to be problematic.

Even charismatic worship, which often lays claim to spontaneity inspired by the Holy Spirit, has repetitive forms.[17] These forms, if experienced negatively, can effectively be triggers to the trauma of past spiritual encounters.

Daniel Albrecht has described the behaviour of Pentecostal and charismatic churches as ritualized in their understanding of time, space and identity.[18] Ritual time concerns the repetitious nature of weekly and annual events and service. Ritual spaces are the physical boundaries of churches that relate to the worship spaces. Although usually eschewing the 'sacred spaces' per se, the arena where worship occurs takes on a type of ritual space in the way it is used – the creation of a 'micro-world' where the experience of God is particularly ritualistic.

Yet charismatic practices are also spontaneous, Thomas Allan Smail claims.[19] By this, I understand him to mean that there is (despite obvious repetitive features) potential always for difference and change. This is being led by the Spirit in the charismatic language. Smail claims that charismatic worship 'escapes from a complicated conceptuality and a second-hand dependence on such liturgical resources as prayer-books and hymn-books, and in immediacy and freedom to the contact with the living Lord'.[20]

Charismatic worship is relentlessly predictable in its unpredictability. It is ritualized because of the use of space and sacred acts but spontaneous in the disruptive and changing nature of worship. This is credited as good because of the immediacy of encounter with the divine. The human self is stood, exposed, before the overwhelming demonstration of God's power. This immediacy is complicated for the autistic individual because it is potentially overwhelming and is unpredictable. Yet it is proposed as the best way, the most faithful way, to encounter God. Liturgical resources can be inhibitors, says Smail, that interfere with the believer's encounter with God as God would wish it.[21]

To make the point that this method of spirituality is potentially traumatizing I refer to the notion of sensory processing. Autistic people experience the world differently through their senses. They may be sensorially seeking or sensitive, which means they may need more sensory stimulation or much less. This is in part to do with the role of normative discourse surrounding acceptable sensory input. Fulton, Reardon, Richardson and Jones illuminate this by describing an autistic person's response to a door slamming. If the response is to be startled, as it would be for this author, that is considered to be a hyper-reactive state.[22] This is because it is not considered normal to respond to a door slamming with a fight-or-flight response. If it is considered acceptable in a church to suddenly begin a song with a crash of drums, the squeal of the electric guitar and three different vocalists singing into their microphones, it is not considered acceptable to have a hyper-reactive response, even if that is normal for the individual concerned. Sensory input is understood on a normative spectrum despite the existence of individuals who do not receive such stimulus in that way. Fulton et al. say that sensory affordances, the opportunities for perception and action of stimulus, are varied and can be received by someone on the spectrum of autism as akin to pain, for example. This can result in something as invisible as a panic response or as visible as a response of terror that causes the person to curl into a ball or attack the person next to them.[23] That level of fear and terror in any other circumstance would be called traumatic. However, it occurs in a situation that others do not find to be traumatic and therefore it is ignored, thus causing stigma and shame as well as fear.

Alongside these traumas is the very real potential that it might happen again. The systematizing response kicks in and fear persists, 'the ongoing, embodied experience of threat and lack of safety inherent in real-time autistic sensory experience'.[24] Immediately after the music begins with a bang, the leader of the service requires everyone, sensing the move of the Spirit, to walk around the church and pray for someone – ideally someone they've never met before. Threat upon threat occurs.

The charismatic stance is that the way in which God wishes to interact with his people is a way that an autistic person finds challenging, difficult, impossible and potentially traumatic. Not only is the experience of charismatic worship overwhelming and risky, the relationship with the divine is fractured. The autistic person is potentially unable, because of their very self, to encounter God. We see the damage to their humanity via their relationships, their sense of shame at being inadequate as well as the trauma of sensory overload in the moment itself.

This brief overview introduces trauma in a theological frame with a particularized nuance in autism. I have illustrated that trauma can be understood as a relational breakdown, one that incorporates disruption of relationship with the divine as well as human. It is particularized in autism because of the unique presentation of traumatic potential and situations. It is pertinent to a theology of trauma that understands the role of the church because these things draw together and create potentially traumatic situations that are found and enacted *within* the walls of the church.

Silence

The conference that I am attending has been quite fun. I am surrounded by a group of people I know and I feel safe with. We are all gathered in a huge auditorium to sing songs and hear the kind of encouraging talks that I usually enjoy picking apart for theological error (which is a terrible habit). However, the current speaker – who is famous – has other plans. I thought that this would be a fairly predictable event, partially because we are hemmed in and gathered from so many different churches that the usual triggers of charismatic worship that cause me anxiety can't happen. I won't have to get up and go anywhere and the songs are probably more organized and less likely to break from tradition. The speaker gives his thoughts, quite funny actually, and then moves into a time of prayer. I sit back. I'm probably not going to be able to do much of this; I never seem to feel the right things. However, today is the day the speaker decides to ramp things up a bit. Suddenly people are having 'experiences' everywhere. There is shouting and screaming, falling about and wailing. I've seen war films with parts like this in it. I feel fearful, the sudden noises are terrifying and sound otherworldly, although not in a particularly good way. It persists. More and more outlandish and unusual behaviour happens; none of this I predicted and I've rarely seen it before. My fear and discomfort escalate – it is so loud, staccato and aggressive. There is a fire door to my right and I push past the people I'm with, who very obviously see me leave and move to stand in the stairwell. I look back through the glass door. I don't really care what the conference organizers think of me but I'm keenly aware that my group know I've left and that I didn't like it. This wonderful move of God scared me. I am angry and cross and ashamed. Why is it that when God 'turns up', I have to leave?

'Trauma and narrative theorists have posited trauma as a decimation of speech and demonstrated the central role of narrative in person/al remaking.'[25] Scarsella's words are particularly concerning for a charismatic theologian. The oral tradition of the Pentecostal/charismatic spirituality is not focused only on the transmission of thoughts and ideas via spoken stories, but on the positioning of individuals within those stories. The biblical story and God's ways in the world are narrated with each individual believer's role within it. Salvation history is the history of God's people caught up into the drama of God's purposes and plan. The inbreaking of the kingdom, the realized eschatology, the experiential spirituality are all transmitted in actions and behaviours that locate the believer in the story of God. However, the silence of failed encounter with charismatic practices is a silence that transcends the ability to speak in any given moment; it is the silence of having no story to tell – no ability to place oneself in the charismatic narrative of glory. It is traumatic because there is no hope of the remaking that Scarsella finds to be important after trauma. Not only is there the fractured relationship with God via the ineffective (at the very least) spiritual practices, there is no hope of place in the redemption narrative, no restoration because the way back is barred and the way forward is impossible. Participation in the great story of salvation that is enacted and spoken about in church and faith community is prevented. Silence is all that remains.

Shame

The shame remains, the shame of failed friendships and brittle relationships, broken by my own inadequate being. I am damaged and damaging, such that even God cannot look upon me. The story of the failed conference is one of many such accounts I can give. Alongside these accounts of charismatic spirituality are the feelings of shame and unacceptability. I may be forgiven but I am not acceptable, not worthy of impartation of the divine in my own small life, that noisy, disruptive, explosive gifting that rends apart worship services proclaiming holiness and mystical experience. My inability to participate in the church that welcomes all, the only club that exists for the benefit of those who aren't members, compounds my alienation.

The narrative, that the disabled person's self is an embodied example of the fall of humanity, is deeply painful and disruptive to the identity of that person.[26] Theories of the social construction of disability state that disabled people only experience the world as disabled because of the way in which society dis-ables them.[27] Trauma theology stands as a challenge to the normative values of practice that the Church presents. Broadly speaking, if some disability models find that society's construction causes disability on top of their impairments, then the Church can be found accountable for its own dis-abling influence. The practices of the charismatic church are a metaphor as well as a concrete situation for the trauma that the Church is capable of inflicting on those who are restricted from meeting God.[28]

Gates finds that autistic people experience shame when they are invalidated and excluded. The stigma of the autistic person's being-in-the-world as constructed as incompatible with God's outrageous breaking into the experience of humanity has devastating consequences.

Shame is also associated with worth, especially in a community that values the state of being forgiven and accepted. Worth in the charismatic community stems from ability to participate and demonstrate signs of redemption. It is a productive state, where the spiritual outcome illustrates a deeper truth about the individual. The demonstration of the spiritual gifts, long held in high regard by both the Pentecostal and charismatic traditions as evidentiary, is produced as a sign of membership in the kingdom. Of what value and worth are those who cannot produce these signs? Karen Bray calls this 'inscriptional violence' that requires the populace to act and produce to be worthwhile.[29] Work and production, in line with the Protestant work ethic, is redemptive. What of those who cannot produce, cannot *do*? As well as sweeping political and theological questions that this understanding generates, it also is pertinent to this particular form of spirituality, one that requires action as evidence of participation and of redemption.

Damage

The Church has long clung to a vision of the healing Christ who takes sins away and makes people clean and whole. The charismatic church continues this narrative with the practices of healing associated with the tradition. The message this gives is that people are deemed to be disabled either through their sin or the sin of humanity in need of healing. Once healed they will be able to enter the church life completely and participate fully.

I am expecting my first child. This causes me no small amount of anxiety. I don't want my child to be like me. If they have my life, or worse, have my mothering, they will be unhappy. We must pray, pray against it. Declare the truth of God and renounce the lies and the sins that you have believed or taken part in. Delve through all of your life and find those sins and renounce them. Like a genetic disease, sin will crawl down the family tree until it leaves no one standing. If you don't do anything about it. Words have power so I must state all the awful things about me to someone else and then they won't steal my child's hope away. I think of how wrong I am and all the wrongness that might have preceded me. I haven't got a name for what I am yet, that comes a long while after; but for now with this tiny ball of life inside me I must do something to mitigate the damage I could do. I declare until there is no breath left in me, repent until I am imagining sins and hope that I will not be found wanting, for the sake of this tiny hope.

The practices of charismatic theology trumpet triumph,[30] whether it is through the assumptions of healing ministries or the certainty with which God's voice can be heard. Charismatic practices also assume normative behaviours around communication and voice – an oral culture, not only in its theological manoeuvres, but also in its practices.

I have described the identity of an autistic body-mind as being silent, shameful and damaged when viewed through the lens of charismatic spiritual practices. These are practices that create an understanding of the world, a vision of the good life via a social imaginary.[31] The ritualized behaviours of the charismatic church are socially and sensorially overloading.

As she narrates the trauma of pregnancy loss, Serene Jones highlights the need for acts of agency.[32] Pregnancy loss, she writes, can come with feelings of guilt and responsibility for this loss. In the same way, I have described the shame of autism and the responsibility that can be felt for failed encounters with the divine. Pregnancy loss features the sense of loss of hope and of future, and this is also the case for autism. There is no 'cure' for autism, nothing can be essentially changed about the autistic person. What agency, therefore, can they have to effect spiritual change in their lives? The disruption of the anticipated future in pregnancy loss is similar to my experiences of diagnosis with autism. All my life I had battled and fought to create a future that did not look like me. Little changes and enormous shifts – all were attempted in a battle to make a future that did not contain my peculiar self but a transformed, redeemed, *normal* self. A diagnosis of autism destroyed that striving. There could not be my imaginary future.

A still small voice

Then He said, 'Go out, and stand on the mountain before the LORD.' And behold, the LORD passed by, and a great and strong wind tore into the mountains and broke the rocks in pieces before the LORD, but the LORD was not in the wind; and after the wind an earthquake, but the LORD was not in the earthquake; and after the earthquake a fire, but the LORD was not in the fire; and after the fire a still small voice. So it was, when Elijah heard it, that he wrapped his face in his mantle and went out and stood in the entrance of the cave. Suddenly a voice came to him, and said, 'What are you doing here, Elijah?' (1 Kings 19.11–13 NKJV)

Trauma theology offers a mode of conversation about such questions of humanity and practice. It challenges the script that there is a way to explain difference according to fallen humanity – that disability is the result of sin in humanity and a flaw in the human.

What resources exist to narrate a meaningful existence from this damaged, silent and shameful self? I want to suggest a different narrative that responds to this. It does not directly correlate to the three features of the self I have described here, rather it is a fragmentary reflection, incomplete, not settling in one place and resisting an urge to fix, remedy or resolve.[33] It corresponds with Rambo's Holy Saturday and 'crip time'. I do not offer these as resolutions or solutions to the problematic transections of trauma autism and the Church. Rather, along with Shoop I propose 'our willingness to be honest about the impossibility of tidying this all up'.[34]

Charismatic spirituality is a spirituality of production. Spiritual experiences are sought and generated through the actions of charismatic practice: for example speaking in tongues as a production of the Holy Spirit; a word of knowledge or a prophecy as a production of an encounter with the divine. Trauma caused by the failure to produce such experiences can be narrated differently via the use of 'crip time'. This is the deliberately provocative phrase to describe the experiences of disability.[35] It is an outlandish and offensive term to embrace the difference of disability in an ableist society. It is profoundly useful for the narration of different experiences in the Church. It speaks against the need for evidence of divine interaction in the standard frame but authenticates a different approach to God, one that is equally valid and has its place in the charismatic church. It is grace-filled.

Crip time is existing in a different key – a different time frame. It is delayed or late.[36] It relates to the charismatic experience in a radical way. In the same way as 'queer time', it understands that events do not always occur when they are expected. In the same way that Judith Halberstam says that queer time defies the linear progression of dependent childhood, independent adulthood through to marriage and reproduction, so crip time says that the future is questionable.[37] This is a future that is not imaginable or is overridden by the disability that has robbed the imagined future from us. The disability, be it acquired or born into, permanently distorts the future.

How does this narrate a charismatic understanding intersecting with autism? Alison Kafer quotes Halberstam's category of 'eccentric economic practices', the moderation of time and energy to preserve future energy and output. For autism this can mean managing sensory overload so as to avoid the impact of such overload in subsequent days and weeks. Among the autism community it is commonly called 'burnout'. A church service that is a sensory overloading experience is overridden by crip-time economics that declare the investment of energy to be fundamentally disabling. The encounter with the divine on the schedule of ableism is distorted by crip time.

Crip time also requires that these difficulties with different accounts of time are not healed. The optimist charismatic eschatology that foresees the inbreaking kingdom as having curative potential needs challenging. My personal experience of charismatic healing theology is a profound optimism for even the most impossible medical situation. This does not always 'work' but it is sought nonetheless. Autism fits into the category of medical impossibilities – it cannot be cured. It would be tempting to seek healing from God for such a condition, notwithstanding the norma- tive values applied to such a request of God (after all, should I even want to be healed?); crip time challenges our understanding of a future that does not seek healing. That future resides in the Holy Saturday time of Rambo, the time where trauma survivors exist.[38] For autism in a non-autistic world, Holy Saturday offers an alternative to the narratives of improvement that so often dominate charismatic triumphalism. In Holy Saturday time, love remains, says Rambo. Love exists in that middle space where healing and redemption do not. Autism is not healed, the trauma of existing in a charismatic environment is not overcome but instead time is understood differently. It is crip time during Holy Saturday.

Holy Saturday is not waiting until the resurrection for healing for what of my autistic self might remain. My identity would be lost in the escha- tology of redemption that sees the troubles with who I am and what the Church is resolved by *my* healing. As has already been shown, that sort of collapse of identity is traumatizing in itself. Rather, my future under- standing of myself is caught up in the crip futurology that understands the standard expectation of what comes next in charismatic eschatology as being dark and unclear. I'm in the middle because I am not *waiting* for a brighter future where I am not myself, rather I am being. I am existing in the crip time of Holy Saturday.

Productive time is re-imagined in crip terms. Spirituality that does not produce an outcome is acceptable. When Bray tells of the effects of overstimulation of the productive economy on fragile body-minds, she describes autistic burnout inadvertently ('depression and exhaustion'[39]). Her solution is to make use of crip time. 'Bipolar time' resists the demands of productivity and resists notions of redemption and cure. It is a time that defies charismatic triumph.

Hence, bipolar temporality refuses the cruel optimism and happy efficiency of neoliberalism and affirms a different sense, one that is enacted through microtactics of the self: collapsing into bed, embracing one's feelings of overwhelming exhaustion; or living into one's porosity to the world, collectivizing connections and so insisting that we need not be alone in facing that which has got us so tired.[40]

Flora Keshgegian suggests that time is understood not as linear with a telos but with outcomes that are unknown. This is a hopeful stance, surprisingly, because it is not aiming at triumphant future accomplishment in a linear narrative time but at being and stability.[41] Stability speaks of a willingness to remain and a hope that is not directed towards accomplishments. This is a futurology that corresponds to crip time, where future is not the imagined future of productivity or achievement but of acceptance and love. Love remains, says Rambo.[42]

This draws me back to 1 Kings and Elijah's encounter with God in his despair. God is not found in the noise and external action, and Elijah does not have a dramatic and charismatic encounter. The inbreaking of God in the moment of hopelessness is quiet and still and appropriate for Elijah's state. Yet still God is active and present in the life of the believer. God offers a hopeful encounter via presence. Elijah participates by being fully himself in the moment of his misery and accepting the encounter. The divine act is not overwhelming, it makes no particular demands on Elijah but is gentle and probing. It is an act of love and of knowing; it is accepting.

I have made use of the theory of crip time to offer a meaningful narrative of the trauma associated with autism and charismatic spiritual practices. There is scope for hopeful theological moves that offer possibilities in the midst of traumatic memory. 'What are you doing here?' is God's question to Elijah and perhaps to everyone. To which my reply is 'To whom else shall I go?'

Bibliography

Adams, Tony E., Stacy Linn Holman Jones and Carolyn Ellis, *Autoethnography*, Oxford: Oxford University Press, 2015.

Albrecht, Daniel E., *Rites in the Spirit: A Ritual Approach to Pentecostal/Charismatic Spirituality*, Journal of Pentecostal Theology Supplement, Sheffield: Sheffield Academic, 1999.

Baron-Cohen, Simon, *The Pattern Seekers: A New Theory of Human Invention*, London: Allen Lane, 2020.

Boynton, Eric (ed.), *Trauma and Transcendence: Suffering and the Limits of Theory*, New York: Fordham University Press, 2018.

Bray, Karen, *Grave Attending*, New York: Fordham University Press, 2020.

Cartledge, Mark J., *Encountering the Spirit*, London: Darton, Longman & Todd, 2006.

Cross, Katie, Wren Radford and Karen O'Donnell, 'Fragments from within the Pandemic: Theological Experiments in Silence, Speech, and Dislocated Time', *Practical Theology* 14, 1–2 (4 March 2021), pp. 144–58, https://doi.org/10.108 0/1756073X.2020.1861802.

Denzin, Norman K. and Yvonna S. Lincoln (eds), *Collecting and Interpreting Qualitative Materials*, 2nd edn, Thousand Oaks, CA: Sage, 2003.

Dreyer, Elizabeth and Mark S. Burrows (eds), *Minding the Spirit: The Study of Christian Spirituality*, Baltimore, MD: Johns Hopkins University Press, 2005.

Eiesland, Nancy L., *The Disabled God: Toward a Liberatory Theology of Disability*, Nashville, TN: Abingdon Press, 1994.

Finkelstein, Vic, 'The "Social Model of Disability" and the Disability Movement', 2007, https://disability-studies.leeds.ac.uk/wp-content/uploads/sites/40/library/finkelstein-The-Social-Model-of-Disability-and-the-Disability-Movement.pdf, accessed 25.2.2022.

Fisk, Anna, *Sex, Sin, and Our Selves: Encounters in Feminist Theology and Contemporary Women's Literature*, Eugene, OR: Pickwick Publications, 2014.

Fulton, Rorie, Emma Reardon, Kate Richardson and Rachel Jones, *Sensory Trauma: Autism, Sensory Difference and the Daily Experience of Fear*, Gwernogle, Wales: Autism Wellbeing Press, 2020.

Ganzevoort, R., 'Scars and Stigmata: Trauma, Identity and Theology', *Practical Theology* 1, 1 (22 February 2008), pp. 19–31, https://doi.org/10.1558/prth.viii.19.

Gates, Gordon S., *Trauma, Stigma and Autism: Developing Resilience and Loosening the Grip of Shame*, London and Philadelphia, PA: Jessica Kingsley Publishers, 2019.

Griffiths, Sarah, Carrie Allison, Rebecca Kenny, Rosemary Holt, Paula Smith and Simon Baron-Cohen, 'The Vulnerability Experiences Quotient (VEQ): A Study of Vulnerability, Mental Health and Life Satisfaction in Autistic Adults', *Autism Research* 12, 10 (October 2019), pp. 1516–28, https://doi.org/10.1002/aur.2162.

Haruvi-Lamdan, Nirit, Danny Horesh and Ofer Golan, 'PTSD and Autism Spectrum Disorder: Co-Morbidity, Gaps in Research, and Potential Shared Mechanisms', *Psychological Trauma: Theory, Research, Practice, and Policy* 10, 3 (May 2018), pp. 290–9, https://doi.org/10.1037/tra0000298.

Jones, Serene, *Trauma + Grace: Theology in a Ruptured World*, 2nd edn, Louisville, KY: Westminster John Knox Press, 2019.

Kafer, Alison, *Feminist, Queer, Crip*, Bloomington, IN: Indiana University Press, 2013.

Keshgegian, Flora A., *Time for Hope: Practices for Living in Today's World*, New York: Continuum, 2006.

MacKenney-Jeffs, Frances, *Reconceptualising Disability for the Contemporary Church*, London: SCM Press, 2021.

National Autistic Society, 'What is Autism?', *National Autistic Society*, www.autism.org.uk/advice-and-guidance/what-is-autism, accessed 24.4.2021.

O'Donnell, Karen and Katie Cross, *Feminist Trauma Theologies: Body, Scripture and Church in Critical Perspective*, London: SCM Press, 2020.

Rambo, Shelly, *Spirit and Trauma: A Theology of Remaining*, Louisville, KY: Westminster John Knox Press, 2010.

Rumball, Freya, Francesca Happé and Nick Grey, 'Experience of Trauma and PTSD Symptoms in Autistic Adults: Risk of PTSD Development Following DSM-5 and Non-DSM-5 Traumatic Life Events', *Autism Research* 13, 12 (December 2020), pp. 2122–32, https://doi.org/10.1002/aur.2306, accessed 25.2.2022.

Slee, Nicola M., *Praying like a Woman*, London: SPCK, 2004.

Smith, James K. A., *Desiring the Kingdom: Worship, Worldview, and Cultural Formation*, Volume 1 of Cultural Liturgies, Grand Rapids, MI: Baker Academic, 2009.

Weiss, Jonathan A. and Michelle A. Fardella, 'Victimization and Perpetration Experiences of Adults With Autism', *Frontiers in Psychiatry* 9 (25 May 2018), p. 203, https://doi.org/10.3389/fpsyt.2018.00203, accessed 25.2.2022.

Notes

1 From 'Litany to a dark God', Nicola M. Slee, *Praying like a Woman* (London: SPCK, 2004).

2 Quoted in Karen O'Donnell and Katie Cross, *Feminist Trauma Theologies: Body, Scripture and Church in Critical Perspective* (London: SCM Press, 2020), p. 13.

3 Nancy L. Eiesland, *The Disabled God: Toward a Liberatory Theology of Disability* (Nashville, TN: Abingdon Press, 1994), p. 69.

4 Thereby following Fisk in attempting to avoid privileging my own voice over others: Anna Fisk, *Sex, Sin, and Our Selves: Encounters in Feminist Theology and Contemporary Women's Literature* (Eugene, OR: Pickwick Publications, 2014).

5 The telling of evocative stories was first developed by Caroline Ellis and Art Bochner (in Denzin and Lincoln, 2003). The aim of the stories told by the researcher is to provoke empathy and feelings. The stories told were used to reflect upon culture via the accounts of personal transformations. The writing of these accounts is a crucial part of the research from which deeper understandings and views are drawn. Autoethnographic work endeavours to understand the self in relation to culture, to describe emotions and feelings and to use the intersection between self and society as a descriptive tool and to make the world better. It is both creative and methodologically rigorous (Adams, Holman Jones and Ellis, 2014). Autoethnographic work is now recognized as a qualitative method that addresses issues of representation and also is an interpretative tool for research findings (Adams, Holman Hones and Ellis 2014, p. 23).

6 'What is Autism?', *National Autistic Society*, www.autism.org.uk/advice-and-guidance/what-is-autism, accessed 24.4.2021.

7 Marcia Mount Shoop, 'Body-Wise: Re-Fleshing Christian Spiritual Practice in Trauma's Wake' in *Trauma and Transcendence: Suffering and the Limits of Theory*, ed. Eric Boynton (New York: Fordham University Press, 2018).

8 Shoop, 'Body-Wise', p. 243.

9 Jonathan A. Weiss and Michelle A. Fardella, 'Victimization and Perpetration Experiences of Adults With Autism', *Frontiers in Psychiatry* 9 (25 May 2018), p. 203, https://doi.org/10.3389/fpsyt.2018.00203, accessed 25.2.2022. Sarah Griffiths et al., 'The Vulnerability Experiences Quotient (VEQ): A Study of Vulnerability, Mental Health and Life Satisfaction in Autistic Adults', *Autism Research* 12, 10 (October 2019), pp. 1516–28, https://doi.org/10.1002/aur.2162, accessed 25.2.2022.

10 Hilary Jerome Scarsella, 'Trauma and Theology: Prospects and Limits in Light of the Cross' in *Trauma and Transcendence: Suffering and the Limits of Theory*, ed. Eric Boynton (New York: Fordham University Press, 2018).

11 Scarsella, 'Trauma and Theology', p. 271; emphasis original.

12 Shelly Rambo, *Spirit and Trauma: A Theology of Remaining* (Louisville, KY: Westminster John Knox Press, 2010).

13 Gordon S. Gates, *Trauma, Stigma and Autism: Developing Resilience and Loosening the Grip of Shame* (London and Philadelphia, PA: Jessica Kingsley Publishers, 2019).

14 Gates, *Trauma, Stigma and Autism*, p. 23.

15 Simon Baron-Cohen, *The Pattern Seekers: A New Theory of Human Invention* (London: Allen Lane, 2020).

16 Scarsella, 'Trauma and Theology'.

17 Mark J. Cartledge, *Encountering the Spirit: The Charismatic Tradition* (London: Darton Longman & Todd, 2006).

18 Daniel E. Albrecht, *Rites in the Spirit: A Ritual Approach to Pentecostal/Charismatic Spirituality*, Journal of Pentecostal Theology (Sheffield: Sheffield Academic, 1999).

19 Thomas Allan Smail et al., *Charismatic Renewal: The Search for a Theology* (London: SPCK, 1993).

20 Smail et al., *Charismatic Renewal*, p. 110.

21 Smail et al., *Charismatic Renewal*, p. 114.

22 Rorie Fulton et al., *Sensory Trauma: Autism, Sensory Difference and the Daily Experience of Fear* (Gwernogle, Wales: Autism Wellbeing Press, 2020).

23 Fulton et al., *Sensory Trauma*, p. 16.

24 Fulton et al., *Sensory Trauma*, p. 30.

25 Scarsella 'Trauma and Theology', p. 274.

26 Nancy Eiesland, in *The Disabled God*, writes that the Church has explained disability as either a symbol of sin or an example of superhero-like spirituality. The biblical record, she notes, explains the propensity towards understanding disability as sin-related, referring to the Levitical law (21.17–23) that prohibits those physically disabled from entering the temple. See also Luke 5.18–26, John 5.14, John 9.1–3. The superhero state refers to virtuous suffering and the incidences that disability allows for kindness from able-bodied people, e.g. Acts 3.1–10.

27 Vic Finkelstein, 'The "Social Model of Disability" and the Disability Movement', 2007, https://disability-studies.leeds.ac.uk/wp-content/uploads/sites/40/library/finkelstein-The-Social-Model-of-Disability-and-the-Disability-Movement.pdf, accessed 25.2.2022. Frances MacKenney-Jeffs, *Reconceptualising Disability for the Contemporary Church* (London: SCM Press, 2021), pp. 27–32.

28 Theologies of disability have contested the readings of Scripture that support the continued dis-abling and othering of difference. For example, MacKenney-Jeffs, *Reconceptualising Disability for the Contemporary Church* and Eiesland, *The Disabled God*.

29 Karen Bray, *Grave Attending* (New York: Fordham University Press, 2020).

30 See also Catherine Keller, 'Foreword' in Rambo, *Spirit and Trauma*.

31 James K. A. Smith, *Desiring the Kingdom: Worship, Worldview, and Cultural Formation*, Volume 1 of Cultural Liturgies (Grand Rapids, MI: Baker Academic, 2009).

32 Serene Jones, *Trauma + Grace: Theology in a Ruptured World*, 2nd edn (Louisville, KY: Westminster John Knox Press, 2019), p. 135.

33 Katie Cross, Wren Radford and Karen O'Donnell, 'Fragments from within the Pandemic: Theological Experiments in Silence, Speech, and Dislocated Time', *Practical Theology* 14, 1–2 (18 January 2021), pp. 1–15, https://doi.org/10.1080/1 756073X.2020.1861802, accessed 25.2.2022.

34 Shoop, 'Body-Wise', p. 254.

35 Alison Kafer, *Feminist, Queer, Crip* (Bloomington, IN: Indiana University Press, 2013), pp. 15–17.

36 Kafer, *Feminist, Queer, Crip*, p. 26.

37 Quoted in Kafer, *Feminist, Queer, Crip*, p. 35.

38 Rambo, *Spirit and Trauma*.

39 Bray, *Grave Attending*, p. 83.

40 Bray, *Grave Attending*, p. 60.

41 Flora A. Keshgegian, *Time for Hope: Practices for Living in Today's World* (New York: Continuum, 2006).

42 Rambo, *Spirit and Trauma*.

11

The Traumatization of Reproductive Loss in Christian Pro-life Discourse and Rituals

MARGARET KAMITSUKA

Memorializing reproductive loss is not new. Families throughout history and across cultures have commemorated these deaths in funerary and other ritual practices. The particular topic of women's religious mourning practices after miscarriage and child death has garnered attention in both secular scholarship[1] and in religious studies in recent years.[2] In Christian communities, there is a widespread recognition that the Church today is lacking in official liturgies and well-resourced pastoral care for reproductive loss.[3] Women rarely find in their Christian communities an opportunity to ritualize a pregnancy that has ended – however it happens – in ways that match their experience of that ending, whether it be grief or relief, loss of faith or hope for the future, shame or resolve. Those who turn to chaplains, pastors or priests with questions about a Christian burial after a stillbirth or miscarriage find that liturgical resources are thin.

There are complicated historical reasons why sacramental and theological materials only sporadically discuss newborns and hardly mention those who die before birth. In general, the issue of pregnancy was avoided, in part because wombs (with the exception of Mary's inviolate one) were associated by most church theologians with the culturally and religiously polluting factors of 'foul smell, excrement, and women's genital blood'.[4] Moreover, unbaptized infant salvation was dubious for most of Western church history. Miscarried foetuses or infants who died without that sacrament were thought to go to an anteroom in hell that eventually came to be known as limbo.[5] These kinds of historical views about filthy wombs and unbaptized infants languishing in hell created a discursive gap in the Church's response to reproductive loss – a gap that has lingered to this day.

Into this gap have stepped pro-life proponents, who offer reassuring answers and a well-choreographed path for memorializing the preborn baby, as they call it, lost to miscarriage or abortion, who now resides in heaven. These religious assurances and ritual pathways, however, come at a cost. Namely, a woman who experiences an ended pregnancy must accept the pro-life view that what she lost was a person – her child – from the moment of conception. Those who suffer a miscarriage get the subtle or overt message that good mothers will make the effort to save the remnants of her miscarriage for a church burial, and good parents will appropriately name and memorialize every miscarried being. A woman who has an abortion gets the subtle or overt message that she killed her child and thus, whether she recognizes it or not, is traumatized by her actions.

This chapter critically examines the morally, theologically and pastorally problematic ways in which pro-life Christian discourses about reproductive loss construct abortion as traumatizing. I will first examine the cultural phenomenon of the foetal memorialization movement and how it attempts to inculcate a message of the spiritual and psychological damage incurred by women who terminate a pregnancy. This messaging spreads a mythology, based on anecdote and pseudoscience, that abortion has such adverse psychological effects as to deserve a diagnosis of post-abortion traumatic stress syndrome. I then examine how conservative Christian ministries for reproductive loss, while ostensibly trying to comfort those who have suffered miscarriage, stillbirth or neonatal death, end up perpetuating the pro-life assumption that the only acceptable view parents should have is grief for a lost preborn child. For either group, intentionally terminating a pregnancy would be anathema. Thus, the pro-life memorialization movement and the miscarriage support movement both end up reinforcing a binary between appropriately bereaved women who have miscarried and supposedly culpable women who have procured an abortion and do not even know they are traumatized.[6] In section three of this chapter, I deconstruct this damaging binary and argue that abortion and miscarriage are two sides of the same coin of reproductive loss. I offer a few final reflections on why this binary is amiss from a theological perspective.

Memorializing foetal demise: a pro-life cultural phenomenon

Pro-life discourses about and activities for memorializing foetal demise after abortion have become a cultural phenomenon. In recent years there has been a surge in post-abortion memorial sites (virtual and actual), post-abortion recovery and repentance retreats, and even international post-abortion pilgrimages. In various media – including books, sermons, online blogs and YouTube videos – one can find references to foetuses as cherubs in heaven, awaiting the repentance of their abortive mothers. One pro-life blog advertising post-abortion spiritual counselling depicts aborted foetuses as infants in an idyllic heavenly landscape and tells women readers that they are for ever linked to their baby by a 'motherly bond that even abortion cannot dissolve'.[7] A website for a Catholic memorial shrine features an image of two babies with Photoshopped angel wings posed on clouds[8] and tells women who had an abortion, 'We want you to memorialze (*sic*) your baby'.[9]

Pro-life groups also want to interact more directly with women who have had abortions in a pastoral capacity. This approach has been referred to as the 'pro-woman/pro-life' approach that purports to advocate for '*both* the woman and her unborn child' and focuses on post-abortion healing.[10] The Catholic-affiliated pro-life organization Rachel's Vineyard offers a ceremony conducted at their post-abortion counselling retreats, which their website describes as an opportunity for parents to 'give dignity to the eternal life and memory of your child in heaven. It is a time to bring a precious bereavement doll and [place] this symbol of your child to rest in a cradle. It is also an act of entrusting the soul of your lost child to God.'[11] Another post-abortion 'healing programme' concludes with a ceremony where participants are encouraged to name their babies and 'formally recogni[ze] their humanity'. One participant remarked that she was now assured that her 'children are alive in heaven with Christ'.[12] A coalition of pro-life groups advertises a national 'day of remembrance for aborted children'.[13] They also publish a massive national registry of cemeteries with dedicated gravesites or shrines for aborted children.[14] The organization Lumina uses the traditional Catholic practice of devotion to the Virgin Mary and pilgrimage to notable Marian shrines as a means to highlight post-abortion trauma and its healing.[15]

One finds counselling-orientated reproductive-loss groups in the UK as well. An organization called Open presents itself as a place of compassion and healing after miscarriage and abortion.[16] Open is run under the auspices of the evangelical Christian Action Research and Education organization (CARE), one arm of which engages in intensive anti-abortion legislative work,[17] most recently in attempting to block abortion liberalization in Northern Ireland.[18] Visitors to the Open website, however, might not know about that institutional connection. Instead, they will probably be struck by the messages of gratitude expressed in personal testimonials by participants who attended Open's post-abortion counselling retreats. One woman said she was able finally to come to 'an acknowledgement that I'd suffered a loss which I had never had considered before'.[19] Another woman said she finally accepted that 'Jesus forgives me and so does my baby [whom] I'll get to meet … in Heaven.'[20] The impression is that they were guided to an awareness that their abortion had caused unresolved pain and guilt, from which they were released by admitting their transgression and receiving forgiveness.

This script of healed trauma is echoed in most pro-life Christian organizations with this so-called pro-woman approach; however, some post-abortion organizations adopt a more severe tone. The order of the Oblates of St Joseph, which oversees a memorial shrine in Santa Cruz, California, states on its website that abortion is the 'denial of the humanity of the child in the womb', a message that sits uneasily with the shrine's claim to offer a place of solace for all reproductive losses. The shrine features a bronze statue of Joseph (husband of Mary the mother of Jesus) holding what is supposed to be a 'six-month-old foetus'. The pro-life logic is that the post-abortive mother will only find peace after becoming 'painfully aware of having denied God's gift of love' in taking the life of a her child.[21] The statue is evocative, but does not reflect the factual reality of abortion since very few abortions in the USA are performed on foetuses older than 13 weeks.[22] It would appear that the statue is meant to trigger, perhaps traumatically so, the awareness that any abortion kills a foetus that looks like a small infant.

The religious studies scholar Maureen Walsh notes the 'growing popularity' of memorialization rituals and shrines, which indicates that many women whose pregnancy losses have been ignored by the Church find 'meaning and comfort' in such commemorations.[23] She presents the hard-line anti-abortion messages she encountered in her research as a few bad apples that should not take away from the healing possibilities that the memorialization movement may provide for women with various experiences along the 'continuum of pregnancy loss'.[24] At the parish or congregational level where priests and ministers may act compassionately towards their own members and listen empathetically to their stories, Walsh may be right. I am less sanguine about being able to separate compassion-orientated intentions from the trope of murdered babies. It is doubtful that women participating in these post-abortion events miss the latter message, even if it is not overt.

The strategy of trying to trigger post-abortion distress must be flagged as morally questionable; nevertheless, the claim about abortion trauma is an increasingly emphasized aspect of the pro-life movement. The Catholic self-professed psychologist David Reardon and the Eastern Orthodox writer Frederica Mathewes-Green are among many who promote the notion that 'post-abortive women' experience deep psychological and spiritual distress. Reardon writes: 'one could argue that the harm that the woman suffers is greater since her soul is damaged by abortion, while the child only suffers physical death and remains spiritually untouched.'[25] Reardon has co-authored scores of articles promoting the theory of post-abortion psychological disorders.[26] In her book *Real Choices*, Mathewes-Green interviewed women recruited from church-based post-abortion counselling groups and claims to have found anecdotal evidence that many women suffer symptoms of PTSD such as 'self-hate, even self-destructiveness and suicidal thoughts'.[27]

While some pro-life evangelicals accept that abortion in cases of rape, incest or threat to the mother's life is morally justifiable, there is an increasingly aggressive campaign to argue that abortion after rape injures the mother psychologically – even more than the rape itself. One brochure published by the Pro-Life Action League claims, 'Not only is it untrue that most victims of sexual assault want to abort their babies, the small minority who do are nearly always regretful', and rape victims themselves see that 'Abortion is a form of "medical rape" – an unwanted, violent intrusion into their bodies.'[28] Serrin Foster, the founder of Feminists for Life, has called abortion 'a second act of violence against a woman who is raped'.[29] In other words, women who terminate a pregnancy from rape risk being affected by a trauma more severe than that brought on by the rape. One scientific study of women who became pregnant from rape found that while a third kept the baby, half of the women opted to terminate the pregnancy. This study also reported that the negative effects of falling pregnant from rape can be wide-ranging and long-lasting, with high incidents of PTSD.[30] Another study noted that some rape survivors 'described abortion itself as a necessary step toward healing, before which they could not begin addressing the emotional trauma of the assault'.[31] Rape trauma is real, its treatment is complicated, and no reputable psychologist would assert that it can be averted by carrying the pregnancy to term. In fact, studies of the horrendous incidence of rape and impregnation as a tool of war in the Serbian invasion of Croatia and Bosnia/Herzegovina show that women's rape and torture trauma was aggravated by the pregnancy.[32]

Sustaining the fabricated claim that carrying a baby after rape would be psychologically better for the woman takes considerable effort. David Reardon and his associates have been at the forefront in popular and scholarly writing that promotes the notion of abortion-caused trauma, upon which most pro-life writers depend. Reardon's publications, websites and public lectures present a litany of adverse psychological, physical and emotional effects of abortion, including suicide, depression, eating disorders, sleep disturbances and sexual dysfunction.[33] No matter that the credentials of Reardon and his fellow researchers have been called into question,[34] or that Reardon's co-authored studies have been tagged as using faulty methods.[35] No matter that rigorous statistical analysis shows that 'Rates of total reported psychiatric disorder were no higher after termination of pregnancy than after childbirth.'[36] No matter that requiring abortion providers to tell their patients 'that abortion increases their risk of anxiety, depression, and suicide lack[s] an evidence base'.[37] Reardon's rhetorical strategy and alternative facts are surprisingly effective in fending off scientific studies whose longitudinal data show that women report few adverse psychological effects of abortion. Faced with this data, Reardon simply claims that 'any post-abortive women without any symptoms of [PTSD] were simply in denial and too mentally unstable to recognize the effects of their abortions.'[38] Reardon and others of his ilk have been relentless in spreading these myths, and his research is cited as authoritative by most popular pro-life writers and organizations – and even by a number of otherwise reputable academic scholars writing on abortion.[39]

It is not hyperbole to say that there is a drumbeat of pro-life preaching that most women will eventually not only regret but will likely be traumatized by their abortion. Given the widespread nature of this pro-life claim in conservative Christian circles, one wonders why there is so little literature in mainstream pastoral care regarding abortion. In 2003, the Canadian scholars Roy Jeal and Linda West published an essay on 'post-abortion women'.[40] Jeal and West bemoan the 'relatively small body of writing that, from a pastoral and biblical point of view, addresses the emotional and spiritual problems some women experience' after an abortion.[41] Because 'many women who have had abortions go through a grieving process exactly like those who have lost children who were already born', it is important not to discount the emotional impact of some abortions.[42] They rightly push to the side claims about a putative 'post-abortion syndrome' by citing authoritative literature that debunks this myth, and they focus instead on women's spiritual pain and isolation from their Christian communities.[43] While the pastoral theological literature on miscarriage and neonatal loss is slowly but surely increasing, only a few scholars and organizations have followed in the footsteps of Jeal and West to address pregnancy termination in ways that are not already dogmatically pro-life.[44]

Christian pro-life miscarriage ministry

Christian groups have been proactive in taking up the slack where the Church has been slow in addressing bereavement after reproductive loss. A plethora of books (mostly by women) have been published,[45] and a number of (mostly women-run) websites and organizations have been created. This section focuses on an organization called Mommies Enduring Neonatal Death (MEND), which is a non-profit Christian (apparently conservative evangelical-leaning) ministry, whose intention is to provide 'a place for families to connect, share their unique story of loss, and learn to live life without your precious baby'.[46] The organization maintains a website and Facebook page, publishes a newsletter and has a number of local chapters in US cities that hold meetings and plan various events. Here, I conduct a discourse analysis of the MEND materials in order to show how MEND sends subtle and not so subtle anti-abortion messages in the midst of their bereavement support. This anti-abortion view is evidenced by the way MEND: 1) reinforces, through a pattern of testimonials, that an appropriate Christian manifestation of miscarriage grief affirms the baby's personhood at conception; and 2) directs readers to pregnancy-loss memorial organizations that are overtly anti-abortion.

It makes sense that the women who frequent a website like MEND, or get involved in events organized by its local chapters, would be those who experience their loss, no matter how early in the pregnancy, as the death of a beloved baby. Their voices are represented in the organization's newsletter, which reserves space for birthday wishes to the baby who died, as if he or she is alive and maturing in heaven year by year.[47] There are personal testimonials from readers recounting how their miscarriage or stillbirth happened and how they are learning to live with their grief. Some of the stories even include a photo of the tiny body that was presented to the grieving parents in the hospital, tenderly wrapped in a blanket for final farewells.[48] Other stories emphasize that even an early miscarriage is still a child to be mourned. In one case, the parents gave a name and assigned a sex to one of the embryonic sacs in a twin pregnancy (shown on their five-week ultrasound) that subsequently never developed.[49] In addition to these testimonials, the president of MEND makes the point theologically, saying, 'to me, an embryo is a life – the beginnings of a little person whom God created in the image of Himself, and a life that He cherishes.'[50] I could not find any testimonial in the MEND material of an early pregnancy loss in which the parents did not experience the miscarriage as the death explicitly of a child who is now growing up in heaven.

The traditional pro-life theme that a baby comes into existence at conception is pervasive in MEND materials; however, MEND goes further and directs readers to websites that are overtly anti-abortion, though without warning their readership of that fact. On the MEND webpage listing 'Infant Loss Organizations', one finds some mainstream national, non-political organizations such as Birthwaves (a pregnancy-loss doula service[51]), but many of the list are involved in anti-abortion advocacy of various kinds that promote the notion of post-abortion trauma. MEND disingenuously describes these organizations as benign and non-political. MEND touts the American Pregnancy Association (APA) as providing 'education services for infertility, pregnancy health, and pregnancy complications'[52] when, in fact, the APA is well known for pursuing anti-abortion lobbying under a guise of medical science. For example, it urges the use of non-FDA-approved procedures such as so-called abortion reversal medication.[53] The American College of Obstetricians and Gynaecologists has deemed the pharmacological attempt to reverse a medical abortion already underway to be unscientific and therefore unethical for medical providers to promote.[54]

MEND also highlights an organization called A Place for Hope, which has a memorial sculpture garden that MEND describes as 'a place of peace and solace where families can come for a quiet time of reflection, prayer, or even to celebrate the life of their loved one'.[55] However, by following the link provided to the Garden of Hope webpage, one finds a very different tone and message. The founder of the organization describes her intention for the garden as ministering to '"post-abortive" women' whose 'lives have been scarred by abortion'. She explicitly asserts that abortion causes deep and long-lasting psychological damage: 'The pain of abortion doesn't just go away; it lies deep inside and torments. Some of its victims try to suffocate it with alcohol, drugs and even suicide attempts.'[56] MEND does not reference these subjects, but it does include several photos of the garden's sculptures and provides a link for patrons who wish to buy a commemorative paving brick.

I do not doubt that many evangelical Christian women who are looking for a place where they can physically commemorate their loss might find the Garden of Hope a good fit. However, one cannot forget that statistically speaking, it is likely that some of the MEND women who have miscarried also had an abortion at some point in their reproductive years. While MEND can be commended for not spreading the baseless and guilt-inducing myth that abortion causes subsequent miscarriage, that myth is a pervasive talking point in pro-life literature and social media. While some MEND members might not be affected by the anti-abortion messaging articulated by the garden's founder, there may be others carrying the secret of a past abortion, for whom those ominous warnings about trauma might add to the painful burden they already carry regarding their miscarriage.

MEND is successful in portraying a sense of community where the visceral and literally bloody experience of reproductive loss can be explicitly voiced and compassionately heard without squeamishness. I have no doubt that women who find their way to MEND chapter meetings or the website find a sense of belonging that is largely absent from their church circles. That upside of an organization, however, does not make up for other problematic aspects of the group's message. I have pointed out the problematic aspect of MEND's dogmatic portrayal of personhood in the womb and its anti-abortion innuendos. When one looks at the ministry of organizations like MEND, alongside the activist post-abortion memorialization movement discussed in the previous section, I detect another troubling issue. Taken together, these discourses about reproductive endings have the effect of corralling women into two opposing groups, which are then pitted against each other: the innocent victims of miscarriage and psychologically damaged perpetrators of abortion.

Miscarriage and abortion: two sides of the same reproductive-loss coin

Pro-life responses to reproductive loss – whether orientated towards post-abortion recovery or comfort after miscarriage – create stereotypes of appropriate maternal mourning and insert decisive wedges between women who suffer a miscarriage and those who terminate a pregnancy. In this section I argue for why this damaging binary runs contrary to the reality of reproductive loss, phenomenologically understood.

One wedge is a moral one that pits passive victim against active sinner. Sympathy is extended to those who are perceived as innocently and tragically suffering a spontaneous miscarriage; opprobrium is voiced towards those who intentionally (whether of their own accord or succumbing to pressure) procure an abortion and do not repent of it. Another wedge is related to a particular normative view of women's maternal nature. Pro-life proponents present women as maternally devastated by miscarriage, yet also spiritually virtuous for having taken their maternal identity so seriously. Correlatively, women who have had an abortion are presented as traumatized psychologically (whether they admit it or not), and having gone against their essential and God-given maternal nature.[57] Another pro-life wedge forecasts two opposing eschatological futures. The woman who miscarries is given the hope of a joyful reunion in heaven; whereas the woman who aborts faces uncertainty in the afterlife unless she repents of having taken the life of her child. These wedges are based on damaging caricatures that breed disinformation about women's lives and misrepresent many women's actual reproductive experiences, with a potential negative impact on both those who miscarry and those who have an abortion.

This section takes a phenomenological approach to pregnancy loss, which enables us to see past the widespread 'cultural assumption of the enormous difference between miscarriage and abortion'.[58] It is not too strong to say that, experientially, miscarriage and abortion are two sides of the same coin of women's reproductive lives. Women are ill-served by societal (including religious) attitudes and practices that pit women against each other. Christians deserve spaces to commemorate religiously their reproductive losses in the manner to which they feel called, and they should not be forced into self-identifying with a moralistic stereotype – victim or repentant sinner – in order to gain access to those spaces. Looking beyond simplistic binaries reveals women's unmet needs for ritualizing all types of pregnancy losses without recrimination.

The binary between miscarriage and abortion runs deep. While the majority of Americans still favour keeping abortion legal, the number of people who also think it is morally problematic has increased.[59] It is difficult to identify the root of this increasing moral concern about abortion. Publicly pervasive pro-life discourses have probably played a role. Whatever the cause, the notion that abortion means an anti-maternal and selfish act is widespread and surfaces, inadvertently or not, in the comments of women who lose a desired pregnancy. Studies show that women with a wanted pregnancy, who subsequently undergo a termination for foetal anomaly, react strongly to having their procedure described as an abortion. As one woman explained, calling her 'TFA' (termination because of foetal anomaly) an abortion 'implies our baby was unwanted and unloved'.[60] Moreover, even those people who understand that their TFA was, technically, a selective abortion will not speak about it openly as such, fearful of condemnation from pro-life family and friends. This 'self-silencing' in light of anti-abortion sentiments is detrimental and, in one woman's words, 'has severely compromised my ability to seek support for my loss in a public way'.[61]

In an examination of pastoral approaches to early pregnancy loss, a Church of Scotland minister found that his informants recoiled strongly against any language that associated the medical treatment for their miscarriage with abortion. Indeed, some were 'horrified' when their medical providers called their miscarriage a spontaneous abortion.[62] For some women, abortion-related terminology contributed to feelings of culpability. One woman in this study remarked: 'I think if you use that terminology then you feel you are guilty.'[63] The author's pastoral recommendation was to use the language preferred by each patient. Individualized medical care that respects the patient's terminology is usually best; however, monitoring language about miscarriage in order to avoid terms linked to abortion may mask a deeper cultural problem – namely, the stigmatizing of abortion that inevitably spills over on to other reproductive losses.

The Church has a history of comforting women who feel guilty about their miscarriage by telling them how different they are from women who procure abortions. The sixteenth-century Protestant reformer Martin Luther gave these instructions regarding pastoral care for women who miscarry:

> We ought not to frighten or sadden such mothers with unkind words. It is not their fault. It is not their carelessness or neglect that caused the birth of their child to go wrong. One must distinguish between them and a woman who resents being pregnant, deliberately neglects her baby, and even goes so far as to strangle or destroy it.[64]

This type of good-mother/bad-mother message may very well contribute to why women who have a miscarriage feel that suspicion surrounds them. They internalize the guilt and try to fend it off by strongly disassociating their experience from that of women who abort.

My suggestion that abortion and miscarriage are two sides of the same coin is not intended to discount the particular grief of people who suffer the loss of a wanted baby. No one would dispute that there are real differences in intentionality and context between the loss of a desperately wanted child and the intentional termination of an unwanted and unwelcome pregnancy. Nevertheless, to think of miscarriage and abortion only in terms of this binary promotes an inaccurate picture of the experience of reproductive endings. Just because a woman who miscarries wishes to distance her experience from any abortion-related terminology does not necessarily mean that she wishes to distance herself from all women who have abortions or to oppose abortion rights. A phenomenological examination of miscarriage and abortion reveals important medical, psychological and emotional similarities. Let me offer three fact-based but fictional vignettes to illustrate.

Vignette 1

In terms of the medical procedure, treatment for a miscarriage and an abortion may be indistinguishable. Imagine a woman who is happily pregnant. Suddenly, she begins to miscarry spontaneously at home, but after several days the bleeding increases drastically. She requires a D&C (dilation of the cervix and curettage) that will empty her uterus to prevent sepsis or haemorrhage. She is distressed that she lost the baby but relieved that the miscarrying is over. She had been alone, frightened and in pain at home, passing wads of bloody tissue sitting on the toilet. Several days later she recounts her harrowing experience to her two long-time friends. One revealed that she had had a medical abortion at home a year ago; the other shared about her past clinic abortion. They could relate to what each others' bodies went through.[65]

Vignette 2

The emotional after-effects of miscarrying an unwanted pregnancy and the after-effects of abortion may have similarities, in that women may feel relief in both contexts. Imagine a teenager busy with her life activities who is not planning on having a child before college, marriage or beginning her career. She has an unusually heavy, late menstrual cycle where she passes some large clots. When she checks her calendar and her sexual activity that month, she realizes that she may very well have been pregnant, despite the use of birth control. She is enormously relieved that the possible pregnancy failed on its own and that she did not have to face an abortion. Her friend was not so lucky. Her friend did not realize she was pregnant until she was well into her first trimester. When her own gynaecologist refused to do the procedure, she ended up going to Planned Parenthood. Even with her mom there for support, it was an experience she never wants to repeat, but she is enormously relieved that she found a safe abortion provider where she was not refused treatment.[66]

Vignette 3

There can be similarities between miscarriage and abortion having to do with the stigma women feel.[67] Imagine a woman finds herself unexpectedly pregnant with her third child at age 40. Her husband is over the moon that it's finally a boy. She is starting to get excited too, but she sometimes complains to her women's Bible study group that her gynaecologist recommended no alcohol and stopping her marathon training (half-jokingly, she admits she still sneaks a glass of wine and a short jog occasionally). Then, unexpectedly, she miscarries. She is conflicted – feeling sad, feeling it was probably for the best, but also worried about being blamed by her Christian friends. She is uncertain about whom to confide in regarding these mixed feelings. Finally, she calls an old friend who had once spoken openly of her abortion and was then subtly snubbed by some of the people at church. Somehow, she had the feeling that her old friend would understand.

These vignettes are fictional but based on medical facts and social scientific studies about the many facets of miscarriage and abortion. My vignettes only referenced religion in passing, though if I were trying to be statistically representative for the US context, over half of the women in those stories would have had a Christian affiliation.[68] I did not include a vignette showing a woman who had an abortion suffering subsequently from infertility, repeated miscarriages, ectopic pregnancy and other such medical problems, because that would not be a fact-based story. The notion that an abortion will cause later reproductive difficulties is a myth but is repeated in many pro-life writings.[69] Statistically speaking, losing a pregnancy is common and the rate of miscarriage increases significantly for a woman no longer in her twenties who is using her own (not previously frozen) ova.[70] A past abortion has no bearing on this age-related reality. When pro-life groups spread the myth that abortion causes later reproductive problems, they inadvertently cast aspersions on any woman experiencing fertility problems, implying that a past secret abortion might be a contributing factor.

I did not include a vignette showing women deeply traumatized by abortion, based on their awakening to the fact that they caused the death of their preborn child. As discussed above, a supposed post-abortion trauma syndrome is widely acknowledged to be based on faulty science. Miscarriage is a different matter. Scientific research does indicate that the death of a wanted future child does correlate with a risk of developing mental health problems.[71] That the death of a loved one is deeply disturbing and may cause trauma, we can all understand. Some of the trauma may be caused by the stigma linked to reproductive endings. One nationwide miscarriage survey found that over 40 per cent of women who had a miscarriage 'reported feeling that they had done something wrong'.[72] When one adds pro-life messages to this general cultural stigma, then Christian women who miscarry may well experience added moral and spiritual guilt that they did something to interfere with God's plan or endanger an unborn child created in God's image.

Some distinctions between miscarriage and abortion are valid, but these distinctions do not justify propagating the moralistic and erroneous binaries one finds in pro-life discourses. A fact-based and phenomenological approach shows that drawing moralising distinctions between miscarriage and abortion misrepresents what actually transpires in many people's reproductive lives. In terms of family planning, fertility management, contraceptive use and sexuality, there is more of a continuum between miscarriage and abortion than many would care to admit. Trying to pit so-called innocent maternal women who miscarry against the so-called guilty anti-maternal women who have abortions turns out to be a political tactic rather than a window into real peoples' reproductive lives that extend over decades. The reproductive experience of bodies that can get pregnant include many types of pregnancies: unwanted-and-prevented, wanted-yet-spontaneously-lost, wanted-but-terminated, unwanted-then-wanted, unwanted-but-prevented-from-terminating, and so on.

Pro-life writers imply that the woman who now mourns the miscarriage of her wanted pregnancy has never been the woman who needed an abortion at some point in her life; or that the woman who now wants an abortion has never grieved over a previous miscarriage; or that the woman who needs an abortion today never chose to continue an unplanned pregnancy at an earlier point in her life. As one pro-life writer asserts, 'The woman who aborts is a different woman from the one who chooses not to.'[73] On the contrary, statistically speaking, she may very well be the same woman. The dividing line between miscarriage and abortion for women, even pro-life Christian ones, can be very narrow and fuzzy, as a recent news story reveals.

Shannon Dingle, a mother of six, including several special-needs children, is well known in Christian pro-life circles for writing and speaking on disability and the sanctity of life. Dingle discovered she was pregnant a mere one week after a freak tragic accident took the life of her husband. Grieving and battling her own medical complications, she began making plans to have an abortion. Then she miscarried. Dingle reveals the details of this painful period of her life in order to counter distorting pro-life caricatures about reproductive decision-making. Such caricatures 'make for good propaganda but terrible policy. People, real people, become pregnant' and may need not to be pregnant. As Dingle writes, 'I knew I couldn't have this baby.'[74] I cite Dingle's story not to argue that some pregnancies happen in such tragic contexts and to such otherwise exemplary mothers that they meet some casuistic criteria for a morally permissible abortion. Rather, I am arguing that the dichotomy between miscarriage and abortion is a phenomenologically and scientifically misleading one. Miscarriage and abortion are more appropriately seen as two sides of the same coin of people managing their fertility and making parenting decisions in different contexts and at different times in their reproductive lives.

I also am not using Dingle's story to prove that if you scratch the surface of a pro-life woman of reproductive age, you will find someone who secretly wants abortion to stay safe and legal – just in case. Dingle says she is 'not pro-life anymore, not in the political sense',[75] and her story may indicate that there are other pro-life Christian women who secretly want to 'exhale' in a non-judgemental context about having had an abortion.[76] Nevertheless, I am not interested in trying to find out if there are more Shannon Dingles out there. In my opinion, theological, ethical and pastoral discussions about miscarriage and abortion do not move forward by merely quoting statistics or anecdotes about pro-life Christian women who considered having or have had an abortion and are not traumatized. Rather, meaningful discussions about reproductive loss will begin to move forward when those engaged in these discussions support both the moral agency of pregnant women to manage their pregnancy as well as the desire these women sometimes have to memorialize the pregnancy's ending.

Reproductive loss and God

Finally, let me make a few theological points in favour of resisting these damaging binaries, which I believe stand at odds with a Christian understanding of God's nature. I do not have the space to elaborate, but I will list three doctrinal loci that militate against such binaries: creation, providence and pneumatology.

A key principle of a doctrine of creation is the goodness of whatever has being – whether animate or inanimate. In a repeated poetical biblical phrase, God saw that the unfolding of creation 'was good' (Gen. 1.4, 10, 12, 18, 21, 25) and 'indeed ... very good' (v. 31). These verses contribute to a view of the creator God who values an abundant and diverse natural world. It is a world we experience as teeming with life, sometimes chaotic and cruel but also often beautiful. A woman who mourns a foetus that died in her womb, with all the promise that tiny life held, is not being sentimental, hysterical or hormonal. That woman's experience reflects something about the goodness of being, and her grief should be respected in whatever mode in which it emerges. To affirm foetal life as part of creation's blessed abundance and to mourn its loss, however, does not mean that Christians have been given a clear and unequivocal scriptural and doctrinal understanding of the meaning and status of uterine beings.[77] We do not know why God ordained their lives to unfold in such a precarious way. To put it bluntly, God allows more embryos and foetuses to die naturally than come to birth. We cannot deduce the moral status of embryos and foetuses from this aspect of the created order. Therefore, a doctrine of creation militates against dividing women into two camps: those cooperating with God's creation and those supposedly undermining it.

Pregnancy and birthing have always been precarious matters for women as well, and for that reason I do not interpret a doctrine of creation prenatally. God allows humans to be fruitful and multiply but does not ensure it or require it. For scientific and theological reasons we do not fully understand, the nature of human biology is that most embryos do not survive to a live birth – even in an era of modern medicine. Moreover, most women and newborns come away from pregnancy and birthing with some kind of health complication, some of them serious.[78] The very curse of the Edenic fall (Gen. 3.16) seems almost to warn women away from the pains of pregnancy. The basis for procreative flourishing is, thus, not found in a doctrine of creation alone, but requires insight from a doctrine of providence.

In the doctrine of providence, God is affirmed to be not a divine watchmaker who sits back and passively observes the world tick but, rather, God is affirmed as exercising care over the creation. That said, God's providence is cloaked in mystery, especially when pregnancy is concerned. As Martin Luther asserted in his letter on miscarriage, 'we may not and cannot know the hidden counsel of God in such a case – why, after every possible care had been taken, God did not allow the child to be born alive.'[79] Luther's point, as I see it, is that the believer should humbly accept the miscarriage event not because one knows what God's will is but, rather, because one does *not* know God's will. God has not deigned to reveal – with very few biblical exceptions – God's plan for each embryo that comes to be. Only in a few biblical pregnancies did God express a direct preference for a pregnancy outcome, and there is no indication that these special callings of notable foetuses should be universalized and seen as ontologically determinative.[80] There is no biblical basis for a divinely ordained right to life from conception.[81]

The Bible analogizes God's will and personhood in the womb to emphasize the mysteries of both: 'Just as you do not know how the breath comes to the bones in the mother's womb, so you do not know the work of God, who makes everything' (Eccles. 11.5 NRSV). A doctrine of providence thus affirms that God is involved in creation, but we do not always, or even ever, know how and to what end. Dividing pregnant women into two groups – one that is obedient to God's will and one that is not – has no basis in a doctrine of providence.

The mystery surrounding God's providential ways in the world makes pneumatology even more important for moral decision-making. One aspect of a doctrine of the Holy Spirit is the role of the Spirit in aiding the believer to seek the truth.[82] The pouring out of God's Spirit at Pentecost is testified in the Bible as an event in which all believers participated, regardless of gender or any other status (see Acts 2). Any pro-life Christian who affirms the ongoing work of the Holy Spirit should think twice when doubting that God gives women a spirit of discernment regarding all the many and complicated reproductive decisions they have to face in their 30- to 40-some years of potential fertility. One pregnant woman may receive a diagnosis of a massive foetal anomaly incompatible with life and say unequivocally, 'I want to have this baby', even if it cannot live beyond birth. Her wish to be able to hold and say goodbye to her child should be respected. Another woman who discovers she is unexpectedly pregnant may say, 'I cannot be a mom to another child'. Her wish that there never be a future child she might hold should also be respected. The only reason to doubt the mental stability, moral rectitude and spiritual gravitas of either woman is because one has decided in advance, and contrary to the movement of God's Spirit, which kinds of reproductive decisions are Spirit-guided and which are not.

When making reproductive decisions, one researcher found that 68 per cent of the conservative Christian women she interviewed 'said they "turned to" prayer for guidance' before their abortion.[83] Many women in this study still struggled with their decision, and one woman felt she had sinned.[84] Asking forgiveness privately from God was sufficient in her mind; she did not need to name and memorialize her foetus or ask its forgiveness in order to avert some kind of post-traumatic syndrome. In another anthology about abortion, one woman spoke of how she came to her decision by 'relying on … "the spirit of power and of love and of a sound mind"' as the biblical passage says. In reflecting back on that decision, she says, 'I feel no guilt ... I only feel sadness.'[85] This woman was acquainted with pregnancy-related trauma, which she experienced after having previously giving up a baby for adoption; she was not traumatized by the abortion.

It is patronizing to accuse these women, and those like them, of some kind of false consciousness masking their abortion trauma. I do not doubt that some women are afflicted by mental health issues after having an abortion; however, the scientific literature overwhelmingly documents, as noted above, that abortion is not correlated with more psychiatric problems than childbirth – and sometimes, even less. If neither the doctrine of creation nor providence point convincingly towards foetal personhood, a right to life from conception or a woman's maternal obligation to gestate every pregnancy, then pregnant believers must make their own decision, relying in part on prayer and the Holy Spirit for guidance. There is little theological reason to doubt that a believer's difficult decision-making regarding her pregnancy is spirit-guided. Indeed, a robust pneumatology leads one to assume that the Spirit is at work in her life.

This brief discussion of creation, providence and pneumatology indicates that there are untapped theological resources for resisting pro-life attempts to triage pregnant women into acceptable and unacceptable maternal roles. The goodness of God's creation, the mystery of God's ways in the world and the promise of the Holy Spirit point decisively away from binaries and towards a morality of walking humbly with God, without recrimination for the path one's sister has taken.

Increased scholarly interest in reproductive loss reveals the depth and diversity of pregnancy-loss experiences and the Church's feeble response to the needs of grieving families. Pro-life proponents, already attuned to abortion death, have been quick to respond with rituals and resources meant to address all kinds of reproductive loss – though rarely do these proponents miss the opportunity to single out the sin of abortion. Professional pastoral counsellors are beginning to address the grief of reproductive losses in non-judgemental ways. However, pro-life rhetoric has already inculcated a damaging binary between spontaneous miscarriage and abortion. I have suggested that from a phenomenological perspective, setting up judgemental moral wedges between and among women will only exacerbate the trauma of miscarriage and the stigmatizing of abortion. Such wedges cannot contribute to any woman's well-being in the long term. Pregnant believers who miscarry or abort, and wish to commemorate that ending Christianly, deserve memorial rituals that do not denigrate their moral agency, pit them against each other or channel their experiences into roles that fit a politicized pro-life rhetoric. There is little psychological or theological basis for imposing the discourse of trauma on those believers who decide to end their pregnancy. On the contrary, these women's often difficult decision-making processes should be respected and supported, so that they will have the spiritual space to make peace with God in their own way and time.

Bibliography

'Abortion for Victims of Rape or Incest?', *Pro-life Action League*, https://prolife action.org/wp-content/uploads/docs/RapeAbortion.pdf.

'Abortion Pill Reversal', *American Pregnancy Association*, https://americanpregnancy.org/unplanned-pregnancy/abortion-pill-reversal-26744/.

Advancing New Standards in Reproductive Health, 'Turnaway Study', University of California, San Francisco, https://turnawaystudy.com/.

American College of Obstetricians and Gynecologists. 'Facts are Important: Medication Abortion "Reversal" is not Supported by Science', ACOG Advocacy (2021), www.acog.org/advocacy/facts-are-important/medication-abortion-reversal-is-not-supported-by-science.

——, 'Early Pregnancy Loss, ACOG Practice Bulletin No. 200', *Obstetrics and Gynecology*, 132, 5 (2018), e197–e206.

Bardos, Jonah et al., 'A National Survey on Public Perceptions of Miscarriage', *Obstetrics and Gynecology* 125, 6 (2015), pp. 1313–20.

Beiting, Christopher, 'The Idea of Limbo in Thomas Aquinas', *The Thomist: A Speculative Quarterly Review* 62, 2 (1998), pp. 217–44.

'Birthday Tributes', *MEND Newsletter* 26, 2, (2021), pp. 4–7, https://static1.squarespace.com/static/56036884e4bocb7ca5d8973a/t/603c4fb54f7eff1aa5ff6bf3/1614565329868/20210304-mend-magazine+v2.pdf.

Birthwaves, http://birthwaves.org/about-us/.

Bommaraju, Aalap et al., 'Situating Stigma in Stratified Reproduction: Abortion Stigma and Miscarriage Stigma as Barriers to Reproductive Healthcare', *Sexual and Reproductive Healthcare* 10 (2016), pp. 62–9.

Bonopartis, Theresa, 'The Souls of Aborted Babies and the "Hope" of Heaven', *Reclaiming Our Children* blog (2 November 2018), https://reclaimingourchildren.typepad.com/lumina_a_ray_of_light_aft/2018/11/be-not-afraid.html.

Brier, Norman, 'Anxiety after Miscarriage: A Review of the Empirical Literature and Implications for Clinical Practice', *Birth* 31, 2 (2004), pp. 138–42.

Brock, Brian, *Wondrously Wounded: Theology, Disability, and the Body of Christ*, Waco, TX: Baylor University Press, 2019.

Cahill, Ann J., 'Miscarriage and Intercorporeality', *Journal of Social Philosophy* 46, 1 (2015), pp. 44–58.

Camosy, Charles C., *Beyond the Abortion Wars: A Way Forward for a New Generation*, Grand Rapids, MI: Eerdmans, 2015.

Carey, Lindsay B. and Christopher Newell, 'Abortion and Health Care Chaplaincy in Australia', *Journal of Religion and Health* 46, 2 (2007), pp. 315–32.

'Carole's Story', *Open*, https://www.weareopen.org.uk/caroles-story/.

Cockrill, Kate et al., 'The Stigma of Having an Abortion: Development of a Scale and Characteristics of Women Experiencing Abortion Stigma', *Perspectives on Sexual and Reproductive Health* 45, 2 (2013), pp. 79–88.

'Compassionate Care', *Religious Coalition for Reproductive Choice*, https://rcrc.org/compassionate-care/.

Craven, Christa, *Reproductive Losses: Challenges to LGBTQ Family-Making*, New York: Routledge, 2019.

Cuffel, Alexandra, *Gendering Disgust in Medieval Religious Polemic*, Notre Dame, IN: University of Notre Dame Press, 2007.

Dingle, Shannon, 'I was in the Pro-Life Movement. But then, Widowed with 6 Kids, I Prepared for an Abortion', *USA Today*, Opinion (11 October 2020).

Eggebroten, Anne (ed.), *Abortion: My Choice, God's Grace: Christian Women tell their Stories*, Pasadena, CA: New Paradigm, 1994.

Elixhauser, Anne and Lauren M. Wier, 'Complicating Conditions of Pregnancy and Childbirth, 2008: Statistical Brief # 113', Rockville, MD: Agency for Healthcare Research and Quality, 2011, https://www.ncbi.nlm.nih.gov/books/NBK56037/.

Ellison, Linda, 'Abortion and the Politics of God: Patient Narratives and Public Rhetoric in the American Abortion Debate', ThD dissertation, Harvard Divinity School, 2008.

Erlick, Gail et al., 'Is there an "Abortion Trauma Syndrome"? Critiquing the Evidence', *Harvard Review of Psychiatry* 17, 4 (2009), pp. 268–90.

Exhale, 'What is Pro-voice?', *Exhale*, https://exhaleprovoice.org/pro-voice/.

'Frequently Asked Questions', *The Shrine of the Holy Innocents*, https://www.shrineholyinnocents.org/frequently-asked-questions.

Gallagher, Mallory, 'Olivia Abigail', *MEND Newsletter* 25, 3 (2020), p. 9, https://static1.squarespace.com/static/56036884e4b0cb7ca5d8973a/t/5ec-458b551ee4c738e115bb6/1589926075843/20200506-mend-magazine.pdf.

MEND, 'Garden of Hope', *MEND*, https://www.mend.org/garden-of-hope.

Heydrick, Debbie, *I'll Hold You in Heaven Remembrance Book: Words of Comfort, Peace, Healing and Hope*, Ventura, CA: Regal, 2003.

Holmes, Melisa M. et al., 'Rape-related Pregnancy: Estimates and Descriptive Characteristics from a National Sample of Women', *American Journal of Obstetrics and Gynecology* 175, 2 (1996), pp. 320–5.

Howard, Agnes R., 'Comforting Rachel: How Christians Should Respond to Prenatal Death', *Commonweal*, 140, 18 (2013), p. 9.

Jeal, Roy R. and Linda A. West, 'Rolling Away the Stone: Post-Abortion Women in the Christian Community', *Journal of Pastoral Care & Counseling* 57, 1 (2003), pp. 53–64.

Jerman, Jenna, Rachel K. Jones and Tsuyoshi Onda, 'Characteristics of US Abortion Patients in 2014 and Changes since 2008', Guttmacher Institute (2016), pp. 1–28.

John Paul II, *Mulieris Dignitatem*, Apostolic Letter on the Dignity and Vocation of Women, Rome: Libreria Editrice Vaticana, 1998.

Jones, David Albert, 'An Unholy Mess: Why "The Sanctity of Life Principle" should Be Jettisoned', *The New Bioethics* 22, 3 (2016), pp. 185–201.

Jones, Robert P., Daniel Cox and Rachel Laser, 'Committed to Availability, Conflicted about Morality: What the Millennial Generation tells us about the Future of the Abortion Debate and the Culture Wars', *Public Religion Research Institute* (2011), pp. 1–41.

Justes, Emma, 'A Response to "Rolling Away the Stone: Post-Abortion Women in the Christian Community"', *Journal of Pastoral Care and Counseling* 57, 1 (2003), pp. 69–70.

Kaczor, Christopher, *The Ethics of Abortion: Women's Rights, Human Life, and the Question of Justice*, New York: Routledge, 2011.

Kamitsuka, Margaret D., *Abortion and the Christian Tradition: A Pro-choice Theological Ethic*, Louisville, KY: Westminster John Knox Press, 2019.

Kelly, Kimberly, 'The Spread of "Post-Abortion Syndrome" as Social Diagnosis', *Social Science and Medicine* 102 (2014), pp. 18–25.

Layne, Linda L., *Motherhood Lost: A Feminist Account of Pregnancy Loss in America*, New York: Routledge, 2003.

Lee, Patrick, *Abortion and Unborn Human Life*, 2nd edn, Washington DC: Catholic University of America Press, 2010.

Lind, Emily R. M. and Angie Deveau (eds), *Interrogating Pregnancy Loss: Feminist Writings on Abortion, Miscarriage and Stillbirth*, Bradford, ON: Demeter, 2017.

Lončar, Mladen et al., 'Psychological Consequences of Rape on Women in 1991–1995 War in Croatia and Bosnia and Herzegovina', *Croatian Medical Journal* 47, 1 (2006), pp. 67–75.

Luther, Martin, 'Consolation for Women whose Pregnancies have not gone well, 1542' in *The Annotated Luther, Volume 4: Pastoral Writings*, ed. Mary Jane Haemig, Hans J. Hillerbrand, Kirsi I. Stjerna and Timothy J. Wengert, Minneapolis, MN: Fortress Press, 2016.

Major, Brenda et al., 'Abortion and Mental Health: Evaluating the Evidence', *American Psychologist* 64, 9 (2009), pp. 863–90.

Mathewes-Green, Frederica, *Real Choices: Offering Practical Life-Affirming Alternatives to Abortion*, Sisters, OR: Multnomah, 1994.

McCoyd, Judith L. M., 'Women in No Man's Land: The Abortion Debate in the USA and Women Terminating Desired Pregnancies due to Foetal Anomaly', *British Journal of Social Work* 40, 1 (2010), pp. 133–53.

Meehan, Mary, 'Rape and Abortion: A Double Injustice', *Human Life Review* 39, 2 (2001), pp. 31–9.

'Memorial Service', *Rachel's Vineyard*, https://www.rachelsvineyard.org/weekend/memorial.aspx.

MEND, 'Loss and Outreach Organizations', *MEND*, https://www.mend.org/infant-loss-organizations.

Mitchell, Rebekah, 'Infertility/Loss of Life at Embryo Stage', *MEND Newsletter* 21, 1 (2015), p. 1, https://static1.squarespace.com/static/56036884e4bocb7ca5d8973a/t/56c80ba4c2ea51c475eceddb/1455950759594/20150102-mend-newsletter.pdf.

Mitchell, Stormy, 'Vanished: Gone without a Trace', *MEND Newsletter* 23, 4 (2018), pp. 20–1, https://static1.squarespace.com/static/56036884e4bocb7ca5d8973a/t/5b42ecef88251beed8c40ed5/1531112708993/20180708-mend-newsletter.pdf.

'National Day of Remembrance for Aborted Children', http://abortionmemorials.com/press.php.

Nuzum, Daniel, Sarah Meaney and Keelin O'Donoghue, 'Pregnancy Loss: A Disturbing Silence and Theological Wilderness', *Modern Believing* 60, 2 (2019), pp. 133–46.

O'Donnell, Karen, 'Theology and Reproductive Loss', *Modern Believing* 60, 2 (2019), pp. 146–59.

Ohnuma, Reiko, 'Mother-love and Mother-grief: South Asian Buddhist Variations on a Theme', *Journal of Feminist Studies in Religion* 23, 1 (2007), pp. 95–116.

Open, 'Home', *Open*, https://www.weareopen.org.uk/#.

Paddleford, Beverly, 'To My Sisters and Brothers in Christ', *A Place of Hope*, http://www.hopemonument.com/styled-2/styled-3/letter.html.

Parsons, Kate, 'Feminist Reflections on Miscarriage, in Light of Abortion', *International Journal of Feminist Approaches to Bioethics* 3, 1 (2010), pp. 1–22.

Paterson, Shaw James, 'How Might Parish Ministers (and other Pastoral Care-givers) better support Women who have Experienced an Early Miscarriage?', PhD dissertation, University of Glasgow, 2010.

Oblates of St. Joseph, 'Patron of the Unborn', *Oblates of St. Joseph*, https://osjusa.org/about-us/apostolates/patron-of-the-unborn/.

Pazol, Karen et al., 'Abortion Surveillance – United States, 2011', *Morbidity and Mortality Weekly Report: Surveillance Summaries* 63, 11 (2014), pp. 1–42.

Perry, Rachel, '"One Problem Became Another": Disclosure of Rape-Related Pregnancy in the Abortion Care Setting', *Women's Health Issues* 25, 5 (2015), pp. 470–5.

Planned Parenthood, 'What is a Miscarriage?', *Planned Parenthood*, https://www.plannedparenthood.org/learn/pregnancy/miscarriage.

——, 'What Happens During an In-clinic Abortion?', *Planned Parenthood*, https://www.plannedparenthood.org/learn/abortion/in-clinic-abortion-procedures/what-happens-during-an-in-clinic-abortion.

——, 'How Does the Abortion Pill Work?', *Planned Parenthood*, https://www.plannedparenthood.org/learn/abortion/the-abortion-pill/how-does-the-abortion-pill-work.

Reardon, David C., 'A Defense of the Neglected Rhetorical Strategy (NRS)', *Ethics and Medicine* 18, 2 (2002), pp. 23–32.

——, 'Research', *Unchoice.com*, http://www.theunchoice.com/pblresearch.htm.

——, 'Psychological Risk: Traumatic Aftereffects of Abortion', *Unchoice.com*, http://www.theunchoice.com/pdf/OnePageFactSheets/PsychologicalRisksSheet1.pdf.

Rose, Melody, 'Pro-life, Pro-woman? Frame Extension in the American Anti-abortion Movement', *Journal of Women, Politics and Policy* 32, 1 (2011), pp. 1–27.

Samson, Judith, 'The Scars of the Madonna: The Struggle over Abortion in the Example of an American Post-abortion Pilgrimage to Mary', *Journal of Ritual Studies* 28, 2 (2014), pp. 42–4.

Open, 'Sandra's Story', *Open*, https://www.weareopen.org.uk/sandras-story/.

Sered, Susan Starr, 'Mother Love, Child Death and Religious Innovation: A Feminist Perspective', *Journal of Feminist Studies in Religion* 12, 1 (1996), pp. 5–23.

Shaw, Alison, 'Rituals of Infant Death: Defining Life and Islamic Personhood', *Bioethics* 28, 2 (2014), pp. 84–95.

Shrine of the Holy Innocents, https://www.shrineholyinnocents.org/.

Steinberg, Julia R., Charles E. McCulloch and Nancy E. Adler, 'Abortion and Mental Health: Findings from the National Comorbidity Survey-Replication', *Obstetrics and Gynecology* 123, 2 part 1 (2014), pp. 263–70.

Sullivan, Francis A., 'The Development of Doctrine about Infants who die Unbaptized', *Theological Studies* 72, 1 (2011), pp. 3–14.

Thomas Aquinas, *Summa Theologica*, translated by the Fathers of the Eastern Dominican Province, New York: Benzinger, 1947.

Virk, Jasveer, Jun Zhang and Jø Olsen, 'Medical Abortion and the Risk of Subsequent Adverse Pregnancy Outcomes', *New England Journal of Medicine* 357, 7 (2007), pp. 648–53.

Vredevelt, Pam, *Empty Arms: Hope and Support for those who have suffered a Miscarriage, Stillbirth, or Tubal Pregnancy*, Colorado Springs, CO: Multnomah, 2009.

Walsh, Maureen L., 'Emerging Trends in Pregnancy-Loss Memorialization in American Catholicism', *Horizons* 44, 2 (2017), pp. 368–98.

Welker, Michael, 'Holy Spirit' in *The Oxford Handbook of Systematic Theology*, ed. John Webster, Kathryn Tanner and Iain Torrance, Oxford: Oxford University Press, 2007, pp. 236–48.

Woggon, Kelley M., 'A Response to "Rolling Away the Stone: Post-Abortion Women in the Christian Community"', *Journal of Pastoral Care and Counseling* 57, 1 (2003), pp. 65–7.

Woodcock, Jane, 'Referral of Unlawful Prescription of Dangerous Abortion Pill Reversal', *Campaign for Accountability* (20 May 2020), https://campaign foraccountability.org/wp-content/uploads/2020/05/FDA-Letter_Abortion-Reversal_5_20_2020.pdf.

Wunnenberg, Kathe, *Grieving the Child I Never Knew: A Devotional Companion for Comfort in the Loss of Your Unborn or Newly Born Child*, Grand Rapids, MI: Zondervan, 2001.

Notes

1 Linda L. Layne, *Motherhood Lost: A Feminist Account of Pregnancy Loss in America* (New York: Routledge, 2003); Emily R. M. Lind and Angie Deveau (eds), *Interrogating Pregnancy Loss: Feminist Writings on Abortion, Miscarriage and Stillbirth* (Bradford, ON: Demeter, 2017); Kate Parsons, 'Feminist Reflections on Miscarriage, in Light of Abortion', *International Journal of Feminist Approaches to Bioethics* 3, 1 (2010), pp. 1–22.

2 See Susan Starr Sered, 'Mother Love, Child Death and Religious Innovation: A Feminist Perspective', *Journal of Feminist Studies in Religion* 12, 1 (1996), pp. 5–23; Reiko Ohnuma, 'Mother-love and Mother-grief: South Asian Buddhist Variations on a Theme', *Journal of Feminist Studies in Religion* 23, 1 (2007), pp. 95–116; Alison Shaw, 'Rituals of Infant Death: Defining Life and Islamic Personhood', *Bioethics* 28, 2 (2014), pp. 84–95.

3 See Daniel Nuzum, Sarah Meaney and Keelin O'Donoghue, 'Pregnancy Loss: A Disturbing Silence and Theological Wilderness', *Modern Believing* 60, 2 (2019), pp. 133–46; Karen O'Donnell, 'Theology and Reproductive Loss', *Modern Believing* 60, 2 (2019), pp. 146–59; Agnes R. Howard, 'Comforting Rachel: How Christians Should Respond to Prenatal Death', *Commonweal*, 140, 18 (2013), p. 9.

4 See Alexandra Cuffel, *Gendering Disgust in Medieval Religious Polemic* (Notre Dame, IN: University of Notre Dame Press, 2007), p. 66.

5 See Francis A. Sullivan, 'The Development of Doctrine about Infants who die Unbaptized', *Theological Studies* 72, 1 (2011), pp. 4–5; Christopher Beiting, 'The Idea of Limbo in Thomas Aquinas', *The Thomist: A Speculative Quarterly Review* 62, 2 (1998), pp. 217–44.

6 It is important to clarify that cisgender women are not the only people who suffer reproductive loss. I am focusing on those designated as female in pro-life Christian discourses. On reproductive loss in the LGBTQ community generally, see Christa Craven, *Reproductive Losses: Challenges to LGBTQ Family-Making* (New York: Routledge, 2019).

7 Theresa Bonopartis, 'The Souls of Aborted Babies and the "Hope" of Heaven',

Reclaiming Our Children blog (2 November 2018), https://reclaimingourchildren.typepad.com/lumina_a_ray_of_light_aft/2018/11/be-not-afraid.html.

8 See the website of the Shrine of the Holy Innocents, Saugerties, NY, https://www.shrineholyinnocents.org/.

9 'Frequently Asked Questions', Shrine of the Holy Innocents, https://www.shrineholyinnocents.org/frequently-asked-questions.

10 David C. Reardon, 'A Defense of the Neglected Rhetorical Strategy (NRS)', *Ethics and Medicine* 18, 2 (2002), p. 24.

11 'Memorial Service', Rachel's Vineyard, https://www.rachelsvineyard.org/weekend/memorial.aspx.

12 Linda Ellison, 'Abortion and the Politics of God: Patient Narratives and Public Rhetoric in the American Abortion Debate', ThD dissertation, Harvard Divinity School (2008), p. 121.

13 See the website for the 'National Day of Remembrance for Aborted Children', http://abortionmemorials.com/press.php.

14 The website claims that there are over 800 such cemeteries or shrines. See 'National Day of Remembrance for Aborted Children', http://abortionmemorials.com/sites.php.

15 Judith Samson describes the group's trip to pay homage to the shrine of the Black Madonna of Częstochowa, Poland. See, 'The Scars of the Madonna: The Struggle over Abortion in the Example of an American Post-abortion Pilgrimage to Mary', *Journal of Ritual Studies* 28, 2 (2014), pp. 42–4.

16 See https://www.weareopen.org.uk/#.

17 Their website says it 'upholds the value of the lives of all human beings from conception' and calls for 'greater protection for them in legislation'. See https://care.org.uk/cause/abortion.

18 My thanks to Kellie Turtle, a PhD Researcher at Ulster University in Belfast, who provided background information on these issues (email correspondence, 3 May 2021).

19 'Carol's Story', *Open*, https://www.weareopen.org.uk/caroles-story/.

20 'Sandra's Story', *Open*, https://www.weareopen.org.uk/sandras-story/.

21 See 'Patron of the Unborn', Oblates of St. Joseph, https://osjusa.org/about-us/apostolates/patron-of-the-unborn/.

22 A 2011 CDC report states that 'most (64.5%) abortions were performed by ≤8 weeks' gestation, and nearly all (91.4%) were performed by ≤13 weeks' gestation'. Karen Pazol et al., 'Abortion Surveillance – United States, 2011', *Morbidity and Mortality Weekly Report: Surveillance Summaries* 63, 11 (2014), p. 1.

23 Maureen L. Walsh, 'Emerging Trends in Pregnancy-Loss Memorialization in American Catholicism', *Horizons* 44, 2 (2017), p. 398.

24 Walsh, 'Emerging Trends in Pregnancy-Loss Memorialization', p. 372.

25 Reardon, 'A Defense of the Neglected Rhetorical Strategy', p. 25.

26 For a list of Reardon's co-authored studies, see the 'Research' page on his website, *Unchoice.com*, http://www.theunchoice.com/pblresearch.htm.

27 Frederica Mathewes-Green, *Real Choices: Offering Practical Life-Affirming Alternatives to Abortion* (Sisters, OR: Multnoma, 1994), p. 94. She quotes a publication by Reardon in support (p. 71, n. 1).

28 'Abortion for Victims of Rape or Incest?', *Pro-life Action League*, https://prolifeaction.org/wp-content/uploads/docs/RapeAbortion.pdf. This brochure relies exclusively on publications by David Reardon for its data.

29 Foster quoted in Mary Meehan, 'Rape and Abortion: A Double Injustice', *Human Life Review* 39, 2 (2001), p. 31.

30 See Melisa M. Holmes, Heidi S. Resnick, Dean G. Kilpatrick and Connie L. Best, 'Rape-related Pregnancy: Estimates and Descriptive Characteristics from a National Sample of Women', *American Journal of Obstetrics and Gynecology* 175, 2 (1996), pp. 322, 320.

31 Rachel Perry et al., '"One Problem Became Another": Disclosure of Rape-Related Pregnancy in the Abortion Care Setting', *Women's Health Issues* 25, 5 (2015), p. 473.

32 In this study, of the 29 women who got pregnant from rape, 17 had abortions, 12 had the baby but gave it up for adoption; only one kept her baby. Mladen Lončar et al., 'Psychological Consequences of Rape on Women in 1991–1995 War in Croatia and Bosnia and Herzegovina', *Croatian Medical Journal* 47, 1 (2006), pp. 72–3.

33 See the factsheet on Reardon's website: 'Psychological Risk: Traumatic Aftereffects of Abortion', *Unchoice.com*, http://www.theunchoice.com/pdf/OnePageFactSheets/PsychologicalRisksSheet1.pdf.

34 See Melody Rose, 'Pro-life, Pro-woman? Frame Extension in the American Anti-abortion Movement', *Journal of Women, Politics and Policy* 32, 1 (2011), pp. 1–27.

35 Brenda Major et al., 'Abortion and Mental Health: Evaluating the Evidence', *American Psychologist* 64, 9 (2009), pp. 863–90; Gail Erlick et al., 'Is there an "Abortion Trauma Syndrome"? Critiquing the Evidence', *Harvard Review of Psychiatry* 17, 4 (2009), pp. 268–90.

36 Major et al., 'Abortion and Mental Health', p. 880.

37 Julia R. Steinberg, Charles E. McCulloch and Nancy E. Adler, 'Abortion and Mental Health: Findings from the National Comorbidity Survey-Replication', *Obstetrics and Gynecology* 123, 2 part 1 (2014), p. 269.

38 Kimberly Kelly, 'The Spread of "Post-Abortion Syndrome" as Social Diagnosis', *Social Science and Medicine* 102 (2014), p. 21.

39 See Charles C. Camosy, *Beyond the Abortion Wars: A Way Forward for a New Generation* (Grand Rapids, MI: Eerdmans, 2015), p. 185, n. 26; Christopher Kaczor, *The Ethics of Abortion: Women's Rights, Human Life, and the Question of Justice* (New York: Routledge, 2011), p. 10; Patrick Lee, *Abortion and Unborn Human Life*, 2nd edn (Washington DC: Catholic University of America Press, 2010), pp. 160–3.

40 Roy R. Jeal and Linda A. West, 'Rolling Away the Stone: Post-Abortion Women in the Christian Community', *Journal of Pastoral Care and Counseling* 57, 1 (2003), pp. 53–64. See Kelley M. Woggon, 'A Response to "Rolling Away the Stone: Post-Abortion Women in the Christian Community"', *Journal of Pastoral Care and Counseling* 57, 1 (2003), pp. 65–7. Woggon speaks approvingly of Jeal's and West's non-judgemental pastoral compassion, which make her recommendation for women to contact Project Rachel for post-abortion support confusing (p. 66).

41 Jeal and West, 'Rolling Away the Stone', p. 53.

42 Jeal and West, 'Rolling Away the Stone', p. 61.

43 Jeal and West, 'Rolling Away the Stone', pp. 54–5.

44 See Emma Justes, 'A Response to "Rolling Away the Stone: Post-Abortion Women in the Christian Community"', *Journal of Pastoral Care and Counseling*

57, 1 (March 2003), pp. 69–70; Lindsay B. Carey and Christopher Newell, 'Abortion and Health Care Chaplaincy in Australia', *Journal of Religion and Health* 46, 2 (2007), pp. 315–32; 'Compassionate Care' curriculum for clergy to address parishioners' reproductive needs offered by the Religious Coalition for Reproductive Choice, https://rcrc.org/compassionate-care/.

45 Some sample titles include: Pam Vredevelt, *Empty Arms: Hope and Support for those who have suffered a Miscarriage, Stillbirth, or Tubal Pregnancy* (Colorado Springs, CO: Multnomah, 2009); Kathe Wunnenberg, *Grieving the Child I Never Knew: A Devotional Companion for Comfort in the Loss of Your Unborn or Newly Born Child* (Grand Rapids, MI: Zondervan, 2001); Debbie Heydrick, *I'll Hold You in Heaven Remembrance Book: Words of Comfort, Peace, Healing and Hope* (Ventura, CA: Regal, 2003).

46 See the MEND webpage at https://www.mend.org/.

47 Some examples of birthday messages to a miscarried foetus: 'You are 6 years old today … I hope you are enjoying being with Jesus. Mommy and Daddy miss you every day'; 'We ALL love you so much and hope you have a good birthday with your great-grandma up in heaven!' 'Birthday Tributes', *MEND Newsletter* 26, 2 (2021), p. 4, https://static1.squarespace.com/static/56036884e4b0cb7ca5d8973a/t/603c4fb54f7eff1aa5ff6bf3/1614565329868/20210304-mend-magazine+v2.pdf.

48 Mallory Gallagher, 'Olivia Abigail', *MEND Newsletter* 25, 3 (2020), p. 9, https://static1.squarespace.com/static/56036884e4b0cb7ca5d8973a/t/5ec458b551ee4c738e115bb6/1589926075843/20200506-mend-magazine.pdf.

49 'A twin had vanished. Without a trace … This baby who I loved so much already. Gone. Just gone. No physical evidence of his/her existence except for an ultrasound picture … We gave her a name. Joy'. Stormy Mitchell, 'Vanished: Gone without a Trace', *MEND Newsletter* 23, 4 (2018), pp. 20–1, https://static1.squarespace.com/static/56036884e4b0cb7ca5d8973a/t/5b42ecef88251beed8c40ed5/1531112708993/20180708-mend-newsletter.pdf.

50 Rebekah Mitchell, 'Infertility/Loss of Life at Embryo Stage', *MEND Newsletter* 21, 1 (2015), p. 1, https://static1.squarespace.com/static/56036884e4b0cb7ca5d8973a/t/56c80ba4c2ea51c475eceddb/1455950759594/20150102-mend-newsletter.pdf.

51 See the Birthwaves website at http://birthwaves.org/about-us/.

52 'Infant Loss Organizations', *MEND*, https://www.mend.org/infant-loss-organizations.

53 'Abortion Pill Reversal', American Pregnancy Association, https://americanpregnancy.org/unplanned-pregnancy/abortion-pill-reversal-26744/. Watchdog groups have petitioned the FDA to crack down on groups promoting abortion reversal. See the letter to the FDA by Jane Woodcock from the Campaign for Accountability, 'Referral of Unlawful Prescription of Dangerous Abortion Pill Reversal' (20 May 2020), https://campaignforaccountability.org/wp-content/uploads/2020/05/FDA-Letter_Abortion-Reversal_5_20_2020.pdf.

54 See American College of Obstetricians and Gynecologists, 'Facts are Important: Medication Abortion "Reversal" is not Supported by Science', ACOG Advocacy (2021), https://www.acog.org/advocacy/facts-are-important/medication-abortion-reversal-is-not-supported-by-science.

55 See https://www.mend.org/garden-of-hope.

56 Beverly Paddleford, 'To My Sisters and Brothers in Christ', *A Place of Hope*, http://www.hopemonument.com/styled-2/styled-3/letter.html.

57 A classic articulation of this viewpoint is the encyclical of Pope John Paul II, *Mulieris Dignitatem*, Apostolic Letter on the Dignity and Vocation of Women (Rome: Libreria Editrice Vaticana, 1998), pp. 18, 19.

58 Ann J. Cahill, 'Miscarriage and Intercorporeality', *Journal of Social Philosophy* 46, 1 (2015), p. 56.

59 Robert P. Jones, Daniel Cox and Rachel Laser, 'Committed to Availability, Conflicted about Morality: What the Millennial Generation tells us about the Future of the Abortion Debate and the Culture Wars', Public Religion Research Institute (2011), pp. 22–4.

60 Judith L. M. McCoyd, 'Women in No Man's Land: The Abortion Debate in the USA and Women Terminating Desired Pregnancies due to Foetal Anomaly', *British Journal of Social Work* 40, 1 (2010), p. 142.

61 McCoyd, 'Women in No Man's Land', p. 144.

62 Shaw James Paterson, 'How Might Parish Ministers (and other Pastoral Caregivers) Better Support Women who have Experienced an Early Miscarriage?' (PhD dissertation, University of Glasgow, 2020), p. 143.

63 Paterson, 'How Might Parish Ministers (and other Pastoral Caregivers) Better Support Women', p. 146.

64 Martin Luther, 'Consolation for Women whose Pregnancies have not gone well, 1542' in *The Annotated Luther, Volume 4: Pastoral Writings*, ed. Mary Jane Haemig, Hans J. Hillerbrand, Kirsi I. Stjerna and Timothy J. Wengert (Minneapolis, MN: Fortress Press, 2016), p. 422.

65 See Planned Parenthood 'What is a Miscarriage?', https://www.plannedparenthood.org/learn/pregnancy/miscarriage; 'What Happens During an In-clinic Abortion?', https://www.plannedparenthood.org/learn/abortion/in-clinic-abortion-procedures/what-happens-during-an-in-clinic-abortion; 'How Does the Abortion Pill Work?', https://www.plannedparenthood.org/learn/abortion/the-abortion-pill/how-does-the-abortion-pill-work.

66 For research into the effects of being denied an abortion, see the 'Turnaway Study' project by Advancing New Standards in Reproductive Health, University of California, San Francisco, https://turnawaystudy.com/.

67 See Aalap Bommaraju et al., 'Situating Stigma in Stratified Reproduction: Abortion Stigma and Miscarriage Stigma as Barriers to Reproductive Healthcare', *Sexual and Reproductive Healthcare* 10 (2016), pp. 62–9; Kate Cockrill et al., 'The Stigma of Having an Abortion: Development of a Scale and Characteristics of Women Experiencing Abortion Stigma', *Perspectives on Sexual and Reproductive Health* 45, 2 (2013), pp. 79–88.

68 See Jenna Jerman, Rachel K. Jones and Tsuyoshi Onda, 'Characteristics of US Abortion Patients in 2014 and Changes since 2008', Guttmacher Institute (2016), p. 1.

69 See Jasveer Virk, Jun Zhang and Jø Olsen, 'Medical Abortion and the Risk of Subsequent Adverse Pregnancy Outcomes', *New England Journal of Medicine* 357, 7 (2007), pp. 648–53.

70 See American College of Obstetricians and Gynecologists, 'Early Pregnancy Loss, ACOG Practice Bulletin No. 200', *Obstetrics and Gynecology* 132, 5 (2018), e197–e206.

71 Norman Brier, 'Anxiety after Miscarriage: A Review of The Empirical Literature and Implications for Clinical Practice', *Birth* 31, 2 (2004), pp. 138–42.

72 Jonah Bardos et al., 'A National Survey on Public Perceptions of Miscarriage', *Obstetrics and Gynecology* 125, 6 (2015), p. 6.

73 Brian Brock, *Wondrously Wounded: Theology, Disability, and the Body of Christ* (Waco, TX: Baylor University Press, 2019), p. 95.

74 Shannon Dingle, 'I was in the Pro-Life Movement. But then, Widowed with 6 Kids, I Prepared for an Abortion', *USA Today*, Opinion (11 October 2020).

75 Dingle, 'I was in the Pro-Life Movement'.

76 See the Exhale website, which provides a 'pro-voice' non-judgemental place for speaking about abortion experiences, positively and negatively: https://exhale provoice.org/pro-voice/.

77 My detailed argument for why the historical tradition cannot be read as unequivocally or even primarily affirming personhood from conception, see Margaret D. Kamitsuka, *Abortion and the Christian Tradition: A Pro-choice Theological Ethic* (Louisville, KY: Westminster John Knox Press, 2019), ch. 1.

78 Anne Elixhauser and Lauren M. Wier, 'Complicating Conditions of Pregnancy and Childbirth, 2008: Statistical Brief# 113' (Rockville, MD: Agency for Healthcare Research and Quality, 2011), https://www.ncbi.nlm.nih.gov/books/NBK56037/.

79 Luther, 'Consolation for Women whose Pregnancies have not gone well', p. 423.

80 For example, Jacob and Esau in Genesis 25.23; the prophet in Jeremiah 1.5; John the Baptist in Luke 1.13–17; Jesus in Luke 1.31–33. Church theologians have warned against drawing universalizing conclusions from these uterine sanctifications. See Thomas Aquinas, *Summa Theologica*, tr. Fathers of the Eastern Dominican Province (New York: Benzinger, 1947), III Q. 27, a. 6, respondeo.

81 Although this is a popular claim, even some pro-life scholars see the theological flaws in the concept. See David Albert Jones, 'An Unholy Mess: Why "The Sanctity of Life Principle" should be Jettisoned', *The New Bioethics* 22, 3 (2016), pp. 185–201.

82 See Michael Welker, 'Holy Spirit' in *The Oxford Handbook of Systematic Theology*, ed. John Webster, Kathryn Tanner and Iain Torrance (Oxford: Oxford University Press, 2007), pp. 236–48.

83 Ellison, 'Abortion and the Politics of God', p. 91.

84 'Frannie', a Methodist black woman, stated, 'I consider myself to be a smart, well-educated woman … But I'm also the sinner choosing to have an abortion … I made a choice and asked God to support me' (Ellison, 'Abortion and the Politics of God', p. 180).

85 2 Timothy 1.7, NKJV. Anne Eggebroten (ed.), *Abortion: My Choice, God's Grace: Christian Women tell their Stories* (Pasadena, CA: New Paradigm, 1994), pp. 32, 33.

12

A Twelve-Step Guide to Resurrection

M. COOPER MINISTER

Dia Dynasty: I made a list, a special list with a special pen and entered into a special place to make this list, of all the things I wanted to do instead of doing photography, so there were things that were counter to my photographic experience, which were to get to wear sexy clothes and dress up and wear high heels and be revered as a goddess for my intelligence and my creativity and my deviousness.
Pam Grossman: How old were you when you came up with this list?
Dia: I was 32 or 33. I believe 33 is Jesus' age when he was crucified.
Pam: That is correct.
Dia: So entering into this new phase of my life I made this list ...
Pam: You went through your own resurrection!
Dia: I did![1]

Resurrection begins when we decide to no longer do the things that have held us in the past and begin to try something new, creative, intelligent, even devious. It can begin in the darkness of night, where nightlife emerges as an opportunity for a shared refusal of certain social norms and the creation of a different world. New beings emerge from the darkness of dungeons and dancefloors. Unlike rave imagery created by Hollywood, featuring glow-sticks and various other self-made light supplements, my favourite dancefloors are filled with people wearing things that absorb light (black) or subtly reflect light without creating it, a mirror-finish, floor-length jacket, neon fishnet, or bright yellow joggers. Good doms, too, reflect the lights of their submissive. Reflectiveness is part of the transformative magic of the dark. Gathering strength from my experiments in nightlife spaces, I determined my own relationship to cancer treatment and began to ask what might enable life in the midst of death. This chapter, formed in relation to my experience with cancer and written during a pandemic, is my current answer to that question.

In summary, here is my twelve-step guide to resurrection: 1) Expand our imagination of what can happen in darkness and our capacity to see in the dark. 2) Reinvigorate affective attachments and learn to live together once again. 3) Fuck resurrections that overinvest in the past. 4) Repeat, with a difference. 5) Stop rehearsing the narratives that killed us (without forgetting them entirely). 6) Fuck. 7) Dance. 8) Make an appearance. 9) Do it now, in the present moment. 10) End gender through creative strangeness and unexpected mergers. 11) Affirm death as a creative, life-giving force. 12) Reconstruct Holy Saturday as a space of preparation, getting ready for what is on the other side. In what follows, I move through these steps drawing on the feminist trauma theologies of Shelly Rambo and Karen Bray, the queer theologies of Marcella Althaus-Reid and Elizabeth Stuart, Sharon Betcher's disability theology and Madison Moore's cultural theory of fabulousness. Working in conversation with these scholars, some also creatures of the night, I offer one possible path to resurrection. This is a path that worked for me in the wake of cancer and that I am working with again in the context of the Covid-19 pandemic.

Steps 1 and 2: alternatives to bearing witness on Holy Saturday

In recent years, feminist theologians have developed Holy Saturday as a space of bearing witness to trauma. These theologies acknowledge the difficulties of traumatic experience and the importance of bearing witness to that experience. Both Rambo and Bray make space for grief within a tradition that works to overcome loss in a way that forecloses grief. Rather than accept nostalgic theologies of the resurrected Christ or demand hope grounded in our own future resurrections, Rambo and Bray attend to present suffering. In this section, I describe the arguments of Rambo and Bray with particular attention to the potential and limitations of their arguments towards the first two steps of resurrection: expanding our capacity to see in the dark and reinvigorating our affective attachments.

In *Spirit and Trauma: A Theology of Remaining*, Shelly Rambo develops a trinitarian pneumatology centred on Holy Saturday. Rambo states:

> Looking through the lens of trauma, it is important to revisit the Spirit not as a figure who secures love between death and life but rather as one who witnesses to what remains – what persists – between them ... The Spirit provides a distinctive way of orienting oneself between death and life, a way of witnessing the fractured dimensions of word and body between death and life.[2]

According to Rambo, we have the potential to follow the Spirit into the abyss in order to glimpse a vision of life as remaining:

> This transformation, this redemption in the abyss of hell, is not about deliverance from the depths but, instead, about a way of being in the depths, a practice of witnessing that senses life arising amid what remains.

The middle story is not a story of rising out of the depths, but a trans-formation of the depths themselves.[3]

Focusing on the middle story of Holy Saturday, Rambo concludes *Spirit and Trauma* without offering an opening to resurrection. In this conclusion, Rambo invites readers into the depths and asks them to remain there with the Spirit.

Karen Bray takes up Rambo's work on Holy Saturday, particularly around the questions of time and affect. Bray asks, 'How does this Holy Saturday *feel*?'[4] Following this question, Bray suggests: 'Bipolar time and disordered affect ask us to feel what it is to be that which neoliberalism has worked so hard to suppress.'[5] To do this, Bray contends that we have to be attentive, what she calls grave attending:

> Grave attending is a caring for the gravity, the pulling down to the material world, the listening and feeling for what all its myriad emotions have to tell us and where they have to lead us. It is also a witnessing to those identities, collectivities, and possibilities assumed to be buried over and gone, the ghosts that haunt us and so gift us a sense of what we might have been and an imagination of what we might become. Acts of grave attending refuse to efface the material mattering of others on the way to our own redemption.[6]

For Bray, witnessing refuses the repetitive cycles of crisis and trauma where a new trauma hits before we have the opportunity to let the last trauma move through our bodies. Bray argues: 'Neoliberalism relies on crucifixions (crisis, trauma) in order to establish meaningful and profitable selves.'[7] Witnessing disrupts these cycles. Like Rambo, Bray asks us to remain in the depths, to witness what happens there, to refuse an easy resurrection and, instead, make ourselves over in the process of remaining with the suffering.

While both Rambo and Bray expand our capacity to remain in difficult spaces, their focus on witnessing and attention require a separation between self and other, between victim-survivor and witnesser. In this separation, the witness becomes a key character in the story. Following the logics of criminal justice, the witness may even become more central to the justice story than the victim insofar as the testimony of a witness to a crime may be taken more seriously than someone whose memory is obviously affected by the trauma. Both attend to how witnessing and attending are traumatic experiences, attempting to dissolve this separation, but in a way that still centralizes the experience of the witness or attender. Witnessing or attending becomes, at least in part, about making sense of the traumatic histories of the witness. Such a positioning centres the role of the privileged who remain in doing the systematic change.

This positioning also requires people to rehearse traumatic stories in order to enable others to bear witness. This requirement forces survivors not only to rehearse their stories, but also to put their stories into the new feminist narrative that challenges the crisis→resolution framework by describing a stuckness in trauma that cannot be resolved until it is witnessed. In a review of Hannah Gadsby's stand-up comedy special *Nanette*, Yasmin Nair asks:

> But what if, instead of trying to 'bear witness,' we simply set about creating systems that allowed those wounded by brutality to receive whatever they needed without having to constantly perform what happened to them? Nanette and Hannah Gadsby are part of a growing movement that seeks to seal us into a public discourse of eternal and constantly re-enacted trauma, which paradoxically claims that the pain of reliving and revealing your trauma is the only way to ease it.[8]

Rambo and Bray argue that practices such as bearing witness and grave attending resist capitalist demands for productivity. But that resistance comes, in part, from the stickiness of trauma, the way it takes up space that needs to be held. Holding space, however, eventually shifts into a melancholic holding back.

In order to hold space, to witness and attend, we have to develop our capacity to see the expanded possibilities for both pain and pleasure that occur in the wake of trauma. This is the first step towards resurrection. With the expanded capacity to see in the dark that we can cultivate on the path to resurrection, we learn how to do the type of witnessing that Rambo and Bray describe and to extend that by seeing the pleasure and joy that people in pain create in the dark. Rambo and Bray teach us to see pain and to stay with it, but our capacity to see in the dark must include the capacity to see delight as well. If we fail to see the delights of the darkness, our witnessing becomes a repetition of what we expect to see when we encounter trauma.

How might expanding our imagination of what can happen in darkness and our capacity to see in the dark open up space to live together? In asking this question, I am interested in the ways in which trauma becomes a cultural narrative and how we might shift what Sharon Betcher refers to as a fixation on cultural traumas. Betcher attempts to 'loosen a certain crisis-mongering fixation on cultural traumas – the death of nature, the "end of humanism," the death of God. Such traumatic recitals can further freeze affective engagement just as we need, rather, to invigorate affective attachment.'[9] Betcher does not claim that these cultural traumas are not real or that they do not require attention but, rather, asks how we can move beyond fixation on these traumas, or a stuckness in these traumas, in order to invigorate affective attachment. This question is even more pressing in light of the Covid-19 pandemic, during which our attachments have been required to shift in order to accommodate a new threat. In the wake of the quarantines and isolation of Covid-19, we must learn to reinvigorate our affective attachments and learn to live together once again. And so the second step to resurrection is to reinvigorate our affective attachments, learning to enjoy and delight in the presence of others, to create space for the articulation of pain and then to move out of that space together.

Steps 3–7: resurrection Sunday and its refusals

Once we have begun to expand our capacity to see what happens in the dark and are reinvigorating our affective attachments, we can revisit resurrection theology. Through this revisiting, I have learned what I offer as the next four steps towards resurrection: Step 3) to reject resurrections that overinvest in the past, Step 4) to repeat with a difference, Step 5) to stop rehearsing the narratives that killed us in the first place, Step 6) to fuck, and Step 7) to dance. This section traces these steps by putting Marcella Althaus-Reid and Elizabeth Stuart in conversation with Rambo.

Rambo's next book, *Resurrecting Wounds*, asks how this extended engagement with Holy Saturday transforms dominant understandings of the resurrection. In this text, Rambo questions Christian assumptions that life triumphs over death and that resurrection necessarily points to the future. According to Rambo:

> Resurrection appears as an invitation to weave a new kind of body, less pure, pristine, and perfected than the resurrected body often presented in the tradition. It appears as an invitation to multilayered witness, involving senses beyond seeing, which in the tradition became the dominant sense to convey truth, faith, and knowledge of God. As the wounds of history return, reappearing in the present, Christian theology might offer a vision of resurrection that addresses these wounds, precisely because the wounds return.[10]

Wounds that continue to wound need to be witnessed and it is through this process, Rambo suggests, that wounds will cause less harm.

At first glance, Marcella Althaus-Reid's *Indecent Theology* seems to make a similar point:

> Resurrection was not a theme for my generation. We seldom discussed it in my years of theological studies, at least in its overspiritualised classical form. *Los desaparecidos* (the disappeared) was our theme, not illusory tales of leaving graves. We did not even know the graves of the disappeared![11]

Here, Althaus-Reid suggests that it is difficult if not impossible to talk of resurrection when we do not have the graves. Because resurrection links us to the wounds of the past, for both Rambo and Althaus-Reid, it requires some kind of reckoning with the past.

While this reckoning must be done, it threatens to leave us stuck in the loops governed by the past. Althaus-Reid says that the resurrected Bi/Christ is 'A Christ who gives us something to think about, who is not a closed discourse and premature death without resurrection, because resurrection has become a mere reproduction or continuous videotape of definitions and regulations.'[12] Reproductive resurrections overinvest in the past and invite into the stickiness of what has been. The third step asks us to reject this loop and resurrection theologies that get us stuck in the past.

As an alternative to getting stuck in the past, we can take the fourth step of attending to how resurrection repeats but with a difference. Elizabeth Stuart links this repetition with a critical difference to how the Church renews itself. According to Stuart:

> Repetition with critical difference is how the church performs. It is how it interacts with culture, it is how it keeps itself open to the renewal of the Holy Spirit. And this performance begins in death. Christians die, but that is all they do for death; they are not consumed by death, they die to enter life.[13]

Resurrection repeats but with a difference. In this way, resurrection comes to serve life instead of repeating the cycles of crisis and trauma.

Resurrection also comes to serve life by refusing to overinvest in the future, as suggested by Althaus-Reid's critique of resurrection theology:

> The over-spiritualising of resurrection ... has produced this outcome, that resurrections seem not to be about relationships, for the resurrected Christ is present only in some departure mode, the end of the lusty body and the beginning of an 'angelic body'. The sacrament of lust and intimacy is not present, it is lost. In the end, resurrection theology ends up achieving the contrary to life: it ends negating it.[14]

In a paradoxical move, Althaus-Reid argues that resurrection theology and its accompanying disembodiments negate life. This negation occurs through a focus on a body that takes on more ghostly qualities, such as some interpretations of the resurrected body in John that focus on a body that appears and disappears without clear entrances or exits. Overinvesting in this understanding of the body is an overinvestment in the future at the expense of lusty bodies in the present.

We can extend Althaus-Reid's critique of resurrection theology to Rambo and Bray. If it is possible for theologies of the resurrection to negate the very thing they intend to affirm (life), then it is possible for theologies of Saturday to do the same. These attempts to bear witness sometimes preclude the embodiments they intend to produce. In this case, resurrection means an end to the rehearsal of the narratives that killed us. Ending these narratives offers a fifth step. In this end, we can create space for those who have been traumatized to invent and design what they need without having to continually perform their trauma in order to defend or rationalize their needs.

In Althaus-Reid's critique of resurrection theology, we have a clue for what Althaus-Reid suggests might enliven us – lusty bodies. Where resurrection theology deadens, we can find life through the sacraments of lust and intimacy. This is an ethical imperative: 'We join then Christ's resurrection with our own coming out for the obscene Christ in a per/verted Christology which reminds us of the ethical need for resurrection.'[15] Althaus-Reid does not skip the possibilities of Saturday but instead expresses a deep familiarity with the needs of bodies that have watched their loved ones die, have nearly died themselves, to lust and express intimacy and, intuiting what Althaus-Reid implies, to fuck (my sixth step) and to dance (my seventh step).

That we remember resurrections and resurrect ourselves through the sacraments of lust and intimacy is the reason that Elizabeth Stuart can claim that 'Death is essential to the queer project.'[16] While Stuart suggests that the queer project requires a reckoning with death, I am arguing that death also supports the queer project by reinforcing the urgency of pleasure and intimacy (à la Althaus-Reid). This solidifies Stuart's claim: 'The resurrection of Christ is the archetypal, primordial queer moment.'[17] In her commitment to the change that resurrection requires, Stuart's argument resists the celebratory nature of Easter Sunday. In its commitment to the fact of resurrection, Stuart's argument resists the risk of getting stuck rehearsing the trauma.

We live in a world that has learned to profit from crisis and trauma. One way of resisting this is to follow Rambo and Bray in witnessing the crisis and trauma, refusing to move on to the next cycle. Another way of resisting the profiteering cycles of crisis is to embrace not the cycles themselves, but the state of in-betweenness in which we are immersed as a result of these cycles. We learn to see the cycles for what they are and, through this immanent seeing, find a kind of transcendence. It is not a transcendence of the body. It is a transcendence through the flesh.[18]

Learning to inhabit this space in-between requires us to spread wings and grow feathers that allow the view from below to merge with the view from above, re-enacting the collapse of space and time that crisis provokes but, following Stuart, with a difference. We learn to understand the cycles for what they are and, through this knowledge and a willing entering in, transform them, transform ourselves. This is not a failure, not a failure even on the terms of the world, but a radical taking up of space. Not a resistance through refusal or negation, just choosing to become something different. We are not forced to live in-between. We choose to live in-between. Christians can enter into this state following a Christ who resisted cycles of trauma by breaking them with a resurrection and, in the Gospel according to John, a series of fabulous appearances.

Step 8: the fabulous risen Christ appears

Feminist theologians have attempted to take wounds seriously, to attend to them, to witness them, to notice that Jesus and those who have experienced trauma do not appear whole and complete. I have experienced more acts of witnessing than I can count and I am grateful for everyone who has seen me as I have figured out what it means to live with stage IV cancer. As important as these acts of witnessing have been and as grateful for them as I am, I have needed more than witnessing in order to approach something like healing. I have needed to live bigger, to immerse my sensorial body in the mysteries of the universe, to appear after everyone thinks I should be dead while insisting on my ongoing proximity to death. Yes, this is a process of disorientation and reorientation, but it is ongoing and to what I am reorientating changes through this process. Tracing my own series of resurrections, I am interested in the insistence, the persistence, the work of Jesus in appearing. In this way, Jesus becomes an active participant in this process and not merely or simply a passive sacrifice. The eighth step is, therefore, to make an appearance.

John 20.24–28, titled in the New International Version as 'Jesus Appears to Thomas,' describes the reappearance of Jesus to the disciples, this time including Thomas, who claimed, 'Unless I see the nail marks in his hands and put my finger where the nails were, and put my hand into his side, I will not believe' (John 20.25 NIVUK). Jesus has died and now people are saying they have seen him. Thomas's quite reasonable claim here is often framed as one of doubt, to the point that Thomas has come to be known as 'Doubting Thomas'. This is one of a series of resurrected appearances Jesus makes after his death. These appearances are often understood to validate the resurrection of Jesus: he is in fact alive, which we can affirm because many people saw. These appearances, in addition to validating the miraculous, demand an attention that reconfigures space. This reconfiguration happens as people shift to make room for an unexpected person, as a good dancefloor shifts to accommodate a new presence.

Rambo describes the appearances of Jesus:

The Gospel of John's account of the resurrection features the return of Jesus to his disciples. He appears as one who is both familiar to them and yet unfamiliar. He appears to them as they once knew him and yet in ghostly form, as one who can enter a room through locked doors. From the gospel's account of Mary mistaking him for the gardener to the Thomas encounter in which he makes his identity known by inviting Thomas to touch his wounds, resurrection is a period of disorientation and reorientation ... The fact that the gospel narrative provides testimony to the challenges of recognizing the risen Christ underscores how difficult it is to resurrect, to come to life again. The testimony to the challenges of locating the body, of determining whether the body is there or not there, can be read as a sacred witness to the complexities of healing.[19]

Resurrection is difficult, complex and requires disorientation and reorientation, but I disagree that these appearances evidence a not-quite-there body in the way of a ghost that might be slowly and painstakingly reincorporating, becoming more and more physical as time produces distance from the event. While Rambo reads these cases of mistaken identity as evidence of a ghostly, barely there body, I am interested in exploring these cases of mistaken identity as evidence of a body that is no longer legible within existing frameworks. This body has changed and invites others to change with it.

Caravaggio's painting *The Incredulity of Saint Thomas* offers a challenging interpretation of this encounter. According to Rambo:

> While other visual representations emphasize the gap between the finger and the body, Caravaggio presents a simultaneously intrusive and intimate scene. Placing the biblical disciples – and viewers – at eye level with the wound, he paints an almost glassy-eyed Thomas who seems to be staring past the wound, as if not to see it.[20]

I first learned of this painting through Rambo and a reproduction of it hung on my wall for many years following this introduction. I have always appreciated Rambo's attention to the touch that occurs in this painting, the literal grotesqueness of the bodies present, the half of the finger that disappears into the wound. But I must depart from Rambo's interpretation here. Thomas sees the wound. He is stunned not because he stares past the wound, refusing to see it. He is stunned because of this close encounter with the wound, because of his seeing, because of his touching. In the Caravaggio painting, I do not see Thomas seeing past this presence, but being so immersed in it that he cannot see anything else. In this scene, Jesus' appearance stops Thomas in his tracks and the grief is shifted from the specific loss of Jesus to a loss of a world view in which death is always an end and not a transformation. This is disorientating and we see that disorientation in Caravaggio's depiction of Thomas's eyes, but it is a disorientation produced by seeing an appearance that demands change.

Instead of reading this resurrected body as a ghostly, barely there, almost see-through, body, I follow Madison Moore's description of what it means to make a fabulous appearance to understand these appearances. In *Fabulous*, Madison Moore describes fabulousness as a gesture, primarily one of queer and trans people of colour, that demands space through the creation of a look in a world that threatens their existence. If we read John with Moore, appearing becomes an intentional way of taking up space, demanding attention. According to Moore, 'Appearing is to visually and physically demand space, attention, and to announce oneself through the creative labor of self-expression. "Appearing" is a rush of visual and sensorial intensification into normative social space.'[21] Certainly the post-crucifixion appearances of Jesus created a rush of visual and sensorial intensification for those to whom he appeared. Moreover, these appearances interrupted the grieving process, interrupted the community gathered around loss and demanded a reorientation of attention. The appearances of Jesus do demand that they be witnessed but Jesus is not playing hide and seek with the disciples. Jesus demands attention and Thomas sees this resurrected Jesus, this Jesus who has appeared, demanding space and attention, announcing his presence through the creative labour of self-expression.

Appearing, rather than performing trauma, attempts to break our assumptions, assumptions that a resurrected body would not be wounded, assumptions that fleshy breasts must be contained or pushed up for the male gaze, assumptions that people with a broken knee or late-stage cancer cannot be found falling out of a warehouse as dawn breaks after dancing all night. In the hands of Caravaggio, Christ becomes a 'spectacle that creates visual damage'.[22] As Thomas sticks his finger into the side of Jesus, the scar becomes sensual, even sexy. By creating a spectacle out of a scar, this appearance invites an erotic attachment in the wake of disorientating and isolating loss.

We further reinvigorate these attachments with joy and pleasure, fun and flow. In the particular late-pandemic moment in which I write this chapter, resurrection means reopening spaces where people can experiment with their identities, taking pleasure in the seeing and being seen and in the fun and flow of music and energy. I am not saying that it was not necessary to close these spaces; I think it was. But reinvigorating affective attachment means increasing the possibilities for life-giving flows of energy. Remembering this will be important to our navigation of future crises.

Steps 9–11: the fabulous risen Christ

Fabulousness defiantly steps out of line as a political gesture that refuses to accept the world as it exists not by demanding another world, but by creating one. In this stepping out, fabulousness threatens both time and gender. In this section, I trace these challenges through time to creatively reimagine the resurrection of Christ and offer three more steps in the resurrection process: Step 9) to attend to the possibilities of the resurrections that are occurring right now, in the present moment, Step 10) to end gender through creative strangeness and unexpected mergers, Step 11) to affirm death as a creative, life-giving force.

Fabulousness threatens social agreements around time. According to Moore, 'With fabulousness, dreams and theories of stylish utopias are yanked from the future and brought to the present. Any suggestion otherwise regulates queer people and queer people of color to a life of waiting, taking a number, and holding on for better times.'[23] Fabulousness occurs in the present, although it is deeply determined by both the past and the future. Moore offers a hope for the future rooted in the present.

In this undoing of time, fabulousness can extend Sharon Betcher's description of crip as an 'aesthetic practice of attentively weaving relations with gravity and time'.[24] According to Betcher, this way of being offers one way to learn how to live the art of the flesh and, through this learning, to reveal a desire to still believe in this world. Taking this ninth step, resurrection becomes a present possibility and not a future hope. Resurrection is urgent, without being an emergency that cycles us through the loops of crisis→resolution.

As fabulousness undoes time, it also undoes gender. According to Moore:

Fabulousness lets us tap out of toxic masculinity, and that means it's less about upholding or adhering to any gender norms and more about ending gender through what I'll call 'creative strangeness.' At its heart, creative strangeness is simple: it is a style that surprises because it makes fashion out of things that are not made for fashion, or it merges things together in unexpected ways.[25]

These acts of creative strangeness and unexpected mergers end gender as a response to systems that justify violence against people who fail to conform to expectations around gender and sexuality. Ending gender through creative strangeness and unexpected mergers is the tenth step.

There is a long history of speculating on the sexuality of Jesus, from *The DaVinci Code*'s theory that Jesus fathered a child to speculations about the nature of the relationship between Jesus and the Beloved Disciple. I am less interested in continuing these speculations here. Rather, I am interested in the ways in which these speculations about the sexuality of Jesus point towards the possibilities of theologies that frame resurrection as an act of creative strangeness. In this, I continue to follow Althaus-Reid and Stuart. Althaus-Reid says:

our theological dealings with Jesus are queer, of an indecent nature, precisely because Jesus' gender performance is blurred with a sexuality which depends on a subtle divinity consciousness (his own, and that projected on him by friends, family, enemies, and admirers) and on location … Queer theologians like Goss and Stuart, amongst others, have been focussing on a Christ who is neither this nor that, a Christ who embraces and shows life as fluid, changing, outside the reductionist patterns which confront people with irrelevant options.[26]

Althaus-Reid's Bi/Christ queers both gender and sexuality. Putting Althaus-Reid in conversation with Moore (and imagining a club where the two might meet), I am arguing that a fabulous Christ presents people with more options. Through this fluid presentation, this series of openings (literal and metaphorical), the resurrected Christ emerges from the grave.

Resurrection as an act of creative strangeness offers new support around death, as Daniel Lavery intuits as he writes about his own gender transition through the language of his childhood Christianity in *Something That May Shock and Discredit You*. Lavery describes responses to gender transitioning that draw on the language of death, particularly in the form of 'It feels like someone has died' as a response to someone who transitions. Extending this concern from non-transitioners to transitioners, Lavery states: 'I sometimes think of the phrase "deadnaming" as a capitulation to the sometimes-fatal language other people use about our transitions – an attempt to reroute the language of death, if we can't clear it away entirely.'[27] Lavery continues:

> But whenever I hear someone refer to death-as-transition or transition-as-death, I think of Paul's second letter to the Corinthians on the subject of resurrection ... Here there are persons with multiple bodies that give way to one another ... capable of change and regeneration that necessarily involve death but do not end with it – here death is a creative power in service to a greater force, the greater reality of life. Here life swallows up death, and everyone is invited to look at it, to see the evidence of the persistence of life with their own new eyes.[28]

While Lavery is resistant to the language of death in relation to transitioning, he finds space for it through the reframing of resurrection. In this reframing, death becomes a creative, life-affirming force. We may resist death but that will not prevent it and so the question becomes: What can become when we imagine death as a creative power that serves living bigger? Figuring out how to answer this question is the eleventh step.

Step 12: Holy Saturday, redux

This understanding of resurrection changes how we interpret Holy Saturday and returning to it is our twelfth and final step. If we read the appearance of the resurrected Jesus with Moore, then it becomes possible to read Holy Saturday as a kind of preparation, that time spent browsing the closet and trying different combinations of pieces until landing on the look that will make an appearance, that will demand viewers to pause (even possibly exclaim!). People who play with gender rise every time they emerge from this effort.

Stuart writes that resurrection's ending of the dualism between life and death also ends the dualisms of gender, sexual orientation, race and class: 'With the end of the dualism between life and death comes the end of the dualisms between gender and sexual orientation, the dualisms of race and class.'[29] Stuart echoes Paul's oft-quoted letter to the Galatians: 'There is no longer Jew or Greek, there is no longer slave or free, there is no longer male and female; for all of you are one in Christ Jesus' (Gal. 3.28 NRSV). These parallel visions offered by Stuart and Paul still feel too romantic, too utopian to me, but the resurrections enabled by nightlife have given me space to imagine their possibility.

Bibliography

Althaus-Reid, Marcella, *Indecent Theology: Theological Perversions in Sex, Gender, and Politics*, New York and London: Routledge, 2000.

Betcher, Sharon V., 'Crip/tography: Disability Theology in the Ruins of God', *Journal for Cultural and Religious Theory* 15, 2 (2016).

Bray, Karen, *Grave Attending: A Political Theology for the Unredeemed*, New York: Fordham University Press, 2019.

Grossman, Pam, 'Dia Dynasty, Dominatrix Witch', *The Witch Wave Podcast* no. 4, 2017.

Lavery, Daniel, *Something That May Shock and Discredit You*, New York: Atria Books, 2020.

Moore, Madison, *Fabulous: The Rise of the Beautiful Eccentric*, New Haven, CT: Yale University Press, 2018.

Nair, Yasmin, 'No, No, Nanette: Hannah Gadsby, Trauma and Comedy as Emotional Manipulation', *Evergreen Review* (Spring/Summer 2019), https://evergreen review.com/read/your-laughter-is-my-trauma/.

Rambo, Shelly, *Spirit and Trauma: A Theology of Remaining*, Louisville, KY: Westminster John Knox Press, 2010.

Rambo, Shelly, *Resurrecting Wounds: Living in the Aftermath of Trauma*, Waco, TX: Baylor University Press, 2017.

Stuart, Elizabeth, 'Queering Death' in *The Sexual Theologian: Essays on Sex, God, and Politics*, ed. Marcella Althaus-Reid and Lisa Isherwood, London and New York: T&T Clark International.

Notes

1 Pam Grossman, 'Dia Dynasty, Dominatrix Witch', *The Witch Wave Podcast* no. 4 (2017), minute 54.

2 Shelly Rambo, *Spirit and Trauma: A Theology of Remaining* (Louisville, KY: Westminster John Knox Press, 2010), p. 79.

3 Rambo, *Spirit and Trauma*, p. 172.

4 Karen Bray, *Grave Attending: A Political Theology for the Unredeemed* (New York: Fordham University Press, 2019), p. 46; emphasis original.

5 Bray, *Grave Attending*, p. 46.

6 Bray, *Grave Attending*, p. 27.

7 Bray, *Grave Attending*, p. 50.

8 Yasmin Nair, 'No, No, Nanette: Hannah Gadsby, Trauma and Comedy as

Emotional Manipulation', *Evergreen Review* (Spring/Summer, 2019), https://ever greenreview.com/read/your-laughter-is-my-trauma/.

9 Sharon V. Betcher, 'Crip/tography: Disability Theology in the Ruins of God', *Journal for Cultural and Religious Theory* 15, 2 (2016), p. 113.

10 Shelly Rambo, *Resurrecting Wounds: Living in the Aftermath of Trauma* (Waco, TX: Baylor University Press, 2017), p. 14.

11 Marcella Althaus-Reid, *Indecent Theology: Theological Perversions in Sex, Gender, and Politics* (New York and London: Routledge, 2000), p. 121; emphasis and parentheses original.

12 Althaus-Reid, *Indecent Theology*, p. 118.

13 Elizabeth Stuart, 'Queering Death' in *The Sexual Theologian: Essays on Sex, God, and Politics*, ed. Marcella Althaus-Reid and Lisa Isherwood (London and New York: T&T Clark International, 2004), p. 67.

14 Althaus-Reid, *Indecent Theology*, p. 122.

15 Althaus-Reid, *Indecent Theology*, p. 123.

16 Stuart, 'Queering Death', p. 61.

17 Stuart, 'Queering Death', p. 58.

18 Betcher, 'Crip/tography'.

19 Rambo, *Resurrecting Wounds*, p. 9.

20 Rambo, *Resurrecting Wounds*, p. 19.

21 Madison Moore, *Fabulous: The Rise of the Beautiful Eccentric* (New Haven, CT: Yale University Press, 2018), p. 91.

22 Moore, *Fabulous*, p. 93.

23 Moore, *Fabulous*, pp. 100–1.

24 Betcher, 'Crip/tography', p. 113.

25 Moore, *Fabulous*, p. 14.

26 Althaus-Reid, *Indecent Theology*, p. 114.

27 Daniel Lavery, *Something That May Shock and Discredit You* (New York: Atria Books, 2020), p. 193.

28 Lavery, *Something That May Shock and Discredit You*, p. 193.

29 Stuart, 'Queering Death', p. 67.

13

Attending to the Fragments: The Implications of Trauma Theologies for the Practice of Christian Spiritual Direction

CATHERINE WILLIAMS

Humanity experiences and can endure the most extraordinary suffering. Bessel van der Kolk, in *The Body Keeps the Score*, describes human beings as an 'extremely resilient species'.[1] Catastrophes and violence causing suffering to body, mind and soul are experienced variously: some caused by humanity, others by nature or environment. Some are carefully planned and executed, others are random. Some suffering is caused by one-off single experiences, some is ongoing, multilayered and complex. Theologians have explored and debated suffering from the very beginning of Christianity: the event of the cross making the experience of suffering foundational to being a follower of Jesus Christ.[2]

Despite this long history, theology specifically exploring and linked to trauma – both violent events and ongoing oppression and abuse – is a relatively new area. Serene Jones, in *Trauma and Grace*, indicates that trauma is more than suffering, more than everyday disturbing and unsettling or stressful events that can happen to us.[3] Traumatic events are those in which our very existence is under threat, we become aware of this and internalize the experience. Events can be traumatic not just for those who experience them, but also for close witnesses. Trauma can be experienced by individuals, groups, nations, ethnicities and generations. Trauma can cause deep physical and overwhelming psychic wounds that are very slow to heal, requiring ongoing specialist attention.

Arising after the Second World War and coming to fruition in the twenty-first century, trauma theologies have developed through the recognition of the need to reflect theologically in the light of extreme events, including the Holocaust, terrorist attacks such as 9/11,[4] devastating natural disasters and the long-term effects of various forms of abuse. Ways of talking and thinking about God are needed to address the wide range of traumatic experiences that humanity encounters. The recognition in 1980 of post-traumatic stress disorder (PTSD) as a specific medical diagnosis requiring professional intervention has placed trauma firmly on modern medical and psychological agendas.[5] But humans are not simply bodies and minds, important though both are in the treatment of trauma. What of the soul? Ministry to the injured soul and its ongoing relationship with God can also be seen as an essential part of post-traumatic recovery.[6] The work of accompanying Christians and facilitating their growth in relationship with God has traditionally fallen to ministers, especially those working as spiritual directors.

As an experienced Anglican priest and spiritual director working in the UK, I find myself drawn to explore and consider how trauma theologies might inform situations with which I am currently dealing, as well as resourcing future encounters. Despite having worked in this field for many years, I have not been trained to work with trauma, nor is trauma currently covered in the initial and continuing training for spiritual directors that I have encountered in the UK, though the current climate, set within the context of the Covid-19 pandemic, has brought issues of ongoing trauma to the fore. Might it be the moment to explore appropriate responses to the traumatized in spiritual direction?

I write against the backdrop of the Covid-19 worldwide pandemic, which has now been raging for well over a year. The total number of deaths from Covid-19 in the UK stands at 127,000,[7] while the worldwide figure is very nearly three million.[8] Following a significant vaccination programme, the UK is cautiously beginning to emerge from the third period of lockdown, where many have been shielding and self-isolating. Social distancing, the wearing of masks and regular sanitizing have become standard everyday practices for most. Early in 2020, in the town in which I minister, a Chapel of Rest was opened and blessed by the Bishop of Gloucester,[9] in order to store bodies before burial. It was with a certain degree of horror that we realized that a meat-processing plant was commandeered for this new mortuary since it had the correct type of refrigeration equipment. It held the dead for 72 hours prior to burial. Several of our parishioners passed through this chapel, and local churches provided chaplains to say prayers there regularly, ensuring dignity for the deceased, and comfort for those working in this demanding environment. Families were unable to attend the bedsides of the dying and only a handful were allowed at funerals. This is an unprecedented situation for current UK clergy. Dr Ray Middleton, writing in April 2020, identified that the pandemic has led to everyone experiencing ongoing traumatic threat, either directly or at second hand. Therefore, what started for me as an interest and desire to learn from trauma theologies has become during the last year a necessity and current reality, as spiritual director and directees alike experience elements of trauma, and bring these into spiritual direction sessions. It has become very timely to investigate some of the ideas expressed by trauma theologians and consider how these might inform and enhance the practice of the Christian spiritual director.

I bring to this research questions and situations from my professional role as a spiritual director and priest, my personal experience of suffering from PTSD following a local disaster in 2007, and the current traumatic situation in which I find myself during the Covid-19 pandemic. Therefore, autoethnographic methodology informs this work, as I draw on my experiences to bring together in dialogue elements from both trauma theologies and spiritual direction.[10] By using the autoethnographic approach, I am exploring the personal experiences of myself as a spiritual director together with the experiences of directees, so as to explore links between 'human dilemmas and divine horizons'.[11] This reflexive approach enables new understanding for my own practice and offers ways to resource the ongoing practice of spiritual accompaniment on a broader canvas, through my engagement with various forums.[12]

My research suggests there are significant resources within trauma theology that can aid both the practice of Christian spiritual direction and the broader response of the Christian community to the experience of trauma. These inform and enhance my priestly ministry as a spiritual director.

Trauma theologies arising from trauma theory

First, let us look at the way trauma theologies have arisen from trauma theory. Trauma theory is not new. As early as the late nineteenth century, Charcot and Janet were researching the area of 'hysterical' women who presented with convulsions and sudden paralysis, thought to be emanating from the uterus.[13] Explorations by Freud on seduction theory and the repressed memories of child sexual abuse followed.[14] Further development in trauma theory occurred during the First World War, when English soldiers exhibiting shell-shock were treated psychologically at the Craiglockhart war hospital.[15] Following the Holocaust, Professor Dori Laub, a Holocaust survivor, set parameters for trauma theory, and these have been developed and expanded by Judith Herman in *Trauma and Recovery* and Bessel van der Kolk in *The Body Keeps the Score*.

Traumatology indicates that trauma is an acute form of suffering, in which the psychic defences are overwhelmed, leading to loss of control, a constant experience of threat and intense fear. A significant danger to life is experienced and may include extreme or ongoing violence and violation of body and/or mind. Trauma may come from a single event or an ongoing threat. Trauma leaves a deep imprint on the body – so much so that memories that would normally be stored in long-term memory banks remain lodged in the short-term memory. This leads to recurrent experiences of the trauma, which break into the present through uncontrollable flashbacks and hyper-vigilance long after the potential threat has ceased. The body can remain primed for fight-or-flight responses, undergoing physical and hormonal changes. The recent development of brain-imaging tools has allowed scientists to view such changes.[16] Psychological therapies are not sufficient for recovery: the physical body must process its somatic memory for some measure of recovery to be possible. Thus, individual and community post-traumatic remaking require an interdisciplinary approach.[17]

The need to reflect on traumatic experiences has led to the rise of trauma theologies in the twenty-first century. Global reporting of violent events, together with a series of catastrophic natural disasters, and the rise in reporting of domestic and child abuse, violent crime, sexism, racism, ongoing poverty and systemic abuse, has brought traumatology to the fore. Trauma is various, complex and multilayered, and this is reflected in the breadth of approaches by trauma theologians. Dominated by women theologians, such as Serene Jones and Shelly Rambo in the USA, and Katie Cross, Karen O'Donnell and others in the UK, many reflect in response to particular situations, and from personal experience. Could it be that women have deeper and more urgent questions regarding faith in situations of trauma, and are less easily satisfied with traditional Christian answers to suffering? As the majority of those who come to see me for spiritual direction are women, this seems important to note for ministerial practice.

In *Trauma and Recovery,* Judith Herman indicates three vital steps that are necessary for a trauma survivor to achieve some level of recovery. These are the establishment of safety, remembrance and mourning, and the reconnection with ordinary life.[18] Theology exploring trauma has needed to look beyond the boundaries of traditional Christian systematics predominantly formulated by and from the position of privileged white Western men, to find answers to questions of traumatic suffering. For some, traditional Christian teaching hasn't addressed the difficulties of constructing a narrative, meaning-making and post-traumatic remaking, and has moved too swiftly to the supplying of what Catherine Keller calls 'disappointing promises' and 'dishonest resolutions' – formulaic and simplistic stories of a God who saves, in a way that doesn't ring true with the experiences of the traumatized.[19]

The practice of spiritual direction

Just as trauma theories and theologies are complex and multilayered, so the practice of spiritual direction is also complex, with no single definition. It is also often misunderstood and caricatured.[20] Some form of the spiritual guidance of others has been undertaken from the earliest days of Christianity. From the Christian women and men who withdrew to the desert and were sought out for their wisdom and guidance, to the development of monastic orders with fixed rules of life, to Celtic *anam cara* (the 'soul-friend'), to modern-day professionally trained spiritual directors, a wide variety of techniques and practices have developed.

Ignatius of Loyola (1491–1556) gave new impetus to spiritual accompaniment, developing a standard form of guidance. Interestingly his *Spiritual Exercises*, which are recognized as a significant tool for spiritual direction and have been developed to great effect by the Jesuits, were devised while Ignatius was recovering from a serious wound received in battle. His method for spiritual discernment, which has been used success-fully for more than 450 years, was therefore conceived following what was probably a traumatic experience together with a long period of conva-lescence.[21] The full *Spiritual Exercises* take place over a period of 30 days and are designed to enable an imaginative immersion in the Scriptures, significantly deepening one's relationship with God and refuelling engage-ment with both the Christian community and the world.

Briefly, in general the role of a spiritual director is to enable and facilitate the growth of the directee in their relationship with God.[22] The director accompanies the directee as they move together in a spiritual direction. Availability, loving openness and hospitality are all marks of the rela-tionship of the director to her directees.[23] Margaret Guenther speaks of the director as midwife – who encourages the birthing and nurturing of God within the life of the directee, alongside the labouring directee, while facilitating, holding and occasionally intervening with expertise in times of danger.[24] The centrality of the spiritual experience of the directee is key in spiritual direction and the director honours this – seeking and listening for the Holy Spirit.[25] There are links with the practice of psychotherapy, and all spiritual directors should aim to have understanding and knowledge of the human psyche, but the two practices are not the same.[26] The spiritual director's aim is not to heal or 'fix', but to journey with the directee as they grow in faith, hope and love, towards God, self and others.[27]

In my practice of spiritual direction, I draw on a variety of approaches, including that which is broadly Ignatian. Having explored trauma theolo-gies, it seems fruitful to investigate three areas of useful dialogue between trauma theologies and Ignatian spirituality. These are testimony, the wit-ness and remaining; the concept of time; and the use of imagination – and they broadly correlate with Ignatian practices of deepening, recollection and contemplation.

Testimony, the witness and remaining (Ignatian: deepening)

Judith Herman points to the importance of the trauma survivor remember-ing and reconstructing a narrative for the process of post-traumatic remaking[28] – yet Cynthia Hess indicates that testimonies may be painful, slow, inaccurate and inconsistent. The story that emerges may be unstable, but what matters is giving space to the traumatized to find their voice and locate themselves in the present.[29]

This resonates with my personal experience of PTSD in 2007, follow-ing severe flash flooding in my home town of Tewkesbury. The town was surrounded by flood water for a week, cut off from the outside world, and its medieval abbey, which I live alongside and where my husband and I worship and minister, became an iconic picture that made international headline news. Three people died tragically in the flood waters, and the experience of seeing waters rise and not being able to stop them haunted me.[30] My experience felt as if a jigsaw puzzle had been emptied into my head; no pieces fitted together, and persistent flashbacks made for significant confusion and ongoing anxiety. In therapy, photographs enabled me to reconstruct a story, to tame details and to make a mostly coherent narrative of the traumatic events. It was a slow process, building a picture of the events as they unfolded, and then allowing that narrative to find a stable place in my memory so that I could continue to live and work in the abbey's vicinity without the danger of being retraumatized.

The psychoanalyst and Holocaust survivor Dori Laub indicates the importance to the traumatized of having a witness – someone to hear the narrative, attend and listen both to and through the story as it unfolds, however demanding this may be.[31] Shelly Rambo's theology focuses on the role of this witness and its location. In my own experience of PTSD, the witness was a counsellor who listened and reflected back, gently teasing out the fear I was experiencing while providing a stable, safe and non-judgemental environment. She was, however, less comfortable discussing questions of faith such as: 'Where was God?' and 'Why did God allow this to happen?'

Witnessing certainly takes place in spiritual direction, but who is the witness for the directee? The director hears stories haltingly unfold and sits with them. Trauma theory indicates that trauma narratives may be inconsistent, take time to articulate and may never be wholly reconstructed, but this is immaterial.[32] The importance is in enabling the survivor to give their testimony and to hear it.[33] For Rambo, the witness to trauma is the Spirit, who leads people into truth and enables the voiceless to communicate.[34] Rambo's extended exploration of the Spirit's role within the process of redemption focuses on Jesus on the cross breathing out the Spirit,[35] who remains as the thread of love between the Father and the Son, even in the grave.[36] The Spirit, therefore, holds the space between death and life and 'attends to the fragments': remaining when everything seems lost.[37] When Jesus (the Word) dies, he is in solidarity with the silenced dead.[38] The Spirit, however, remains. Even in silence, the Spirit bears witness. The Ignatian practice of deepening, 'staying with', or repetition encourages directees to remain with an image or idea that resonates, pondering and praying until they perceive God within. The director asks not 'Where is God in this?' but 'How are you experiencing God in this?' – acknowledging that God is present even if not discernible, and that experiences, however complex or traumatic, may be a source of revelation. Discerning feelings of 'consolation' or 'desolation' enables the director and directee to locate the movement of the Spirit and discern whether the directee is moving towards or away from God.[39]

Therefore, though the director is the witness to the directee, she is doing so to represent the Holy Spirit, who is the ultimate spiritual director and witness.[40] This means that even if the narrative is incoherent, or unarticulated, the Spirit is attentive and holding that which is muddled or disassociated. Whatever happens to directees, it's impossible for the thread of God's love for them to be broken. The Spirit holds the person within the love of God, however fragile that love appears, and however weary life has become. What is of significance here for spiritual direction is that nothing is beyond God's reach.[41] The directee cannot fall out of God's love, which is witnessed to even in the grave. Thus, the directee has the freedom to say anything about God and their mutual relationship, and the director has nothing to fear from the directee's testimony since there is no place where God cannot dwell.[42] The directee too need not fear expressing thoughts that may seem dangerous or irreverent, since God already knows the directee's thoughts and continues to love unconditionally, while there is also nothing to fear from the non-judgemental spiritual director.[43] Take for example the deeply bereaved person who, bearing significant loss, cannot believe that God's love can console them. They sense that God must be some sort of monster; that they must have done something heinous to be punished in this way. They may even cease to believe that God exists since the separation from their loved one is so painful. The director can have confidence that God's love is constant through the Spirit's witness, even when the directee cannot – in the moment – access that love.

Drawing on the work of Hans Urs von Balthasar, Rambo writes of the importance of Holy Saturday as the place of empty waiting with the weary Spirit that the traumatized may find themselves in as they move from death to life, from trauma to post-traumatic remaking. It is a place in the middle of events that contains the full horror of Good Friday with no hint of the realized joy of Easter Sunday.[44] The spiritual director needs to recall that though the Church celebrates the journey from death to life in the scant three days of the Triduum, for the first disciples many days of confusion, doubt, grief and hurt occurred before the resurrection was grasped and celebrated.[45] Meanwhile, the disciples carried the Spirit within them through the breath of the resurrected Jesus as a foretaste of the Pentecostal outpouring to come.[46] This Spirit is referred to in John's Gospel variously as Advocate, Comforter, Counsellor and Sustainer.[47] Deep breathing is an important part of realigning the traumatized body, enabling it to reach a place of safety and be fully within the moment.[48] So spiritual exercises that focus on the breath, such as learning the Jesus Prayer[49] or developing Centring Prayer,[50] may prove fruitful. While the traumatized directee may not be ready to embrace a hope-filled future, the director knows that the resurrection has happened and can eventually be accessed, even if the directee cannot bear it yet.[51] Spiritual director and Holy Spirit hold the promise of new life confidently for the directee, bearing witness to it at the appropriate time. Thus, the spiritual director aims to model the Spirit who remains, listens and loves, celebrating survival but not rushing headlong into resurrection, acting as the 'hinge' between death and life.[52] This leads us to another area for consideration – that of time.

Time (Ignatian: recollection)

Traumatic events are destabilizing experiences in which bodies, minds and souls can be ruptured or even shattered. In *Broken Bodies*, Karen O'Donnell points to the ruptures in body, time and cognition that trauma may cause.[53] For those experiencing a traumatic event, time can cease to function linearly, with past and present eliding through flashbacks and nightmares.[54] In extreme cases, the person may relive a traumatic event and become retraumatized. This is due to the memories and bodily responses created during traumatic events being stored in the amygdala in the brain stem rather than being processed in the hippocampus, the brain's long-term memory banks. Simply put, this means that the memory recalls trauma as a present reality rather than a past event.[55] When this occurs it becomes almost impossible for someone to imagine a future beyond the ongoing effects of the traumatic experience, and to move forward on the path of post-traumatic remaking.

An area that can be readily explored and developed in spiritual direction is the directee's understanding of time. Time is marked by moving between events in the belief that we are progressing forward. The Christian story of redemption moves step by step: creation to fall, incarnation to cross, resurrection to second coming. As mentioned before, crucifixion to resurrection is celebrated over three days: a very short time for traumatic events to be survived, grasped and integrated. Rambo suggests that trauma survivors will always carry elements of the past within them – returning to before the event and wiping the slate clean is impossible.[56] This is surely true of all we experience, traumatic or otherwise. The appearances of the resurrected Christ are helpful here as Jesus retains the wounds – 'haunted reality' – of the crucifixion.[57] Death is still present in life. Christ's wounds enable the disciples, especially Thomas, to grasp the resurrection, as the physical presence of scars that can be touched and held earths and makes real this new experience of a resurrected 'remade' Jesus.[58] Jesus' experiences through arrest, torture and crucifixion were traumatizing ones,[59] and thus Christians who enter into the body of Christ through symbolic and mystical death and resurrection in the sacrament of baptism carry this trauma within them. Thus, the body of Christ is shaped by trauma.

Regularly in spiritual direction, I accompany those who have experienced significant loss or journey with various forms of anxiety or depression. In some cases, though the church community has shown compassion and care in the early stages of the presenting situation, too often the expectation is that those with a strong Christian faith should be able to 'pull themselves together', to 'get over' their troubles or even to rejoice that their dead loved one is in heaven. These unhelpful voices can leave the directee feeling inadequate, a failure or struggling with guilt.[60] Graphs – such as Figure 13.1 – which plot the phases of disaster or trauma response indicate that beyond the heroic first phase of surviving the initial trauma and the honeymoon elation of coping with what has happened, lies a deep and irregular period of disillusionment and a lengthy journey to travel until a new way of living and flourishing can be embraced. The graph suggests that beyond the phase of remaking, a place of restoration and wiser living can be arrived at, though some trauma theologians suggest that a new beginning is not always possible in this life. Resolution may not be arrived at until the eschaton, and so it can be important in spiritual direction to hold open a vision that includes life after death.

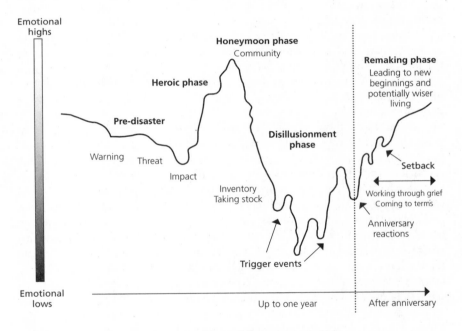

Figure 13.1. Phases of disaster response[61]

Biblical stories that speak of long struggles or unrealized hope, such as the book of Job, the Israelites' wandering for 40 years in the wilderness, learning to trust God for daily provision while not being confident that they will reach the Promised Land,[62] or Paul's very lengthy and hazardous journey to testify to Jesus in Rome,[63] may prove more realistic biblical reflection for some.

O'Donnell reminds us that Christianity is full of time ruptures.[64] These are moments when heaven and earth collide; when people and angels appear together;[65] when the elderly bear children;[66] when people are raised from the dead.[67] Helping directees embrace the concept of God's eternal time – *kairos* – which breaks into our earthly constructed time – *chronos* – reminds us that we are not ultimately in control of events and their out-working.[68] The spiritual director can encourage directees not to be wedded to the linear but to openly embrace God moving in and out of time, and to recognize that a moment of new life can come in the present – from the middle – rather than some elusive future.[69] Catherine Keller speaks of time being helical – a spiral that moves backwards to move forward, revisiting and gathering up before proceeding, and with multiple beginnings and entry points.[70] This one step forward, two steps back pattern resonates well with our human experience of life. In Ignatian spirituality, the exercise of recol-lection encourages directees to consciously bring past positive experiences of God into the present to inform and shape current difficulties. Recalling that God has acted for good and been faithful and loving in past encounters builds confidence and hope that God will remain constant in the present and future. Both the Jewish Passover and the Christian Eucharist with their concept of *anamnesis* – recognizing the past becoming real and effective in the present – are potent symbols of this.[71]

Time is also an important factor when considering the possibility of intergenerational trauma. Rosie Andrious explores the violence towards and objectification of early female Christian martyrs, indicating how the accounts of their experiences differ markedly from the heroic and victorious accounts of male martyrs.[72] Andrious suggests that much of the subjugation of women, overt and subtle, enacted by the Church for centuries can be traced to these early accounts, which have led to significant female psychological and spiritual trauma exhibited in a variety of ways, including medieval ascetic self-harm.[73] She suggests that women carry the psychic legacies of the traumas experienced by their forebears, and this leads to a chronic lack of self-worth in women generally and Christian women in particular.[74] Many of the directees I work with identifying as female have significant issues with self-worth and some have an associated lack of confidence regarding their place and validity within the body of Christ. These are issues that arise for me too from time to time. Andrious' work, together with O'Donnell's assertion that the whole body of Christ is traumatized,[75] incorporating the incarnate and crucified Jesus, lead me to question whose trauma I am encountering in spiritual direction. Might it be possible that the recognition of the body of Christ's shared trauma enables individuals within the body to allow other members to share and relieve the effects of intergenerational trauma? Furthermore, what role might the great Cloud of Witnesses[76] have to offer the body of Christ here on earth? The recognition of this shared heritage of trauma within the Church may aid the stage of post-traumatic remaking that relies on the reconnection of self with the community: both temporal and eternal. This consideration is of particular importance following the ongoing trauma sustained by the pandemic, when church congregations have been dispersed and physical connection to the body of Christ and the sacraments at times compromised. This leads to a third area to consider from trauma theologies – that of courageous imagination.

Courageous imagination (Ignatian: contemplation)

Rambo suggests that the process of post-traumatic remaking requires imagination.[77] A significant step on the journey is the ability to imagine something different from the traumatic environment in which one finds oneself. Serene Jones suggests that this may be beyond some survivors,[78] though Natalie Collins challenges this assertion.[79] Drawing on Judith Herman, Jones indicates that establishing safety enables people to begin to imagine freely. The Jesuit training programme for spiritual directors in South Africa recognizes the complex traumatic impact of years of apartheid, the HIV/AIDS pandemic and poverty on the population of South Africa and recommends that directors create as safe a space as possible for spiritual direction sessions.[80] Suggestions include having a calm, uncluttered environment, not changing furniture and furnishings without warning, and structuring sessions with a definite beginning and end. These practical elements are important to take on board when enabling a safe environment.

Within safe space, Jones encourages both mourning and wonder – the ability to grieve for what has happened or been lost and to imagine what might emerge, seeing death and life not as binaries but as part of a whole that may be integrated.[81] A developed theological example of this is the holding together of death and life within the Trinity. Following the crucifixion, the first person of the Trinity embraces the dead Jesus (the second person of the Trinity) within the ongoing life and love of the Trinity.[82] Jones links this to the experience of reproductive loss: the live mother holding the dead child within herself. This imagination requires courage and reveals deep truth that has resonance for those who have experienced such trauma. For a more traditional expression, some find the image of the Pieta – Mary holding the dead Jesus at the foot of the cross – helpful when experiencing the loss of a child. Spiritual direction is a courageous setting for directees to think creatively of ways in which God may be revealed and understood within their specific experiences. I find that new directees often require permission to push the boundaries of traditional systematic Christian teaching, question biblical accounts and rework long-held beliefs. Creating a non-judgemental space for directees to explore widely and deeply encourages them to take responsibility for their relationship with God, recovering agency rather than remaining dependent on either the Church or the director.[83] In this way, directees find themselves led by the Spirit into truth and potential liberation.[84]

Heather Walton writes of two ways in which imagination can be used to construct a narrative.[85] First, the narrative can be constructed within the canonical teaching of the Church, locating it within the Christian meta-narrative. The Ignatian practice of contemplation encourages directees to enter imaginatively into Gospel stories and to interact with Jesus within them, finding meaning and a deeper relationship with Jesus through the encounter. This gazing on the Scriptures can also be applied to the created order, and human creative endeavour to locate God who dwells within all and brings life.[86] Among the more positive experiences of lockdown during the pandemic has been, for some, a new connection with the natural world, experienced through daily walks and gardening, promoting mental well-being.[87] Such engagement has also led to a greater aware-ness of environmental issues, climate change and the interweaving of all life.[88] In addition, creative activities such as craftwork and baking have reassured, settled and relaxed people as they have worked from home, been home-schooled or lived in isolation.[89] For the Christian, these experiences can reveal new images of God in daily and domestic life, leading to new searches for truth that speak into one's unique situation.

The second of Walton's suggestions is that a new narrative can be con-structed that takes one to a new place, sometimes outside the structures of traditional Christian believing. This may create challenges for the spiritual director, who will require discernment and humility to trust that the Spirit is leading directees to develop their relationship with God.[90] Pushpa Joseph, writing in *Calling for Justice throughout the World: Catholic Women Theo-logians on the HIV/AIDS Pandemic*, notes how a group of South Indian women in Chennai, suffering the trauma of living with HIV/AIDS, found that turning from traditional Christianity to a broader more fluid spiritual-ity enabled them to tap into universal energy and strength that deepened their relationship with God, gave them new dignity and courage and enabled them to reconnect with both their communities and the healing nature of the cosmos.[91] Using whatever tools one can to encourage life and reconnection to God, self and community requires imagination from the director and the directee. Remembering that trauma affects somatic memory, and that integration requires work with body, mind and soul, should encourage the director to mention as possibilities a wide variety of verbal and non-verbal aids to prayer, such as poetry, art, exercise and drama. It should also remind the director of the need to refer her directees to other medical and psychological professionals when necessary,[92] and of the importance of undertaking regular professional supervision.[93]

Practical application

Evidently, there is a wealth of material in trauma theologies that can con-tribute to the practice of spiritual direction, when the director encourages dialogue between the two disciplines. Indeed, this chapter is only a first foray into this area. What might the practising spiritual director extract and distil from this academic and detailed exploration of trauma theologies? What lessons and insights can be taken into the work of spiritually accompanying others? This is of increasing importance as we recognize that many people suffer trauma, that the majority of people will have experienced some form of ongoing low-key chronic trauma during the Covid-19 pandemic, and that the body of Christ itself is traumatized and continues to bear the marks of trauma even in resurrection.

The following are practical suggestions arising from this study.

Safety

The spiritual director and direction session need to be places of safety. The physical space should be simple, uncluttered and constant. Appropriate boundaries should be adhered to and respected. The session should have a clear beginning and end, and the directee be aware of the time allotted. The director should understand and hold appropriate confidentiality, be non-judgemental, reliable, unshockable, acutely aware of power dynamics, consistent and kind. Directors and spiritual guides should also know their limits, be in regular direction and undertake supervision with an experienced director, watching particularly for the dangers of becoming enmeshed in patterns of dependency or heroic rescue, and understanding of the subconscious dynamics of projection, transference and counter-transference. Working with trauma is likely to be a multidisciplinary undertaking, potentially including medical care, psychotherapy, physiotherapy and, on occasion, legal intervention. Spiritual directors need to make wise decisions about when to make referrals and to whom, to know when to step back and when spiritual guidance will be best accessed or temporarily halted. On occasion, something may be revealed that requires mandatory reporting. A safe place is one in which healing can begin to be accessed, and in which people are free to say and think anything, asking the most demanding questions of both God and self, and exploring in whichever way works best for them as individuals. They do this in the knowledge that the director has the directee's very best interests at heart, and is working with skill and compassion, listening for the thread of the Spirit's guidance, which may be experienced in such ways as an unexpected thought, a moment of inspiration, dissonance in the conversation or a puzzling question.

Testimony and witnessing

We have already explored the importance of constructing a narrative for those who have been traumatized, and for the narrative to be heard and held. The story needs to emerge at the directee's own pace, and in the way that they wish to tell it, so as to minimize the risk of being retraumatized. The story that emerges may be painful, slow, inaccurate, inconsistent, muddled and unstable. The story may shift and change. The person may need to tell parts of it many times, and in different ways. This does not matter – it is the telling of it and the being heard that matters. Directors and spiritual guides need to listen patiently and non-judgementally and be with the directee in the moment. Whatever we may feel, this is not the time to say: 'You've already told me that', 'That's not what you said last time', 'Is that really true?' We may wonder where the truth lies, and we may never fully arrive at it, though we hold in our hearts and minds the understanding that the Holy Spirit knows where the truth lies and is leading to it. This process of mourning, remembering and longing needs to be assembled and rehearsed. It may be undertaken by speaking, but also through art or creative work – writing, poetry, journaling or rituals. The director needs to be intuitive, open and creative in order to encourage the story to emerge in the way that is best for the directee. And the directee needs to know that Holy Saturday – the in-between, middle ground of waiting and emptiness between death and life – is real and potent. There need be no expectation of a headlong rush into resurrection.

Embodied spirituality

As we've seen, trauma is a somatic experience, connected deeply with the body. Encouraging physical spirituality can be very helpful in post-traumatic remaking, enabling the body, mind and soul to realign. Prayer exercises that encourage stillness and deep breathing are helpful. So teaching the Jesus Prayer or Centring Prayer can be beneficial, but also playing musical instruments, singing or bell-ringing have similar effects on the body. Physical activities that easily combine with prayer include walking, running, yoga, swimming, cycling and mountain climbing. Connecting with the awe and wonder of God in the natural world can bring a new zest for life. Undertaking art and craft activities can enable directees to experience being co-creators with God. Questions such as 'What brings you life?' 'What brings you joy?' 'What do you long for?' can give permission for people to follow their heart and connect with the Spirit who is active within them, bringing energy and new life. Sometimes remembering and reconnecting with a childhood hobby or passion can bring new energy and curiosity. A less constructed and more fluid understanding of time can relieve the pressure on directees to 'recover', try to control the future or reach for a goal. Living fully in the moment and responding to prompts from the Spirit can aid integration and produce experiences of current joy amid ongoing struggle. Regular times for reflection such as the Examen will help to locate and capture experiences of God in the ongoing ordinariness of life, thus building and deepening relationship. For some, the rituals of the church may help, but this is not always the case and, depending on the trauma, may indeed be very unhelpful. In these cases, directees may need to be encouraged to develop their own new rituals for their journey.

Reconnection

As we've seen, part of the process of post-traumatic remaking is reconnection – with God, self and others. This may be a physical reconnection – the joining of a group, the return to church, the rebuilding of relationships. These all take time, energy and courage. This is where Ignatian contemplation can be used to good effect. Entering imaginatively into a Bible passage, joining in with the action, connecting with spiritual forebears and having imaginary conversations with Jesus can be revealing, challenging and comforting. Reminding directees that others in faith who have gone before have also suffered traumatic experiences can bring a sense of solidarity with the Christian community, and help to relieve some of the sense of isolation that trauma may bring. Those who have suffered trauma, such as bereavement, loss, a harrowing event, even the pandemic – may find previously supportive groups difficult places. There are times when others in groups struggle to behave appropriately and place unrealistic expectations on the one who is hurting. This can happen in churches too, where there can be the expectation that people of faith will somehow 'get over' difficult experiences. Formulaic and simplistic platitudes, such as 'Forgive and forget', 'It's all part of God's plan', 'You should be happy your loved one is with Jesus', while well meant can be less than helpful. Enabling directees to see that they need not return to a particular group or church, but that they have freedom and agency to choose where and how they continue their relationship with God, can be liberating. Moving to a new way of worshipping or a different theological stance can be part of remaking and reconnection. With the rise of digital worship during the Covid-19 pandemic, many more opportunities for reconnection at a variety of levels are possible, and exploration can be encouraged. There is also always the possibility that a directee may wish to sever the relationship with the divine. As directors, we know that nothing can separate any of us from God's love. We can have confidence in God's love for others, whatever their decision, and we can hold that love for them when they no longer wish to hold it for themselves. As spiritual directors, we need to have wisdom and humility to trust that the Spirit leads people into truth and new life, which might not look like what we expect or know. God's eternal kingdom is an extraordinary place, and God works in many ways beyond our understanding. Courageous imagination together with openness to surprise, delight and growth is called for when we work in tandem with the Spirit.

Conclusion

Many people are affected by trauma and carry the effects of traumatic experiences within their bodies, minds and souls to a greater or lesser extent. The current situation that we find ourselves in during this time of worldwide pandemic indicates that most people will be currently feeling the effects of trauma. We need to be aware of how this may play out in ongoing issues in people's lives, possibly for many years to come. Studying trauma theory and exploring trauma theologies may be essential parts of the training of spiritual directors and should be encouraged in the future.

We may keep in mind too the idea that the body of Christ is itself traumatized.[94] If this is so then we reflect on sacred texts written by the traumatized for the traumatized, receive sacraments that in some way contain trauma, and witness to ongoing intergenerational trauma in the Christian community and beyond. This raises fascinating and significant questions about the nature of post-traumatic remaking for the Church. How should we begin to address this need for remaking? And will there be a time when trauma will cease? We need to begin now with the weary Spirit – in the middle – right here.

Our final words come from Annemarie Paulin-Campbell, Head of the Jesuit Institute School of Spirituality in Johannesburg, South Africa, who has written her daily experiences of the Covid-19 pandemic through a series of prayer poems in a slim, as yet unpublished volume. In 'Anguish', she articulates the low-level ongoing trauma of the pandemic, and her turning to God for the remaking she senses is needed.

ANGUISH

Beloved,
When anguish
makes it hard to breathe.
When grief, like a tidal wave,
crashes on the shore of
my heart,
shattering the tiny shells
of ordinary moments;
shifting sands beneath my feet.
When anxiety grips my heart,
and sleep is an elusive friend.

Enfold me in your protective cloak,
synchronize my breath with yours,
whisper words of comfort,
tell me of my strength.

Nourish me with foods
I can eat.
Satisfy my senses
with sights and sounds that soothe.

Stir-up cherished memories
that bring calm.
Let me see the light,
break through dark clouds.

Heal the disconnects,
within me.
Let your grace
flow into my veins,
transfusing my being
with Love.[95]

Bibliography

Arel, Stephanie N. and Shelly Rambo, *Post-Traumatic Public Theology*, Cham: Springer, 2016.

Atkins, Wendy, 'The Use of the Arts in Trauma Healing Ministry', *GIA Lens* 7, 1 (April 2013), https://www.diu.edu/documents/gialens/Vol7-1/Atkins_Arts.pdf, accessed 21.4.2020.

Ball, Peter, *Anglican Spiritual Direction*, Harrisburg, PA: Church Publishing, 2007.

Barker, Pat, *Regeneration*, London: Penguin, 2008.

Barry, William A. and William J. Connolly, *The Practice of Spiritual Direction*, New York: HarperCollins, 2012.

BBC, 'Temporary Morgue to Be Set up in County', *BBC News*, 9 April 2020, https://www.bbc.com/news/uk-england-gloucestershire-52224073, accessed 22.4.2022.

BBC, 'UK Hospital Coronavirus Deaths Pass 20,000', *BBC News*, 25 April 2020, https://www.bbc.com/news/uk-52424413.

Chandler, Diane J. (ed.), *The Holy Spirit and Christian Formation: Multidisciplinary Perspectives*, Christianity and Renewal – Interdisciplinary Studies, London: Palgrave Macmillan, 2016, https://doi.org/10.1007/978-3-319-42667-9.

Conroy, Maureen, *The Discerning Heart: Discovering a Personal God*, Chicago, IL: Loyola Press, 1993.

Eberle, Gary, *Sacred Time and the Search for Meaning*, Boston, MA: Shambhala, 2002.

Fischer, Kathleen, *Women at the Well: Feminist Perspectives on Spiritual Direction*, London: SPCK, 1989.

Fleming, David, *Christian Ministry of Spiritual Direction*, St Louis, MO: Review for Religious, 1988.

Gloucestershire Live, 'The Floods 10 Years On', *Gloucestershire Live*, http://thefloods.gloucestershirelive.co.uk, accessed 27.4.2020.

Graham, Elaine, Heather Walton and Frances Ward, *Theological Reflection: Methods*, 2nd edn, London: SCM Press, 2019.

Grant, Robert, 'Spiritual Impact of Trauma: Trauma and Spiritual Direction', *Spiritual Impact of Trauma* (blog), 18 June 2013, http://in-sighttherapy.blogspot.com/2013/06/trauma-and-spiritual-direction.html.

Grant, Robert, 'Innerwords Newsletter: Trauma and the Spiritual Journey', *Innerworks Publishing*, https://www.innerworkspublishing.com/news/winter2017/trauma.htm, accessed 27.3.2020.

Guenther, Margaret, *Holy Listening: The Art of Spiritual Direction*, London: Darton, Longman & Todd, 1992.

Harborne, Lynette, *Psychotherapy and Spiritual Direction: Two Languages, One Voice?*, London: Karnac Books, 2012.

Herman, Judith L., *Trauma and Recovery: The Aftermath of Violence – From Domestic Abuse to Political Terror*, London: Hachette, 2015.

Hess, Cynthia, *Sites of Violence, Sites of Grace: Christian Nonviolence and the Traumatised Self*, Washington DC: Lexington Books, 2008.

Ignatian Spirituality, 'Discernment of Spirits', *Ignatian Spirituality*, https://www.ignatianspirituality.com/making-good-decisions/discernment-of-spirits/, accessed 20.4.2020.

The Inner Journey, 'Holding Trauma as a Spiritual Director', *The Inner Journey*, http://innerjourneyblog.weebly.com/1/post/2017/04/april-25th-2017.html, accessed 27.3.2020.

Iozzio, Mary Jo with Mary M. Doyle Roche and Elsie M. Miranda (eds), *Calling for Justice throughout the World: Catholic Women Theologians on the HIV/AIDS Pandemic*, London: Continuum, 2008.

Jeff, Gordon H., *Spiritual Direction for Every Christian*, London: SPCK, 1987.

Jones, Serene, *Trauma and Grace: Theology in a Ruptured World*, Louisville, KY: Westminster John Knox Press, 2009.

Meichenbaum, Donald, 'Trauma, Spirituality and Recovery: Toward a Spiritually-integrated Psychotherapy', n.d., p. 39.

Nemeck, Francis Kelly and Marie Theresa Coombs, *The Way of Spiritual Direction*, Collegeville, PA: Liturgical Press, 1993.

O'Donnell, Karen, *Broken Bodies: The Eucharist, Mary and the Body in Trauma Theology*, London: SCM Press, 2019.

O'Donnell, Karen and Katie Cross (eds), *Feminist Trauma Theologies: Body, Scripture and Church in Critical Perspective*, London: SCM Press, 2020.

Paulin-Campbell, Annemarie, *Prayer Poems for a Pandemic*, self-published e-book, 2020.

Paulin-Campbell, Annemarie, 'Teaching Spiritual Accompaniment in the Context of Trauma', n.d., p. 16.

Pickering, Sue, *Spiritual Direction: A Practical Introduction*, London: Canterbury Press, 2008.

Rambo, Shelly, *Spirit and Trauma: A Theology of Remaining*, Louisville, KY: Westminster John Knox Press, 2010.

Jayme R. Reaves, David Tombs and Rocío Figueroa, *When Did We See You Naked? Jesus as a Victim of Sexual Abuse*, London: SCM Press, 2021.

Rosenwink, Andreas A., 'How Body Awareness Informs the Practice of Spiritual Direction', n.d., p. 31.

van der Kolk, Bessel, *The Body Keeps the Score: Mind, Brain and Body in the Healing of Trauma*, London: Penguin, 2014.

Vest, Norvene, *Still Listening: New Horizons in Spiritual Direction*, Harrisburg, PA: Church Publishing, 2000.

von Balthasar, Hans Urs, *Mysterium Paschale: The Mystery of Easter*, San Francisco, CA: Ignatius Press, 2000.

———, *You Crown the Year with Your Goodness: Radio Sermons*, San Francisco, CA: Ignatius Press, 1989.

Wallis, Ian G., *Holy Saturday Faith: Rediscovering the Legacy of Jesus*, London: SPCK, 2000.

Walton, Heather, 'Speaking in Signs: Narrative and Trauma in Pastoral Theology', *Health and Social Care Chaplaincy* 5, 2 (28 May 2013), pp. 2–5, https://doi.org/10.1558/hscc.v5i2.2.

Walton, Heather, *Writing Methods in Theological Reflection*, London: SCM Press, 2014.

Warner, Megan, Christopher Southgate, Carla Grosch-Miller and Hilary Ison (eds), *Tragedies and Christian Congregations: The Practical Theology of Trauma*, London: Routledge, 2019.

Notes

1 Bessel van der Kolk, *The Body Keeps the Score: Mind, Brain and Body in the Healing of Trauma* (London: Penguin, 2014), p. 1.

2 Luke 9.23.

3 Serene Jones, *Trauma + Grace: Theology in a Ruptured World* (Louisville, KY: Westminster John Knox Press, 2009), pp. 13–15.

4 Jones, *Trauma + Grace*, p. 28.

5 Karen O'Donnell, *Broken Bodies: The Eucharist, Mary and the Body in Trauma Theology* (London: SCM Press, 2019), p. 5.

6 Kathleen Fischer, *Women at the Well: Feminist Perspectives on Spiritual Direction* (London: SPCK, 1989), p. 168.

7 'Official UK Coronavirus Dashboard', *Gov.uk*, https://coronavirus.data.gov.uk/details/deaths, accessed 14.4.2020.

8 'Coronavirus Update (Live): 138,113,914 Cases and 2,974,677 Deaths from COVID-19 Virus Pandemic – Worldometer', *Worldometer*, https://www.worldometers.info/coronavirus/, accessed 14.4.2021.

9 BBC, 'Temporary Morgue to Be Set up in County', *BBC News*, 9 April 2020, https://www.bbc.com/news/uk-england-gloucestershire-52224073.

10 Heather Walton, *Writing Methods in Theological Reflection* (London: SCM Press, 2014), p. xxxii.

11 Elaine Graham, Heather Walton and Frances Ward, *Theological Reflection: Methods*, 2nd edn (London: SCM Press, 2019), p. 6.

12 Such forums include supervision both individual and group, spiritual direction development groups, training sessions and ongoing dialogue with the spiritual direction community: local, national and international.

13 van der Kolk, *The Body Keeps the Score*.

14 S. Freud and J. Breuer, 'The Etiology of Hysteria' in *Standard Edition of the Complete Psychological Works of Sigmund Freud*, vol. 3, ed. J. Strachy (London: Hogarth Press, 1962), pp. 189–221, quoted in van der Kolk, *The Body Keeps the Score*, p. 180.

15 For an imaginative insight into the work of Craiglockhart Hospital with traumatized First World War soldiers, see the novel by Pat Barker, *Regeneration* (London: Penguin, 1991).

16 Hilary Ison, 'Working with an Embodied and Systemic Approach to Trauma and Tragedy' in Megan Warner et al., *Tragedies and Christian Congregations: The Practical Theology of Trauma* (Routledge, 2019), p. 48.

17 Norvene Vest, *Still Listening: New Horizons in Spiritual Direction* (Church Publishing, 2000), p. 19.

18 Judith L. Herman, *Trauma and Recovery: The Aftermath of Violence – From Domestic Abuse to Political Terror* (London: Hachette, 2015), p. 155.

19 Catherine Keller, 'Foreword' in Shelly Rambo, *Spirit and Trauma: A Theology of Remaining* (Louisville, KY: Westminster John Knox Press, 2010), p. x.

20 William A. Barry and William J. Connolly, *The Practice of Spiritual Direction* (London: HarperCollins, 2012), p. 9.

21 'Discernment of Spirits – IgnatianSpirituality.com', https://www.ignatian spirituality.com/making-good-decisions/discernment-of-spirits/, accessed 20.4.2020.

22 There are many terms used to describe those who deliver and those who receive spiritual direction, and terms used are open to debate. For the purposes of this chapter, I am using the standard terms throughout: spiritual director and directee.

23 Peter Ball, *Anglican Spiritual Direction* (Harrisburg, PA: Church Publishing, 2007), p. 14.

24 Margaret Guenther, *Holy Listening: The Art of Spiritual Direction* (London: Darton, Longman & Todd, 1992), ch. 3.

25 Barry and Connolly, *The Practice of Spiritual Direction*, p. 8.

26 Lynette Harborne, *Psychotherapy and Spiritual Direction: Two Languages, One Voice?* (London: Karnac Books, 2012), p. 119.

27 Francis Kelly Nemeck and Marie Theresa Coombs, *The Way of Spiritual Direction* (Louisville, KY: Liturgical Press, 1993), p. 64.

28 Herman, *Trauma and Recovery*, p. 7.

29 Cynthia Hess, *Sites of Violence, Sites of Grace: Christian Nonviolence and the Traumatized Self* (Washington DC: Lexington Books, 2008), p. 70.

30 Gloucestershire Live, 'The Floods 10 Years On', *Gloucestershire Live*, http://thefloods.gloucestershirelive.co.uk, accessed 27.4.2020.

31 Rambo, *Spirit and Trauma*, p. 35.

32 Hess, *Sites of Violence, Sites of Grace*, p. 70.

33 See Fischer, *Women at the Well*, ch. 8, 'Violence against Women' for an interesting discussion about the importance of the spiritual director not closing down difficult and painful discussions about violence and abuse.

34 Rambo, *Spirit and Trauma*, p. 144.

35 John 19.30.

36 Rambo, *Spirit and Trauma*, p. 74.

37 Rambo, *Spirit and Trauma*, p. 151.

38 Hans Urs von Balthasar, *Mysterium Paschale: The Mystery of Easter* (San Francisco, CA: Ignatius Press, 2000), p. 165.

39 'Discernment of Spirits – IgnatianSpirituality.com'.

40 Barry and Connolly, *The Practice of Spiritual Direction*, p. 89.

41 Vest, *Still Listening*, p. 28.

42 Rambo, *Spirit and Trauma*, p. 68.

43 Guenther, *Holy Listening*, p. 129.

44 Hans Urs von Balthasar, *You Crown the Year with Your Goodness: Radio Sermons* (San Francisco, CA: Ignatius Press, 1989), p. 87.

45 Ian G. Wallis, *Holy Saturday Faith: Rediscovering the Legacy of Jesus* (London: SPCK, 2000), pp. 11–12.

46 John 20.22.

47 John 14.15ff.

48 van de Kolk, *The Body Keeps the Score*, p. 80.

49 The Jesus prayer is an ancient Orthodox Christian threefold mantra that encourages deep breathing while praying on the breath. Once the practice is learned, the words may be adapted to reflect current necessity.

50 Centring prayer is a form of silent contemplation developed by the Trappist monk Fr Thomas Keating. It encourages one to sit in deep stillness and imagine oneself being held in the love of God.

51 John 16.12.

52 Rambo, *Spirit and Trauma*, p. 40.

53 O'Donnell, *Broken Bodies*, p. 6.

54 Stephanie N. Arel and Shelly Rambo, *Post-Traumatic Public Theology* (Cham: Springer, 2016), p. 7.

55 For a fuller and more scientific explanation of the brain and trauma, see van der Kolk, *The Body Keeps the Score*.

56 Rambo, *Spirit and Trauma*, p. 6.

57 Jones, *Trauma + Grace*, p. 41.

58 John 20.24–29.

59 Jayme R. Reaves, David Tombs and Rocío Figueroa, *When Did We See You Naked? Jesus as a Victim of Sexual Abuse* (London: SCM Press, 2021).

60 Hess, *Sites of Violence, Sites of Grace*, p. 104.

61 I am grateful to Harrison Williams for this reproduction of a graph charting the 'Phases of Disaster Response', ICTG – Getting Leaders' Restorative Strategies to Grow after Loss, https://www.ictg.org/phases-of-disaster-response.html, accessed 28.5.2021. Various examples based on the original work of Zunin and Myers (as cited in Deborah J. DeWolfe, *Training Manual for Mental Health and Human Service Workers in Major Disasters* (US Department of Health and Human Services, 2000), p. 5) can be found at https://www.ictg.org/phases-of-disaster-response.html and https://embodiedawareness.com/tag/disaster-recovery/.

62 Exodus 16ff.

63 Acts 22—28.

64 O'Donnell, *Broken Bodies*, p. 11.

65 Luke 1.26–38; 2.8–15.

66 Genesis 18.1–15; Luke 1.57–66.

67 1 Kings 17.17–24; John 11.1–44.

68 For a more detailed exploration of *kairos* and *chronos* time, see Gary Eberle, *Sacred Time and the Search for Meaning* (Boston, MA: Shambhala, 2002), ch. 3.

69 Rambo, *Spirit and Trauma*, p. 139.

70 Catherine Keller, *On the Mystery*, p. 74, quoted in Rambo, *Spirit and Trauma*, p. 126.

71 For further exploration of the concept of anamnesis within the Eucharist, see ARCIC, *The Final Report* (Oxford, CTS/SPCK, 1981), pp. 18–20.

72 Rosie Andrious, 'Violating Women in the Name of God: Legacies of Remem-

bered Violence' in *Feminist Trauma Theologies: Body, Scripture and Church in Critical Perspective*, ed. Karen O'Donnell and Katie Cross (London: SCM Press, 2020), p. 141.

73 Andrious, 'Violating Women', p. 146.

74 Andrious, 'Violating Women', p. 150.

75 O'Donnell, *Broken Bodies*, pp. 11–12.

76 Hebrews 12.1.

77 Rambo, *Spirit and Trauma*, p. 162.

78 Jones, *Trauma + Grace*, p. 155.

79 Natalie Collins, 'Broken or Superpowered? Traumatised People, Toxic Doublethink and the Healing Potential of Evangelical Christian Communities' in *Feminist Trauma Theologies: Body, Scripture and Church in Critical Perspective*, ed. Karen O'Donnell and Katie Cross (London: SCM Press, 2020), p. 198.

80 Annemarie Paulin-Campbell, 'Teaching Spiritual Accompaniment in the Context of Trauma'.

81 Jones, *Trauma + Grace*, p. 161.

82 Jones, *Trauma + Grace*, pp. 147–9.

83 Fischer, *Women at the Well*, p. 161, attests to the importance of women finding their own answers.

84 Guenther, *Holy Listening*, p. 128.

85 Heather Walton, 'Speaking in Signs: Narrative and Trauma in Pastoral Theology', *Health and Social Care Chaplaincy* 5, 2 (28 May 2013), pp. 2–5, https://doi.org/10.1558/hscc.v5i2.2.

86 Sue Pickering, *Spiritual Direction: A Practical Introduction* (London: Canterbury Press, 2008), p. 27.

87 Food Tank, 'Home Gardening as Self-Care during the Pandemic', *Food Tank* (blog), 24 August 2020, https://foodtank.com/news/2020/08/home-gardening-promotes-mental-health-during-covid-19/.

88 Jeffrey Frankel, 'Covid-19 and the Climate Crisis Are Part of the Same Battle', *The Guardian*, 2 October 2020, http://www.theguardian.com/business/2020/oct/02/covid-19-and-the-climate-crisis-are-part-of-the-same-battle.

89 Katherine Gammon, 'Kneading to Relax? How Coronavirus Prompted a Surge in Stress Baking', *The Guardian*, 19 April 2020, http://www.theguardian.com/us-news/2020/apr/19/coronavirus-stress-baking-sourdough-kneading-relax.

90 Barry and Connolly, *The Practice of Spiritual Direction*, p. 60.

91 Pushpa Joseph, 'Retrieving Spirituality as a Resource for Coping with HIV/AIDS' in *Calling for Justice throughout the World: Catholic Women Theologians on the HIV/AIDS Pandemic*, ed. Mary Jo Iozzio with Mary M. Doyle Roche and Elsie M. Miranda (New York: Continuum, 2008), pp. 192–200.

92 Ball, *Anglican Spiritual Direction*, p. 114.

93 Vest, *Still Listening*, pp. 19, 25.

94 O'Donnell, *Broken Bodies*, p. 11.

95 Annemarie Paulin-Campbell, *Prayer Poems for a Pandemic*, self-published, 2020, p. 24, reproduced with permission from the author.

Poverty and Privilege in Conversation with Trauma Theology

14

The Grenfell 72: Austerity, Trauma and Liberation Theology

CHRIS SHANNAHAN

Introduction

The inferno that engulfed Grenfell Tower in North Kensington in June 2017 symbolizes the cruel inequality of the 'age of austerity' that followed the global financial crash. In spite of Conservative Chancellor George Osborne's claim that 'We are all in this together', it is the poetry of Ben Okri that better captures the fractured nature of contemporary British society – 'If you want to see how the poor die, come see Grenfell Tower.'[1] Okri's critique stimulated the two questions to which this chapter responds. First, to what extent does the collective trauma unleashed by the Grenfell Tower fire reflect the intersectional violence of poverty during the 'age of austerity'? Second, how might an understanding of collective trauma provide political theologians with a hermeneutical framework capable of resourcing a liberative theology of austerity-age poverty?

Life on the Breadline is the first empirically based interdisciplinary analysis within academic theology of the impact of the 'age of austerity' on the nature and scope of Christian engagement with UK poverty since the 2008 financial crash.[2] The project is an example of liberative, fieldwork-led contextual theology. Our triangulated approach to data collection between 2019 and 2021 combined interviews with the national leaders of more than a dozen Christian denominations, an online survey of over 100 regional church leaders from across the UK, interviews with approximately 60 grassroots activists and six themed ethnographic case studies in Birmingham, London and Manchester within which we held informal conversations with approximately a further 400 people. This chapter draws on our case study of Christian responses to the Grenfell Tower fire and the wider questions about social housing, equality and housing justice that the tragedy highlighted.

In order to respond to the key questions above I explore the political and economic discourse of austerity that has defined UK government policy since the 2010 General Election. Second, I analyse the intersectional nature of austerity-age poverty. Third, I argue that a critical examination of the collective trauma that the Grenfell Tower fire unleashed can facilitate a more holistic analysis of the multidimensional nature of contemporary poverty. Fourth, I show how an understanding of collective trauma can enable a fresh reading of housing injustice as an expression of intersectional and ideologically driven austerity-age poverty. Fifth, I begin to sow the seeds of an intersectional theology of poverty that wrestles honestly with austerity's systemic violence and unresolved trauma.

An age of austerity

A year before becoming Prime Minister, David Cameron told the 2009 Conservative Party Conference that the implementation of austerity policies was an economic necessity in the aftermath of the global financial crash.[3] This claim has been widely critiqued over the last decade and it has become clear that austerity was, in fact, a political choice, as the former Chancellor of the Exchequer Philip Hammond acknowledged in 2018.[4] The introduction of austerity policies by the then Chancellor George Osborne exemplified broader neoliberal practice within which the private sector is valorized. Collective or state-based solutions to social problems such as inequality were depicted as barriers to entrepreneurship and competition, which were framed as the drivers of meritocracy and social mobility.[5] Such neoliberal tropes were used to justify the onset of the 'age of austerity', a retreating welfare state and calls for a resurgent but localized and largely apolitical 'big society'.

In the decade that followed the 2008 financial crash, welfare spending was cut by 25 per cent, while average incomes remained lower than they had been before the crisis unfolded. In 2011, Child Benefit was frozen for three years and the following year the Welfare Reform Act introduced the so-called Bedroom Tax, which saw people lose 25 per cent of their benefits if they had a spare room in their homes.[6] Then 2013 brought with it cuts in Legal Aid that impacted most heavily on people on low incomes, and the government's welfare reform flagship, Universal Credit, which rolled six pre-existing benefits into one, began its phased national roll-out in 2014.[7] The 2016 Welfare Reform and Work Act deepened the hold of austerity on social policy as it froze benefit levels for four years and removed Housing Benefits from 18–21-year-olds.[8] One of the impacts of earlier spending cuts following the 2008 crash was the closure of a large number of Sure Start Centres, which were introduced by the Blair Labour government in 1999 to provide educational support for children in socially excluded neighbourhoods. Between 2010 and 2019 just over 600 Sure Start Centres were closed as state support was withdrawn, according to the Department for Education.[9] Over the same period the number of people employed on insecure zero-hours contracts rose dramatically to almost one million people in

2020.[10] Furthermore, as the Trussell Trust demonstrate in their analysis of the rising number of people using their foodbanks after Universal Credit was introduced, the flagship benefit change is clearly worsening rather than alleviating in-work poverty.[11]

Throughout the age of austerity Cameron and Osborne repeatedly asserted that 'We are all in this together' to suggest that everyone needed to make sacrifices as part of the collective effort to reduce the UK's economic deficit. As we demonstrate in our Life on the Breadline research, we have definitely not all been in this together. Austerity policies have been targeted at groups within society who were already marginalized.[12] As Philip Alston, the United Nations Special Rapporteur on Poverty, made clear during his 2018 visit to the UK, people already in poverty, Black and Brown Britons, women, single parents and people with disabilities were hit far harder by austerity policies than other groups within society.[13] While many people have been cushioned from the impact of austerity, Hall notes that for millions across the UK, 'austerity is woven into the fabric of everyday life'.[14] Justin Welby, the Archbishop of Canterbury, put it this way: 'Austerity is a theory for the rich and the reality of suffering for the poor.'[15] Austerity is not neutral – it has been targeted at people who are already left out or left behind in breadline Britain. Austerity was not an unavoidable economic necessity but a conscious political choice that has destroyed the social fabric of British society, ruptured the social contract by which we negotiate our common life and deepened pre-existing structural injustice, leaving communities wounded as they wrestle with unresolved collective trauma.

The octopus of poverty

Standing to speak after receiving his Nobel Peace Prize in 1964, Martin Luther King Jr suggested that poverty was like an octopus whose tentacles reached into every corner of our lives and our world. According to the Joseph Rowntree Foundation, 14.5 million people were living in poverty in the UK in 2020, of whom 2.4 million were destitute.[16] The Institute for Public Policy Research found that a record 11.7 million people in paid work were in poverty in 2021 and that working families with children have seen poverty rise by 42 per cent since 2010.[17] The convergence of structural injustice, the unequal impact of austerity and deepening levels of social exclusion during the Covid-19 pandemic represented a perfect storm for people who are left out or left behind in contemporary Britain. However, in spite of the multidimensional nature of poverty, most theological analysis of austerity is largely one-dimensional. A liberative theology of austerity-age poverty needs to correct this oversight in three ways.

First, in order to provide the resources needed to engage with collective trauma, a theology of austerity-age poverty needs to recognize its intersectional nature. It is not new to suggest that poverty is multidimensional, but we need to take a further step if we are to grasp the interwoven nature of its different faces. Kimberlé Crenshaw's articulation of the concept of intersectionality emerges from the struggle against structural racism in the USA but it can enrich theological analyses of austerity-age poverty in the UK. Writing about the experience of African American women, Crenshaw highlighted the multiple, intersecting forms of oppression they faced. Sexism, racism and classism overlapped to create a perfect storm.[18] Crenshaw describes intersectionality as 'a metaphor for the ways in which multiple forms of inequality combine and compound themselves'.[19] May suggests that intersectionality reflects a 'matrix worldview [which] contests "single-axis" forms of thinking about subjectivity and power', approaching 'lived identities as interlaced and systems of oppression as enmeshed and mutually reinforcing'.[20] By embracing an intersectional framework, theologians can cultivate a matrix mindset capable of facilitating the holistic analyses needed to respond effectively to austerity-age poverty in general and the communal trauma that the Grenfell Tower fire left in its wake in particular. A generation ago the pioneer of liberation theology, Gustavo Gutiérrez, pointed the way: 'Poverty means death: lack of food and housing, the inability to attend properly to health and education needs, the exploitation of workers, permanent unemployment, the lack of respect for one's human dignity.'[21] Are we ready to take up the challenge Gutiérrez laid down?

Second, contemporary theologians need to recognize the systemic nature of poverty if they are to grasp the impact of the communal trauma it leaves in its wake. Such a step relies on a willingness to fashion a countercultural narrative that critiques the individualizing of poverty, the promotion of unreflective binary thinking, which contrasts the so-called 'deserving' and 'undeserving' poor, and the moralizing of poverty within popular political discourse. Ahead of the 2019 General Election, the Home Secretary Priti Patel exemplified this neoliberal discourse in her denial that rising levels of poverty were related to government austerity policies.[22] The Blair Labour government elected in 1997 introduced sweeping policy reforms that placed social exclusion centre stage and reduced child poverty dramatically, as well as introducing a National Minimum Wage.[23] However, as Levitas notes in her analysis of the Blair government, New Labour moved from a clear focus on economic redistribution to an emphasis on individual ethical responsibility and ultimately to the presentation of poverty as 'pathological … rather than endemic'.[24] A comparable perspective was articulated by George Osborne at the 2012 Conservative Party Conference just months after the Welfare Reform Act, which instituted a raft of austerity policies, passed into law. Osborne echoed the language of the late New Labour years, contrasting so-called 'strivers', who worked hard, with people whom he called 'skivers', who enjoyed a comfortable life, he claimed, on benefits.[25] Such myths moralized poverty, painting it as the consequence of moral fecklessness and lack of hard work.[26] This binary thinking scapegoated people living in poverty and echoed the older dichotomy of the 'deserving' and 'undeserving' poor, but it did not reflect reality, as the Joint Public Issue Team's 2013 report *The Lies We Tell Ourselves* demonstrated.[27] In spite of JPIT's incisive and perceptive critique, the moralizing and individualizing of poverty retains cultural traction. In this context theologians and theorists need to be bold and explain again and again that poverty is not accidental, nor the result of an individual's moral inadequacy. As Castells and Sassen remind us, poverty results from the processes and structures that underpin neoliberal capitalism.[28] Such embedded oppression can be described as systemic sin, what Gutiérrez calls 'a social, historical fact, the absence of brotherhood'.[29] Sin, he argues, 'is evident in oppressive structures ... as the root of a situation of injustice'.[30] This perspective can help us to see austerity poverty as a form of structural injustice that results in collective trauma, and it is essential if we are to fashion a theology of austerity poverty that can respond to the enormity of the Grenfell Tower disaster.

Third, in an age of austerity, theologians need to frame poverty as a form of grinding and debilitating violence. I have argued elsewhere that the pioneering work of Galtung within peace studies on the multidimensional nature of violence provides political theologians with a new framework for analysing poverty.[31] In his triad of violence Galtung speaks of the interrelationship between direct, structural and cultural violence. Galtung speaks of the ways in which face-to-face violence – indirect violence that is woven into the fabric of systems and practices and the unspoken fomenting of injustice, discrimination and social exclusion within art, film, music, worship, the media or television – feed into each other.[32] Mahatma Gandhi argued that poverty is the worst form of violence.[33] More than half a century later Davies suggested that 'Poverty kills with subtlety and skill ... Poverty will use the damaged emotions of its victims as a deadly weapon, driving them to ... violence against each other.'[34] Gutiérrez agrees, suggesting that 'Material poverty is a sub-human situation ... to be poor means ... to be exploited by others ... not to know you are a person.'[35] In a similar vein Tamez speaks of the existential damage caused by poverty, which leads to the 'degradation of the human being, a seizure, as it were, of the divine image in the person'.[36] Powers and Rakopoulos refer to the deployment of austerity policies as a form of 'slow violence' that seeps into the fabric of broader and longer-lasting policy culture.[37] In their analysis of UK social policy, Cooper and Whyte speak of 'the devastatingly violent consequences of government policy conducted in the name of austerity'.[38] Grover agrees, suggesting that UK austerity policies exemplify structural violence – 'Un- and underemployed people are enduring the violence of deepening inequalities ... as a consequence of capital's need for commodified labour ... The outcome is social murder.'[39] The most graphic example of such social murder in recent decades is the Grenfell Tower fire, to which I now turn.

'Where the poor die today' – a reflection on the Grenfell Tower fire

At 1 a.m. on 14 June 2017, a fridge caught fire in a flat on the fourth floor of Grenfell Tower. Two hours later the entire tower was engulfed in flames but the Grenfell fire was not ultimately caused by a faulty fridge, broken sprinklers or even combustible cladding. It resulted from decades of underinvestment in social housing and the harsh impact of neoliberal austerity. The poet Ben Okri summarized: 'In this age of austerity the poor die for others' prosperity.' Okri raised the cry of lament: 'It was like a burnt matchbox in the sky ... You saw it in the tears of those who survived ... You heard it in the cries howling for justice ... If you want to see how the poor die come see Grenfell Tower.'[40] Sitting in the shadow of the Westway, Grenfell Tower is in the Notting Dale local government ward in the Royal Borough of Kensington and Chelsea, one of the 10 per cent most multiply deprived neighbourhoods in England.[41] Life expectancy in Notting Dale is 14 years lower for men and 12 years lower for women than it is just a few miles away in South Kensington, and 39 per cent of children are living below the poverty line.[42] The rap musician and activist Akala suggested that the tragedy was not an accident but 'the product of a philosophy that says some lives have value and others do not'.[43] Just a day after the fire, with the tower still smouldering, Akala insisted that 'the people who died here died because they were poor.'[44]

Cooper and Whyte argue that the Grenfell fire represents a form of 'institutional violence' that arose from the impact of unequal power relations. This 'institutional violence', they suggest, was the direct result of conscious political decisions made by the leadership of Kensington and Chelsea Borough Council in their imposition of austerity cuts in the years before the 2017 fire.[45] Shildrick amplifies this point, suggesting that the roots of the Grenfell tragedy pre-date the onset of austerity and can be dated to the adoption of neoliberal monetarist policies in the early 1980s by the then government of Margaret Thatcher.[46] The Grenfell fire is a tragically graphic reminder that poverty is a systemic form of violence. Until there is justice for Grenfell, the cry of the 72 will continue to echo down the years as an iconic expression of collective trauma.

The video for Lowkey's track 'Ghosts of Grenfell', which features people who lived in the tower, exudes despair, weariness, anger, loss, confusion and a deep sense of solidarity with the 72 and their families. Released in August 2017, the track resembles a collective cry of lament arising from the traumatic splintering of individual, family and community narratives.[47] Fleeing from the burning tower, people found immediate refuge in makeshift rescue centres and places of worship near the Lancaster West estate, which was overlooked by Grenfell Tower. In the following weeks it became clear that large numbers of people who had been directly or indirectly affected by the fire were suffering from post-traumatic stress disorder. This was not a war zone, a violent rape or mugging but a social cohesion cri-sis resulting from the implementation of ideologically driven austerity in the UK and the logic of neoliberal capitalism. In December 2017 the BBC reported that more than 1,000 people who lived near Grenfell Tower had been screened for PTSD.[48] By the time a public health report was published for the National Health Service and Kensington and Chelsea Council in late 2018, this figure had risen to 2,200.[49] Three years after the tragedy the impact of the Grenfell fire continued to reverberate. In January 2020, ITV News reported that as many as 10,000 people had been screened and 2,000 people had been treated for PTSD, including 744 children.[50]

The symptoms traditionally connected with trauma in general and PTSD in particular include ongoing and unpredictable feelings of anxiety, flash-backs, night-terrors, survivors' guilt, confusion, anger, isolation, loss and a lost sense of value and direction. The studies referred to above, in par-ticular the *Journey to Recovery* report for the NHS and Kensington and Chelsea council, clearly demonstrate the ongoing social impact of PTSD and secondary trauma more than four years after the Grenfell fire on people directly affected, but also on those who live in Notting Dale and were impacted more indirectly.

The study of trauma has become increasingly common within the arts and humanities but, as Radstone and Farrell remind us, its roots lie in the work of early psychoanalysts like Freud and Charcot and, much more recently, in the development of 'trauma theory' by Caruth.[51] Three inter-related insights drawn from the multidisciplinary world of trauma studies speak to the communal trauma of the Grenfell tragedy and its relation-ship with austerity and contemporary theology. First, the work of Garland invites us to see trauma as a wound that damages, disturbs and disrupts individual and collective well-being.[52] By envisaging the Grenfell tragedy as an unresolved communal trauma that has inflicted an unhealed wound on the people of North Kensington, we can see neoliberal austerity-age poverty in a fresh light. Second, as Hirschberger argues, collective trauma is 'a cataclysmic event that shatters the basic fabric of society', causing a 'crisis in meaning' that can have an impact on the 'ontological security' of people who were not directly or even indirectly affected by a traumatic event.[53] By understanding the Grenfell Tower fire in this way we are able to express the iconic nature of the tragedy, its status as an archetype of neoliberal austerity and the extent to which this fire in North Kensington stimulated a broader commitment to housing justice across the UK. Third, collective trauma can, as Sewell and Williams suggest, rupture the sociality that underpins shared meanings and identities, thereby breaking the narratives that bind us.[54]

Faith-based responses to the collective trauma of Grenfell Tower

The 2018 *Journey of Recovery* NHS report team commented on the networks of support they encountered in the community around Grenfell Tower – 'There is a palpable sense of community in North Kensington ... The diversity and many communities within it ... make it a place with a strong sense of identity, social capital and a depth of social networks.'[55] More residents in the neighbourhood around Grenfell Tower self-identify as people of faith than in any other part of Kensington and Chelsea. According to *Journey to Recovery*, 57 per cent self-identified as Christian, 28 per cent as Muslim and 12 per cent as 'No Religion'.[56] As the report noted, local faith groups lie at the heart of community life in the streets around Grenfell Tower: 'Recovery for many people is interconnected with religious belief and notions of justice and for some people religion can be an overarching framework for recovery.'[57] It is, therefore, to the role that faith communities played on the night of the fire and in the years since that I now turn, as I begin to identify the tentative shape of a theology of austerity-age poverty capable of challenging endemic housing injustice. In summarizing this response I draw on qualitative data from our Life on the Breadline research and the report *After Grenfell* published by the Theos think tank.

Plender suggests that in the aftermath of the Grenfell fire, local faith groups responded 'practically, emotionally and spiritually to a moment of pain and confusion', noting that 15 local faith groups offered space or support on the night of the fire and in the following weeks. Such support, they observe, included providing and staffing evacuation centres; receiving and sorting donations of money, food, clothes and blankets; providing emergency accommodation and feeding approximately 6,000 people in the three days following the fire.[58] In recent decades the acknowledgement that faith groups continue to play a key role in civil society politics at a neighbourhood level because of their enduring social capital has challenged the assumption among secularists that religion was withering on the vine. While debates about social capital were popularized by Putnam, it is the research of Skinner and Baker into the social action of churches in Manchester that is most relevant in the case of Grenfell Tower.[59] Two forms of social capital should be noted: religious capital and spiritual capital. Skinner and Baker suggest that religious capital refers to faith groups' resources and the practical contribution they make to the communities in which they are set. Such practices, they argue, are shaped by foundational ethical or spiritual values, or spiritual capital.[60] With reference to the Grenfell fire, Plender notes that:

> faith groups were able to respond in the way they did because they were *trusted*. They were *embedded in the communities* they served ... they

were *long-standing institutions* ... They were in it for the long haul ... faith groups were committed [to] preaching and practicing an ethos of openness and hospitality to those in need.[61]

Plender identifies immediate responses to the fire and long-term engagement. Immediate responses included the collection and distribution of food, clothes and blankets; what they call 'pastoral first-aid' and unconditional hospitality.[62] One Muslim leader summarized: 'Open [the] doors, welcome anyone who comes. We are open to all.'[63] Alongside immediate support for anyone in need, Plender points to the long-term commitment of faith groups to rebuilding and reweaving community in North Kensington, quoting one faith leader: 'When the journalists and emergency services go, we'll still be here.'[64] Plender makes it clear that their report was not intended to analyse the contested cause of the Grenfell fire, although they do note the perception that one faith leader shared with them about Kensington and Chelsea Borough Council:

> The Council collapsed. Groups like St Helen's Church, the Clement James Centre and the Westway Centre 'became' the local government as people lost trust in the council. But people don't lose trust suddenly. It was lost before.[65]

Plender summarizes the practical caring responses faith groups made after the blaze. However, their lack of critical engagement with the broader socio-economic and political context minimizes the impact of their report, which includes just one brief comment about the current crisis in social housing.

Our Life on the Breadline case study of the work of Notting Hill Methodist Church in the years since the Grenfell tragedy adds specificity to the summary provided by Plender. Following a phone call in the early hours of 14 June 2017, Revd Mike Long, minister at Notting Hill, spent the night sitting with people who had fled the fire engulfing Grenfell Tower just a few hundred yards from the church. Notting Hill Church became a focal point for gatherings, emergency support and vigils in the weeks, months and years following the Grenfell fire. Its response to the tragedy has reflected four of the expressions of Christian engagement with poverty that we have encountered during our Life on the Breadline research.

First, Notting Hill provided emergency pastoral support. Initially Mike Long sat quietly with survivors in the nearby Rugby Portobello Trust building until the police lifted the cordon and allowed him to open Notting Hill Church, which was closer to Grenfell Tower. Once he opened the church doors, 'people began to stream in', looking for refuge and the chance to support people fleeing from the fire. In a 2018 interview with *The Guardian* newspaper reflecting back on a year since the tragedy, Long recalled that opening the church doors 'began a whole impromptu community response, mostly led by people I'd never met before, a very significant portion of them Muslim'.[66] Huge amounts of food, clothing and blankets were donated and distributed in this emergency response phase. Long recognizes the pressure that Kensington and Chelsea Borough Council were under in the immediate aftermath of the fire. However, like others he voices the frustration felt by many about what is widely recognized to be the piecemeal and inadequate response of the Council to the tragedy, as well as its apparent lack of response to countless warnings about the safety of Grenfell Tower in the months and years preceding the fire:

> They were trying to put the fire out, to rescue and accommodate people. But after a week, what we needed was some visible sign of coordination, which at least would have reassured the public. It might have actually calmed down a lot of the aggro on the street. Because it looked like the council didn't care.[67]

Second, in part because it was so close to the Tower, in part because the church building became a vital distribution centre in the aftermath of the fire and in part because of Mike Long's visibility as a key community leader, Notting Hill Methodist Church has become a centre of spiritual support and solidarity since the fire. On the evening of 14 June 2017, with Grenfell still burning, Long led a candlelit vigil on the steps of the church – a moment of lament and loss.[68] Similar moments of quiet reflection have been held in 2018 and 2019, and Long offered a reflection at a virtual vigil at the height of the Covid-19 pandemic in 2020.[69] In a neighbourhood where faith continues to be a major influence on individual and communal life, these moments to pause and reflect provided an opportunity for the community to let out a collective cry of lament but also for the quiet assertion of cross-cultural interfaith solidarity.

Third, Mike Long's work since 2017 reflects Notting Hill's historic commitment to community engagement in North Kensington and to an incarnational model of ministry characterized by long-term relationship building.[70] This commitment to solidarity with a marginalized inner-city community abandoned again by those with power is seen in the support Long and the Notting Hill congregation have offered to local residents associations and the Grenfell United pressure group, which is made up of the bereaved, the displaced and the survivors of the fire.[71]

Fourth, the response of Notting Hill Church to the Grenfell disaster exemplifies an advocacy and campaigning tradition of Christian anti-poverty activism that prioritizes an ethic of social justice over a more limited welfare model of discipleship. Such a perspective reflects the commitment to transform structural injustice articulated in the Marks of Mission, which were first developed within the Anglican Communion in 1984.[72] Long's work with the UK homelessness charity Shelter since the Grenfell fire exemplifies this advocacy and campaigning tradition, and roots the disaster in a longer history of underinvestment in social housing in poor communities and the economic logic of austerity-age neoliberalism. In 2018 Long was asked to chair the public commission established by Shelter to investigate the crisis of social housing across the UK in the aftermath of the Grenfell fire. The task was enormous and included consultations with more than 31,000 people. In the resulting 2019 report, *Building for our Future: A Vision for Social Housing*, Long wrote of the need to end the UK's 'housing crisis' and of a determination that the Grenfell disaster should become 'a catalyst for positive change'. He summarized the commissioners' conclusion that social housing had been 'devalued and neglected' in the UK, and their conviction that 'everyone, no matter their income, deserves a decent place to live ... The time for the government to act is now.'[73]

Trauma, poverty and forgotten communities: doing theology after Grenfell Tower

The death of the 72 in the Grenfell Tower tragedy is more than the embodiment of austerity economics. It is a *kairos* moment for contemporary theology. The enormity of this moment cannot be addressed in a credible manner until the roots of the fire in endemic structural injustice, deep-seated poverty and neoliberal austerity economics are recognized. How can the dialogue between analyses of austerity, the violent, systemic and intersectional nature of poverty and collective trauma begun here enable contemporary theologians to forge a liberative theology of austerity-age poverty? In the closing section of this chapter I draw on photographs from our Life on the Breadline fieldwork to begin to sketch out some of the themes that need to take centre stage in a liberative theology of austerity-age poverty. Here I offer four glimpses, each of which hints at a larger narrative.

Glimpse 1 – embracing intersectionality

During the Life on the Breadline project we have worked with a UK artist called Beth Waters. One of the images she created for us articulates the need for contemporary theologians to grasp the intersectional jigsaw of poverty. Theoretical and theological engagements with intersectionality emerged from the experiences of African American women and have largely focused on analyses of racism and sexism. However, as Kim and Shaw note, engagement with the concept of intersectionality can provide contemporary theologians with the matrix-like theoretical, hermeneutical and methodological framework needed to grapple effectively with broader and wider experiences of oppression. In the aftermath of the Grenfell fire and a decade of neoliberal austerity economics, the cultivation of the intersectional gaze needed to forge a liberative theological response that shines a light on the interconnectedness of the jigsaw of poverty is vital.[74] Are contemporary theologians ready to embrace the opportunity and the challenge of this *kairos* moment?

Figure 14.1. *The Jigsaw of Poverty*, Beth Waters, 2018.[75]

Glimpse 2 – anger and lament

If the 'social murder' that culminated in the Grenfell Tower fire does not make us angry then nothing will. I have shown that austerity-age poverty is a form of direct and structural violence that is underwritten by forms of cultural violence that remain largely unacknowledged. A theology of austerity-age poverty that engages meaningfully with structural injustice must prioritize the cries of lament that emerged from the smoke of Grenfell Tower and the simmering anger that remains because of the ongoing absence of justice.

Too often the carefully finessed language of academic theology smoothes away the visceral cry of anger in the face of unbearable oppression. In this photograph of a sign hung on a railing just a few yards from Grenfell Tower, pain and despair are entwined with rage. Dialogues between theology and trauma studies can provide theologians with the tools needed to engage in an authentic manner with the collective trauma of outrages like the Grenfell Tower fire and the dull anger of never-ending austerity. Rambo suggests that an embrace of the presuppositions of trauma theory can help theologians to engage with traumatic experience in a more pastorally sensitive manner than classical approaches to theodicy. Whereas theodicy seeks to rationalize the problem of pain, trauma theologies, says Rambo, warn

Figure 14.2. A cry of angry lament.[76]

against platitudes and prescriptive answers that smoothe suffering away.[77] Writing in a different context, Pinn's exploration of music as a means of engaging with historic and contemporary African American suffering can also help contemporary theologians to engage with the wounding trauma of austerity-age poverty in a manner that does not hide from the question: 'Why do we the working class have to suffer again?' Pinn suggests that even liberative hermeneutical frameworks have a tendency to shoehorn cries of angry lament into predefined theological tropes. For Pinn, 'Nitty-gritty hermeneutics and its interpretative roughness free enquiry from the restrictions imposed by "theodicy".' Such a perspectative, he argues, 'seeks a clear and unromanticized understanding of a hostile world [and] ... entails "telling it like it is" and taking risks'.[78] If theologies of austerity-age poverty are to be genuinely liberative it is essential that lament, anger and the wounds of collective trauma are not spiritualized, hidden or smoothed away. The years since the Grenfell fire have illustrated the multidimensional language of contemporary lament with which theology needs to engage. The incisive protest music and films of the London Hip-Hop artist Lowkey, the informal people's art gallery underneath the nearby Westway and annual candlelit vigils and memorial services encapsulate the lament, the anger, the solidarity and the unlikely hope of the Grenfell community. A theology of austerity poverty needs to be formed of sources such as these.

Glimpse 3 – unmasking austerity

The austerity economics that made the Grenfell Tower fire possible and which leave countless thousands of people living in substandard housing across the UK challenges theologians to reimagine the apocalypse. I am not referring to the widely understood use of this term to denote the 'end-times' but to the deeper existential function of apocalypse as a process of unmasking and uncovering hidden realities. Such a theological trope may not, at first glance, appear to speak to the age of austerity and discussions about social housing. However, I suggest that paying attention to the apocalyptic tasks of unmasking, uncovering and revealing can attune our minds to the ways in which Osborne's disingenuous 'skiver'/'striver' narrative moralized poverty and persuaded us that it was caused by an individual person's own inadequacy, rather than structural injustice and government policy. An apocalyptic turn in contemporary political theology is needed if we want to see behind the austerity curtain. The image below of a child's painting of the Grenfell tragedy serves such a function. Located on a wall in the people's art gallery beneath the Westway, the picture, which was part of the local 'Art 4 Justice' project, provides us with an example of raw apocalyptic reflection on the trauma of Grenfell.

Figure 14.3. A child's painting unmasks the reality of the Grenfell fire.

The twisted burnt-out shell of Grenfell Tower stood untouched and uncovered for almost a year – a stark reminder of lives lost, a community wounded, the corporations who cut corners to fit cheaper cladding, the unheeded warnings to the local council and the structural injustice that made it culturally acceptable to build unsafe housing for people living in poverty. An apocalyptic turn in political theology will enable us to uncover the cultural violence that justifies austerity as an economic necessity, and begin the weaving of a new liberative narrative within which all people can flourish because nobody is left out or left behind.

Glimpse 4 – dignity and solidarity

A theology of austerity-age poverty will reaffirm the goodness of creation and the inherent dignity of every human being. Anything less would dishonour the memory of the Grenfell 72. Such an assertion may appear obvious but in the face of the unequal impact of a decade of austerity policies largely directed at poor and minority communities, the conscious neglect of social housing, the silent structural violence of systemic intersectional poverty and a cultural narrative that demonized people living in poverty, the reaffirmation of the inherent dignity of every human being is a subversive countercultural act. We inhabit a society where some lives clearly matter more than others. The Grenfell tragedy was only possible because of the prevalence of such binary thinking. The combustible cladding, broken fire doors and faulty sprinkler system that was considered acceptable in social housing for people living in poverty in Notting Dale would never have been tolerated a mile away in Notting Hill Gate. Yet as we have discovered in our Life on the Breadline research, such a disjunction between the included and the excluded is not confined to North Kensington. The Grenfell fire, therefore, does not just shine a light on austerity-age poverty, housing injustice and structural inequality. It exemplifies a mindset that normalizes and justifies injustice.

Muers' exploration of the 'moral categorization of people in poverty' can help us to find a way out of the maze.[79] Muers examines the binary thinking that provides ethical justification for the asymmetric categorization of the 'deserving' and the 'undeserving' poor and the ways in which this process empowers those who are already powerful and disempowers those without power. Muers' analysis can help us to resist the dominant practice of attributing dignity, worth and agency on the basis of a fixed binary, which makes demonizing people in poverty, the imposition of austerity and the housing injustice that led to the Grenfell disaster morally acceptable. In this context, theologians' witness to the central claim of the creation narrative – that all people are made in the image of the one God – becomes a subversive act. A line drawing of Mary the mother of Jesus from the people's art gallery beneath the Westway encapsulates the appetite for such a subversive theology.

The Westway image of Mary praying for justice just a few hundred yards from the shell of Grenfell Tower subverts asymmetric binary thinking and the economic oppression it enables. The praying Madonna is an image of unity that reasserts the inherent dignity and worth of all people. The street art challenges us to join the figure of Mary in solidarity with the Grenfell community and with all who are still denied housing justice. Is theology up to the task?

Figure 14.4. The Virgin in prayer beneath the Westway.

Conclusion

The Grenfell Tower fire challenges contemporary theologians, church leaders and Christian congregations up and down the land to take sides in the battle to beat oppressive austerity and death-dealing poverty. Are we ready to walk the walk, as well as talking the talk? Our UK-wide engagement with grassroots activists, local congregations, regional and national Church leaders within Life on the Breadline provides the clearest evidence to date of the immense but underestimated value of Christian action on poverty during the 'age of austerity'. The impact of caring responses to poverty, the support for social enterprise and skills-based vocational education, while often hidden, is huge and, quite literally, life-saving. In the years since the 2008 global financial crash, national Church leaders have become advocates and spoken truth to power in relation to ballooning personal debt, child poverty, holiday hunger, Universal Credit, the exponential growth of foodbanks and the Grenfell Tower tragedy. However, our research also suggests that the Church continues to be hesitant, uncomfortable and often ill-equipped to challenge the structural injustice it commits itself to transform in the Marks of Mission. Tamez wrote a world away and a generation ago, but her words strike home in breadline Britain – 'God identifies himself with the poor to such an extent that their rights become the rights of God himself.'[80] In the aftermath of the debilitating collective trauma of the Grenfell Tower disaster and a decade of austerity policies that have punished people already living in poverty, the time has come for theology to be bold and to nail its colours to the mast. Whose side are we on? Surely, for the sake of the 72, there can only be one answer.

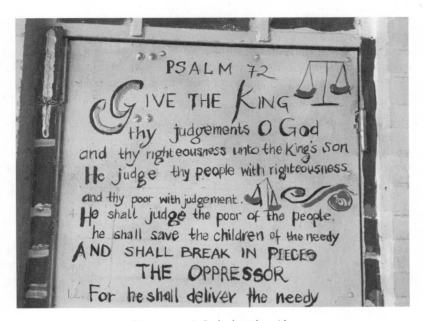

Figure 14.5. A God who takes sides

Bibliography

Alston, Phillip, 'Statement on Visit to the United Kingdom, Philip Alston, United Nations Special Rapporteur on Extreme Poverty and Human Rights', 2018, https://www.ohchr.org/sites/default/files/Documents/Issues/Poverty/EOM_GB_16Nov2018.pdf.

Baker, Christopher and Hannah Skinner, *Faith in Action: The Connection Between Spiritual and Religious Capital*, Manchester: William Temple Foundation, 2014.

Bhatia, Ravi P., 'Violence and Non-Violence Today: How Gandhian Principles can Help in Reducing Violence', *Mahatma Gandhi's Writings, Philosophy, Audio, Video and Photographs*, 2012, https://www.mkgandhi.org/articles/nonviolence2.html.

Bomford, Andrew, 'Grenfell Fire: Worrying Number of PTSD cases among Survivors and Locals', *BBC News*, 14 December 2017, https://www.bbc.co.uk/news/uk-42338725.

Butler, Paul, 'Universal Credit: What is it and What Exactly is Wrong with it?', *The Guardian*, 25 January 2018, https://www.theguardian.com/society/2018/jan/25/universal-credit-benefits-scheme-iain-duncan-smith.

Cameron, David, 'David Cameron: The Age of Austerity', *SayIt*, 2009, https://conservative-speeches.sayit.mysociety.org/speech/601367, accessed 23.4.2022.

Caruth, Cathy, *Unclaimed Experience: Trauma, Narrative and History*, Baltimore, MD: Johns Hopkins University Press, 1996.

Castells, Manuel, *The Rise of the Network Society. The Information Age: Economy, Society and Culture, Vol. 1*, Oxford: Blackwell, 1996.

Chakelian, Anoosh, 'Everything Wrong with Priti Patel's Denial that the Government is Responsible for Poverty', *The New Statesman*, 21 November 2019.

Channel 4 News, 'Musician Akala: People Died in London Fire "Because they were Poor"', *YouTube*, 15 June 2017, https://www.youtube.com/watch?v=n9NWK7VOLig, accessed 23.4.2022.

Cooper, Vickie and David Whyte (eds), *The Violence of Poverty*, London: Pluto Press, 2017.

Cooper, Vickie and David Whyte, 'Grenfell, Austerity, and Institutional Violence', *Sociological Research Online* 27, 1 (2022), pp. 207–16.

Crenshaw, Kimberlé, 'Mapping the Margins: Intersectionality, Identity Politics, and Violence against Women of Color', *Stanford Law Review* 43, 6 (1991), pp. 1241–99.

——, 'Kimberlé Williams Crenshaw: What is Intersectional Feminism?', *Youtube*, 2007, https://www.youtube.com/watch?v=oTFy4zRsItY.

Davies, Nick, *Dark Heart: The Shocking Truth About Hidden Britain*, London: Vintage, 1998.

Everett, Alan, 'Grenfell: After the Fire, Anger; After the Anger, What?', *Church Times*, 8 June 2018, https://www.churchtimes.co.uk/articles/2018/8-june/features/features/grenfell-after-the-fire-anger-after-the-anger-what, accessed 21.07.2021.

Farmsworth, Kevin and Zoe Irving, 'Austerity: Neoliberal Dreams come True?', *Critical Social Policy* 38, 3 (2018), pp. 461–81, https://doi.org/10.1177%2Fo261018318762451.

Farrell, Kirby, *Post-traumatic Culture: Injury and Interpretation in the Nineties*, Baltimore, MD: Johns Hopkins University Press, 1998.

Fox, Killian, 'Grenfell One Year On: The Reverend who Opened his Church to Survivors', *The Observer*, 10 June 2018.

Galtung, Johann, 'Violence, Peace and Peace Research', *Journal of Peace Research* 6, 3 (1969), pp. 167–91.

Garland, Caroline (ed.), *Understanding Trauma: A Psychoanalytical Approach*, Abingdon: Routledge, 2019.

Grover, Chris, 'Violent Proletarianization: Social Murder, the Reserve Army of Labour and Social Security "Austerity" in Britain', *Critical Social Policy* 39, 3 (2019).

Gutiérrez, Gustavo, *A Theology of Liberation*, London: SCM Press, 1974.

——, *A Theology of Liberation*, rev. edn, Maryknoll, NY: Orbis Books, 1988.

Hall, Sarah Marie, 'A Very Personal Crisis: Family Fragilities and Everyday Conjunctures within Lived Experiences of Austerity', *Transactions of the Institute of British Geographers* 44, 3 (2019), pp. 479–92.

Hills, John, *Good Times, Bad Times: The Welfare Myth of Them and Us*, Bristol: Policy Press, 2015.

Hirschberger, Gilad, 'Collective Trauma and the Social Construction of Meaning', *Frontiers in Psychology* 9, 1441 (2018).

Joint Public Issues Team, *The Lies We Tell Ourselves: Ending Comfortable Myths about Poverty*, London: Joint Public Issues Team, 2013.

Joseph Rowntree Foundation, *UK Poverty 2020–2021*, London: Joseph Rowntree Foundation, January 2021.

Kim, Grace Ji-Sun and Susan M. Shaw, *Intersectional Theology: An Introductory Guide*, Minneapolis, MN: Fortress Press, 2018.

Levitas, Ruth, *The Inclusive Society: Social Exclusion and New Labour*, Basingstoke: Palgrave Macmillan, 2005.

Lowkey, featuring Mai Khalil, 'Lowkey ft. Mai Khalil – Ghosts of Grenfell (Official Music video)', *YouTube*, 8 August 2017, https://www.youtube.com/watch?v=ztUamrChczQ, accessed 23.4.2022.

May, Vivian, *Pursuing Intersectionality: Unsettling Dominant Imaginaries*, New York: Routledge, 2015.

McCloskey, Stephen, 'Stereotyping the Poor: Why Development Educators Need to Challenge the Myths of Austerity', *Policy and Practice: A Development Education Review*, 17 (2013).

McNeil, Clare, Henry Parks, Kayleigh Garthwaite and Ruth Patrick, *No Longer 'Managing': The Rise of Working Poverty and Fixing Britain's Broken Social Settlement*, London: Institute for Public Policy Research, 2021.

Muers, Rachel, 'Always with You: Questioning the Theological Construction of the Un/Deserving Poor', *International Journal of Public Theology* 15, 1 (2021).

Okri, Ben, 'Grenfell Tower 2017 – A Poem by Ben Okri', *Ben Okri*, 2017, https://benokri.co.uk/news/grenfell-tower-2017-poem-ben-okri/, accessed 23.4.2022.

Plender, Amy, *After Grenfell: The Faith Groups' Response*, London: Theos, 2018.

Powers, Theodore and Theodorus Rakopoulos, 'The Anthropology of Austerity: An Introduction', *Focaal: Journal of Global and Historical Anthropology* 83 (2019), pp. 1–12.

Rambo, Shelly, 'How Christian Theology and Practice are being Shaped by Trauma Studies', *Christian Century*, 1 November 2019, https://www.christiancentury.org/article/critical-essay/how-christian-theology-and-practice-are-being-shaped-trauma-studies.

Pinn, Anthony, *Why Lord? Suffering and Evil in Black Theology*, London: Continuum, 1999.

Putnam, Robert, *Bowling Alone: The Collapse and Revival of American Community*, New York: Simon & Shuster, 2000.

Radstone, Susannah, 'Trauma Theory: Contexts, Politics, Ethics', *Paragraph* 30, 1 (March 2007), pp. 9–29.

Sassen, Saskia, *Cities in a World Economy*, Thousand Oaks, CA: Pine Forge Press, 1994.

Sewell, Kenneth W. and Amy M. Williams, 'Broken Narratives: Trauma, Meta-constructive Gaps and the Audience of Psychotherapy', *Journal of Constructivist Psychology* 15, 3 (2002), pp. 205–18.

Shannahan, Chris, 'The Violence of Poverty: Theology and Activism in an Age of Austerity', *Political Theology* 20, 3 (2018), pp. 243–61.

Shelter, *Building for our Future: A Vision for Social Housing*, London: Shelter, 2019.

Shildrick, Tracy, 'Lessons from Grenfell: Poverty Propaganda, Stigma and Class Power', *The Sociological Review Monographs* 66, 4 (2018).

Siddique, Haroon, 'The Bedroom Tax Explained', *The Guardian*, 26 January 2016.

Strelitz, Jason, Chris Lawrence, Clare Lyons-Amos and Tammy Macey, *A Journey of Recovery: Supporting Health and Wellbeing for the Communities Impacted by the Grenfell Tower Fire Disaster*, London: Public Health Department, 2018.

Strong, Samuel, 'Food Banks, Actually Existing Austerity and the Localisation of Responsibility', *Geoforum* 110 (2020), pp. 211–19, https://doi.org/10.1016/j.geoforum.2018.09.025.

Tamez, Elsa, *The Bible of the Oppressed*, Maryknoll, NY: Orbis Books, 1982.

Waters, Beth, 'Life on the Breadline Project Resources', *Life on the Breadline*, 2018, https://breadlineresearch.coventry.ac.uk/resources/.

Welby, Justin, *Reimagining Britain: Foundations for Hope*, London: Bloomsbury Continuum, 2018.

Williams, Rachel, 'Budget 2010: Child Benefit Frozen', *The Guardian*, 22 June 2010.

Wintour, Patrick, 'Welfare Reforms: We will Make Work Pay, says George Osborne', *The Guardian*, 2 April 2013.

Notes

1 See George Osborne, 'George Osbourne's Speech to the Conservative Party Conference', *The New Statesman*, 2012, https://www.newstatesman.com/blogs/politics/2012/10/george-osbornes-speech-conservative-conference-full-text, accessed 29.04.2021, in contrast to Ben Okri, 'Grenfell Tower – June 2017', https://benokri.co.uk/news/grenfell-tower-2017-poem-ben-okri/, accessed 27.04.2021.

2 The Life on the Breadline: Christianity, Poverty and Politics in the 21st Century City research project is funded by the Economic and Social Research Council. Details about the project and the resources and outputs developed can be found at https://breadlineresearch.coventry.ac.uk/, accessed 29.04.2021.

3 David Cameron, 'The Age of Austerity', *SayIt*, 2009, https://conservative-speeches.sayit.mysociety.org/speech/601367, accessed 30.04.2021.

4 Phillip Hammond, 'Evidence to the Treasury Committee, House of Commons, 5 November 2018', *House of Commons* (5 November 2018), http://data.parliament.uk/writtenevidence/committeeevidence.svc/evidencedocument/treasury-committee/budget-2018/oral/92275.html, accessed 1.05.2021.

5 Kevin Farmsworth and Zoe Irving, 'Austerity: Neoliberal Dreams Come True?', *Critical Social Policy* 38.3 (2018), pp. 461–81, https://doi.org/10.1177%2F0261018318762451.

6 Rachel Williams, 'Budget 2010: Child Benefit Frozen', *The Guardian*, 22 June 2010, https://www.theguardian.com/uk/2010/jun/22/budget-child-benefit-frozen, accessed 7.06.2021; 'Welfare Reform Act 2012', see https://www.legislation.gov.uk/ukpga/2012/5/contents with reference to the 2012 Welfare Reform Act and P. Butler and Haroon Siddique, 'The Bedroom Tax Explained', *The Guardian*, 26 January 2016, https://www.theguardian.com/society/2016/jan/27/the-bedroom-tax-explained, accessed 7.06.2021.

7 On the impact of cuts in legal aid, see Citizen Advice Bureau, '"Nowhere to turn" – Citizens Advice Speaks out on Impact of Legal Aid Cuts', *Citizens Advice Bureau*, https://www.citizensadvice.org.uk/about-us/about-us1/media/press-releases/nowhere-to-turn-citizens-advice-speaks-out-on-impact-of-legal-aid-cuts/; P. Butler, 'Universal Credit: What is it and What's Wrong with it', *The Guardian*, 25 January 2018, https://www.theguardian.com/society/2018/jan/25/universal-credit-benefits-scheme-iain-duncan-smith, accessed 7.06.2021.

8 Andrew Mackley, 'Effect of Welfare Reform and Work Act 2016', *House of Commons Library* (19 March 2018), https://commonslibrary.parliament.uk/research-briefings/cdp-2018-0072/, accessed 8.06.2021.

9 Department for Education, *Number of Children's Centres 2003–2019*, London: Department for Education (2019), https://assets.publishing.service.gov.uk/government/uploads/system/uploads/attachment_data/file/844752/Number_of_Children_s_Centres_2003_to_2019_Nov2019.pdf, accessed 8.06.2021.

10 Office for National Statistics figures note that in December 2020, 978,000 people were on zero-hours contracts: https://www.ons.gov.uk/employmentand labourmarket/peopleinwork/employmentandemployeetypes/datasets/emp17people inemploymentonzerohourscontracts, accessed 7.06.2021.

11 Trussell Trust, 'Universal Credit and Food Banks', https://www.trusselltrust.org/what-we-do/research-advocacy/universal-credit-and-foodbank-use/, accessed 7.06.2021.

12 John Hills, *Good Times, Bad Times: The Welfare Myth of Them and Us* (Bristol: Policy Press, 2015); S. Strong, 'Food Banks, Actually Existing Austerity and the Localisation of Responsibility', *Geoforum* 110 (2020), pp. 211–19, https://doi.org/10.1016/j.geoforum.2018.09.025.

13 Phillip Alston, 'Statement on Visit to the United Kingdom, Philip Alston, United Nations Special Rapporteur on Extreme Poverty and Human Rights', 2018, https://www.ohchr.org/sites/default/files/Documents/Issues/Poverty/EOM_GB_16Nov2018.pdf, accessed 26.05.2022.

14 Sarah Marie Hall, 'A Very Personal Crisis: Family Fragilities and Everyday Conjunctures within Lived Experiences of Austerity', *Transactions of the Institute of British Geographers* 44, 3 (2019), pp. 479–92.

15 Justin Welby, *Reimagining Britain. Foundations for Hope* (London: Bloomsbury Continuum, 2018).

16 Joseph Rowntree Foundation, *UK Poverty 2020–2021*, London: Joseph Rowntree Foundation (January 2021), https://www.jrf.org.uk/report/uk-poverty-2020-21, accessed 11.07.2021.

17 Clare McNeil, Henry Parks, Kayleigh Garthwaite and Ruth Patrick, *No Longer 'Managing': The Rise of Working Poverty and Fixing Britain's Broken Social Settlement*, London: Institute for Public Policy Research, 2021.

18 Kimberlé Crenshaw, 'Mapping the Margins: Intersectionality, Identity Politics, and Violence against Women of Color', *Stanford Law Review* 43, 6 (1991), pp. 1241–99.

19 Kimberlé Crenshaw, 'Kimberle Williams Crenshaw: What is Intersectional Feminism?', *YouTube*, 19 February 2016, https://www.youtube.com/watch?v=0TFy4zRsItY, accessed 13.07.2021.

20 Vivian M. May, *Pursuing Intersectionality: Unsettling Dominant Imaginaries* (New York: Routledge, 2015), p. 3.

21 Gustavo Gutiérrez, *A Theology of Liberation*, rev. edn (Maryknoll; NY: Orbis Books, 1988), p. xxi.

22 Anoosh Chakelian, 'Everything Wrong with Priti Patel's Denial that the Government is Responsible for Poverty', *The New Statesman*, 21 November 2019, https://www.newstatesman.com/politics/uk/2019/11/everything-wrong-priti-patel-s-denial-government-responsible-poverty, accessed 13.07.2021.

23 Chris Shannahan, 'The Violence of Poverty: Theology and Activism in an Age of Austerity', *Political Theology* 20, 3 (2018), pp. 243–61.

24 Ruth Levitas, *The Inclusive Society: Social Exclusion and New Labour* (Basingstoke: Palgrave Macmillan, 2005), p. 7.

25 Patrick Wintour, 'Welfare Reforms: We will Make Work Pay, says George Osborne', *The Guardian*, 2 April 2013, https://www.theguardian.com/politics/2013/apr/02/george-osborne-work-welfare-tax, accessed 13.07.2021.

26 Stephen McCloskey, 'Stereotyping the Poor: Why Development Educators Need to Challenge the Myths of Austerity', *Policy and Practice: A Development Education Review* 17 (Autumn 2013), https://www.developmenteducationreview.com/issue/issue-17/stereotyping-poor-why-development-educators-need-challenge-myths-austerity, accessed 13.07.2021.

27 Joint Public Issues Team, *The Lies We Tell Ourselves: Ending Comfortable Myths about Poverty* (London: Joint Public Issues Team, 2013).

28 Manuel Castells, *The Rise of the Network Society. The Information Age: Economy, Society and Culture, Vol. 1* (Oxford: Blackwell, 1996), pp. 164ff. and Saskia Sassen, *Cities in a World Economy* (Thousand Oaks, CA: Pine Forge Press, 1994), p. 4.

29 Castells, *The Rise of the Network Society*, p. 175

30 Castells, *The Rise of the Network Society*, p. 175.

31 Shannahan, 'The Violence of Poverty'.

32 Johann Galtung, 'Violence, Peace and Peace Research', *Journal of Peace Research* 6, 3 (1969), pp. 167–91.

33 The origins of this quotation are not clear but it is widely cited. See for example Ravi Bhatia, 'Violence and Non-Violence Today: How Gandhian Principles Can Help In Reducing Violence', *Mahatma Gandhi's Writings, Philosophy, Audio, Video and Photographs*, 2012, https://www.mkgandhi.org/articles/nonviolence2.html, accessed 14.07.2021.

34 Nick Davies, *Dark Heart: The Shocking Truth About Hidden Britain* (London: Vintage, 1998), p. 187.

35 Gustavo Gutiérrez, *A Theology of Liberation* (London: SCM Press, 1974), p. 289.

36 Elsa Tamez, *The Bible of the Oppressed* (Maryknoll, NY: Orbis Books, 1982), p. 12.

37 Theodore Powers and Theodorus Rakopoulos, 'The Anthropology of Austerity: An Introduction', *Focaal: Journal of Global and Historical Anthropology* 83 (2019), pp. 1–12.

38 Vickie Cooper and David Whyte (eds), *The Violence of Poverty* (London: Pluto Press, 2017), p. 1.

39 Chris Grover, 'Violent Proletarianisation: Social Murder, the Reserve Army of Labour and Social Security "Austerity" in Britain', *Critical Social Policy* 39, 3 (2019), p. 344.

40 Ben Okri, 'Grenfell Tower 2017 – A Poem by Ben Okri', *Ben Okri*, 16 Febru-

ary 2018, https://benokri.co.uk/news/grenfell-tower-2017-poem-ben-okri, accessed 27.04.2021.

41 According to the UK's government's 2019 Indices of Multiple Deprivation, the Notting Dale local government ward is ranked 3,215th most deprived of 32,844 local neighbourhoods in England and 2,065th in relation to housing deprivation, 2,102nd in relation to income and 2,473rd in relation to employment. See Ministry of Housing, Communities and Local Government, 'English Indices of Deprivation 2019, File 2 Domains of Deprivation', 2019, https://www.gov.uk/government/statistics/english-indices-of-deprivation-2019, accessed, 16.07.2021.

42 Hatch Regeneris, 'Westway Trust Socio-economic and Community Research' (May 2019), https://www.westway.org/wp-content/uploads/2019/12/Westway-Trust-Socio-Economic-and-Community-Research-Final-Report.pdf, accessed 16.07.2021 and London Councils, Kensington and Chelsea Demographics, https://directory.londoncouncils.gov.uk/demographics/rbkc/, accessed 16.07.2021.

43 Grenfell United, 'Akala Demands Change for Grenfell', *YouTube*, 17 June 2019, https://www.youtube.com/watch?v=aGodDel9uGA, accessed 16.07.2021.

44 Channel 4 News, 'Musician Akala: People died in London Fire "Because they were Poor"', *YouTube*, 15 June 2017, https://www.youtube.com/watch?v=n9NWK7VOLig, accessed 16.07.2021.

45 Vickie Cooper and David Whyte, 'Grenfell, Austerity, and Institutional Violence', *Sociological Research Online* (October 2018), doi:10.1177/1360780418800066, pp. 4ff.

46 Tracy Shildrick, 'Lessons from Grenfell: Poverty Propaganda, Stigma and Class Power', *The Sociological Review Monographs* 66, 4 (2018), pp. 784ff.

47 VoiceOver, 'Lowkey, ft. Mai Khalil – Ghosts of Grenfell (Official Music Video), 8 August 2017, *YouTube*, https://www.youtube.com/watch?v=ztUamrChczQ, accessed 16.07.2021.

48 Andrew Bomford, 'Grenfell Fire: Worrying Number of PTSD Cases among Survivors and Locals', *BBC News*, 14 December 2017, https://www.bbc.co.uk/news/uk-42338725, accessed 19.07.2021.

49 Jason Strelitz, Chris Lawrence, Clare Lyons-Amos and Tammy Macey, *A Journey of Recovery: Supporting Health and Wellbeing for the Communities Impacted by the Grenfell Tower Fire Disaster* (London: Public Health Department, 2018), pp. 45–6.

50 ITV News, 'Grenfell Uncovered: Hundreds of Children Treated for Trauma after the Grenfell Fire', *ITV News*, 24 January 2020, https://www.itv.com/news/london/2020-01-24/grenfell-uncovered-hundreds-of-children-treated-for-trauma-after-the-grenfell-fire, accessed 19.07.2021.

51 Susannah Radstone, 'Trauma Theory: Contexts, Politics, Ethics', *Paragraph, Trauma, Therapy and Representation* 30, 1 (March 2007), pp. 9–29; Kirby Farrell, *Post-traumatic Culture: Injury and Interpretation in the Nineties* (Baltimore, MD: Johns Hopkins University Press, 1998); and Cathy Caruth, *Unclaimed Experience: Trauma, Narrative and History* (Baltimore, MD: Johns Hopkins University Press, 1996).

52 Caroline Garland (ed.), *Understanding Trauma: A Psychoanalytical Approach* (Abingdon: Routledge, 2019).

53 Gilad Hirschberger, 'Collective Trauma and the Social Construction of Meaning', *Frontiers in Psychology* 9, 1441 (2018), doi: 10.3389/fpsyg.2018.01441, p. 1.

54 Kenneth W. Sewell and Amy M. Williams, 'Broken Narratives: Trauma,

Metaconstructive Gaps and the Audience of Psychotherapy', *Journal of Constructivist Psychology* 15, 3 (2002), pp. 205–18, doi: 10.1080/10720530290100442.

55 Strelitz et al., *A Journey of Recovery*, p. 37.

56 Strelitz et al., *A Journey of Recovery*, p. 26.

57 Strelitz et al., *A Journey of Recovery*, p. 94.

58 Amy Plender, *After Grenfell: The Faith Groups' Response* (London: Theos, 2018), p. 9.

59 Robert Putnam, *Bowling Alone: The Collapse and Revival of American Community* (New York: Simon & Shuster, 2000) and Christopher Baker and Hannah Skinner, *Faith in Action: The Connection Between Spiritual and Religious Capital* (Manchester: William Temple Foundation, 2014).

60 Baker and Skinner, *Faith in Action*, p. 4.

61 Plender, *After Grenfell*, p. 9; emphasis original.

62 Plender, *After Grenfell*, p. 29.

63 Plender, *After Grenfell*, p. 25.

64 Plender, *After Grenfell*, p. 34.

65 Plender, *After Grenfell*, p. 32.

66 Killian Fox, 'Grenfell One Year On: the Reverend who Opened his Church to Survivors', *The Observer*, 10 June 2018, https://www.theguardian.com/uk-news/2018/jun/10/reverend-opened-church-grenfell-survivors-mike-long, accessed 21.07.2021.

67 Fox, 'Grenfell One Year On'.

68 Agency Staff, 'Grenfell Tower Fire: Pictures Show Crowds Gathering for Vigil in Tribute to Victims', *MyLondon*, 14 June 2017, https://www.mylondon.news/news/west-london-news/grenfell-tower-fire-pictures-show-13187834, accessed 21.07.2021.

69 Revd Mike Long, 'Grenfell Anniversary Sermon', *Notting Hill Methodist Church*, http://nottinghillmc.org.uk/grenfell/anniversary-gallery/, with reference to 2018; Christian Today staff writer, 'Churches Open for Quiet Reflection on Grenfell Anniversary', *Christian Today*, 14 June 2019, https://www.christiantoday.com/article/churches-open-for-quiet-reflection-on-grenfell-anniversary/132618.htm with reference to 2019 and Grenfell United, 'Rev Mike Long, Notting Hill Methodist Church', *YouTube*, 19 July 2020, https://www.youtube.com/watch?v=Qviyl4QtriU in relation to 2020. All accessed 21.07.2021.

70 Alan Everett, 'Grenfell: After the Fire, Anger; After the Anger, What?', *Church Times*, 8 June 2018, https://www.churchtimes.co.uk/articles/2018/8-june/features/features/grenfell-after-the-fire-anger-after-the-anger-what, accessed 21.07.2021.

71 For more about Grenfell United, see Grenfell United website, https://www.grenfellunited.org.uk/, accessed 21.07.2021.

72 See 'Marks of Mission', *Anglican Communion*, https://www.anglicancommunion.org/mission/marks-of-mission.aspx, accessed 21.07.2021.

73 Shelter, *Building for our Future: A Vision for Social Housing* (London: Shelter, 2019), p. 5.

74 Grace Ji-Sun Kim and Susan M. Shaw, *Intersectional Theology: An Introductory Guide* (Minneapolis, MN: Fortress Press, 2018), pp. 79ff.

75 *The Jigsaw of Poverty* is available from Beth Waters, 'Life on the Breadline project resources', *Life on the Breadline*, 2018, https://breadlineresearch.coventry.ac.uk/resources/, accessed 22.07.2021.

76 All of the photographs in this chapter were taken by Chris Shannahan in March 2020.

77 Shelly Rambo, 'How Christian Theology and Practice are being Shaped by Trauma Studies', *Christian Century*, 1 November 2019, https://www.christian century.org/article/critical-essay/how-christian-theology-and-practice-are-being-shaped-trauma-studies, accessed 22.07.2021.

78 Anthony Pinn, *Why Lord? Suffering and Evil in Black Theology* (London: Continuum, 1999), p. 116.

79 Rachel Muers, 'Always with You: Questioning the Theological Construction of the Un/Deserving Poor', *International Journal of Public Theology* 15, 1 (2021), https://doi.org/10.1163/15697320-12341641, p. 42.

80 Tamez, *The Bible of the Oppressed*, p. 73.

15

Colonization, Trauma and Prayers: Towards a Collective Healing

CLÁUDIO CARVALHAES

Introduction – A prayer project

I had the chance to travel to four continents with a project designed to listen to poor people and turn their stories into prayers, songs, poems and rituals. The project was called Re-Imagining Worship as Acts of Defiance and Alternatives on the Context of Empire and was funded by the Council for World Mission under the leadership of Sudipta Singh. This project travelled to Manila, Philippines; Johannesburg, South Africa; Kingston, Jamaica; and Scicli, Italy. More than 100 people participated: pastors, lay people, seminarians, scholars and artists. On each continent, a group of foreigners and local people from that same continent joined hands to listen to local people. In each place, we visited local communities struggling in many ways who were willing to receive us and tell us their stories. As much as they wanted, and in the way they wanted. At the end, some people from these communities joined the larger group to shape those stories into liturgical material that could be used by any Christian church in the world.[1]

This project had several components, among them: (1) to invert the forms of prayer creation in the Christian tradition that is often orientated by universalized books of worship. The idea was to create prayers from a specific place, from a patch of land, with its own specific traits, historical aspects, assemblages of power, dynamics of religious creation and political conditions. From those places, we were wondering how hearts, minds and bodies would create and orientate a certain language, create symbols and relation with God; (2) to move away from extemporaneous prayers that centre the individual as a discrete being and their own needs as the fundamental source that shapes prayers; (3) in that way it wanted to offer a third space, a religious alternative where prayer would be a voice from concrete conditions and situations that would create collective alternatives to the lived world at hand, responding to specific pain and needs. Just like, then, the slavery work songs,[2] or freedom songs or spiritual songs of African and

African American people in United States, where the narrative of the song/ prayer was both the condition of bodies living in pain and oppression and also the dreaming and hopes to escape from these conditions.

If prayer is the grammar of faith, then the hope was to create a new language so faith, its beliefs and actions can also bring possible changes through these networks of prayer solidarity. The globalization of the world with its economic neoliberalist creed is dramatically crushing the diversity of local people's ways of living. Everywhere the story is the same: a few local people getting rich while everybody else is becoming poor; the natural world being devoured by extractivism, which poisons fields, pollutes rivers, devastates oceans and deforests every last forest that took thousands of years to be conceived; immigrants and refugees running for dear life and hoping to find new homes; working conditions becoming more and more debilitating with extra hours of work without good salaries and rights. Our global situation is simply calamitous. These complex backgrounds were the larger contexts from which these prayers were created. However, since they were created in very specific locations, they carried the very breath of the people living under many forms of violation and destitution. In this project there is the belief that local prayer can connect diverse communities throughout the world. Also, it is local prayer that can and must become universal and not the other way around.

Colonization and liturgical theologies

It is within this context that trauma can be visited. Only by knowing the traumas of a local place can we find the healing leaves of local trees. The conditions of living in these places are filled with various kinds of violence that intends to traumatize people to break their power of creation, resistance and sustenance. Colonization is a historical machine of trauma creation and perpetuation that is fully alive in our times. The hope of the *Liturgies from Below*[3] book was to find ways in which liturgy can break the centre of coloniality within Christianity. Surely trauma can be read in and through biblical texts,[4] and it seems that the whole Christian edifice has been rebuilt under the notion of trauma.[5] This chapter wants to show the dialectical ways colonization and Christianity work through destruction and trauma. Perhaps, the best way to understand the processes of colonization are through Jesus' words in the Gospel of John 10.10: 'The thief comes only to steal and kill and destroy (NRSV).' In a nutshell, that is the process of colonization.

The thief continues to steal, kill and destroy. What remains are people left without land, spaces filled with devastation and traumatized people: land, animals, waters, forests and human people. The South of the world is still a big colony, colonized by several thieves: Europe, the United States, Canada and China. With the help of local corrupt thieves, elected politicians of the South, the thieves of the North continue the process of plundering, destruction and the ongoing realization of trauma. Christianity has been perhaps one of the major allies to the thieves, being a thief itself. The work of trauma by colonization, and the Christian liturgical work of reinstating trauma, are fundamental to continued erasure of local forms of thinking, praying, living and resisting. The ongoing colonization is making people more and more fragile, turning them into easy buyers of meagre resources if they sell their lands. Wars are always displacing people everywhere.

To figure out the dialectics of the colonization is not an easy task. I carry in my body many forms of the colonial dialectic project. Christianity stole my belonging to my own people, severed the memories of my historical relations with the land and left me with ghosts of belonging I cannot publicly claim. What I know about my belonging lives in the deepest parts of my cells that nobody can steal away from me. Yet it is a belonging of the heart and not of a group of people I can fight with as equal. Divide and conquer say the empires! At the same time, through the church, Christianity gave me a place in the world: not land, but 'other' people, institutions, job, salary, forms of survival. My local and extended family are foreign to me and yet they are fully myself and all I have. I belong to them and they to me.

The notion of colony carries the notion of *cultus*, which is both the stealing of the land and the expropriation of the rituals of the dead, which entail the memory of the land and those who lived there. The institutionalizing of Christian services (or any other colonizing religion) also meant appropriate forms of funeral services, which was a powerful way of detaching people from land, god and people. Rites of funerals have been one of the most powerful weapons of colonial destruction. The *cultus* of the local dead people were replaced by the *cultus* of the bodies of another people, namely Christian martyrs, and from then on the resemblance of those who died had nothing to do with those who were uprooted from their lands. The process of funeral rites kept on detaching people from the earth as it now seemed unnecessary to have the presence of bodies in many funerals. A picture will do. So much so that the recollection of the body into funeral services in Christian funerals has been all we can do to restore a real Christian *cultus* to the dead.[6] However, even this liberal theological sense of the rite of the dead understands the body as a discrete presence in relation to people but not to the land. Within Christianity, there is not the slightest sense that a body has to be deeply related to the land, to the community of the land, its enchanted beings and its entire complex of relations.

Having stolen, killed and destroyed any semblance of memory with the land, the Christian *cultus* in the Eucharist still fills us up with memories of another people, the Jewish people, as God's salvific history. That story continues with the life of Jesus but is cut short from the local forms of resilience and resistance where the Eucharist is celebrated. Even the dead Jesus is to be understood within the liturgical grid of the Christian *cultus* as to protect it from the politization of the gospel. Theologies of the cross and death of Jesus compete for a different narrative. The field is complex. For example, the current attempt to turn theologies of sacrifice into forms of thanksgiving end up helping perpetuate the avoidance of naming people killed by colonization. In Pedro Casaldáliga's eucharistic prayer, the local martyrs are named again and again,[7] like naming the immigrants who are killed crossing borders. In some ways and not all the ways, local martyrs can be too bloody for a middle class that cannot stand violence. A nice meal of thanksgiving is much better than the naming of people killed.

On the other hand, there are attempts to reorganize the works of the Eucharist by reinstating the place and power of the cross. Dirk Lange brings the cross into the origin of the Christian traumatic story, and in that, he reframes our own collective trauma.[8] Rebecca Ann Parker and Rita Nakashima Brock try to say that that atonement theology wasn't there in the beginning and that savaged our theological thinking.[9] Women everywhere, and especially our precious editors Karen O'Donnell and Katie Cross, have given us so much to bring feminist theological perspectives into the violence perpetrated against women.[10] Jon Sobrino reads the cross of Jesus as the cross of all of the losers of the world.[11] Delores Williams says Christianity does not need the cross for it has been used as a weapon against women and especially Black women.[12] James Cone gives us a powerful account of the cross, associating it with the lynching tree where Black people were murdered.[13] What kind of eucharistic prayer would come out of these accounts?

What is often missed, it seems, is a relation between theology and the land, something vividly present in Pedro Casaldáliga's ministry, where martyrs are tied together with the loss of land. Most theologies, however, are circumscribed in language that does not attend the dynamics of the ownership of the land and the naturalized sense of private property. It remains in the givenness of beliefs, where the suffering of the people is often detached from its relation to the earth. Nonetheless, from a colonial perspective, the earth has to be the very account of where the trauma is understood. We are earth but there is no earth in our theologies. In terms of the eucharistic prayers, we are concerned with language and ritual process, all of it floating above the earth, as if the land we inhabit does not matter or we have no real relation. Why have theologies never taken hold of the eucharistic celebrations that recollect the memory of the land where we are staying: first people's lives, animals, trees, birds, rivers, mountains? We prefer to construct theology and celebrate sacraments through a discrete relation to God, which is focused on the celebrant's actions.[14] In all of that, the restitution of a collective memory is never one that relates memory with the land but rather a memory that pertains to a discrete set of beliefs and faith. The sacrament is for humans, self-enclosed in its *arché*, filled with bracketed memories, voided of genocides, stealing, death and destruction and destitute of any memory that might offer ways of restitution, transformation and reimagining other worlds from the land where we literally stand. In that way, Christianity and its sacraments are weapons of colonization that keep intact the structures of stealing, killing and destruction.

Still in that way, the past becomes a commodity of the powerful who control the *cultus*, the memory, the ideas and the people they choose to sustain. Controlling the memory of the *cultus*, the colonizer keeps controlling the present and its dynamics of power, as well as the future and any possibility to envision new forms of living. And healing. In controlling the religious narrative (and thus the political, cultural and economic narratives), even the origin of life is not grounded on the origin myths of local people, but rather in a universal story of a God of a people who created everything *ex nihilo*. This story would not be damaging if held in relation to other stories of local people. Besides, this notion of nothing at the beginning of times severs cyclical forms of time and demands a notion of end, a telos where everything will find a pre-organized form of end. As a result, a cosmological sense of life where the pluriverses are intentionally living together in billion forms of relations, are extremely reduced to a single story of a single God of a single people in a single ritual with a single narrative with a single ritual. With all of the rituals now exploded in thousand forms of the same. With Covid-19, these processes got worse, with people being buried without any form of funeral, any memory, any narrative, any relation, any form of sorrow. When one would think necrophilia necropolitics had already staged its worst act throughout these 500 or so years of colonization, Covid-19 opened up ways for necrophilia and necropolitics to expand its actions that were unheard of before.

In the midst of Brazil live the Xingu, a populous indigenous nation. With Covid-19 and the absence of the government to support their ways of living and dying, this nation has seen an immense impact in their lives. The people are struggling with the need to bury people who die of Covid-19. Some are saying the *Kuarup*, the funeral rite of the people of the Xingu. By burying in their land, they follow the precepts and the ways of honouring the person who died, the people who bury the person and the land that lives and dies with them. But Covid-19 has suspended the *Kuarup* and that has destabilized a whole cosmological structure in their lives. Without the *Kuarup*, one never leaves the mourning period and cannot do several things that sustain their lives. Covid-19 can be seen as a form of colonization, uprooting the indigenous people from their lands, and facilitating the approaching of extractivist corporations that are devastating the land and the rivers.

Again and again, the uprooting of people from the land continues to be the necessary colonizing process of dismantling thinking/living/being from the earth. It is no wonder that the vast majority of theologies and even decolonial forms of thinking have no sense of earth in their writings. What is left in a slow violent process of destruction? How will the lingering of years of trauma unfold in the lives of the people and the faith they follow now?

Walking through absences[15]

The indigenous thinker Ailton Krenak said that '[O]ur time is specialist in producing absences.'[16] This is the work of trauma from the perspective of coloniality: to have land, Spirit and people taken away from us; to have those we love and care and live with, and who constitute who we are, taken away. The land/people from which we were born, belonged and/or once related to are absent from us. We have become paid workers of a land that used to be ours. We walk amid ghosts and precious enchanted people who were here for too short a time and were taken away by violence. We are haunted by the presences of their absences.

This was the feeling I had walking with mothers who lost their boys, 15 to 21 years old, to the war on drugs – all killed by identity mistake. They were killed just because the police could kill whomever they thought were involved in the drug wars. But the kids were not and the police knew they made mistakes. And yet they would never say they did. We visited the cemetery for the seventh-day mass of one of these boys. When we got there, I realized that the cemetery was a living community, with people sleeping on tombstones and graveyards. There was a full community living there: children, adults, elderly people, dogs – people who were expelled from places of belonging. As we were driving in our small car around the cemetery, somebody with a rifle stopped us and pointed it at us, asking what we were doing there. The local leader said we were heading to a mass at a nearby graveyard. He invited us to come.

While mass was being said, it rained so hard we got all wet. Water got above our feet. Later on, the local leaders told me to take a hot bath because there was an outbreak of leptospirosis. We had a beautiful mass. The priest was furious at the death of that precious boy. His preaching was powerful. After the mass, the mother provided us all with pasta and dessert. It felt like a eucharistic offering. We all ate together under shared umbrellas and improvised plastic covers. I went to the mother saying, 'I pray for peace.' And she immediately replied: 'I don't want peace, I want justice.' In the morning of the next day, we went to a home funeral where another mother had the casket of her son in her living room. We all sat down around him with her, and she offered to tell his history. We spent some time with her and her family. There were several young chickens on top of the coffin, and we were told it was to bring the same fate to the person who committed that crime. The mother said: 'He was with me until yesterday … He was working and then I heard my son was murdered by the police.' We listened. The council of churches created a group of women who had lost their children and she was invited. Later in the day she and six other women were at the council of churches' building for a time of a common meal and worship, honouring their kids and mourning together. It was three to four hours' worship. On the floor of our circle, there were pictures of the boys and objects that told stories of their lives. Each mother told the histories of their precious sons and the ways they disappeared from their lives. Their testimonies were heart-wrenching, their weeping just like the cry of the whales: poignant, devastating, announcing worlds that have collapsed, lands devastated by unexpected hurricanes of police violence. These women do not have land, they are country-less, they do not have their children, they do not have justice. Mothers dealing with these traumas without closure, without reason, without much agency. 'Our time is specialist in producing absences.'

In another place, a group of us were dropped in a neighbourhood where we were supposed to be picked up. Nobody came and we stayed waiting in the middle of a road. A local resident passed by us and said, 'You better leave, you are going to be mugged.' We started walking and found a Christian church behind a locked gate. We approached and asked: 'Can we come in?' The people inside said, 'No, we don't know you.' We said, 'We are pastors, teachers, members of churches too, can we come in?' And they said, 'No, we are sorry, we don't know you.' Having no other place to go we glued ourselves to that church gate until somebody could come and pick us up. We had a good conversation with the members inside that church. One question was: 'What is the church for you?' And one of the people inside said: 'Church is the safest place to be and the most dangerous place to be.' We were all baffled by this apparent contradictory saying and asked if she could explain that:

> The church is the most dangerous place because we can be mugged here. Nobody can bring anything to church or they will have it stolen. We have to lock our doors otherwise we can't finish our worship. But the church is the safest place to be because here I have people that I can trust, here I can cry and be heard. Here I have a place I don't need to worry about my life when I kneel to pray. We are always losing so much, I can't lose my church, I can't lose my faith.

Later in the day we were able to visit another church not too far from that place. The church was open and the pastor waiting for us. That church was an institution for the neighbourhood. The whole building of the church was covered in wires and high fences. Just outside the church walls there were rugged places with marks of violence and abandonment. The pastor told us how ministry there meant mostly to be able to stay open and to insist that there can be another way of living. That church was a beloved place for the neighbourhood, a kind of assurance that not everything has been taken away, dismantled, killed, destroyed.

The absence of a safe place to live, a community without the vivid sense of danger, of being at risk, of not knowing what tomorrow will bring. Those churches were both witnesses to absences and places where some absences were turned into presences. Uprooted people were trying to find their nexus in the cultural ways of the people through songs, Bible verses, preaching, rituals. Amid so many absences, these churches were roots of belongings and memories lost, taken away, denied.

Forward to another place. We visited a street market where the smells were intense. People moving around and offering simple things. Everything was for sale: used dolls, socks, sandals, wigs, cloths, fish, meat, livestock, cutlery, tables, boxes, necklaces, books, candles, everything you can imagine. A church nearby was open offering healing for all the wounds of the world. When we entered a different neighbourhood, we witnessed a place where not long ago, police shot 200 times against local people, saying they were searching for a drug dealer. More than 200 people were killed. With the bullet marks still on the walls, to this day none of those murders has been solved or justice achieved in any way. A local mother told us: my son was killed by a bullet right here and my uncle there. And there was silence. Not far off was a community living behind a dumpster. Completely abandoned, the men were all marked by police attack about 20 years ago, when they were raped and thrown out of empty buildings. That community was mostly silent. Very little was said. There was so much absence in that community. 'Our time is specialist in producing absences.'

Let us move to another place. We were hearing the testimony of a boy who was a refugee who was able to live in this country. His story was a treacherous one. He had a good life and private school until his father was killed and war took his country. He remained with his mother, hiding, but he could not stay. At 17 he left his country with the little money he had and crossed many country borders to get to a point where he could get into a boat and leave in search for a possible life. After crossing more borders, he had spent all his money and had to do work for people at the next borders he found. Whatever people wanted him to do he had to do. All kinds of things. When he finally arrived at a seaport he was locked into a container without light or food, with many other people, and there he stayed for a time he did not know how to count. One day he was offered work for his boat ticket. He accepted. After months working for nothing, he was finally able to be placed into a rubber boat and was sent off. However, these boats do not carry enough fuel, and when its occupants tried communicating with the coastguard, they were told, 'You are not within our borders, we can't help you.' This was when help was still possible. Today people die on high seas and nobody cares or even knows about it. He said he stayed on the sea for several days, the rubber burning everybody's skin with the scorching sun. The boat had a leak and people had to take turns bailing the water out of the boat. After a few weeks, they were able to be rescued. A Protestant mission received him and is helping him to find study and work. He is still not sure if he will be able to continue and stay in this new country but he is there now. His testimony was so soft, his voice so low we could barely hear him. It was as if he had a lump in his throat.

These are just a few of the stories that this project allowed me to witness. This project showed how all of the issues of colonization are intertwined: wars, injustice, corruption, violence, nation-states' necropolitics, neoliberalism and economic dominion over politics and rewriting of countries' constitutions to allow corporations to rule countries, extreme poverty, extractivism, the war against women, religious exploitation, plundering of resources, uprooting people from their lands, destruction of social threads of life, lack of access to basic services, education systems falling apart and so on. With Covid-19 all these issues have increased exponentially, with the continued concentration of money in the hands of few people. There are traumas everywhere, small and big, fast and slow, deep and wide, spoken and unheard of, devastating and with long-term results. All of them piling up on the backs and the erased stories of so many local people.

(Traumatic) prayers, songs, stories

I remember the day when our group was being directed by local leaders on how we should proceed, be with others and follow the organizer's leading, as local people would always be with us. At the end of the instructions, one of the guides handed us a folder with information about what to do if police were to stop us. If they asked questions, we should ask our local leaders to respond. And in the unlikely case that we were put in jail, the council had lawyers to work on our behalf. People had the choice not to do anything, but everybody went forward. Before I travelled, I had read about religious people being put in jail for social activism, and one of our groups were going to join a workers' strike where the police were breathing down their necks. When I heard about jail, it was too much for me. Claustrophobic as I am, I started feeling anxious and an intermittent sound came to my ears. Soon this sound was non-stop. It was hard to go with the groups but later in the day I joined them. Coming back home after our intense time there, I went to the doctor and learned I had tinnitus, an endless sound in my ears. My doctor asked me what had happened to me in recent days and I told him my experience. He promptly gave an unexpected diagnosis: 'Your experience might have traumatized you; your body needed to respond to it in some ways and that is how it chose to deal with it.' It made sense to me.

After I left the doctor's, I remembered that when I was still in Brazil I had written a thesis on the work of the Algerian-French writer Albert Camus. I think the trajectory of Camus' thought was mine too: absurd, revolt, love. In my research, I realized that the word *absurd* had two parts in Latin: *ab-surdus*, a sound so loud, so off, so unbearable that it makes one *surdus*, deaf. All that I had heard in these trips was too much for me to make sense of. Too many absurdities, too many ruins all along, too many worlds devastated, too many threads of life ripped apart, so many lives wasted, brutalized, so many places destitute of any breath of life. The *ab-surdus* was that which cannot be mended, put together, organized properly.

It reminds me of the art of Doris Salcedo.[17] I remember the first time I saw Doris Salcedo's work and immediately felt a lump in my throat.[18] There was something there that was way too recognizable, too vivid, too real and yet was lost in the qualifications and distinctions of both the art itself and oceanic feelings. Her work on violence and loss is a work of mourning. A lump in the throat of humanity.

Salcedo's work is a mirror of our inward guts after having been shuffled and revolved by the filthy dirty hands of violence, convulsing our inner organs, shutting down the light that shines on us and leaving us speechless or with very little to say. The connections of household furniture with cement shows the results of trauma that is fully there, heavy, impossible to speak about, to make sense of, to undo. Absences are shown in unrecognizable assemblages of presence. Salcedo's work represents the telling of the stories of people and their own traumas. As the art exhibition text says: 'Immobilized in cement, the dresser and chairs in this untitled work suggest the replacement of presence with absence.'[19]

Her work does not restore to people what they had lost but helps them, and us, to mourn and do the work of mourning. Salcedo makes us engage our wounds and the violence that, suddenly or slowly, become the very threads of our existence. Salcedo also helps us create a sense of solidarity with those who have been hurt. It could have been us. They are us.

As we set about the liturgical work of listening to the stories of people who have been traumatized by so much violence, we wanted to turn these stories into prayers and songs and rituals. We also wanted to show solidarity, to say it could have been us, to learn that they are us. So we used the liturgical structure of the Church to try to mend, offering paths that would lead us to healing places, creating spaces where people would feel safe to engage, and build structures where the gentle sounds of grace could somewhat, somehow, appease some of the roaring sounds of death.[20] The people who composed this book were incredible. They had seen it all and yet they were able to find language to pray. The work of a collective praying group from places where vivid forms of death were all around us begged us all for feelings, languages and different forms of prayers.[21]

What we had all learned was a paradoxical truth: in creating a different language to deal with the pain of the world, we realized the power of the Christian faith anew, how much we can carry within this faith that can respond to the traumas of our time in strength, sustenance, resilience and power. On the other hand, we realized that the liturgical prayers we can offer are too frail, too weak, not enough to deal with the massive pain of the world. When I talk about this, people often ask me if I believe in prayer and I say this: I have learned that in situations of death, destitution, disasters and plundering, where there is no one to help, prayer means nothing. It cannot do anything; it is a drop of saliva in a desert of sand. Prayer, my friend, does nothing. On the other hand, I have learned that prayer in these exact situations has such a power that can indeed change everything! It is like Hagar praying in the desert, being alone with a child and nobody else there. When we pray, angels come to us in some way or another but mostly by bringing us together. Then, everything can change! Absolutely! Oh yes, I do believe in prayer!

The liturgical spaces in churches are privileged places to deal with that which cannot be tamed, controlled or mastered. Liturgy mumbles words and actions, songs and forms of life that infuse our bodies and might reshape our minds, hearts and souls, filling our bodies with life. In worlds where dreams are forever deferred, there is still the urgency and the struggle that we can and must create something. As Shelly Rambo says:

> The experience of trauma dismantles notions of theology as a fixer, a provider of solutions. A move to 'fix' things may interfere rather than assist in the process of healing. Theologians who have learned from trauma theory emphasize the importance of accompaniment, truth telling, and wound tending. Acts of witness and testimony acknowledge the reality of traumatic experiences that can never be fully brought to the surface of consciousness. This posture is not focused confidently on conveying theological or moral certainty. Instead, its confidence is in the healing power of giving a witness to suffering.[22]

Yes, this project's hope was to offer witness to people's suffering, to create a liturgical solidarity. This project intended to offer presence to a world that specializes in producing absences. Here is one eucharistic prayer made during these visits from the perspective of women who lost their sons:

Mary Remembers Her Son

(A Communion Prayer dedicated to Nanette Castillo and her son, Aldrin)[23]

Five bullets and a hundred lashes on my son's body;
I greet you still, the Lord be with you.
    And also with you.
Five bullets and a hundred more they stopped his heart and cancelled
    my own,
I bid you still, lift up your hearts:
    We lift them up to God.
Five times and hundred more I ask God if it is still right to give God
    thanks and praise,

_____.

They asked him, 'Are you who they say you are?' He told the truth. Upon him the anger of Rome and their obsession with their peace and their order rained from their whips. And fired from their guns. They have killed my son.

For they have forgotten the God who has breathed upon us the Breath of Life; they have forgotten the One who gave life, when they took his life away.

On the night that my son was to be given up for betrayal, desertion, and death, he took bread from the plate of pancit and gave it to me and said, 'Take this and eat.' And then he gave me something to drink and said, 'Take this and drink.' I will be going away, Mother. Somewhere you cannot follow. And when I return you will not have to work too hard and wash other people's clothes; and our family and friends will live better lives.

Breathe upon these gifts now again, O God, your breath of life. So we may remember again how to live.

For as often as you eat of this bread and drink of this cup, you will remember me and all the sons who have been taken away from their mothers and wives.

For as often as you eat of this bread and drink of this cup, you will remember all the daughters who have been snatched from their homes.

For as often as you eat of this bread and drink of this cup, my son calls to you, 'please remember me,' until I come again.

Remember my Son.

(Song: 'Hele ng Pagtangis'. Alternatively, 'No Woman No Cry', Bob Marley)

[The Rise Up women will distribute servings of bread and pancit and buko juice to those present.]

Rituals cannot be work of individuals or individuals without the land and each other, for the healing lies on the ground we all stand on, as it is in the flowing of rivers, in the leaves of the trees, in the plants of biodiverse biomes. The indigenous thinker Tyson Yunkaporta tells us what lasts for a long time and it is not a response to the eternal newness of neoliberal desires: 'Like all things that last, it must be a group effort aligned with the patterns of creation discerned from living within a specific landscape.'[24] Yunkaporta tells us of the trinity of our common work: Land, Spirit and groups of people or Spirit, law (of the land) and community.[25] It is important to sing the songs and prayers we have in our communities, but more important than the order of the worship or the proper liturgical structure is the community attending to each other's wounds along with the land they live in and with so many other more than human people. As Yunkaporta reminds us again: 'The song itself (within the ritual of a community) is not as important as the communal knowledge process that produces it.'[26]

This is to say that the healing of collective trauma and absences must be a collective work of presence, one where a whole community lives under a gathered subjectivity and offers healing processes and environments where each individual can go deeper into their own wounds. The colonial wound cannot be healed individually for that is the project of liberalism and neo-liberalism. The colonial wound can only be healed if in relation. Land, Spirit and groups of people, human and more than humans.

This chapter did not work much with the land but it does have soil, water, trees and skies in it. This eucharistic prayer we read could be for people whose lives have been stolen, killed, destroyed – or at least start the work or help in the process of healing. It is for people whose spoken and unspoken traumas are addressed directly, symbolically, in tangible and intangible ways. The liturgist, the artist, the theologian is like the historian, in the sense that Rubem Alves gives to it:

> Thus, the historian is someone who recovers lost memories and distributes them, as if it were a sacrament, to those who lost their memory. In truth, what better communal sacrament is there than the memories of a common past, marked by the existence of pain, sacrifice and hope? Collect to distribute. He is not just a memoir archaeologist. He is a sower of visions and hopes.[27]

Sacramental work has the power to connect, to mend, to pull things back, to help heal inflammations of the soul, make sacred again what was desacralized, and sew ropes of healing around open wounds. Memories of hope and life, memories of years past and relations with the earth, memories of birdsong and seeds sprouting. We might not be archaeologists in the exact sense of the word, but we are excavators of past lives that carry our future. We build on memories of the past and memories of the future as we build collective and individual subjectivities back again. We are no longer discrete souls in a world in which we are individually responsible for ourselves alone. We can't live in such world. We need societies that collectively create forms of living together with collective limits, responsibilities, forms of restoration and creation. If somebody made a mistake, we can all fix it together. If one is violated, we can all work for collective restoration. This is the work of a collective religion.

Conclusion

I want to conclude with the words of Ailton Krenak, whom I mentioned at the beginning. After saying 'Our time is specialist in producing absences' he names some of the absences: absences of:

> the meaning of living in society, the very meaning of the experience of life. This generates a huge intolerance towards those who are still able to experience the pleasure of being alive, dancing and singing. And it's full of small constellations of people around the world who dance, sing and make rain fall.[28]

Perhaps Krenak's words remind us that without the joy to live, without dancing, singing and rituals to make the rain fall, we will not be able to survive all of the absences that a very small number of people are perpetrating to all the worlds on earth. In order to do that, we will need to change our *cultus* in so many ways, rethink our memories, pay fundamental attention to the earth and its natural law and processes, to all the people, trees, animals and rocks uprooted from the land. As the Brazilian singer Gilberto Gil poetically said:

> If the fruits produced by the land
> are not yet
> As sweet and mushy as the pears
> of your illusion
> Tie your plow to a star
> And times will give
> Crops and harvests of dreams
> pounds and pounds of love
> on other smiling planets
> and other kinds of pain
>
> If the cultivated fields around this world
> are too hard
> And the lands ravaged by war
> do not produce peace
> Tie your plow to a star
> and then you will be
> The crazy farmer of the stars
> A peasant loose in the skies
> For the farther we go from the earth
> The farther we go from God.[29]

Bibliography

Allen, William Francis, Charles Pickard Ware and Lucy McKim Garrison (eds), *Slave Songs of the United States: The Classic 1867 Anthology*, Mineola, NY: Dover Publications, 1995.

Alves, Rubem, 'Las ideas teológicas y sus caminos por los surcos institucionales del protestantismo brasileño' in *Materiales para una historia de la teología en América Latina*, ed. Pablo Richard, San José: CEHILA-DEI, 1981.

Carr, David M., *Holy Resilience: The Bible's Traumatic Origins*, New Haven, CT: Yale University Press, 2018.

Carvalhaes, Cláudio, *Liturgies from Below: Prayers from People at the Ends of the World*, Nashville, TN: Abingdon Press, 2020.

Carvalhaes, Cláudio, 'Praying Truly, With a Lump in the Throat' in *Praying With Every Heart: Orienting Our Lives to the Wholeness of the World*, Eugene, OR: Cascade Books, 2021.

Cone, James H., *A Black Theology of Liberation*, New York: Orbis Books, 1990.

Cone, James H., *The Cross and the Lynching Tree*, New York: Orbis Books, 2021.

Cross, Katie, *The Sunday Assembly and Theologies of Suffering*, London: Routledge, 2020.

Cruz-Villalobos, Luis, *Posttraumatic Exegesis: Exegetical Commentary of Coping in Second Corinthians*, independently published, 2021.

Gil, Gilberto, 'Amarra o teu arado a uma estrela', from CD *O Eterno Deus Mu Dança*, WEAH Latina, 1989.

Jones, Serene, *Trauma + Grace: Theology in a Ruptured World*, 2nd edn, Louisville, KY: Westminster John Knox Press, 2019.

Krenak, Ailton, *O amanhã não está à venda*, São Paulo: Companhia das Letras, 2020.

Lange, Dirk G., *Trauma Recalled: Liturgy, Disruption, and Theology*, Minneapolis, MN: Fortress Press, 2009.

Long, Thomas G., *Accompany Them with Singing: The Christian Funeral*, Louisville, KY: Westminster John Knox Press, 2009.

O'Donnell, Karen and Katie Cross (eds), *Feminist Trauma Theologies: Body, Scripture and Church in Critical Perspective*, London: SCM Press, 2020.

Parker, Rebecca Ann and Rita Nakashima Brock, *Saving Paradise: How Christianity Traded Love of this World for Crucifixion and Empire*, Norwich: Canterbury Press, 2012.

Rambo, Shelly, 'How Christian Theology and Practice are being Shaped by Trauma Studies. Talking about God in the Face of Wounds that won't go away', *The Christian Century*, 1 November 2019, https://www.christiancentury.org/article/critical-essay/how-christian-theology-and-practice-are-being-shaped-trauma-studies.

Reimagining Worship, https://reimaginingworship.com

Ricci, Giana, 'Doris Salcedo Remembers the Forgotten', *IFA Contemporary*, 8 October 2015, http://ifacontemporary.org/doris-salcedo-remembers-the-forgotten/.

Salcedo, Doris, '*Untitled, 1995*', *MoMA*, https://www.moma.org/collection/works/80767?artist_id=7488&page=1&sov_referrer=artist.

Sobrino, Jon, *Christ the Liberator: A View from the Victims*, New York: Orbis Books, 2001.

Sobrino, Jon, 'La causa de los mártires agradecimiento a Pedro Casaldáliga', *Revista latinoamericana de teología* 25, 73, 2008, pp. 3–19, https://doi.org/10.51378/rlt.v25i73.4979.

Yunkaporta, Tyson, *Sand Talk: How Indigenous Thinking can Save the World*, San Francisco, CA: HarperOne, 2020.

Notes

1 Cláudio Carvalhaes, *Liturgies from Below: Prayers from People at the Ends of the World* (Nashville, TN: Abingdon Press, 2020).

2 William Francis Allen, Charles Pickard Ware and Lucy McKim Garrison (eds), *Slave Songs of the United States: The Classic 1867 Anthology* (Mineola, NY: Dover Publications, 1995).

3 Carvalhaes, *Liturgies from Below*.

4 See David M. Carr, *Holy Resilience: The Bible's Traumatic Origins* (New Haven, CT: Yale University Press, 2018); Luis Cruz-Villalobos, *Posttraumatic Exegesis: Exegetical Commentary of Coping in Second Corinthians* (independently published, 2021).

5 Shelly Rambo, 'How Christian Theology and Practice are being Shaped by Trauma Studies. Talking about God in the Face of Wounds that won't go away', *The Christian Century*, 1 November 2019, https://www.christiancentury.org/article/critical-essay/how-christian-theology-and-practice-are-being-shaped-trauma-studies.

6 Thomas G. Long, *Accompany Them with Singing: The Christian Funeral* (Louisville, KY: Westminster John Knox Press, 2009).

7 Jon Sobrino, 'La causa de los mártires agradecimiento a Pedro Casaldáliga', *Revista latinoamericana de teología* 25, 73 (2008), pp. 3–19, https://doi.org/10.51378/rlt.v25i73.4979.

8 Dirk G. Lange, *Trauma Recalled: Liturgy, Disruption, and Theology* (Minneapolis, MN: Fortress Press, 2009).

9 Rebecca Ann Parker and Rita Nakashima Brock, *Saving Paradise: How Christianity Traded Love of this World for Crucifixion and Empire* (Norwich: Canterbury Press, 2012).

10 Karen O'Donnell and Katie Cross (eds), *Feminist Trauma Theologies: Body, Scripture and Church in Critical Perspective* (London: SCM Press, 2020); Katie Cross, *The Sunday Assembly and Theologies of Suffering* (London: Routledge, 2020).

11 Jon Sobrino, *Christ the Liberator: A View from the Victims* (Maryknoll, NY: Orbis Books, 2001).

12 Delores Williams, 'Afterword' in James H. Cone, *A Black Theology of Liberation* (New York: Orbis Books, 1990).

13 James Cone, *The Cross and the Lynching Tree* (New York: Orbis Books; reprint edn 2011).

14 I heard this several times from high liturgists.

15 I wrote these stories from my selective memory with all its imperious conditions.

16 Ailton Krenak, *O amanhã não está à venda* (São Paulo: Companhia das Letras, 2020), unpaginated, Apple Books.

17 Giana Ricci, 'Doris Salcedo Remembers the Forgotten', *IFA Contemporary*, 8 October 2015, http://ifacontemporary.org/doris-salcedo-remembers-the-forgotten/.

18 See Cláudio Carvalhaes, 'Praying Truly, with a Lump in the Throat' in *Praying With Every Heart: Orienting Our Lives to the Wholeness of the World* (Eugene, OR: Cascade Books, 2021), pp. 21–40.

19 Doris Salcedo, '*Untitled*, 1995', *MoMA*, https://www.moma.org/collection/works/80767?artist_id=7488&page=1&sov_referrer=artist.

20 Serene Jones, *Trauma + Grace: Theology in a Ruptured World*, 2nd edn (Louisville, KY: Westminster John Knox Press, 2019).

21 You can see some of the prayers of the book in this website: https://reimaginingworship.com

22 Rambo, 'How Christian Theology and Practice are being Shaped by Trauma Studies'.

23 Carvalhaes, *Liturgies from Below*, p. 129. Names changed for anonymity.

24 Tyson Yunkaporta, *Sand Talk: How Indigenous Thinking can Save the World* (San Francisco: HarperOne, 2020), p. 61, Kindle edn.

25 Yunkaporta, *Sand Talk*, p. 62.

26 Yunkaporta, *Sand Talk*, p. 62.

27 Rubem Alves, 'Las ideas teológicas y sus caminos por los surcos institucionales del protestantismo brasileño' in Pablo Richard (ed.), *Historia de la teología en América Latina* (San José: CEHILA-DEI, 1981), pp. 363–4.

28 Krenak, *O amanhã não está à venda*.

29 Gilberto Gil, 'Amarra o teu arado a uma estrela' from CD *O Eterno Deus Mu Dança* (WEAH Latina, 1989).

16

'A Stone You Need to Polish': Affect, Inequality and Responding to Testimonies Under Austerity

CL WREN RADFORD

The quiet is difficult to judge in this space. I am aware of wanting to give everyone time to think, to find the words that they feel best represent them, the words that they wish to share here. It's the first time that we have been meeting as this group, and we are tentatively developing a sense of how we will best work together, how to talk and listen to each other respectfully. There are long pauses as we figure out the rhythm of speaking, not wanting to talk over each other or skip too fast past anyone's perspectives. A couple of people have already met, and everyone here has been working with the wider movement, drawing on their various experiences of poverty to work against inequality. Reflecting on this work, Jocelyne talks about how going through the UK asylum system and being told that she must be lying about seeking refuge have influenced her sense that in order for people to be respected, they must be believed when they talk about what they are going through.[1] For her, our group must be based on this premise of believing people. We nod and affirm this, with others chipping in that we need to remember how difficult it is to talk about what you are experiencing, naming this as a brave act. 'No one can share another's pain, take it away', says Eham, reflecting on living with chronic health conditions, 'and we don't always know who to share with, we don't want to be rejected.' He continues, quiet, thoughtful, 'We need to practise and polish empathy.' We are all struck by his statement, and others in the group take up this image, and add to it, so by the end we are working with the phrase, 'Empathy is a stone you need to polish.'

Over the next few weeks of the group sharing together, the phrase plays in my mind. Even as I might feel uneasy about naming empathy, the image is hardly straightforward. It evokes something ordinary, easily overlooked. Something you might pick up – carrying weight, carrying memory – just as easily slipped in a pocket as let go and forgotten. Held by a palm; concealed by a fist. Thrown at a target, it becomes a weapon. Yet alongside statements of the need to be believed, of not wanting to be rejected, the group called for a practice of ongoing, careful attention.

Testimonies of trauma have come to inhabit a particular space in contemporary culture. Activists and academics alike may draw on their own and others' testimonies to make claims about inequality and injustice, raising awareness of particular issues and appealing for changes in policy and practice. Testimonies may take the form of autobiographies, poetry, visual and performance arts, as well as public speeches or short statements over social media. Contemporary forms of testimony are influenced by historical modes of witness, including Holocaust writings, South American *testimonio* literature, and the work of truth commissions across the globe, most notably the South African Truth and Reconciliation Commission. As testimonies of violence and oppression have come to be used by human rights campaigns, attention has been paid to the commodification and circulation of personal testimonies for global publics.[2]

Trauma theologies often seek to hold a space for these testimonies, in various academic, ecclesial and public spaces. Theologians may engage with traumatic testimonies by responding to literary and religious texts, by engaging with cultural analysis to explore contemporary events, or through qualitative methods to record their own and others' experiences. Trauma theologies have been influenced by feminist approaches that seek to be attentive to how particular, embodied experiences are critical of existing theological and ecclesial norms that harm and exclude, and also are generative or disclosive sites for constructing theologies.[3] Both indirect and direct requests may be made that we 'listen carefully' to and learn from traumatic testimonies in our theological work.[4]

However, in being shared with different audiences, a range of public sentiments are impacted, raising significant debate about the role of traumatic testimonies in public and political life, and also in theological meaning-making practices. Both those testifying to trauma and those listening may encounter guilt, empathy, compassion, aversion or disgust as the 'circulation of narratives of trauma and suffering in public domains produces troubled and troubling emotions'.[5] This can lead to those testifying being judged, stigmatized and exposed to further abuse or stereotyped as 'passive victims'.[6] While compassion and empathy are often celebrated virtues in Christian theologies, feminist and queer cultural theorists have debated where such affects create a sentimental politics that focuses on individuals rather than systemic injustices.[7] As suggested above, there is an ambivalence to these emotions, raising questions about the affective and relational dynamics of traumatic testimonies in addressing inequalities and working for justice. Theologians can intentionally and unintentionally play into the affective dimensions of testimonies as they seek to respond to and hold space for traumatic experiences in their academic and activist practices. Trauma-engaged theologies thus need to be attentive to how '[m]ultiple affects play out in both the personal and public spheres'.[8] In this way, the practice of engaging traumatic testimonies requires attention to how public and theological discourses shape our reception to those testifying, and the need to challenge where the circulation of affect reproduces rather than challenges inequalities.

In this chapter, I explore questions responding to traumatic testimonies in the public sphere, highlighting a case study of activists testifying to experiences of poverty in UK austerity. For this, I draw on research collaborations with Poverty Truth groups in Glasgow and Greater Manchester. Poverty Truth is a movement that brings together those living at the sharp end of poverty with civic and political decision-makers to share their experiences and create change. After introducing my framing for this discussion of trauma, testimony and poverty, I draw on Rebecca Chopp's work on the 'poetics of testimony' to reflect the judgements that are made by theological and public discourses that deny the validity of testimonies, and how theological practices may be reshaped in response to traumatic testimony. I examine how embodied, affective responses to testimony are produced by and can reinforce unequal power dynamics between those testifying and those responding. I then move to consider Poverty Truth members' reflections on testifying to their experiences of poverty in the UK; here I do not seek to present these testimonies, but to draw on their critical engagement with the testimonial practices. From this, I reflect on challenges for theologies that are committed to justice, and where theological practices may be remade in holding space for traumatic testimonies.

Poverty, trauma and austerity

In broad discussions around trauma studies, questions are raised about reading poverty and trauma together. Clinical definitions of trauma have been influential in the field in categorizing trauma as 'punctual events', leading to some desires to differentiate between 'structural subordination' and 'trauma', especially when trauma is seen as what 'takes you out of your life shockingly and places you into another one, whereas structural subordination is not a surprise to the subjects who experience it, and the pain of subordination is ordinary life'.[9] As this suggests, it is important not to lose focus on the specific nature of trauma by using the term 'trauma' to apply to any circumstances of hardship. However, Laura Brown's feminist approach has been generative for challenging the idea that trauma is always 'unusual' experiences but also encompasses 'insidious trauma', recognizing that the political and social realities in which we are situated make particular populations more vulnerable to specific harms.[10] Similarly, the queer theorist Ann Cvetkovich's work has resisted a clinical framing, instead engaging with trauma as a way of naming 'experiences of socially situated political violence' in order to create 'overt connections between politics and emotion'.[11] She aims to develop a focus on the 'everyday and insidious', in part because:

> the distinction between everyday and catastrophic trauma is also tied to the distinction between public and private, since what often counts as national or public trauma is that which is more visible and catastrophic, that which is newsworthy and sensational, as opposed to the small dramas that interest me because they draw attention to how structural forms of violence are so frequently lived, how their invisibility or normalization is another part of their oppressiveness.[12]

Furthermore, Cvetkovich notes that trauma puts traditional forms of documentation under pressure, resulting in marginalized groups developing their own practices of expression such as testimony and ritual that can 'call into being collective witnesses and publics'.[13]

My interest here is not in categorizing poverty as a form of trauma, and I am particularly wary of creating any suggestion of pathologized notions of poverty. Rather, my concern is to read Poverty Truth's practices in relation to trauma studies in order to explore the cultural and political dimensions of UK poverty and attempts to address this socio-economic inequality. In the past decade, austerity discourses have blamed people living in poverty for their own problems, with terms such as 'scroungers', 'skivers' and 'frauds' being used by politicians and the media to justify an intensive programme of cuts to welfare and public services that have particularly targeted women of colour, white women, disabled people and people living in poverty.[14] Under austerity, systemic injustices are framed as personal failings, pushing them back from issues of public and political concern into the private sphere. Cvetkovich's comments on everyday trauma are useful for recognizing how the distinctions between private and public concern can themselves reinforce harm, leading to the normalization of structural inequalities. While politicians have announced that austerity is now 'over', the policies and ideologies of austerity are still in place, meaning that austerity continues to impact people's daily lives, and to 'take form in everyday objects, relationships, places, and feelings'.[15] Indeed, the naming of an end may contribute to making it harder to discuss and act on austerity and inequality, highlighting where 'such silence and naming [of an end to austerity] accompanies and contributes to the ongoing violence of austerity'.[16] It is necessary for justice-orientated theologies to keep making visible the material and discursive impacts of austerity, registering the complex and messy affects in which the intimate and the structural aspects of inequality are inseparable. This is to recognize that 'the term trauma provides a different way of voicing the impact of systemic and structural injustice'.[17]

Responding to traumatic testimonies

Reshaping theological and public discourses

In two influential essays on the 'poetics of testimony', the feminist theologian Rebecca Chopp sets out the reshaping of theological and public discourses in response to traumatic testimonies.[18] Chopp considers that testimony includes 'poetry, theology, novels, and other forms of literature that express how oppressed groups have existed outside modern rational discourse'.[19] As with Cvetkovich's comments above, Chopp notes that traumatic testimonies reveal that exclusion and oppressions have occurred through drawing divides between the personal and the public. She notes that when a person 'testifies in and to the public space' about what they have experienced, the 'categories of public and personal do not hold'.[20] Testimonies reveal the power structures surrounding where certain images, narratives and communities have been excluded from shaping how different publics make meaning. Furthermore, she sees that testimony issues a theological and moral summons, rendering a claim on those who 'live Christianity as practices of emancipatory transformation'.[21]

Drawing on trauma theorists who note the impossibility and necessity of writing about the Holocaust, Chopp attends to the fragmentation and failure of language in representing and accounting for traumatic experiences. In her earlier work on liberation theology, Chopp argues that suffering cannot 'be fully expressed in theory or fully represented in symbols'.[22] Traumatic testimonies are thus fragmented and jarring, told through broken speech and silences. Chopp uses the metaphor of the courtroom to describe how modern theologians have taken 'the mantle of judgement, and, robed in various styles, become theorists who decide which witnesses are credible and true'.[23] As a result, the 'jarring witnesses' to suffering are seen as outside the limits of credibility: 'excluded into silence, into powerlessness, as irrational'.[24] Precisely because traumatic testimonies – particularly those arising from already marginalized groups – cannot be contained in the dominant theological language, they are disregarded and not viewed as valuable for creating theological meaning. Similarly, Chopp articulates that such testimonies highlight where dominant narrative identities of national and ecclesial publics have been premised on the exclusion, silencing and forgetting of marginalized groups' experiences and struggles for change.

Chopp articulates that to respond to traumatic testimony is not simply to include these experiences within these existing, exclusionary systems, but to change the frameworks that determine such exclusions. Theological and public discourses must be reshaped in response to these testimonies. The courtroom is refigured in response to traumatic testimony: it is the whole courtroom itself, 'its procedures and power, and its own ability to speak credibly' that is on trial instead.[25] This is a poetic refashioning of theological and public discourses, in which their ways of making meaning through theory, language, images and symbols must be remade in order to serve those who testify. Chopp offers an illustrative move away from the courtroom to suggest that theologies formed by a poetics of testimony are less about judging these testimonies than they are about participation and negotiation, forming 'new discourses as practices of emancipatory transformation'.[26] Being refigured in this mode, theology can then offer 'cultural interventions' to reshape 'the social imaginary', the basic presuppositions, metaphors and rules that frame cultural operations.[27] She gives examples of Black and feminist theologies as intervening in the public sphere in that they have combined art, literature, music 'with an ethical summons to be responsive to those who suffer'.[28] She advocates for a renewed public sphere in which multiple different voices can be heard, enabling empathy and solidarity.

Chopp's refashioning of theology sees a particularly positive role both for testimony and for the possibilities of modes of theological meaning-making being remade. However, Heather Walton argues that traumatic testimony carries 'a far more ambivalent and powerful force than can be discerned in Chopp's optimistic work', indicating that the poetics of testimony is not only 'a means of employing different linguistic gestures to change the idioms of culture' but rather 'opens up a terrifying revelation'.[29] In this way, we need to reflect further on some of the troubling aspects of affective responses of empathy and solidarity, and to be attentive to some of the more ambivalent nature of trauma testimonies. Shelly Rambo questions where the 'shattering of meaning in trauma' impacts theology as a 'meaning-making enterprise'.[30] Theological discourse may be reshaped in attending to trauma, a 'haunted' language that is a 'compelling language not insofar as it contains truths but insofar as it testifies to truths that cannot be contained'.[31] Theology is gathered, with trauma, around 'what is not known', finding 'resonance in this unknowing'.[32] For Rambo, theology is remade in taking up a 'testimonial positioning instead of in its confident proclamations'.[33]

Yet for Chopp, it is not that testimonies themselves undertake this reshaping of theological and public discourses. In her attention to transcendence in trauma testimonies, Chopp does not 'simply locate "God" or "Spirit" within these testimonies' as making 'the experience, the testimony, authoritative (in and of itself), runs the danger of "sacralizing" testimonies. While this is a reversal of the courtroom, more is needed.'[34] Instead, Chopp locates this change as the work of the Spirit, understood as transcendence in the material and social dimensions of life. Chopp articulates transcendence as 'radical alterity' that is 'both the source and the dynamics of transfiguration' in the world.[35] Drawing on examples from feminist and Black theologies, transcendence is named as 'the spirit and power of transfiguration that vetoes the law of slavery, breaks the chains of classism, rewrites social customs that erase and deny women's dignity through various practices of abuse and so-called protection'.[36] Thus the articulation of transcendence and the practising of theology are shifted in this poetics of testimony, as for Chopp, the Spirit is traced not by 'uncovering a depth of God's presence or revealing a substance or essence of God, but through negotiating spaces of solidarity, connection, and new creation'.[37]

Power dynamics in the relationship between testifier and listener

This poetics of testimony provides a generative perspective, not least because it draws attention to the frameworks that deny certain testimonies and testifiers. Engaging with traumatic testimonies, theologians need to examine the power dynamics in constructing the ideals by which such testimonies are judged. Women, and particularly women of colour, 'encounter doubt as a condition of bearing witness', precisely because problematic histories have associated racialized and gendered bodies with doubt so that pre-existing judgements 'taint' both the person witnessing and their testimony.[38] Testimonies offered as part of movements for racial justice, such as Black Lives Matter, have indicated how audiences shaped by Whiteness judge experiences by the standards of respectability politics, which serves to 'dismiss the particular challenges faced by those who do not mimic dominant depictions of deservingness', often encouraging the presentation of only the most 'compelling victims' even as contemporary movements for racial justice seek to dismantle respectability politics.[39] As Anthony Reddie notes, because Black people have come to be seen as 'the other' – transgressive and 'ontologically problematic' – 'sympathy and therefore justice as a response to racialised violence can only become operative when the recipient of such violence is seen to be blameless'.[40] Although often seen as verbal or textual accounts, testimonies are always embodied and it is this broader set of bodily affects and histories of gender, race and class that influence the reception of traumatic experiences. Thus, stating that we should 'listen to' the traumatic testimonies of marginalized groups is not enough; rather, we need to be conscious of how certain testimonies and testifiers encounter doubt and stigma.

One example of how testimonies come under judgement is Cash Carraway's autobiography *Skint Estate* being investigated by *Guardian* journalists for literary fraud after accusations from a 'credible source' who was later found to be lying.[41] Carraway reflects on this experience of having her life story placed in doubt, suggesting that aspects of gender and class influence how her narration of her experiences is questioned by others. She notes that middle-class women can 'hint' at sexual violence, but '[w]orking-class women are only allowed to write – or as the media call it: "Share their story" – if we are willing to lay out every last detail of existence without artistry; delivered with the torpidity of a police statement or the indignity of a boo-hoo scoop.'[42] The investigation itself put Carraway and her daughter in danger, undoing the protections that social services and Women's Aid had put in place by contacting the man she had fled due to domestic violence. In more ways than one, the demand for exacting, verifiable details can reproduce harms for those testifying.

The expectations of those listening and responding place a particular weight on traumatic testimonies. The courtroom metaphor holds a particular sway for publics encountering traumatic testimonies, with legal understandings shaping the notion that testimony is evidence to be judged by those hearing, rather than as a potential call to action, or an artistic way of expressing what one has experienced. Leigh Gilmore articulates that when 'the standard of credibility for bearing witness is measured against an escalating demand for testimonial purity that virtually no one can meet when trauma is involved, those standards ought to be inspected for ideological bias rather than permitted to stand solely as an ethical norm worthy of endorsement'.[43] This is not to suggest that we might be able to be entirely free of bias in either giving or hearing testimonies or that we might do away with notions of truth and truth telling. Rather, it is to critically examine how standards for judging testimony have been constructed, and where these standard legal and theological norms and formats might not be able to bear the weight of certain truths.

In his influential work on the testimonies of Holocaust survivors, Dori Laub identifies where the listener's expectations of testimony influence the response. Noting the importance of testimony having an 'addressable other' without whom the testimony cannot be heard and witnessed, Laub discusses a range of emotional responses, or 'listening defences', in those responding, from a sense of withdrawal and numbness, feelings of outrage and anger at the testifier, to a flood of awe in which the survivor is endowed with a sense of sanctity.[44] He considers how testimonies may be foreclosed through the listener's obsession with detailed facts, either in questioning the witness about these facts in their narrative or positioning themselves as 'knowing it all' in advance; in both situations the testimony is being treated as evidence or information rather than human experience.[45] Laub also identifies that in some circumstances what looks like compassion and caring can be a way of flooding the testifier with the listener's own emotional responses.[46] While this analysis arises from the specific setting of Holocaust testimony and psychoanalytic theory, this identifies how those responding can adversely impact the hearing of traumatic testimonies.

However, just as the sense of a courtroom or legal setting can influence the reception of traumatic testimony, so can notions of therapeutic or clinical settings. When the relationship between the testifier and listener (or reader) is patterned after the model of patient and therapist, which can come about through the influence of psychoanalytic theory in trauma studies, the listener can see themselves in the role of the knowledgeable expert while the testifier is cast as the 'passive victim'. The risk is that such a model for literary or spoken testimony offers no place in which the 'narrator speaks as an expert about his or her experience, making political claims and actively intervening into power relations'.[47] As such, trauma theory needs to account 'for the specific social and historical contexts in which trauma narratives are produced and received' as well as being open to multiple strategies of representation that may be specific to different contexts.[48] Much European and North American trauma theory has emphasized the nature of traumatic testimony as being in jarring and fragmented speech and has pointed to particular literary texts that demonstrate this form; this can require 'authentic' trauma narratives to conform to this aesthetic category.[49] Even as we might agree with Chopp's assessment that broken and fragmented speech has been disregarded by dominant theologies and public discourses, we also need to be aware of how those in positions of power, including theologians, may see themselves as in a position to analyse and identify the aesthetics of these testimonies in ways that judge and dismiss alternative presentations of traumatic testimony from marginalized groups.

Testimonial practices in austerity

Poverty Truth

Poverty Truth groups started as Poverty Truth Commission (PTC) in Glasgow in 2009. This originally used a commission model to bring people with experiences of poverty together with civic and political decision-makers to meet over an 18-month period, spending the first half of the commission building relationships and listening to people sharing their lived experiences, before highlighting specific emerging themes for that commission. In Glasgow, this model ran for four commissions over ten years. They covered kinship care;[50] media representation; welfare cuts and assessments; asylum and refuge; food poverty; and mental health. These commissions held 'closing' events where commissioners presented their findings and recommendations through songs, stories, stand-up comedy, poetry and short films. PTC also host monthly community gatherings and continue long-term projects such as work on the 'cost of school' and 'mutual mentoring' in which Scottish civil servants are partnered with commissioners. Their approach is guided by the ideal that those who are impacted by policies and who experience the daily reality of poverty should be involved in shaping those policies and actions to address poverty, often expressed through the phrase 'Nothing about us, without us, is for us'.[51] In recent years, more Poverty Truth groups have started across the UK, including in Manchester, Salford, Leeds, West Cheshire and Morecambe Bay. In 2019, the group in Glasgow changed their name to Poverty Truth Community (still known as PTC) to reflect moving away from a commission model into new areas of work that are better suited to the time and interests of the movement, ensuring that it is led by people experiencing poverty. Here, I draw on my ongoing involvement as a researcher with this movement, spanning six years and two collaborative research projects with Poverty Truth groups in Glasgow and Greater Manchester. This research has involved a variety of methods, but typically involves reflective workshops in which I facilitate discussions, including the initial articulation and agreement of how we can best listen to and share with one another, as described in the introduction.

It is useful to be clear here that Poverty Truth spend a lot of time working in facilitated small groups to explore their experiences and develop connections with one another; it is this work that then resources larger events with the wider public, or meetings with specific policymakers and politicians. Poverty Truth members often highlighted how much they valued this community space, sometimes contrasting it with negative experiences at sites such as the UK Border Agency and Jobcentres. As noted in the introduction, Jocelyne spoke on various occasions about her experiences of seeking refuge in the UK, where she was disbelieved and told her experiences were not true, resulting in being held in detention and going through a lengthy asylum process; she reflected that this impacted her sense that it is important that Poverty Truth groups be places where people are believed when they share. Another Poverty Truth member, Ben, directly contrasted his sense of being listened to in community meetings with his experiences at the Jobcentre. He gave the example of speaking at an event where, even though it had gone well, he became emotional afterwards and other people came to support him. Ben reflected that if he spoke about his situations of experiencing homelessness and mental health difficulties at the Jobcentre, they were not interested in listening and that if he became emotional at all he would be sanctioned or removed by security.[52] Conversely, people experiencing poverty are frequently asked to 'tell their story' in different situations, often when accessing resources. I witnessed a number of Poverty Truth members speaking about their frustrations with being asked 'Why are you here today?' at foodbanks, along with witty or sarcastic comments that occasioned knowing laughter from others. This was contrasted with food justice models where people can pay a small amount and select their own weekly shop at community pantries without being asked about their situations. This highlights where people can be forced to narrate their lives in particular, *acceptable*, ways in order to access vital resources.

Poverty Truth members are invited to share in group meetings but never forced to do so. On several occasions, I witnessed people gently shake their head or say 'Not today' in community sessions. Similarly, PTC has recognized that for members who are currently having their claims processed in the asylum system, publicly testifying about the system itself may negatively impact their claims, including the possibility of detention and deportation. Thus, while PTC does encourage individuals to share their experiences in public, they also work to provide a sense of testimony as a community, speaking out on issues while enabling specific individuals to remain anonymous. This can also involve using creative arts-based methods that enable a balance between anonymization and ownership, such as the graphic art booklet *Stories of Hope* from people who had been through the asylum process.[53]

Affect and austerity

Within the research workshops, Poverty Truth members frequently reflected on the stigma surrounding poverty and the influence this had on giving testimony about specific issues. They noted that feelings of stigma and shame occurred at particular instances, for example in using foodbanks, welfare assessments and being unable to afford social activities for children; however, they also recognized that experiences of stigma might be different for people depending on family, gender, race and disability. For example, one Poverty Truth member, a man with no children, spoke about feeling such stigma at using a foodbank that he felt he would rather 'walk over broken glass' than have to go back to a foodbank and endure this. While emphasizing that his statement was powerful, the group also reflected that for women with children, particularly single parents, they might feel that they have no other options and find themselves having to live with this stigma in order to feed their families. One Poverty Truth member noted that her experiences were of 'pushing the pram for miles in the rain to go to a foodbank where no one will recognize me'; this also influenced how she felt about publicly testifying about these experiences. In the research groups, women with children regularly reflected on the judgements they encountered about having children and being on benefits or experiencing food poverty. Chloe reflected that, when accessing support or testifying about her experiences, she was often asked, 'Well, why did you have children, then?' as a criticism of being a disabled mother living in poverty, and she noted the specific judgements stemming from being a mother who uses a mobility scooter. Such examples demonstrate the need to reflect on how particular testimonies and testifiers experience greater stigma and hostility related to wider cultural assumptions.

Under austerity, particular testimonies and testifiers incur specific judgements. Tracey Jensen and Imogen Tyler argue that austerity has produced 'anti-welfare commonsense' in which disgust and stigma are attached to austerity figures or characters in order to create a '"technology of consent" for a deeper political programme of welfare reform'.[54] In being presented as 'commonsense', public feelings surrounding these particular figures and the welfare system are covered with the veneer of logical, easily understandable statements that are supposedly interested in fairness. For example, Theresa May, when Prime Minister, stated: 'We believe that people who are in work have to make the same decisions as those people who are out of work, so that people who are on benefits should have to decide whether they can afford more children, just as people in work have to make such a decision.'[55] This was presented as justification for introducing the two-child limit on tax credits, despite research showing that around two-thirds of those claiming child tax credits are in work. Similarly, the then-chancellor George Osborne stated at the Conservative Party Conference in 2012: 'Where is the fairness, we ask, for the shift-worker, leaving home in the dark hours of the early morning, who looks up at the closed blinds of their next-door neighbour sleeping off a life on benefits?'[56] Again, this overlooks the complexity of the situation by presenting a sharp distinction between work and welfare rather than recognizing the far more fluid reality. This has also been echoed in media coverage of welfare. As Louise, an activist working in collaboration with PTC noted:

> We're just examples of the millions of people in poverty out there, who walk past papers like the *Daily Mail* and see words like 'feckless parents' or 'feral children', 'scroungers', 'skivers' and you think 'That's me they are talking about, that hurts, how dare they' ... but they dare, because we're poor, and we don't have the voice of the media behind us ... so they can get away with calling us what they like.

As well as putting forward a negative characterization of welfare, anti-welfare common sense 'misrecognises the lives and experiences of people in poverty, and operates to exclude their voices from discussions about policy changes which directly impact upon their lives'.[57]

The impacts on specific groups who have come to be misrepresented as certain abject figures under austerity are connected to cuts and the withdrawal of protections: the discursive and the material are deeply linked. I briefly highlight three groups here. First, disabled people have come to be labelled as 'fakers', with changes in disability benefits assessments functioning as a way of redrawing and ultimately shrinking the 'disability' category so that disability benefits can be accessed only by this newly defined 'truly disabled' group of people, but without any actual change in people's embodied health.[58] Second, as with May's statement above, parents on benefits are misrecognized through the notion of 'benefits broods', cultural figures of disgust who are portrayed as 'almost pathologically fertile in their desire to secure greater amounts of welfare payments by having more and more children'.[59] Third, UK immigration policy has taken an increasingly strong approach to detention and deportation, accompanied by a 'persecutory regime of welfare disentitlement and social exclusion for those who have managed to gain access', resulting in increased destitution among asylum seekers.[60] In constructing a discourse of the 'bogus asylum seeker as a figure of hate', an uncertainty is introduced: 'How can we tell the difference between a bogus and a genuine asylum seeker?', which is swiftly converted 'into the possibility that any of those incoming bodies may be bogus'.[61] For those who are seeking to testify about their experiences of disability, family, asylum and welfare, this misrecognition means they are already tarnished with disgust and doubt as their testimonies are interpreted through the context of anti-welfare sentiments.

Figure 16.1. *Fear of the Brown Envelope*
Copyright Wren Radford and Anneleen Lindsay
Brown envelopes with torn openings bound together by red thread to form a booklet,
standing upright on a wooden table. White insert can be seen through envelope window, red
stamped lettering reads: 'Oh no, the brown envelope'. The edge of the insert can be seen at
the envelope's torn openings; it has red stitching around the edge, with the word 'fear' in red
ink stamped on to brown paper and stitched to the edge of the insert.

Poverty Truth members spoke about how these assumptions about poverty
influenced how policymakers, politicians and the wider public responded
to them and their testimonies. Louise talked about sharing her experiences
at a particular event and being told by someone in a position of power that
she couldn't be living in poverty as her shoes were polished and she wore
silver rings. She noted that people anticipated 'that we should wear sack-
cloth and ashes and have dirty faces stained with tears and that prove we're
in poverty ... but we don't give up our dignity to anybody, we don't allow
other people to take that away from us'. Betsy, who had been involved in

work with kinship care for Poverty Truth for over a decade, spoke about being at an event where a policymaker tried to raise awareness but, even after listening to various testimonies, spoke about kinship care 'as if it was still 2009, as if no progress had been made' by the kinship network. Betsy felt frustrated that this person only wanted to portray the negatives of the situation, rather than understand that they were activists who had fought for important changes in their own lives, such as the increases in the kinship-carer's allowance. Not only are people judged against harmful images of poverty, but policymakers and politicians may construct figures of the 'deserving poor' in opposition to the 'undeserving poor' in trying to elicit empathy, which all too often conflates 'deserving' with 'helpless'. This characterization not only fails to reflect the activism of those who live this reality and work for change, but also plays into notions of benefits claimants as helpless, as 'passive and inactive, with a defective agency that can only be corrected through highly interventionist and behavioural forms of welfare conditionality'.[62]

Poverty Truth members also gave examples of those in positions of power focusing on specific details or issues in someone's testimony to the detriment of engaging with them as a person with experience and knowledge. Jenny reflected on having seen a testifying commissioner being told in a meeting with a policymaker, whom the person had never previously met, 'I've heard that story before.' Jenny explained: 'You can't just label people for gender, race, sexuality, class ... you can't just say "that's the story from poverty", you have to respect people's individual stories. Hearing a person's story, you can't say "I've heard that story before", you may have heard similar, but not the same, you can't generalize.' In this example, the policymaker was looking for particular facts and details that would be useful to them, valuing 'new' information over talking and learning with those sharing their testimonies. Similarly, it was highlighted that policymakers and politicians might state that while a testimony was important, it could be treated as either a 'homelessness issue' or a 'mental health issue', rather than recognizing the complexity of the person's experiences. Poverty Truth members also discussed sharing their experiences of benefits assessments, being sanctioned, or school-uniform grants not covering the full cost of a uniform and being met with responses of 'There must be a mistake in the system', or with suggestions of not having applied for the 'right' grants, alongside being directed to further information and support services. Poverty Truth members explained that sometimes those in positions of power gave advice, suggesting 'budgeting skills' or 'cookery classes', ideas stemming from the assumption that people are in poverty because they lack skills or mismanage money, framing the issue as personal failings rather than structural inequalities. This reflects the criticisms noted above that those listening can be obsessed with detailed facts or can claim that they are more of an authority on the issue, which ultimately forecloses the possibilities of engaging with testimonies. This power discrepancy was also commented on by Poverty Truth members in noting that it had become popular to have people sharing their lived experiences at events or in community consultations, yet these often listened briefly to people's experiences, but then failed to include the same people in discussing the implications for policy decisions or organizational practices.

However, Poverty Truth members were also keen to note the changes that had arisen from their efforts despite these barriers, and their desire to keep working for justice. These have included changes that have a specific material impact on their lives, for example in the changes to the kinship-care payments, or the increase to the minimum level of school-uniform grants in Scotland. While some may see these as small against the overwhelming backdrop of austerity, they are meaningful and crucial for those who depend on these grants. People in positions of power and privilege, including researchers and theologians, can often treat such small-scale, everyday changes as unimportant when we do not understand the difference that these can make to someone's life, or when we overlook them in favour of only large-scale structural changes.[63] Poverty Truth members also spoke with pride about being part of something that was challenging the cultures around austerity and welfare and creating a movement in which people were valued and where their contributions mattered. In addition, Poverty Truth members recognized the cultural work in showing policymakers and local politicians a different way of working together in building longer-term connections rather than one-off consultations.

In my own work with Poverty Truth groups, we put forward alternative forms of testimony to challenge austerity narratives. As highlighted in Cvetkovich's work, trauma puts traditional forms of documentation under pressure, and marginalized groups often develop their own expressions that can form collective witness. One creative arts-based piece, *Fear of the Brown Envelope* (Figures 16.1 and 16.2), worked with the brown envelopes and benefits assessment forms that are sent by the Department for Work and Pensions (DWP). Using white paint to cover and then write over blank forms, we created a space for people to give testimonies of benefits assessments, countering the austerity narratives that purposefully ignore the complexity of people's lives and bodies. Poverty Truth members used the terms *fear, panic, gut-wrenching, lost, shamed, sick, dread* to explore the very tangible feelings of austerity that are caught up in this material object and the subsequent assessment process. These affects arise on contact with the envelopes, so we stitched these words to the outside of the envelopes to be brushed by fingertips as the viewer picks up the piece. The longer testimonies inside detail the different experiences of benefits assessments within this community, recognizing that there are different interactions of poverty, disability, care, family and work rather than one generalized type of poverty. Participants stated their delight in seeing the envelopes and forms reworked in ways that documented what it was like to engage with the forms physically and emotionally, saying it expressed something of their experiences they hadn't been able to put into words. In showing the piece to policymakers and politicians, Poverty Truth members noted that they felt they were putting forward their creativity and their work for change; interacting with the creative piece often slowed the responses from those in positions of power. The material nature of the piece, the remaking of an everyday object that has come to represent fear and dread for so many people, became a point of connection and a way to document the feelings and experiences produced by the austerity regime.

Figure 16.2. *Fear of the Brown Envelope Insert*
Copyright Wren Radford and Anneleen Lindsay
Hands holding a white insert page over the top of the brown envelope booklet. The insert page shows the boxes of a form that has been lightly painted over with white paint.
Red stamped ink reads 'The process damages my health'. Handwritten text reads 'For the next few days after it arrives all my health problems play up, I just crash'. The edges of the insert are stitched with read thread, and the word 'sick' in red stamped ink on brown paper is dangling from the edge.

Remaking theological practices in response to austerity

In light of the reflections from Poverty Truth members, I want to consider the implications they have for reshaping justice-orientated theologies engaging with poverty and austerity. Trauma testimonies question how justice is understood and negotiated, including how responses of empathy and compassion may fail to address underlying power inequalities. The experiences of Poverty Truth members highlight that power differentials can be reinforced in testimonial practices, with those listening placing themselves in positions to judge the testifier, whether in denying the testimony or in trying to fix an individual's situation. This includes both the immediate response to testimonies, as noted above in comments around applying for the right grants or having cooking and budgeting classes, but also in more widespread practical responses; we might note Poverty Truth members' discussions around how certain foodbank models reinforce stigma. Testimony is responded to not only in the immediate moment, but in how practical responses to particular social issues are constructed and framed. We need to question where faith-based responses to austerity engage specific feelings arising from and responding to stigma, judgement, disgust and notions of anti-welfare common sense or the deserving and undeserving poor; theologies are not immune to but are already enmeshed in and reproduce these affective economies.

All too often theologians and faith practitioners can treat marginalized groups' embodied realities and critical engagement in change as an impediment or an irrelevance to their own theological practices of social justice. Shelly Rambo notes that the 'experience of trauma dismantles notions of theology as a fixer, a provider of solutions. A move to "fix" things may interfere rather than assist in the process of healing', yet theologies often 'remain tied to the theme of recovery.'[64] The disability theologian Sharon Betcher argues that marginalized others are typically met with the desire to remediate flaws, in which responsibility to another may be conflated with the power to judge, 'short circuiting any ethically deliberative interchange'.[65] She notes that 'the power to judge has taken up residency inside Western cultural notions of healing (health care and education have been nearly synonymous with compassion in colonial contact), compassion, social justice, and, even ... human rights.'[66] Betcher is critical of theological notions of redemption and remediation that are entwined with this position of judgement over marginalized people. She articulates that naming this 'conditioned response to deviance "compassion" convinces us that we are doing the right thing',[67] highlighting where such positions of compassion and empathy can be defensive moves that protect the underlying power dynamics in insidious traumas and everyday inequalities. Such modes of compassion are not necessarily or sufficiently oppositional to the disgust that anti-welfare common sense produces around certain figures, as compassion can remain in 'proximity to aversion'.[68] This is particularly true when, as Betcher identifies, marginalized others are often wrongly portrayed in colonial and ableist theologies as not capable of critical thinking, or as lacking the spiritual and rational capacities for subjectivity. Betcher summarizes that this 'politics of compassion appears to mean helping persons into normalcy, into our definition of well-being and our definition of what makes for a good life', and she suggests that undoing this 'will require us to theologize redemption without emplotting the redemptive encounter as the remediation of defect, remediation that hides the power to judge'.[69]

In light of Betcher's diagnosis, we are invited to think carefully about our responses to trauma testimony in the context of austerity. Social justice campaigns from activists and media have sometimes used testimonies to counteract images of the austerity figures of disgust. However, similar to the example of the policymaker at the kinship-care event, these can become the circulation of 'deserving' narratives that 'foreground individual tragedy, victimhood and despair to make this point' or present images of hard workers who contribute to society.[70] While this may mean that people are judged as 'deserving' rather than 'undeserving', changing the judgement does not address the position of judgement itself. Where might we, to engage Chopp's metaphor, put the whole courtroom of judgement on trial? What resources are needed to be able to interrogate our own 'affective attachments to mastery and judgement that we bring to bear on the testimony of another'?[71] In moving away from courtrooms or psychoanalytic metaphors for engaging with testimonies, we need to recognize that testimonial practices make active claims into the political relationship between the testifier and those responding, challenging the responder 'to imagine herself in the ethically and politically complex position of the bystander or potential collaborator', a much more 'compromising and unsettling' position.[72] Testimonial practices need to intervene in the socio-economic structures that rely on and reproduce certain sentiments surrounding different experiences of poverty, particularly by calling those listening to consider their own entanglement in such structures and in the circulation of affective responses.

However, this also highlights the challenges of placing demands on testimonies and testifiers to produce particular justice-orientated and political ends. As noted above, traumatic testimonies are ambivalent and troubling in nature; they cannot be easily managed into certain theological meanings and political outcomes. I highlighted where Poverty Truth members were critical both of generalizations of their testimonies as being 'about' poverty, and also of attempts to categorize testimonies in ways that treat them as themes and issues that can easily be separated out. Testimonies are more than 'data' or 'evidence' to be analysed, but an encounter with the alterity of other persons. In discussing theological engagement with trauma, M. Shawn Copeland notes that theologies have developed 'a way of thinking about the human person where the human person is not reduced to a statistic, a problem, or a social fact. This is the issue of transcendence of the human person that isn't quite captured in psychoanalytic, sociological, or some other language.'[73] However, theologies still have taxonomic impulses that thematize traumatic testimonies, as academic texts and specialisms can be grouped and structured around key issues, often erasing the contradictions and ambiguities in traumatic experiences in search of stable meanings.

This raises tensions surrounding what theological meanings can be produced, what can be known in the midst of insidious, structural trauma. I am drawn to where Rambo articulates the shattering of meaning in trauma and suggests theology is gathered in response to what is not known.[74] However, I am also cautious of where such unknowing needs to be carefully negotiated in relation to marginalized groups; forms of theological unknowing can potentially 'further suppress that which culture holds abject'.[75] As I have argued, austerity discourses have functioned to exclude people experiencing poverty from contributing to public and policy discourses around welfare. Thus, I want to suggest that for trauma theologies to engage with poverty and everyday inequalities, the remaking of theology also requires valuing the critical knowledges of marginalized groups, knowledges that are often bound up in the giving of traumatic testimony. This questions the assumptions around the aesthetic forms of trauma testimony and requires a recognition of the oppositional, resourceful meaning-making that happens for groups who live the daily realities of insidious trauma. Holding these in a generative tension, the remaking of theological practices becomes a collaboration with communities whose experiences have not been seen as significant for public and theological discourses. Engaging with traumatic testimonies in search of justice requires us to move away from one-off events of hearing testifiers, and instead into cycles and movements, challenging where trauma is consumed and circulated by those in positions of power and moving towards affective encounters that bring to light both epistemic and socio-economic inequalities. As described in the introduction, we may need to relearn our ethics of engaging with traumatic testimonies from those who are most impacted, so that those testifying can direct the meanings and not-knowings that we are to find in these events, enabling these settings to remake our justice-orientated practices.

Bibliography

Ahmed, Sara, 'Affective Economies', *Social Text* 79, 22 (2004), pp. 117–39.

Alston, Philip, 'Statement on Visit to the United Kingdom, United Nations Special Rapporteur on Extreme Poverty and Human Rights', London, 16 November 2018, https://www.ohchr.org/sites/default/files/Documents/Issues/Poverty/EOM_GB_16Nov2018.pdf, accessed 26.05.2022.

Berlant, Lauren, 'The Subject of True Feeling: Pain, Privacy, and Politics' in *Cultural Pluralism, Identity Politics, and the Law*, ed. Austin Sarat and Thomas R. Kearns, Ann Arbor, MI: University of Michigan Press, 1999, pp. 49–84.

Berlant, Lauren, 'Introduction Compassion (and Withholding)' in *Compassion: The Culture and Politics of an Emotion*, ed. Lauren Berlant, London: Routledge, 2004.

Betcher, Sharon V., 'Becoming Flesh of My Flesh: Feminist and Disability Theologies on the Edge of Posthumanist Discourse', *Journal of Feminist Studies in Religion* 26, 2 (2010), pp. 107–18.

Boler, Megan, 'The Risks of Empathy: Interrogating Multiculturalism's Gaze', *Cultural Studies* 11, 2 (1997), pp. 253–73.

Bons-Storm, Riet, *The Incredible Woman: Listening to Women's Silences in Pastoral Care and Counseling*, Nashville, TN: Abingdon Press, 1996.

Brown, Laura S., 'Not Outside the Range: One Feminist Perspective on Psychic Trauma', *American Imago* 48, 1 (1999), pp. 119–33.

Carraway, Cash, *Skint Estate*, London: Ebury Press, 2019.

Carraway, Cash, 'Lidl Women (a monologue)' in *DOPE* 11 (2020), https://issuu.com/dogsectionpress/docs/dope11, accessed 5.05.2021.

Chopp, Rebecca, 'Theology and the Poetics of Testimony' in *Converging on Culture: Theologians in Dialogue with Cultural Analysis and Criticism*, ed. Delwin Brown, Shelia Greeve Davaney and Kathryn Tanner, New York: Oxford University Press, 2001.

Chopp, Rebecca, 'Reimagining Public Discourse' in *Black Faith and Public Talk: Critical Essays on James H. Cone's Black Theology and Black Power*, ed. Dwight N. Hopkins, Waco, TX: Baylor University Press, 2007.

Chopp, Rebecca, *The Praxis of Suffering: An Interpretation of Liberation and Political Theologies*, Eugene, OR: Wipf & Stock, 2007.

Craps, Stef, *Postcolonial Witnessing: Trauma Out of Bounds*, Basingstoke: Palgrave Macmillan, 2013.

Cross, Katie, 'I Have the Power in My Body to Make People Sin' in *Feminist Trauma Theologies: Body, Scripture and Church in Critical Perspective*, ed. Katie Cross and Karen O'Donnell, London: SCM Press, 2020.

Crow, Liz, 'Scroungers and Superhumans: Images of Disability from the Summer of 2012: A Visual Inquiry', *Journal of Visual Culture* 13, 2 (2014), pp. 168–81.

Cvetkovich, Ann, *An Archive of Feelings: Trauma, Sexuality, and Lesbian Public Cultures*, Durham, NC: Duke University Press, 2003.

Cvetkovich, Ann, 'Public Feelings', *The South Atlantic Quarterly* 106, 3 (2007), pp. 459–68.

Gilmore, Leigh, *Tainted Witness: Why we Doubt what Women say about their Lives*, New York: Columbia University Press, 2017.

Graham, Elaine, *Transforming Practice: Pastoral Theology in an Age of Uncertainty*, London: Mowbray, 1996.

Gready, Paul, 'The Public Life of Narratives: Ethics, Politics, Methods' in *Doing Narrative Research*, 2nd edn, ed. Molly Andrews, Corinne Squire and Maria Tamboukou, London and Los Angeles: Sage, 2013.

Hitchin, Esther and Ruth Raynor, 'Editorial: Encountering Austerity in Everyday Life: Intensities, Localities, Materialities', *Geoforum* 110 (2020), pp. 186–90.

Jensen, Tracey and Imogen Tyler, 'Benefits Broods: The Cultural and Political Crafting of Anti-Welfare Commonsense', *Critical Social Policy* 35, 4 (2015), pp. 470–91.

Kennedy, Rosanne and Gillian Whitlock, 'Witnessing, Trauma and Social Suffering: Feminist Perspectives', *Australian Feminist Studies* 26, 69 (2011), pp. 251–5.

Kennedy, Rosanne and Tikka Jan Wilson, 'Constructing Shared Histories: Stolen Generations Testimony, Narrative Therapy and Address' in *World Memory: Personal Trajectories in Global Time*, ed. Jill Bennett and Rosanne Kennedy, Basingstoke: Palgrave Macmillan, 2003.

Laub, Dori, 'Bearing Witness, or the Vicissitudes of Listening' in *Testimony: Crisis of Witnessing in Literature, Psychoanalysis and History*, ed. Shoshana Felman and Dori Laub, New York: Routledge, 1992.

Lopez Bunyasi, Tehama and Candis Watts Smith, 'Do All Black Lives Matter Equally to Black People? Respectability Politics and the Limitations of Linked Fate', *Journal of Race, Ethnicity and Politics* 4, 1 (2019), pp. 180–215.

O'Hara, Mary, *Austerity Bites: A Journey to the Sharp End of Cuts in the UK*, Bristol: Policy Press, 2015.

Patrick, Ruth, 'Unsettling the Anti-Welfare Commonsense: The Potential in Participatory Research with People Living in Poverty', *Journal of Social Policy* 49, 2 (2020), pp. 251–70.

Rambo, Shelly, *Spirit and Trauma: A Theology of Remaining*, Louisville, KY: Westminster John Knox Press, 2010.

Rambo, Shelly, '"Theologians Engaging Trauma" Transcript', *Theology Today* 68, 3 (2011), pp. 224–37.

Rambo, Shelly, 'Introduction' in *Post-traumatic Public Theology*, ed. Stephanie N. Arel and Shelly Rambo, Switzerland: Palgrave Macmillan, 2016.

Rambo, Shelly, 'Theology after Trauma: Tending Wounds that won't go away', *Christian Century*, 20 November 2019.

Reddie, Anthony, 'Racial Justice for the Windrush Generation in Great Britain', *The Ecumenical Review* 71, 1 (2020), pp. 73–86.

Rodríguez, Juana María, 'Keyword 6: Testimony', *Differences* 30, 1 (2019), pp. 119–25.

Roulstone, Alan, 'Personal Independence Payments, Welfare Reform and the Shrinking Disability Category', *Disability and Society* 30, 5 (2020), pp. 673–88.

Schaffer, Kay and Sidonie Smith, *Human Rights and Narrated Lives: The Ethics of Recognition*, New York: Palgrave Macmillan, 2004.

Walton, Heather, *Writing Methods in Theological Reflection*, London: SCM Press, 2014.

Women's Budget Group and Runnymede Trust, 'Intersecting Inequalities: The Impact of Austerity on Black and Minority Ethnic Women in the UK', *Women's Budget Group*, 2 November 2017, https://wbg.org.uk/analysis/intersecting-inequalities, accessed 15.05.2021.

Zetter, Roger and Martyn Pearl, 'The Minority within the Minority: Refugee Community-Based Organisations in the UK and the Impact of Restrictionism on Asylum-Seekers', *Journal of Ethnic and Migration Studies* 26, 4 (2000), pp. 675–97.

Notes

1 Throughout this chapter, pseudonyms chosen by the participants have been used.

2 Kay Schaffer and Sidonie Smith, *Human Rights and Narrated Lives: The Ethics of Recognition* (New York: Palgrave Macmillan, 2004).

3 Elaine Graham, *Transforming Practice: Pastoral Theology in an Age of Uncertainty* (London: Mowbray, 1996); Riet Bons-Storm, *The Incredible Woman: Listening to Women's Silences in Pastoral Care and Counseling* (Nashville, TN: Abingdon Press, 1996).

4 For an example of a direct request, see Katie Cross, 'I Have the Power in My Body to Make People Sin' in *Feminist Trauma Theologies: Body, Scripture and*

Church in Critical Perspective, ed. Katie Cross and Karen O'Donnell (London: SCM Press, 2020).

5 Rosanne Kennedy and Gillian Whitlock, 'Witnessing, Trauma and Social Suffering: Feminist Perspectives', *Australian Feminist Studies* 26, 69 (2011), p. 252.

6 Schaffer and Smith, *Human Rights*, pp. 37, 45; Paul Gready, 'The Public Life of Narratives: Ethics, Politics, Methods' in *Doing Narrative Research*, 2nd edn, ed. Molly Andrews, Corinne Squire and Maria Tamboukou (London and Los Angeles: Sage, 2013).

7 See for example Megan Boler, 'The Risks of Empathy: Interrogating Multiculturalism's Gaze', *Cultural Studies* 11, 2 (1997), pp. 253–73; Lauren Berlant, 'Introduction Compassion (and Withholding)' in *Compassion: The Culture and Politics of an Emotion*, ed. Lauren Berlant (London: Routledge, 2004).

8 Shelly Rambo, 'Introduction' in *Post-Traumatic Public Theology*, ed. Stephanie N. Arel and Shelly Rambo (Switzerland: Palgrave Macmillan, 2016), p. 7.

9 Lauren Berlant, 'The Subject of True Feeling: Pain, Privacy, and Politics' in *Cultural Pluralism, Identity Politics, and the Law*, ed. Austin Sarat and Thomas R. Kearns (Ann Arbor, MI: University of Michigan Press, 1999), p. 76.

10 Laura S. Brown, 'Not Outside the Range: One Feminist Perspective on Psychic Trauma', *American Imago* 48, 1 (1999), pp. 119–33.

11 Ann Cvetkovich, *An Archive of Feelings: Trauma, Sexuality, and Lesbian Public Cultures* (Durham, NC: Duke University Press, 2003), p. 3.

12 Ann Cvetkovich, 'Public Feelings', *The South Atlantic Quarterly* 106, 3 (2007), p. 464.

13 Cvetkovich, *An Archive*, p. 7

14 Philip Alston, 'Statement on Visit to the United Kingdom, United Nations Special Rapporteur on Extreme Poverty and Human Rights', London, 16 November 2018, https://www.ohchr.org/sites/default/files/Documents/Issues/Poverty/EOM_GB_16Nov2018.pdf, accessed 26.05.2022; Women's Budget Group and Runnymede Trust, 'Intersecting Inequalities: The Impact of Austerity on Black and Minority Ethnic Women in the UK', *Women's Budget Group*, 2 November 2017, https://wbg.org.uk/analysis/intersecting-inequalities, accessed 15.05.2021.

15 Esther Hitchin and Ruth Raynor, 'Editorial: Encountering Austerity in Everyday Life: Intensities, Localities, Materialities', *Geoforum* 110 (2020), p. 186.

16 Hitchin and Raynor, 'Editorial', p. 187.

17 Shelly Rambo, 'Theology after Trauma: Tending Wounds that won't go away', *Christian Century*, 20 November 2019, p. 24.

18 Rebecca Chopp, 'Theology and the Poetics of Testimony' in *Converging on Culture: Theologians in Dialogue with Cultural Analysis and Criticism*, ed. Delwin Brown, Shelia Greeve Davaney and Kathryn Tanner (New York: Oxford University Press, 2001); Rebecca Chopp, 'Reimagining Public Discourse' in *Black Faith and Public Talk: Critical Essays on James H. Cone's Black Theology and Black Power*, ed. Dwight N. Hopkins (Waco, TX: Baylor University Press, 2007).

19 Chopp, 'Reimagining', p. 155.

20 Chopp, 'Theology and the Poetics of Testimony', p. 62

21 Chopp, 'Theology and the Poetics of Testimony', p. 57.

22 Rebecca Chopp, *The Praxis of Suffering: An Interpretation of Liberation and Political Theologies* (Eugene, OR: Wipf & Stock, 2007), p. 2.

23 Chopp, 'Theology and the Poetics of Testimony', p. 60.

24 Chopp, 'Theology and the Poetics of Testimony', p. 60.

25 Chopp, 'Theology and the Poetics of Testimony', p. 61.

26 Chopp, 'Theology and the Poetics of Testimony', p. 67.

27 Chopp, 'Theology and the Poetics of Testimony', p. 57.

28 Chopp, 'Reimagining', p. 155.

29 Heather Walton, *Writing Methods in Theological Reflection* (London: SCM Press, 2014), p. 162.

30 Rambo, 'Introduction', p. 4.

31 Shelly Rambo, *Spirit and Trauma: A Theology of Remaining* (Louisville, KY: Westminster John Knox Press, 2010), p. 165.

32 Rambo, *Spirit and Trauma*, p. 15.

33 Rambo, *Spirit and Trauma*, pp. 165, 160.

34 Shelly Rambo, 'Theopoetics of Trauma' in *Trauma and Transcendence: Suffering and the Limits of Theory*, ed. Eric Boynton and Peter Capretto (New York: Fordham University Press, 2018), p. 234.

35 Chopp, 'Reimagining', p. 162.

36 Chopp, 'Reimagining', p. 162.

37 Chopp, 'Theology and the Poetics of Testimony', p. 67.

38 Leigh Gilmore, *Tainted Witness: Why we Doubt what Women say about their Lives* (New York: Columbia University Press, 2017), p. 20.

39 Tehama Lopez Bunyasi and Candis Watts Smith, 'Do All Black Lives Matter Equally to Black People? Respectability Politics and the Limitations of Linked Fate', *Journal of Race, Ethnicity and Politics* 4, 1 (2019), pp. 186, 188.

40 Anthony Reddie, 'Racial Justice for the Windrush Generation in Great Britain', *The Ecumenical Review* 71, 1 (2020), p. 82.

41 Cash Carraway, *Skint Estate* (London: Ebury Press, 2019).

42 Cash Carraway, 'Lidl Women (a monologue)', *DOPE* 11 (2020), https://issuu.com/dogsectionpress/docs/dope11, accessed 5.05.2021.

43 Gilmore, *Tainted Witness*, p. 80.

44 Dori Laub, 'Bearing Witness, or the Vicissitudes of Listening' in *Testimony: Crisis of Witnessing in Literature, Psychoanalysis and History*, ed. Shoshana Felman and Dori Laub (New York: Routledge, 1992), p. 68.

45 Laub, 'Bearing Witness', p. 73.

46 Laub, 'Bearing Witness', pp. 72–3.

47 Stef Craps, *Postcolonial Witnessing: Trauma Out of Bounds*, (Basingstoke: Palgrave Macmillan, 2013), p. 42.

48 Craps, *Postcolonial Witnessing*, p. 42.

49 Rosanne Kennedy and Tikka Jan Wilson, 'Constructing Shared Histories: Stolen Generations Testimony, Narrative Therapy and Address' in *World Memory: Personal Trajectories in Global Time*, Jill Bennett and Rosanne Kennedy (Basingstoke: Palgrave Macmillan, 2003).

50 Kinship care is a phrase for children being placed in the care of a family member or close friend, often a grandparent, when a parent is unable to provide care.

51 This phrase has been used by disability movements and also in the South African post-apartheid reconciliation process.

52 'Sanctions' refers to a person having their benefits payments removed for a time period of between four weeks and a maximum three years for higher-level sanctions. For more, see Mary O'Hara, *Austerity Bites: A Journey to the Sharp End of Cuts in the UK* (Bristol: Policy Press, 2015).

53 The *Stories of Hope* booklet can be accessed on the PTC section of the

Faith in Community Scotland website, https://www.faithincommunity.scot/ptc reports-and-resources, accessed 9.09.2021.

54 Tracey Jensen and Imogen Tyler, 'Benefits Broods: The Cultural and Political Crafting of Anti-Welfare Commonsense', *Critical Social Policy* 35, 4 (2015), pp. 470–91.

55 Theresa May, Parliamentary debate, 26 April 2017, Hansard Volume 624.

56 Conservative Party Conference 2012, 8 October 2012.

57 Ruth Patrick, 'Unsettling the Anti-Welfare Commonsense: The Potential in Participatory Research with People Living in Poverty', *Journal of Social Policy* 49, 2 (2020), p. 254.

58 Alan Roulstone, 'Personal Independence Payments, Welfare Reform and the Shrinking Disability Category', *Disability and Society* 30, 5 (2015), p. 675; Liz Crow, 'Scroungers and Superhumans: Images of Disability from the Summer of 2012: A Visual Inquiry', *Journal of Visual Culture* 13, 2 (2014), p. 174.

59 Jensen and Tyler, 'Benefits Broods', p. 479.

60 Roger Zetter and Martyn Pearl, 'The Minority within the Minority: Refugee Community-Based Organisations in the UK and the Impact of Restrictionism on Asylum-Seekers', *Journal of Ethnic and Migration Studies* 26, 4 (2000), p. 675.

61 Sara Ahmed, 'Affective Economies', *Social Text* 79, 22 (2004), p. 122.

62 Patrick, 'Unsettling', p. 252.

63 Ada María Isasi-Díaz, *Mujerista Theology: A Theology for the Twenty-First Century* (Maryknoll, NY: Orbis Books, 1996).

64 Rambo, 'Theology after Trauma', p. 24.

65 Sharon Betcher, *Spirit and the Politics of Disablement* (Minneapolis, MN: Fortress Press, 2007), p. 108.

66 Betcher, *Spirit*, p. 106.

67 Betcher, *Spirit*, p. 110.

68 Kennedy and Whitlock, 'Witnessing', p. 252.

69 Betcher, *Spirit*, p. 110.

70 Lucy Burke and Liz Crow, 'Bedding Out: Art, Activism and Twitter' in *Disability and Social Media: Global Perspectives*, ed. Katie Ellis and Mike Kent (London: Routledge, 2017), p. 62.

71 Juana María Rodríguez, 'Keyword 6: Testimony', *Differences* 30, 1 (2019), p. 123.

72 Kennedy and Wilson, 'Constructing', p. 129.

73 M. Shawn Copeland in Shelly Rambo, '"Theologians Engaging Trauma" Transcript', *Theology Today* 68, 3 (2011), p. 229.

74 Rambo, *Spirit and Trauma*, p. 15.

75 Sharon Betcher, 'Becoming Flesh of My Flesh: Feminist and Disability Theologies on the Edge of Posthumanist Discourse', *Journal of Feminist Studies in Religion* 26, 2 (2010), p. 115. Here, Betcher is referring specifically to apophatic approaches to knowing others, highlighting that that apophatic unknowing can 'disappear' those who are already excluded from social and economic structures.

There is no 'After' with Trauma

KAREN O'DONNELL AND KATIE CROSS

Shelly Rambo begins her book *Spirit and Trauma: A Theology of Remaining* with a quotation from Deacon Julius Lee. She is standing with him in his backyard where everything has been washed away by Hurricane Katrina. He says, 'The storm is gone, but "after the storm" is always here.'[1] Similarly, addressing the first Easter season of the Covid-19 pandemic, Wil Gafney writes that Christ's resurrection, while miraculous, does not 'miraculously heal' the trauma left behind by his death. Grief will fade in time, and there will be space for joy, but for those close to Jesus a 'tender spot' will remain.[2]

This sense of the ongoing-ness of trauma is important to remember, particularly in the case of Christian theology that has traditionally emphasized the victory, triumph and sense of completeness of the resurrection. The experience of trauma may have passed but the trauma remains, ingrained in our bodies, written in our scars and surfacing throughout our lives. Therefore, there is no 'Last Word' or 'Epilogue' or 'Afterword' in this volume because there is no *after* with trauma.

Rather, instead, we offer this open ending where we emphasize the partial nature of this volume. We are delighted with the chapters in this volume but recognize that they are not the final word on trauma theology. They are merely contributions to the conversation. As a form of constructive theology, there is no neat presentation of a system of thought that makes sense of this theological approach. Rather it is messy, partial, fragmented, continually open to revision, and in dialogue with the conversations going on around it both in theology and in the related disciplinary fields – a whole range of which are represented here.

What, then, do we do now? Well, we continue to have these conversations. We continue to hear the voices and stories of trauma within our communities. We continue to listen. We continue to witness. We continue to remain alongside trauma survivors. We continue to bring our theology into dialogue with the realities of the lived experiences of trauma and allow our theologies to be open to hearing these voices. This last point is particularly salient. We must not cling so tightly to tradition that we cannot be open to the need to reimaging theological doctrines in the light of trauma. But nor must we dispense with the goods and riches of the Christian tradition completely. Finding a way forward between these two extremes is essential if we (theologians and the Church more broadly) are to avoid doing further damage to trauma survivors.

Trauma theologians tend to avoid talking about 'recovery' or 'healing' and instead prefer the language of post-traumatic remaking. This language exemplifies that work of the trauma survivor as they attempt to remake themselves in their experience of trauma. Various things are required for this work to be successful: attending to and reconnecting with their body; constructing a narrative of their trauma experience and being witnessed and believed; reconnecting with their community. It is important to recognize that since there is no 'after', this process of remaking will be continuous, perhaps throughout a lifetime. Various elements of remaking might need to be revisited over and over again.

Many of our contributors have written their chapters out of their own experiences of trauma. We are grateful for their bravery in doing this. We know that when trauma survivors break silences about their experiences it can be both painful and redemptive. And when other trauma survivors see their stories witnessed and attested to it can be helpful in their processes of remaking. Some of these chapters are the construction of narratives of trauma experiences, and many begin to attest to what is needed in theology, the Church, and the wider community if we are to become a trauma-informed, trauma-sensitive society that does not cause further damage to people.

There is no 'after' in trauma, but there is a forward motion that can be grounded in hope, peace, community and honesty. We encourage you to attend to these theologies and remain in the Spirit of God.

Notes

1 Shelly Rambo, *Spirit and Trauma: A Theology of Remaining* (Louisville, KY: Westminster John Knox Press, 2010), p. 1.

2 Wil Gafney, 'Three Days Later: A Womanist Midrash', *Womanists Wading in the Word* (blog), 12 April 2020, https://www.wilgafney.com/2020/04/12/three-days-later-a-womanist-midrash/, accessed 19.05.2022.

Index of Names and Subjects